Sport, Culture and Society

An Introduction

Grant Jarvie

 Routledge
Taylor & Francis Group

LONDON AND NEW YORK

First published 2006
by Routledge
2 Park Square, Milton Park, Abingdon, Oxon OX14 4RN

Simultaneously published in the USA and Canada
By Routledge
270 Madison Ave, New York, NY 10016

Reprinted 2006 (twice), 2007

Routledge is an imprint of the Taylor & Francis Group, an informa business

© 2006 Grant Jarvie

Typeset in Perpetua and Bell Gothic by
Florence Production Ltd, Stoodleigh, Devon
Printed and bound in Great Britain by
TJ International Ltd, Padstow, Cornwall

British Library Cataloguing in Publication Data
A catalogue record for this book is available from the British Library

Library of Congress Cataloging in Publication Data
Jarvie, Grant, 1955–
    Sport, culture and society: an introduction/Grant Jarvie.
        p. cm.
    Includes bibliographical references and index.
    1. Sports – Social aspects.   I. Title.
    GV706.5.J383 2005
    306.4'83–dc22   2005015463

ISBN10: 0–415–30646–9 (hbk)
ISBN10: 0–415–30647–7 (pbk)
ISBN13: 978–0–415–30646–1 (hbk)
ISBN13: 978–0–415–30647–8 (pbk)

Governments Change, Policies Change
But the Need Remains the Same

Contents

CONTENTS

Boxes

Figures

Tables

Acknowledgements

This book has been researched during periods of sabbatical research leave granted by the University of Stirling for which I am extremely grateful. I am lucky to work in such a beautiful and supportive research environment. Different groups of students, colleagues, conference audiences, local sports groups and some Ministers of Sport have been invaluable in helping me both refine and challenge my thinking on much if not all of the content of this book.

The following have kindly granted permission to use either photographic or empirical materials. The *Daily Telegraph* is to be thanked for providing the photographs presented in chapters 1, 3 and 18 as is Nan Fang Sports for the photographs presented in chapters 4 and 10. Getty Images provided the photographs for Chapters 5, 6, 7, 8, 9, 11, 12, 13, 15 and 16. The National Museum for Scotland provided the photograph for Chapter 2. SportsBusiness has granted permission to present the empirical material in Tables 6.1 and 13.1. Sport Scotland and Sport England are to be thanked for allowing me to publish the empirical data presented in Tables 15.1 and 15.2 and Figures 15.1 and 15.2. The University of Ottawa Press granted permission to include the material presented in Figure 10.1 as did Human Kinetics Press for the material presented in Table 17.1.

Like all books this one owes its existence to many people. The book has benefited greatly from various sources of information and inspiration. Samantha Grant and Kate Manson at Routledge have been extremely supportive during some very hard times between 2004 and present. Jacqui Baird and Elza Stewart have been very patient and helpful during the entire project. Barbara Kettlewell and Linda Rankin have helped along the way. Many colleagues at Stirling such as Wray Vamplew, Stephen Morrow, David Bell, Paul Dimeo, Raymond Boyle, Richard Haynes, Fred Coalter, Peter Bilsborough, John Field, Philip Schlesinger and Ian Thomson have either read drafts of various chapters or provided advice on many issues. Outside of the University many people have provided invaluable critical comment and intellectual stimulation in relation to the material. Over the years I have been fortunate enough to work with many good people, too many to mention, but in terms of influencing this material either directly or indirectly I should also like to mention Henning Eichberg, Jenny Hargreaves, Ian Henry, Tony Mason, Joe Maguire, Bruce Kidd, George McKinney, Jim Hunter, Donald Meek, Craig Sharp, Sheila Scraton, Alan Bairner,

Lindsay Paterson, Alan Tomlinson, Rick Gruneau, Jim Riordan, David McCrone, Hart Cantelon, Graham Walker and Eric Dunning.

Colin Jarvie, who has acted throughout as photographic consultant, was asked to do the impossible in terms of photograph production but I learned a lot from his interventions and the book is all the better for them. Brora friends have supported me throughout and for that Olive, Bruce, Lesley and the boys – thanks.

Glossary

AEN	Asia-Specific People and Environmental Network
AFC	Asian Football Confederation
ANC	African National Congress
ANOC	Association of National Olympic Committees
ANTENNA	Asian Tourism Network
ASEAN	Association of South-East Asian Nations
ASOIF	Association of Summer Olympic International Sports Federations
AIWF	Association of Winter Olympic International Sports Federations
BBC	British Broadcasting Corporation
BSA	British Sociological Association
BSkyB	British Sky Broadcasting Corporation
BSSH	British Society for Sports History
BWSF	British Workers Sports Federation
CAS	Court of Arbitration for Sport
CAF	Confederation of African Football
CONCACAF	Confederation of North and Central American and Caribbean Football
CONMEBOL	Confederation of South American Football
EEC	European Economic Community
EFTA	European Free Trade Association
ENGSO	European Non-Governmental Sports Organisation
FA	English Football Association
FS	Fabian Society
FIFA	Fédération Internationale de Football Association
GAA	Gaelic Athletic Association
GANEFO	Games of the Newly Emerging Forces
GNAGA	Global Network for Anti-Golf Course Action
IAAF	International Amateur Athletic Federation
ICAS	International Council of Arbitration for Sport
ICC	International Cricket Council
ICCPR	International Covenant on Civil and Political Rights
IESCR	International Covenant on Economic, Social and Cultural Rights

ILO	International Labour Organisation
IMF	International Monetary Fund
INSP	International Network of Street Papers
IOC	International Olympic Committee
ISA	International Sumo Association
JSA	Japanese Sumo Association
KS	Kladt-Sobri Group
MLB	Major League Baseball
MYSA	Mathare Youth Sports Association
NASS	North American Society for the Sociology of Sport
NASSH	North American Society for Sports History
NBA	National Basketball Association
NCAVA	National Coalition Against Violence
NGO	Non-Governmental Organisation
NHL	National Hockey League
OFC	Oceania Football Confederation
OHCHR	Office of the United Nations High Commission for Human Rights
OPHR	Olympic Project for Human Rights
PASO	Pan-American Sports Organisation
ROK	Republic of Korea
RSI	Red Sports International
SNP	Scottish Nationalist Party
SWSI	Socialist Workers Sports International
TNC	Trans-National Corporation
UAE	United Arab Emirates
UEFA	Union of European Football Associations
UN	United Nations
UNEP	United Nations Environmental Programme
UNICEF	UN Children's Fund
USSR	Union of Soviet Socialist Republics
WHO	World Health Organization
WTO	World Trade Organisation

Introduction

*In the 1920s and 1930s the Social Credit Movement made a number of progressive sugges-
tions with regards to the use of sport in society but how should we think progressively
about sport today? © cocopics (2005)*

PREVIEW

Sport, culture and society • The study of sport • Structure and rationale of the book •
Modern sport • The public role of the intellectual • Different levels of analysis in sport,
culture and society • Epistemology • Culture and sport • Sporting sub-cultures • The nation
• Global sport • Neighbourhood and community sport • Policy intervention • Sport • The
historical period • Social inequality • How to use the book.

OBJECTIVES

This chapter will:

- introduce the study of sport, culture and society;
- explain the structure and rationale for this book;
- comment upon the public role of the student, academic and researcher interested in sport;
- introduce different levels of analysis in the study of sport, culture and society;
- explain the main features of the book and how to use them;
- outline the content of the four different parts to *Sport, Culture and Society.*

INTRODUCTION

It is impossible to fully understand contemporary society and culture without acknowledging the place of sport. We inhabit a world in which sport is an international phenomenon, it is important for politicians and world leaders to be associated with sports personalities; it contributes to the economy, some of the most visible international spectacles are associated with sporting events; it is part of the social and cultural fabric of different localities, regions and nations, its transformative potential is evident in some of the poorest areas of the world; it is important to the television and film industry, the tourist industry; and it is regularly associated with social problems and issues such as crime, health, violence, social division, labour migration, economic and social regeneration and poverty.

We also live in a world in which some of the richest and poorest people identify with forms of sport in some way. This can be said without denying the fact that an immense gap exists between rich and poor parts of the world or accepting uncritically the myth of global sport. In some ways global sport has never been more successful. The Sydney 2000 Olympic Games involved 10,300 athletes from 200 countries, attracted more than US $600 million in sponsorship and was viewed on TV by more than 3.7 billion people. Sport's social and commercial power makes it a potentially potent force in the modern world, for good and for bad. It can be a tool of dictatorship, a symbol of democratic change, it has helped to start wars and promote international reconciliation. Almost every government around the world commits public resources to sporting infrastructure because of sport's perceived benefits to improving health, education, creating jobs and preventing crime. Sport matters to people. The competing notions of identity, internationalisation, national tradition and global solidarity that are contested within sport all matter far beyond the reach of sport. At the same time, some have suggested that there is a legitimate crisis of confidence in global sport and those dealing with the pressures of its transformation cannot handle the reform that is required within twenty-first-century sport. Perhaps, as Katwala (2000b) suggests, the crisis of global sport is not one of commercialism, but one of lack of trust in sporting governances at a time when the governance of sport has never been more complex or important.

The study of sport, culture and society is no longer a young and naive area of academic study and research. Generation after generation of sociologists and historians have raised classical sociological and historical questions in relation to sport's organisation, its distribution and the part it has played in the allocation and exercise of power. The study of sport, culture and society today is less of a peripheral element within the social sciences and other subject areas, including geography, political science and history. The scope and content of sport, culture and society can be wide-ranging since various specialised sub-areas have given rise to degree courses, specialist texts, and particular forms of policy intervention and specialist research groupings. The potential eclectic coverage of ideas together with a sound grasp of sport itself provide for a stimulating avenue not only to developing sport, but also to analysing, demystifying it and ultimately attempting to contribute to social change and intervention in the world in which we live in.

STRUCTURE AND RATIONALE OF THE BOOK

The book is written for those researchers, students and teachers, amongst others, who are thinking about sport as a social phenomenon and the extent to which sport contributes to the very social fabric of communities. It examines critically many of the assumptions relating to sport and questions the extent to which the substantive basis for such claims made by sport actually exist. The objective of the book is not only to encourage students and others to reflect upon sport, drawing upon concepts, theories and themes, but also to produce a body of original substantive research from different sports, societies and communities. The position taken throughout this book is that, while it is important to explain and understand sport in society, the more important intellectual and practical questions emanate from questions relating to social change. The book aims in a small way to also influence research agendas involving sport.

Modern sport has been described as (i) a ritual sacrifice of human energy; (ii) providing a common cultural currency between peoples; (iii) a means of compensating for deficiencies in life; (iv) a mechanism for the affirmation of identity and difference; (v) business rather than sport; (vi) a social product; (vii) a contested arena shaped by struggles both on and off the field of play and (viii) being a euphemism for Western or capitalist sport.

A genuine social understanding of sport remains crucial to our understanding of the world in which we live. Sport needs to be contextualised critically and evaluated in order to explain why sport is the way it is today. The approach that differentiates this text from other recent but equally important explanations of sport in society is that it does not just attempt to understand the relationship of sport in society, but also to reassert the question of social change and intervention.

Almost 20 years ago critical commentators on sport were asking *what is the transformative value of sport? Can sport truly make a difference to people's lives?* More recently political scientists and policy experts have been asking *where is the evidence to substantiate the claims made by sport today?* These questions are as important today as they were twenty years ago. The late Palestinian activist and American intellectual Edward Said (2001:5) was explicit about the public role of the intellectual as being 'to uncover and contest, to challenge and defeat both an imposed silence and the normalised quiet of unseen power wherever and whenever possible'. The role of the public intellectual in the field of sport is desperately needed as a partial safeguard against a one-dimensional world of sport in which that which is not said tells you perhaps more than what is actually said. The informed student of sport who can develop the skills of presenting complex issues in a communicative way, participate in public debates about sport and even promote debates about sport is very much needed in the twenty-first century. I hope that the content of this book will help many on that journey and help readers to reflect upon and inform public debates about, for example, sport and the environment, sport and the limits of capitalism, sport and poverty, sport, internationalism and nation building and sport and human rights.

Raising awareness about social issues within sport and answering social problems that arise out of and between different sporting worlds may occur at different levels or entry points.

LEVELS OF ANALYSIS IN SPORT, CULTURE AND SOCIETY

It has already been suggested that the study of sport, culture and society involves a number of complex factors all of which impinge upon the nature of sport at different levels. It has also been suggested that students and researchers alike need to have a number of organising frameworks or at least points of entry and exit into and out of debates about sport. The notion of levels of analysis or entry points offers a useful organising framework for locating any analysis of sport. The levels below are not exhaustive but merely illustrative of different ways of organising and prioritising knowledge about sport, culture and society.

Level 1: Epistemology

Just as different politicians reflect divergent party agendas and philosophies, so too does the body of knowledge that is sport, culture and society champion numerous problematics or approaches to the study of sport. Researchers reflect divergent viewpoints and bodies of knowledge that influence the practice of research and the questions that they want to ask of sport. Indeed, at times the rivalry and tension between different points of view have often been gladiatorial as opposed to being mutually supportive. The different paradigms or perspectives or eclectic approaches to the study of sport include post-modernist, feminist, figurational, functionalist, Confucian, Marxist, post-colonial, nationalist, even 'whiggish' or conservative. All of these approaches raise particular questions and suppress others – a point that is illustrated and developed further in Chapter 1. Students and researchers of sport, culture and society will need to decide and reflect upon where they are coming from in an epistemological sense or at the very least from what standpoint they wish to constructively engage with other bodies of work or knowledge about sport *per se*. (Epistemology is not equated solely with theory, but see Chapter 1 for further comment on the relationship between epistemology, sports theory and the problem of values.)

Level 2: Culture and sport

This mainly refers to the values, ceremonies and way of life characteristic of a given group and the place of sport within that way of life. Like the concept of society, the notion of culture is widely used in the sociological, anthropological and historical study of sport. It encourages the researcher and student to consider the meanings, symbols, rituals and power relations at play within any particular cultural setting. The notion of culture may be operationalised at a national, local or comparative level. Consequently, examples at this level of analysis may include the place of sport within Irish or Kenyan culture; the meaning of the Tour de France to the French or Sumo wrestling to the Japanese; or, as in Clifford Gertz's classic study, the meaning of cock-fighting in Balinese culture; or the extent to which sport in South Africa during the apartheid era actively challenged the dominant definition of sport through politicising and empowering the idea that one cannot have normal sport in an abnormal society; or by examining the extent to which certain representations of culture within the media or readings of cultural texts by audiences reinforce certain cultural messages or meanings about sport.

Level 3: Sporting sub-cultures

Sub-cultural analysis refers to the place of sport within any segment of the population that is distinguishable from the wider society by its cultural pattern. Sub-cultures have at times been referred to in relation to broader parent cultures or host cultures. At one level studies have examined the place of sport or alienation from sport amongst different youth cultures or counter-cultures. In modern cities many sub-cultural communities live side by side, supporting different sports and teams for social, cultural and political reasons. Ethnic or linguistic groupings may be referred to as sub-cultures. The term 'sub-cultures' is very broad in scope and may refer to specific football club supporters, or alternative sporting sub-cultures as in extreme sports or high-risk sports. Historically in certain parts of the world surfing sub-cultures during the 1960s and 1970s were associated with groups searching for alternatives to a mainstream way of life. Social movements or groups of people sharing common lifestyles are powerful forces of change within societies. Sub-cultures allow freedom for people to express and act on their opinions, hopes and beliefs. At a general level the term sub-culture simply refers to any systems of beliefs, or values or norms shared by or participated in by a sizeable minority of people within a particular culture – sporting or otherwise.

Level 4: The nation

The role of sport in the making of nations is one of the most discussed areas in sport, culture and society. The precise nature of nations and nation-states varies, as do the forms of nationalism that are often associated with different sports. The extent to which we understand fully the complex ways in which sport contributes to national identity, civic and ethnic nationalism and internationalism remains an open question. In order to understand sport fully students and others need to comprehend processes and patterns of national and international change in sport as well as the distinct content of national sports policies or the criteria for selection to national teams. At its most celebrated the relationship between sport and the nation is illustrated at one level by the relationship between events, such as the Tour de France and France, the All Ireland hurling final and Ireland, cricket in India or England, and at another level by national world leaders, such as Nelson Mandela who has commented upon sport's role in the building of a new post-apartheid South Africa. (See Chapter 5 for an examination of the part sport has played in nation building and national identity.)

Level 5: Global sport

The notion of global sport implies the processes by which sport reflects the growing interdependence of nations, regions and localities within a global or world political economy. World systems theory has been popular within non-Western areas such as China and Latin America. In studying global sport it is important to identify processes that transcend or cross national boundaries. Maguire's (1999) study of global sport identifies the following processes – ideoscapes, ethnoscapes, mediascapes, financescapes and techno-scapes. International sporting organisations, such as the Fédération Internationale de Football Association (FIFA), often convey the message of marketing, administering and controlling global football. The notion of global sport has tended to be criticised from a number of points of view including those of nationalists and internationalists. The development of global sport should not be considered in isolation from anti-globalisation or anti-capitalism. Protests have targeted global sporting companies, such as Nike, and highlighted the role of cheap labour, often children's labour, in the production of international sporting goods. (See Chapter 4 for a further discussion of global sport, globalisation and anti-globalisation protests.)

Level 6: Neighbourhood and community sport

The neighbourhood geographically has been the area around one's home and usually displays some degree of homogeneity in terms of housing type, ethnicity or socio-cultural values. The term 'neighbourhood' is closely associated with a particular, although not the sole, definition of community. Neighbourhoods usually display strong allegiances to the local sports teams, provide a focus for intergenerational discussions about 'golden sporting eras' and provide a basis for the development of community solidarity, but also rivalry, with other neighbourhoods or communities. Metcalfe's (1996:16) study of the mining communities in the north east of England identifies factors that have impinged upon neighbourhood or community sport, such as population stability and the physical layout of the community, town or village. The term 'community' has tended to denote a social group that is usually identified in terms of a common habitat, common interest and a degree of social co-operation, but it can also in an applied sense refer to a community of sportspeople, artists and students as well as the international or national community. As a term it has been historically associated with the German *Gemeinschaft*. More recently it has been suggested that within left-wing discourses it has become more popular in the twenty-first century than the term social class that used to be the 'holy grail' of various labour movements. The challenge over the use of such concepts as community and neighbourhood is whether they can be resurrected in new ways, in new shapes or in new incarnations to help make sense of the world and sport today.

Level 7: Policy intervention

The term 'policy' is derived from the Greek *politeia* meaning government. The general principles of sports policy, like all policy, guide the making of laws, the administrative and executive governance of sport as well as acts of governance *per se* in international and domestic affairs. Policy intervention in sport takes many forms, such as anti-drug policies or anti-discrimination policies or policies restricting the movement of players from one club to another or one country to another, which may be viewed as anti-competitive. Sports policies may reflect particular political ideologies, but policies in general are not the same as doctrines which may be viewed as the system of values and beliefs that may help to generate policies and that purport to describe the ends to which policy is the means. Nor are policies the same as philosophies which tend to be the underlying justification for doctrines and policies together. Sports policy is one of the major practical means of intervention in sport. The different perspectives on sports policy put it somewhere in the middle ground between sports doctrine and sports philosophy. Houlihan (2003:31) provides a commentary on the term as applying to something bigger than particular decisions but smaller than general social movements. Political outlooks differ radically over whether sports policy is or should be a reflection of some underlying philosophy, but most agree that policy should be consistent, reasonable and acceptable to those with power to oppose it.

One last point is to suggest that there is no choice between the engaged and neutral ways of policy intervention. A non-committal policy is an impossibility. Seeking a morally neutral stance amongst the many forms of sports policy and decision making that impact upon the world of sport would be a vain effort. (See Part 4 of this book for a more in-depth coverage of some of the ways in which policy has been used to bring about social change in sport.)

Level 8: The sport

A particular sport itself may provide the focus for arranging the research material or essay. Many historical, sociological, political and other frameworks for analysing sport have been organised around case studies of particular sports or clubs themselves. Some of the most superficial questions about a particular sport can lead to further investigations and enquiries about gender relations, social inequality, nationhood, the distribution of economic, cultural, and social resources, social change, human rights, the environment, the role of the state, poverty, the urban and the rural, the global and the local, freedom and dependence, insiders and outsiders, and many other areas of investigation which fall within the remit and duty of the socially committed student, academic or politician to explore. Any number of sports or illustrative examples could be provided and I have limited myself here to briefly mentioning the following that have been drawn from both past and more recent contributions

7

to the field of sport, culture and society. Vamplew's (1988) study of horse-racing tells us about the changing nature of professionalism, trade-unionism, the exchange of money and socialisation into the club; Dunning and Sheard's (1979) study of rugby football informs us about social class in Britain, power, the folk origins of football, amateurism and professionalism, violence and figurational sociology; Gruneau and Whitson's (1993) critical investigation into professional ice-hockey explains notions of community, national identity, relations between Canada and the USA, the urban and the rural, and the political economy of sport; Crosset's (1995) investigation into golf explores gender relations, sexuality, discrimination, the body, and social control; Sugden's (1996) study of boxing explores social class, poverty, religion, exploitation and disadvantage; Alabarces' (2000) investigation of football in Latin America raises issues about globalisation, colonialism, tradition and identity; Ray's (2001) study of the Highland Games explores issues of ethnicity, racism, Scottish–American heritage, social networks and power; Guha's (2002) study of cricket in India raises and answers questions about colonisation, the indigenous cricket experience, nation, caste and religion; and Maguire's (2005) study has furthered our understanding of the relationship between sport, power and globalisation.

Level 9: The historical period or theme

The historical study of sport has been one of the most active and interventionist in helping to interpret past and present sport. It has also brought to the study of sport, culture and society the discipline of sustained micro-level archival research methods that have helped to qualify unsubstantiated grand narratives of sport. Chronologically the study of sport, culture and society may be approached century by century or time period by time period, as for example in Vamplew's (1988) study of professional sport and commercialisation between 1875 and 1914; Metcalfe's (1991) study of power in Canadian amateur sport between 1918 and 1936; Pfister's (1990) study of female physical culture in nineteenth and early twentieth-century Germany; Parratt's (1989) study of working-class women and leisure in late Victorian England; Kidd's (1996) account of the struggle to control Canadian sport, or Burnett's (2000) study of sport in lowland Scotland before 1860. The study of what and why in the history of sport has also been influenced by other ways of presenting the history of sport, whether it be thematically or in terms of ancient, modern or post-modern perspectives about sport, culture and society. Hill (2002) concludes that the history of sport may be presented with different emphases; quantitatively, economically, theoretically, semiotically, heroically, whiggishly, reverently and/or chronologically. There are many historical levels of analysis from which to approach the study of sport, culture and society. (See Chapter 2 for further coverage of the historical contribution to the study of sport, culture and society.)

Level 10: Social divisions and inequality

It is impossible to think about sport, culture and society without encountering different ways in which sport means something to different groups of people or different policies or forms of social mobilisation aimed at empowering different groups of people. The meanings that often divide sport are those of class, ethnicity, gender, age, black or white, European or non-European or nationality, and disabled or physically impaired. Many of these social divisions have become separatist and fail to acknowledge the connection between and within different forms of social inequality in sport. Various accounts of sport, culture and society have accorded priority to different forms of social division and social inequality; for example, the relationship between rich and poor parts of the world informs Arbena's (1999) study of sport in Latin America; issues of race, racism and multi-culturalism inform Back, Crabbe and Solomos's (2001) study of the changing face of English professional football; issues of social class and social stratification are central to Scheerder, Vanreusel and Renson's (2002) account of sport in Belgium and other parts of Europe; gender, feminism and different experiences of women are central to Fan Hong's (1997) study of women in sport in China, while notions of imperialism and post-colonialism are crucial to Hwang's (2001) accounts of sport in Taiwan. The question remains: how do these social divisions intersect, should priority be given to any form of social division and should we not at least recognise that the gap between rich and poor in sport remains? The study of sport and social divisions should not simply examine a random selection of different sections of society, but rather the issues of hierarchy, social inequality and social injustice that impact upon all social divisions *per se*. (See Part 4 for a more detailed account of these social divisions in terms of sport.)

ORGANISATION OF THE BOOK

The book is organised into four main sections, with each section providing an introduction for the reader. Part 1 explores the broader epistemological and ontological context in which contemporary sport may be understood, it introduces a number of common concepts and theories which have been utilised in the explanation of sport, it acknowledges the lessons of history and what this brings to the study of sport and it asserts that one of the tasks and promises of sociological theory has always been to help us draw bigger diagnostic pictures of sport, culture and society. How these particular tools, theory and evidence are used, and for what purpose, should be the exclusive prerogative of social-actors themselves in specific social contexts and used on behalf of their values and interests. With these pictures the student of sport can begin to understand and comprehend the socially and politically situated nature of their work and being.

Part 2 examines some of the international, national, post-colonial and local contexts in which sport operates. One of the enduring problems with core introductory texts which have addressed these issues is that the analysis of sport, culture and society has tended to be dominated by or at least sensitive to an American perspective without critically questioning this or alternative points of view (Coakley, 2003; Nixon and Frey, 1996). The interaction between such processes as imperialism, post-colonialism and internationalism may have a much louder voice in any comprehensive analysis of sport in today's world. Just as Kaldor (2001:15) suggests new circumstances call for strengthened international frameworks capable of constraining the use of political violence, equally there should be a call for self-examination by the West of its attitudes towards other worlds of sport and the international role of sport in contributing to humanitarian causes. One of the major advances in the analysis of sport, culture and society over the past decade has been the impact made by social, cultural and urban geographers who have researched and mapped out crucial bodies of work in relation to sport and the city, sport and space, sport and the body, sport and post-colonialism and urban sporting cultures. Part 2 of this book therefore critically examines the relationship between sport, power and globalisation, identifying some of the core international players, organisations and institutions that have impacted upon or brought about social change in sport in many different parts of the world.

Part 3 focuses upon issues of identity and lifestyle. Identity politics through sport seems to have been premised upon the acceptance that all social groups have essential identities. The rise of identity politics in sport forms a convergence of cultural and political style, a mode of logic, a badge of belonging, a claim to insurgency, a recovery from exclusion and/or a demand for representation. The long overdue opening of political initiatives to minorities, women, and a multitude of voiceless people in sport has developed into a method of its own. Identity politics on its own is not enough. At the same time the pressures for alternative forms of sport and physical activity mean that the social and physical profile of sport itself is changing. Research indicates that a crop of activities which might be loosely termed extreme sports are firmly embedded within counter-cultures. Many traditional sports are in decline and therefore there is more space for alternative sport cultures to impinge upon mainstream sports culture. What is the meaning attached to alternative sports cultures? Is their development a reflection of a changing lifestyle or the quest for excitement, risk and the break from alienation (Wheaton, 2004)? Do we need to re-think what we mean by identity through sport and how does sport contribute to the quest for risk, excitement and individualism? These and other issues form the basis of Part 3.

In Part 4 our attention turns to matters of social division and social intervention. While Parts 1, 2 and 3 have been about analysing and substantiating the world of sport, Part 4 is about social change and social intervention. It is based upon the premise that while it is important for students and researchers of sport, culture and society to analyse and empirically test the social world of sport, it is also important to identify areas in which sport has or ought to campaign for change. Much of the existing research carried out by social researchers and students interested in sport has sought to destroy many taken-for-granted myths about sport, critically appraise and evaluate the actions of the powerful in sport and their impact upon the less powerful, and inform and champion the promise of sport in terms of social policy and community welfare. It is only relatively recently that sport's contribution to human rights campaigns has been recognised. It has been said that sociology is the power of the powerless and yet there is no guarantee that having acquired sociological understanding one can dissolve or disempower the resistance put up by the tough realities of everyday life. The power of understanding is no match for the pressures of coercion allied with resigned and submissive common sense (Bauman, 1990:18). If it were not for this understanding the chance of further freedoms being won through and in sport would be slimmer still.

Finally, in conclusion some of the main influences that have informed the thinking behind this book are pulled together. The whole project is mindful that sport can make a difference to communities and societies and that, while policies and governments may change in different parts of the world, the need for many remains the same.

HOW TO USE THE BOOK

The book provides a comprehensive introduction to the study of sport, culture and society. There is a sustained attempt to critically analyse, describe and explain sport today as a social, cultural and political phenomenon. The position taken throughout this book is that while it is important to explain and understand sport in society the more important intellectual and practical questions emanate from questions relating to social change. The core questions at the heart of this text are as follows:

- What empirical evidence can we draw upon to substantiate aspects of sport, culture and society? (What is happening in sport?)
- What theories and concepts can we draw upon to explain and analyse this substantive evidence? (How can we make sense of what is happening in sport?)
- What capacity does sport have to transform or intervene to produce social change? (What can be done to produce change?)
- What is the contemporary role of the student, intellectual or researcher in the public arena? (What are *you* going to do about it?)

One of the objectives of the book is to encourage students to reflect upon sport, drawing upon concepts, theories and themes, but also on a body of substantive research from different sports, societies and communities. It is the constant interplay between theory, explanation, evidence and intervention that is one of the hallmarks of the approach adopted. Put more simply, the student of sport, culture and society will continually be faced with three interrelated challenges. Although the production of knowledge and policy rarely comes in such a neat package or process, these can be summarised as: what evidence do you have, how are you going to make sense of it and what recommendations are you going to make as a result?

The text is supported by a wealth of additional sources of information provided in a number of forms. These include:

- chapter previews and objectives which outline the main areas covered in each chapter;
- photographs that provide visual illustrations from sport, culture and society settings;
- boxes which provide empirical information that complement, where appropriate, the area being covered in each chapter;
- key concepts that act as a guide to the core ideas and concepts covered within each chapter;
- study questions designed to test knowledge and promote critical reflection upon the subject matter of each chapter;
- sample projects which may be used as a databank of exercises to sharpen and refine not only transferable research skills but also a sensitivity to the social world of sport;
- the Internet provides a vast array of potentially useful information, but it must be used with a critical appreciation of the sources. Each chapter is provided with a list of at least five world-wide websites that will assist and support the body of knowledge in each chapter. These websites provide access to a range of information and are not all sports specific. Be prepared to explore each website thoroughly in relation to the topic in which you are interested.

11

SUMMARY

This introductory discussion of sport, culture and society has outlined the structure and rationale that has informed the content of this book. It has highlighted the need not only to draw upon substantive evidence and explain that evidence but also the necessity to link this exercise to policies and attempts to produce social change. It has championed the cause of the researcher, teacher, intellectual and student of sport who really wants to understand more than just superficially the popularity, importance and relevance of sport in today's world. It has provided an introduction to some of the tools of the trade that help to equip and enlighten the enquiring student who is fascinated and caught up in the power, potential and passion of sport and related areas. It is one thing to identify the key areas of concern of our time but it is also vital to identify silences, since what is not being said often tells us as much about sport as that which is being said. None the less, sport is as Nelson Mandela once said a force that mobilises the sentiments of a people in a way that nothing else can and hopefully it will remain a vehicle for social capital, community solidarity, critical scholarship, resources of hope and fun for a long time to come.

KEY CONCEPTS

Community	Neighbourhood
Culture	Policy
Epistemology	Social change
Global sport	Social division
Nation	Sub-cultures

KEY READING

Books

Bauman, Z. (1990). *Thinking Sociologically*. Cambridge: Basil Blackwell.
Coakley, J. and Dunning, E. (eds) (2002). *Handbook of Sports Studies*. London: Sage.
Houlihan, B. (2003). *Sport and Society: An Introduction*. London: Sage.
Levinson, D. and Christensen, K. (1996). *Encyclopedia of World Sport*. Oxford: ABC-CLIO.
Maguire, J., Jarvie, G., Mansfield, L. and Bradley, J. (2002). *Sport Worlds: A Sociological Perspective*. Champaign, IL: Human Kinetics.

Journal articles

Jarvie, G. (2004). 'Sport in Changing Times and Places'. *British Journal of Sociology*, 55(4): 579–587.
Markovits, B. (2003). 'The Colours of Sport'. *New Left Review*, 22 (July/August): 151–160.
McGovern, P. (2002). 'Globalization or Internationalization? Foreign Footballers in the English League 1946–95'. *Sociology*, 36(1): 23–42.

Pfister, G. (1990). 'The medical discourse on female physical culture in Germany in the 19th and early 20th centuries'. *Journal of Sport History*, 17(2) 183–189.

Sassoon, D. (2002). 'On Cultural Markets'. *New Left Review*, 17 (September/October): 113–126.

Sugden, J. and Tomlinson, A. (1999). 'Digging the Dirt and Staying Clean: Retrieving the Investigative Tradition for a Critical Sociology of Sport'. *International Review for the Sociology of Sport*, 34(4): 385–397.

Further reading

Baylis, J. and Smith, S. (2001). *The Globalization of World Politics*: *An Introduction to International Relations*. Oxford: Oxford University Press.

Eitzen, D. (2003). *Fair and Foul*: *Beyond the Myths and Paradoxes of Sport*. New York: Rowan & Littlefield Publishers.

Field, J. (2003). *Social Capital*. London: Routledge.

Marshall, G. (1998). *Dictionary of Sociology*. Oxford: Oxford University Press.

Sugden, J. (1996). *Boxing and Society*: *An International Analysis*. Manchester: Manchester University Press.

REVISION QUESTIONS

1. Outline and develop five different levels of analysis by which you might begin to reflect upon sport, culture and society.

2. Critically discuss in detail the importance of sport in today's world.

3. What is the public role of the intellectual and/or student involved in the study of sport, culture and society?

4. In what ways might you describe modern sport?

5. What are some of the key questions facing the student of sport, culture and society?

PRACTICAL PROJECTS

1. Interview five people who are 10, 20, 30 or 40 years older than yourself and ask them to talk about what sport was when they were your age. Compile a short report on how sport has changed over time based upon your interviews.

2. Read the sports coverage of two national newspapers over a period of a month and count the number of articles and column inches devoted to different sports. Based upon your results write a short report comparing the uneven sports coverage of different sports.

3. Access the web site www.google.co.uk and insert sport+society in the search space. Read the articles listed and then carry out five other searches of your own choice in relation to sports topics such as sport+poverty or sport+environment or sport+politics.

4. Read the manifesto of any political party and see if it refers to sport. Suggest five sports policy recommendations that reflect the core values of the political party you have chosen.

5. Draw a flow chart of networks from key people in your or someone else's life whom you or they have met through sport. Consider and reflect upon the potential for sport to introduce and sustain networks of people.

WEBSITES

American Sports Data Incorporated
www.americansportsdata.com/pr

Sport in Europe
www.sport-in-europe.de

Streetfootball league initiative
www.streetleague.co.uk

The Foreign Policy Centre
www.fpc.org.uk, see discussion on Democratising Global Sport

University of Stirling sport sites
www.sports.stir.ac.uk/NewSite/SportSites.htm

Part 1

The broader context

INTRODUCTION

The three chapters that form the first part of this book examine broader contexts that have informed our knowledge about sport, culture and society.

Sport theory and the problem of values

How does theory help us to understand sport? Theory and empirical research provide ways of explaining and understanding sport. The constant interplay between theory and evidence helps to examine taken-for-granted sporting assumptions. Sporting myths need to be constantly challenged and re-evaluated. How these particular tools, theory and evidence, are used and for what purpose should not be the exclusive prerogative of researchers and students themselves but used in specific social contexts and on behalf of the individual's or group's values and interests. It is important that the accuracy, rigour and relevance of theory and evidence provide a basis for not only critically examining popular and unpopular sports issues but also providing students with solutions and explanation to particular sporting problems.

Sport, history and social change

How does the history of sport help us to understand the development of sport today? The socio-historical development of sport tells students of sport where and when particular sporting practices emerged. It owes as much to acknowledging cross-comparative contexts as it does contemporary historiography. It acknowledges the influence of the past on the present, but also the dangers of thinking solely contemporaneously. By enabling us to know about other centuries and other cultures an understanding of the socio-historical development of sport provides students with one of the best antidotes to any temporal sporting parochialism which assumes that the only time is now, and geographical parochialism which assumes that the only place is here. The emphasis on social change, sporting trends and past solutions to problems forms the core to understanding how sporting worlds are the way they are.

Sport, politics and culture

What are the politics of sport and culture? Chapter 3 seeks initially to identify some of the ways in which sport has figured within the political field. Politics has been variously described as being centrally concerned with sport when sport is involved with: (i) civil government, the state and public affairs; (ii) human conflict and its resolution or (iii) the sources and exercise of power. A contemporary view might be that politics only applies to human beings or at least to those beings that can communicate symbolically and thus make statements, invoke principles, argue and disagree. The politics of sport occurs in practice when people disagree about the distribution of resources and have at least some procedures for the resolution of such disagreements over sport. This is particularly pertinent to the analysis of sport, culture and society where competing definitions of this relationship struggle for dominance within and outside the sporting world.

Chapter 1

Sport, theory and the problem of values

Were athletic heroines such as Cathy Freeman able to make a sustainable difference by highlighting the plight of Aboriginal people in Australia? © Telegraph Group Limited (2000)

PREVIEW

Ideology • Social criticism • Theory and sport • Sociological imagination and sport • Sport within different traditions of social thought • Epistemology and ontology • Functionalism and sport • Symbolic interactionism and sport • Interpretative sociology and sport • Figurational sociology and sport • Political economy and sport • Culture, power and sport • Cultural and social anthropology and sport • Feminism and sport • Racism and sport • Globalisation and sport • Post-modernism and sport • Post-democracy and sport • Historical sociology and sport • Common ground between theories of sport.

OBJECTIVES

This chapter will:

- discuss the role of theory in analysing sport;
- outline the relationship between sports theory and values;
- consider different theoretical approaches to analysing sport;
- evaluate the relationship between sport, power and culture;
- consider the common ground between different traditions of social thought and sport;
- reject the notion of neutral or value-free sport.

INTRODUCTION

In approaching the study of sport for the first time it is useful to begin thinking about some of the many popular theoretical approaches to the study of sport, culture and society. Despite the burgeoning interest in sport, culture and society, one of the peculiarities of most *general* books in this area is that many, not all, are still discussed largely in isolation from a broader context and to a lesser extent the society of which they are part. Many popular sporting texts are not written from the standpoint of the critical thinker, sociologist, historian, geographer, anthropologist, feminist, economist or political scientist, all of whom have used concepts and theories as a basis for explaining and understanding sport as part of social life.

It is no coincidence that the thinker who evokes the promise of sociology to think about sport will draw upon political science, economics, social policy, history and other bodies of knowledge in practising and developing a critical and practical understanding of sporting problems, practices and issues. At the same time, those studies of sport which have helped to provide insights into different ways of understanding the world of sport or some part of it have all made domain assumptions, adopted starting points, prioritised certain questions and marginalised others. In this sense a number of competing problematics have emerged. Some of the most common have been Marxism, feminism, post-modernism, cultural studies, figurational or process sociology, social anthropology, interpretative sociology, positivism, humanism, structuralism and post-colonialism.

It would be a mistake to suggest that the above problematics are simply ideology. There is no agreed understanding of many of the concepts and ideas introduced in this book. Notions of justice, rights, equality, authority and poverty are all essentially contested concepts. The contests over different solutions, policies and approaches to sport that occur between different sports administrators, participants, researchers or teachers may also occur between any two people who subscribe to different political ideologies. The claim that any position can be dismissed on the grounds of ideology does in fact remove the possibility of having any healthy debate over any particular sports issue. If the criticism, writes Nuttall (2002:237), that having a particular ideological position negates what a person has to say, then the same is true of the person making that criticism. In other words, the criticism deprives itself of the context and structure needed for effective criticism. This is not so much an argument against ideology, but a warning against simply accepting uncritically all ideologies as a form of universalism.

All of the aforementioned themes have contributed to the scope and understanding of sport. One of the fundamental roles of the student of sport is to question critically and understand the very nature of why sport is the way it is and what it could or should be. The promise of fully understanding and grasping the complexity of sport, culture and society necessitates a broader understanding of sport and theory which in itself helps to inform not only the sociological imagination, but also the policy advisor, political activist, public speaker or student of sport who wants to think and reflect socially about sport, culture and society.

THE VALUE OF THEORY TO THE ANALYSIS OF SPORT, CULTURE AND SOCIETY

When asked what the value of theory is to the analysis of sport, culture and society, the following are some of the most common answers given: (i) asking theoretical questions is crucial to allowing us to explain or generalise about sport, culture and society; (ii) theoretical or hypothesis testing is a necessary part of approaching or organising research; (iii) theory is capable of illuminating circumstances or equally destroying certain cherished myths that are often taken for granted without being tested; and (iv) a good theory stimulates new ideas and is fruitful in terms of generating further areas of research or study.

Sport, culture and society, like other bodies of knowledge, has its own perspectives, ways of seeing things and of analysing human actions, as well as its own set of principles for interpretation. It is first and foremost a distinct body of knowledge, but it also has fluid boundaries in that it draws upon other bodies of knowledge, for example in the search for solving classical sociological problems. Fundamentally, both practical and scholastic social questions are not about interpreting the world of sport, but about how to change it. As a tentative summation of what is entailed in thinking sociologically about sport it is important to develop the habit of viewing human actions as elements of wider figurations. Sport does not exist in a value-free, neutral social, cultural or political context but is influenced by all of these contexts. The value of sociology to the study of sport, culture and society is primarily that it provides a multitude of different ways of thinking about the human world. The way one chooses to think about sport will ultimately depend upon the values and political standpoint from which one views the human world. Thinking sociologically about sport is more than just adopting a common-sense approach to sport, in that the art of thinking sociologically may help the student of sport to be more sensitive to the human conditions that constitute the different worlds of sport. Thinking sociologically about sport may help us to understand that an individual's personal experience of sport is ultimately connected to broader public issues.

19

As suggested earlier, it has been said that sociology is the power of the powerless and yet, as one leading exponent has pointed out, there is no guarantee that having acquired sociological understanding one can dissolve or disempower the resistance put up by the tough realities of everyday life. The power of understanding is no match for the pressures of coercion allied with resigned and submissive common sense (Bauman, 1990:18). If it were not for this understanding the chance of further freedoms being won through and in sport would be slimmer still. Sociological thinking helps the cause of freedom. In agreement with Bauman and May (2001:180) the service that sociology is well equipped to provide is to render to the human condition the promotion of a mutual understanding and tolerance as a potential condition of shared freedom. Sociology provides a basis for better understanding of not just societies and cultures but also of ourselves. As such it is as much about ontology or a way of being as it is about epistemology or ways of knowing.

The two terms epistemology and ontology are worth elaborating upon at this point. Epistemology, from the Greek word *episteme* meaning knowledge, is concerned with theories or a theory of knowledge that seeks to inform how we can know the world we inhabit. Important divisions within the philosophy of knowledge have been between rationalism or idealism and empiricism. In a sociological sense epistemology tends to emphasise the way in which forms of knowledge have been influenced by social structure. Ontological arguments are also an explicit feature of sociological theory in that they attempt to establish the nature of fundamental things that might exist in the world or of ways of being in the world. Ontology may refer simply to the study of being, yet at times it is worth distinguishing the ontology of a belief or practice from the theory that explains it. Thus at a lived or micro level the practice of sectarianism in Scottish football, for example, might be different from the theories that explain it.

Among the ontological sociological issues that researchers of sport, culture and society may have to consider are where they stand in relation to the nature of social facts, whether sociology is a contemporary or historically based subject, the relationship between materialism and idealism, structure and agency, or what is the essence of social class or social division in the twenty-first century. Thus a theorist attempting to explain the world of sport in society or even what is a social fact will utilise different paradigms of thought or bodies of knowledge to explain the way things are or could be. Some of the most prominent approaches have been symbolic interactionism, structuralism, Marxism, feminism, post-modernism, post-structuralism, post-nationalism and figurational sociology, all of which try to construct knowledge or ways of seeing the world and the place of sport within it.

In order to establish that theory is necessary it might be useful to consider two things: (i) the role and importance of theoretical thinking and (ii) the relationship between theory and research. A point that needs to be made here is that theoretical thinking is not a process divorced from sport or everyday life. Theoretical thinking is not the obscure and esoteric exercise that it is so often characterised as, but rather the rigorous and continual systematic attempt to make use of particular tools in order to interpret the world around us or solve a problem or provide for a programme of change, action or critical thinking. What sociological theory may provide is a mode of critique, a language of opposition and a promise that the potential for radical transformation actually exists. The role of the sociological researcher and student interested in sport is not simply to destroy myths about sport but also to ensure that the choices that are made about sport and the worlds in which it operates are genuinely free regardless of whether these choices are libertarian, on the one hand, or staunchly communitarian, on the other (Bauman 2000:252).

In the same way that the relationship between sport and capitalism was a common theme within much of the critical Marxist or socialist literature on sport produced towards the end of the twentieth century, the notion of global sport and the accompanying language of globalisation have increasingly and uncritically dominated social, cultural and political debates about the nature of sport in the early part of the twenty-first century. It is as if at some point a resolution between the inherent tensions brought about by globalisation and capitalism has been achieved and that sport and its relationship to capitalism has lost its meaningfulness as a way of thinking about sport in the world today. If we reduce the various theoretical forms of appeal to sport – globalisation, capitalism, the third way, or post-colonialism – as a basis for simple abstraction about the social world, then we need to jettison such an approach. If we view theory as useful shorthand for a set of collectively practised prompts to reflection – in other words, if we raise sport through all its activities and forms as a basis for reflexivity about the very nature of sport and the world itself, then we are subjecting sport and the world we live in to a qualitative assessment. Theory can help to lay the foundations for this assessment that in turn may extend to the notion of a critique of sport that is often ignored by mainstream, orthodox and traditional sports practitioners. This is but one of the core healthy progressive functions of theory – the function of criticism.

One of the fundamental functions of theory and sociology is that it contributes to a form of critique of existing forms of culture and society. Putting aside the issues of a sociology dominated by Western thinking, which is itself problematic, there is much credibility in the enduring claim that the practice of sociology demands invoking what C. Wright Mills (1970) referred to as the sociological imagination. This is a threefold exercise that involves an historical, anthropological and a critical sensitivity. The first effort of the sociological imagination involves recovering our own immediate past and understanding the basis of how historical transformation has influenced the social and cultural dimensions of life. The second effort entails the cultivation of an anthropological insight. This is particularly helpful in that it lends itself to an appreciation of the diversity of different modes of human existence and cultures throughout the world and not just those associated with the materiality of life in the West or advancing modern capitalist societies. Through a better understanding of the variety of human cultures and societies it is asserted that we can learn or facilitate a better understanding of ourselves. The third aspect of the imagination is but a combination of the first two in that the exercise of the sociological imagination avoids a critical analysis based upon the here and now and involves the potential of grasping an understanding of social relations between societies throughout the world.

Theory is also a necessary part of the research process and there are a number of possible explanations for this. First, it can inform the type of research that is undertaken in that the particular theoretical approach adopted will influence both the types of questions examined and the particular types of research methods adopted. This is because of the close relationship between certain theories and certain methods or, put more simply, certain

21

theoretical approaches have a disposition to certain methods. Second, theory informs how the data collected may be interpreted, not simply because certain conclusions may be derived as a result of the approach adopted, but also as a result of the type of theoretical scrutiny that is applied to data and empirical evidence. Finally, theory may act as a stimulus to pursue particular research topics and questions. In all of these approaches the accumulation of knowledge is continually evolving, although that which was taken for granted in the past might be superseded by contemporary ways of thinking. Earlier findings and previous ways of knowing may be returned to in the light of changing world conditions or new ways of thinking about data or the fact that the same continuing themes prevail, for example the relationship between rich and poor, or that the genuine transformative capacity of sport has never been realised.

Since at least the 1960s the scope and significance of the study of sport, culture and society has expanded rapidly. The breadth of perspectives that have been brought to bear upon sport has led some to be critical of the multi-paradigmatic rivalry which has been viewed as a source of potential weakness, while others have welcomed the breadth of perspectives as a basis for strengthening sociology's position as an integrative force for research into all social and developmental aspects of sport. While the importance of particular approaches and ways of knowing about sport will ultimately become less eclectic as one develops, in the first instance it is important for students of sport, culture and society to be familiar with some of the main epistemological developments which have shaped the area of study.

SPORT IN SOCIAL THOUGHT

One of the tasks and promises of sociological theory has always been to help us draw bigger diagnostic pictures of sport, culture and society. With these pictures students and researchers can begin to understand and comprehend the socially and politically situated nature of their work and being. Associated with this is the fact that critical analysts of sport, culture and society must also consider or decide upon their preferred entry point into any social or political analysis of sport. In other words, where do you as an individual, club, or group stand upon particular issues in sport such as inequality and social division, the way in which money is controlled and distributed in sport, the processes involved in the long-term development of sport, the way in which research findings are used to create policy decisions which impact upon communities and cultures or the extent to which sport should be used as a way of changing or drawing attention to people's lives in different parts of the world? In a sociological sense does sport help to produce or reproduce social, cultural and/or economic capital?

Sociologists and other groups of social/critical analysts have approached sport from a number of perspectives. The major perspectives which have impacted upon the study of sport since the mid-1960s, according to Coakley and Dunning (2002), have been functionalism, cultural studies, feminism, interpretative approaches, figurational sociology and post-structuralism. Others, such as Jarvie and Maguire (1994), have identified functionalism, interpretative sociology, pluralism, political economy, cultural studies, figurational sociology, feminism, post-modernism, structuralism (associated with the work of Bourdieu) and globalisation theory as the key traditions of social thought that have informed our knowledge about sport, culture and society. More recently Giulianotti (2005) has identified the main tenets of any critical sociology of sport as being Durkheim, Weber, Marx and Neo-Marxism, cultural studies and hegemony theory, race, ethnicity and intolerance, gender identities and sexuality, the body, space, Elias, Bourdieu, post-modernism and globalisation. All of these problematics have highlighted certain questions about sport and marginalised others. In other words, they provide a set of concepts and questions that make up a particular way of seeing the world of sport. In an epistemological sense they provide the tools for ways of knowing about the world of sport, culture and society.

What then are *some* of the main epistemological or theoretical developments that have influenced our understanding of sport, culture and society? It is impossible to adequately cover and evaluate all of the above and there is no one theoretical position that dominates this area. The jostling of divergent theoretical approaches will be viewed here as an expression of vitality. The coverage of various theoretical developments should not simply limit itself to sociology since other trends and influences such as post-colonialism and post-modernism are as much a product of social history and social geography as they are of sociology. Nor is what follows meant to be a simple chronology of the main developments in sociology reflected through sport.

Functionalism

Functionalist perspectives tend to be based upon the notion that social events can best be explained in terms of the function they perform. Society is viewed as a complex system whose various parts work in relationship to each other. Functionalist theories in both sociology and anthropology help to explain social institutions primarily in terms of functions and, consequently, if sport were viewed within this problematic one of the core questions would be what is the function of sport as a social institution today? Some of the central areas of debate have concerned the treatment of social order, power, social conflict and social change with the assertion being that functionalism overemphasises the socialised conception of sport in society at the expense of the human subject or individual agency. The idea of studying social life in terms of its social functions was adopted in the early twentieth century by social anthropology. Society was seen as being made up of different interdependent parts that operated together to meet different social needs. Anthropological functionalism has tended to emphasise methodological issues, while sociological functionalism has tended to be critical of the epistemological rationale informing this body of knowledge.

Commenting upon recent anthropological studies into football, Armstrong and Giulianotti (1997:27) talk of the appeal of football lending itself to Parsonian thinking. They go on to comment that just as players and teams seem to adapt themselves when confronted by difficult opponents to improve their goal attainment, so the system of the game itself continues to modify its shape and form in order to survive and thrive in new cultural circumstances. According to Loy and Booth (2002:17), the theoretical and substantive criticisms of functionalism relate to its consensual and contemporary bias. In other words functionalism as a normative body of knowledge exaggerates harmony, social stability and consensual politics. Its contemporary bias stems from its ahistorical or non-historical change over time. As a particular body of knowledge functionalism has existed for over 40 years and, although not a dominant force, some of the core concepts remain active with certain exponents who argue that explaining social phenomena such as sports practices leads naturally to questioning the existence of social practices and their explicit or hidden functions.

The following are some of the potential functions of sport:

- socio-emotional function, wherein sport contributes to the maintenance of socio-psychological stability;
- socialisation wherein sport contributes to the inculcation of cultural beliefs and mores;
- integrative function, wherein sport contributes to the harmonious integration of disparate individuals and diverse groups;
- political function wherein sport is used for ideological purposes;
- social mobility function wherein sport serves as a source of upward mobility.

Symbolic interactionism

Many would include symbolic interactionism within interpretative sociology. However, I have chosen to deal with them separately because they have each had a distinct contribution to make to the study of sport, culture and society. Symbolic interactionism originated in pragmatist philosophy that held that the truth of theories and concepts depended upon their value in practical terms. Symbolic interactionism places a strong emphasis on the role of symbols and language as core elements of all human interaction. The definitions that people use are constructed from the symbols that are available to them throughout their culture and society. Symbols convey information and are used by people to convey meaning to the situations in which they find themselves. These symbols are learned and communicated through interaction with others. The arguments of William James, George Mead, Erving Goffman and other symbolic interactionists have figured prominently in discussions of self, roles and identity, deviance and social reaction and social construction of health and organisations.

At least four core themes have been associated with symbolic interactionism. The theory highlights the way in which human beings distinctly manipulate symbols. It is through symbols that they alone are capable of producing culture and transmitting history. A further theme relates to the notion of process and emergence in the sense that the social world is viewed as a dynamic and dialectical web in which attention is paid not to rigid structures, but to a fluid process of interaction between self and society. Any understanding of, for example, an athlete's career and the extent to which sport contributes to personal identity or feelings of loss or achievement might be open to a symbolic interactionist approach. A further theme is emphasis on the fact that the social world is interactive and from this point of view there is no such thing as a solitary individual, only an understanding of the self in relation to other humans. Finally, certain strands of thought in the work of Georg Simmel have stressed that interactionists look beneath the symbols and processes and that any interaction is very much a dynamic process that is not necessarily harmonious. It involves the expression of meanings in a multi-layered exchange between social actors that is reciprocal and not simply linear or one-way. Symbolic interactionists may study the life experiences of footballers or baseball players or swimmers or dancers or sports administrators as distinct groups, but they would also detect common processes at work in all these groups, perhaps in terms of how status is negotiated or loss of status is dealt with.

The following are indicative questions that might arise out of a symbolic interactionist approach to sport.

- What does sport mean to oneself or what place has sport played in the individual's biography?
- How has one's personal identity been affected by sport over time?
- To what extent have feelings about sport been influenced by a process of interaction with others?
- How do sports form a pattern of association and interaction?
- How do athletes in certain situations reciprocate with and against one another?

In general symbolic interactionist approaches have attracted criticism because of their general neglect of power, history and social structure, but more recent interventions have shown such critiques to be somewhat misguided.

Interpretative sociology

As mentioned above interpretative sociology has tended to incorporate symbolic interactionism as a basis for looking at core issues, such as meaning, action, status, *Verstehen*, rationality and cultural relativism. While symbolic interactionism mounted an increasingly successful challenge to the excessive claims made by functionalism, it too was challenged in the 1960s by what was claimed to be a more radical perspective on interaction, namely phenomenology and ethnomethodology. Interpretative sociology has been associated with Weber, Simmel, Garfinkel, Schultz and the early work of Anthony Giddens. Phenomenological approaches have focused attention upon the taken-for-granted content of everyday consciousness. When reified these allegedly form the external constraining realities of society. Ethnomethodology attempts to take this one step further by examining the processes through which people sustain a taken-for-granted sense of reality in their everyday lives. It is not difficult to see the potential connections here with more contemporary perspectives such as post-modernism.

In one of the most authoritative overviews of interpretative sociology's contribution to the study of sport, Donnelly (2002) has highlighted a number of strands of work that have been developed within the sport, culture and society literature. In this review Donnelly proceeds to describe, critically examine and evaluate the impact of interpretative sociology upon the sociological study of sport. He outlines a number of areas that have come under the gaze of the interpretative sociologists of sport, including the analysis of media texts, sport sub-cultures, socialisation into sport, and biographical and narrative accounts of life histories and autobiographical accounts of sporting lives. The review concludes by suggesting

25

that perhaps the major impact of interpretative sociology has been 'the way in which it hangs flesh on the skeletons of survey data' (Donnelly, 2002:83).

The following are indicative questions that might arise out of an interpretative approach to sport.

- To what extent are sportspeople conscious of their actions?
- How have sportspeople's careers in reality been experienced?
- What socialisation experiences are involved in the process of becoming an athlete?
- How have media audiences internalised or interpreted the representations of sport in the media, particularly television?
- To what extent is status helpful in explaining sport and social order?

Process sociology

Figurational, sometimes referred to as process or developmental, sociology has grown out of the work of Norbert Elias. Its impact upon the sociology of sport has been sustained in a number of projects in the latter half of the twentieth century and the early part of the twenty-first century. Notions such as 'the civilising process' have been influential within the sociology of sport and also the history of sport. Polley (2003:57) has commented upon the fact that aspects of the civilising process have been influential within those areas of British sports historiography interested in explaining the development of modern sport in Britain. Many of the points of departure within this book reflect some of the concerns of figurational sociology, namely that theoretical accounts of sociology are as unsatisfactory as those accounts of sport that simply exude empirical findings without any theoretical grounding; that original sources were the very substance of history; that the mapping out of various processes was central to explaining how sport had developed more or less over time; that developmental accounts of sport were more than simple evolutionary or linear accounts of sporting progress since sport developed at different rates; that the development of sport and issues of involvement in and detachment from the material of study influenced the plausibility of the sociological account of sport provided.

A central facet of figurational sociology has been the notion of figuration that Elias (1978) referred to as a structure of mutually orientated and interdependent people. Figurations of interdependent people make up many webs of interdependence, which are characterised in part by different balances of power of many sorts, such as families, states, towns or simply groups. Elias used the word figuration as a processual or dynamic term in contrast with more static expressions, such as social system or social structure. Elias preferred to talk of process sociology rather than figurational sociology and this primacy of process, according to Goudsblom (1977:105), has four principled points of departure, namely that sociology is about people in the plural and that people's lives develop within and between the social figurations they form together; these figurations are continually in flux; the long-term developments taking place in human beings have and continue to be unplanned and the development of human knowledge is one important aspect of overall development. The primacy of process then has given rise to the notion of process sociology although the term figurational sociology is what is often referred to within the sport, culture and society literature.

Figurational accounts of sport have been supportive of the links between history and sociology, namely that a developmental approach to sport has made and continues to make an important contribution to historical sociology. The coverage of sport which has been informed by figurational sociology has included studies of the development of rugby in Britain, fox-hunting, global sport, boxing, Highland Games, football hooliganism and violence in sport in general.

The following are indicative questions that might arise out of a process sociology approach to sport.

- What are the principal processes that have been involved with the development of sport?
- Has sport become more or less violent over time?
- What have been the core figurations that have influenced the shifting balances of power in sport?
- How might the globalisation of sport be explained?
- Do we have a reality-congruent body of knowledge about sport?

Political economy

Classical Marxist and liberal theories of political economy have tended to provide a basis for a socio-economic analysis of sport. In short what is the politics that arises out of an analysis of sporting economics? Liberal political economy as opposed to Marxist political economy also developed around several themes more closely associated with the discipline of economics or more precisely the inter-relationship between economic theory and political action. It encompassed several broad themes, such as an economic theory of historical progress; a theory of accumulation and economic growth through the division of labour; a redefinition of wealth as comprised of commerce and not just treasure; a theory of individual behaviour which reconciled the pursuit of self-interest with the collective good and a labour theory of value which argued for labour as a measure and sometimes a source of value.

Marxist theories have tended to deal with a critique of capitalism and, as such, inherent within Marxist notions of political economy are the following questions:

- What is wealth?
- How is wealth produced?
- How did the ownership and means of production fall into the hands of the minority?
- What do we mean by class and how did classes come into being?
- What are the causes of slumps and economic crises under capitalism?
- What is the economic and political significance of the term imperialism?
- What is the economic foundation of socialist and communist societies?

The term political economy is often associated with Marx's critique of political economy, but in reality Marx never had a theory of political economy. He did have a critique of eighteenth- and nineteenth-century thinking about political economy. Any account of Marx's ideas has to be holistic in the sense that it was intensely practical and, unlike academic Marxism, the praxis of Marxism meant that the theories of social change went together with Marx's scientific theory.

The following are indicative questions that might arise out of a political economy of sport:

■ Who profits from sport and how is it organised under global capitalism?
■ How is wealth produced through sport and who benefits from this wealth?
■ Are different social groups – professional athletes, women, and/or black athletes exploited?
■ How have imperialism and colonialism influenced the development of world sport?
■ How might a materialist understanding of sports historiography be produced?

Culture and power

It is to its credit that much of the research into sport, culture and society since at least the 1980s has acknowledged the importance of a cultural politics that moves far beyond analysis of the nation-state. The Gramscian notion of hegemony has been a clarion call for a significant amount of research into sport. In its traditional sense hegemony has literally been taken to mean the ideological/cultural domination of one class by another achieved by engineering consensus through controlling the content of cultural forms and major institutions. In *Sport, Power and Culture*, John Hargreaves (1986) rejected a 'common-sense' approach to British sport on the grounds that it helped to sustain and reproduce rather than challenge particular notions of sport. It was argued throughout that it is precisely because sport played different roles in relation to different cultures that it was able to reproduce existing power relations. Culture, in the sense that we can identify working-class culture, men's and women's culture, black culture, bourgeois culture and youth culture, must be sensitive to the fact that the function and significance of sport within different cultures may vary. The point emphasised by Hargreaves (1986:9) was that the significance of sports varied within and between cultures, and that a comprehensive account of sport, power and culture had to make reference to other forms of culture such as popular culture and consumer culture, more specifically, the relationship between the populist attraction of sport and capitalism. Analysis of sport, power and culture consequently had to acknowledge the transformative potential of sport.

Over the past three decades one of the undoubted strengths of feminist work in the area of sport, power and culture has been the presence of significant differences and, consequently, rich substantive empirical work that has told us so many different stories about women's experiences of sport. These have acknowledged the fact that power is everywhere and that power is not simply an institution or a structure, but rather it is exercised through innumerable points, rather than a single political centre. Foucault (1988) was concerned with an analysis of power within detailed studies of social practices. This approach to power dealt directly with the antagonistic struggles of social movements, arguing that one of the most important aspects of these struggles in contemporary society was the way in which they challenged subjectification. These might include struggles against the power of men over women in sport or the coach over the child or parents over children or of the power of sporting administrative bodies over national sports plans or the way people experience sport.

The advantage of this approach to the study of sport, culture and society is that it allows the student to move beyond the conventional analysis of politics at the level of the state or the ways in which, for example, governments use sport as an instrument of nation-building or as a facet of health policy. This does not mean that the study of the way in which the state uses sport is irrelevant, but that the cultural politics in civil societies, between civil society and the state and within the practices and institutions considered to be of the state must also be taken into account when analysing the politics of sport. Cultural politics is understood to be potentially everywhere and therefore it has a broad social context.

The Canadian writer Richard Gruneau (1999:125) has argued that where there is no truth, only power, and where power is said to circulate everywhere, politics can only be understood as an ongoing localised tactical project. In this sense one form of domination or subordination is as relevant as any other, so political struggles through sport could easily be seen as little more than an arena of choice closely associated with one's self-identity. Without any normative standards for evaluating the politics of sport or when some forms of power are more prevalent than others at any point in time or for evaluating the conditions by which different political agendas come into conflict with one another, social criticism loses its potential. Since such an argument is developed further in Chapter 3, suffice it to say at this point that without such a dimension the idea of broad collective struggle through sport becomes reduced to a question of lifestyle politics.

The following are indicative questions that might arise out of a cultural studies approach to sport:

- What are the cultural politics of sport?
- How does a particular definition of sport become dominant in society at any given point in time?
- What is the relationship between sport, power and culture?
- How is a particular definition of sport challenged, struggled over and transformed?
- What is the meaning and symbolism of sport to different cultures?

Cultural and social anthropology

A resurgence of anthropological studies of sport has emerged from different parts of the world during the late twentieth century. Blanchard's (2002:144) review of the field tends to suggest that conventional anthropology is characterised by a primary focus upon people living in traditional, tribal or folk societies. One of the classical definitions of this approach to culture is provided by Kluckohn (1951:34) who suggests that 'culture consists in patterned ways of thinking, feeling and reacting, acquired and transmitted mainly by symbols, constituting the distinctive achievements of human groups, including their embodiments in artefacts'. The essential core of culture consists of traditional ideas and especially their attached values. The frequent use of cross-cultural comparative field studies provides for a substantive and empirical attention to how sport, games and play have evolved as part of the process of cultural change in different cultures. The study of objective cultural artefacts that contribute to a particular culture, tradition or set of customs is referred to as cultural materialism or etymology. A value of any etymological study of sport, such as Burnett's (2000) study of sport and games in Scotland before 1860, is the potential richness that can be found in the collection and analysis of those cultural artefacts such as songs, rituals, medals, flags, team colours and equipment associated with any grounded study of the sport. Any analysis of the cultural materials that make up sporting settings can contribute to an understanding of the social and cultural fabric of sport in both a contemporary and a historical sense.

Recent anthropological approaches to the study of sport have made a valuable contribution to the ethnography of sport, culture and society and yet such an approach has not been without criticism. In a critique of the anthropological studies of football, King (2002) argued that the failure to situate the ethnography within any critical anthropological or sociological framework led to a descent into forms of uncritical journalism. Anthropological approaches to sport have had the tendency to be all consuming and fail to differentiate and theorise adequately the notion of sport, power and culture. An all-consuming evolutionary approach to culture tends to marginalise issues of power and social differentiation between and within groups or sub-cultures. If everything within a particular way of life is seen as culture it is difficult to distinguish between different aspects of culture or the relationship between sub-cultures. The notions of power or social inequality or social differentiation or social inclusion and exclusion need not be silent within all-embracing anthropological notions of culture. King (2002:14) observes that thinking critically about sport necessitates researchers continually to question why they think the way they do and never taking for granted that the way they think is the correct way. This provides a starting point for any self-conscious reflection.

The following are indicative questions that might arise out of any cultural or social anthropological approach to sport:

- What is the symbolism attached to sporting rituals, customs and traditions?
- What can cultural materialism tell us about sport and games in traditional, tribal, folk or non-Western cultures?
- What are the limits and possibilities of viewing sport as an institution and therefore a component of culture?
- How have sporting ceremonies and festivals evolved?
- What does the anthropological study of play tell us about modern sport?

Feminism

Feminism, according to Ahmed (2000), is not simply one set of struggles in that it has mobilised different women in different places at different times, all of whom are seeking social transformation but who are not necessarily seeking the same thing nor even responding to the same situation. Feminism and theories of feminism therefore speak to different women for different reasons and for different political aims. It is not a single theory or a united political movement, nor is it a static body of knowledge. It is perhaps, argues hooks (2000:144), best described as a theory in the making. Certain key notions might include sexuality, patriarchy, gender logic, gender roles, space, femininity, engendered power relations, notions of the body, social difference and oppression. Just as it is mis-representative to talk of feminist theory and not theories, it is also misguided to state that feminism is a just a matter of women's equality. Yet in the sporting imagination this defin-ition of feminism is persistent within the popular imagination. It is a testament to the ongoing reflexivity inherent in feminism that there is at least recognition of the fact that women may oppress others. Consequently women can be both oppressed and oppressor.

It is evident that sport and for that matter physical activity is a site of contested gender ideology and as such key questions highlighted by feminist analyses of sport might include some or all of the following:

- Can sport reinforce and challenge traditional gender relations?
- How might we explain women's involvement in and alienation from sport?
- How have sporting structures historically exploited, under-valued and oppressed women?
- How have women on the margins of the sporting world experienced sport?
- How are women represented through the sporting media?
- How might we adopt a critical approach to accounts of sport, culture and society that have ignored or justified women's oppression?

In particular, the work of Jennifer Hargreaves (1994:2000) epitomises the complexity and diversity of women's experiences of sport and sporting heroism. At least in terms of sport, culture and society the diversity of women's sporting experiences move well beyond the boundaries of white middle-class feminism to encompass the sporting experiences of, for example, Muslim women and black South African women. This ongoing work on the question of difference, just as it has in feminism, has initiated a process of raising trouble-some questions within feminist politics of sport to the extent that its future directions remain vibrant and hotly debated. This does not mark the demise of feminist accounts of sport, culture and society rather it is, like other bodies of knowledge and ways of seeing the world, constantly shifting and as such is theory in the making (hooks: 2000).

The following are indicative questions that might arise out of feminist approaches to sport:

- How can sport contribute to the emancipation of women?
- What is the engendered nature of sport in different parts of the world?
- How do women in different parts of the world experience sport?
- How have women's sporting histories and biographies differed from other social divisions?
- What are the different sexual politics arising out of a study of body culture?

Racism and ethnicity

Racism is any political or social belief that justifies treating people differently according to their racial origins. Ethnicity refers to a sometimes complex combination of racial, cultural and historical characteristics by which societies are occasionally divided into separate and often hostile political families. Ethnicity often raises the question of national identity, which is why ethnic politics are often at their most virulent when they are attached to the politics of territory, space and place. Popular arguments about sport, racism and ethnicity have contributed to a number of racist beliefs about different people's sporting abilities. Sport has often been implicated in campaigns against racism and sporting organisations in many countries are subject to Race Relations Acts aimed at combating racism. Historically sport played a central role in bringing about change in South Africa during the period of apartheid rule. The African National Congress slogan, 'you cannot have normal sport in an abnormal society', specifically referred to the way in which the politics of apartheid or separateness mitigated against the possibility of multi-racial or anti-racial sport in South Africa. The 1968 Black Power demonstration by black American athletes at the 1968 Mexico Olympic Games was in part a protest against the treatment of black American people, but also an attempt to raise consciousness about the politics of participation in sport by talented black athletes, who were deemed to be first class citizens while running for their country on the athletic track, and second class citizens when they walked out of the athletic stadium. The politics of ethnic identity are evident in the emergence of the Maccabbi Games which is often referred to as the Jewish Olympic Games.

Both racism and ethnicity are closely associated with imperialism and post-colonialism. During the 1990s what were termed the new politics of race and racism displayed a deep ambivalence towards what was termed Eurocentric discourses and the politics of otherness. This approach challenged whiteness as the universal norm and what was at stake was the attempt to create a different vocabulary for representing racism, race and border relations – that is, the relationships that often cross national boundaries.

Norbert Elias presented a comprehensive analysis of prejudice-generating situations in his theory of the established and outsiders. An influx of outsiders always presents challenges to the way of life of established populations and tension arises out of the necessity to make room for newcomers. Anxiety and hostile feelings often reach boiling point between established and outsider groups and yet the established often have better resources to act upon their prejudices. Length of habitation is often invoked as a right to acquire land and outsiders are viewed as alien, different, intruders and often invaders with little or no entitlements. The complex relationship between the established and the outsiders does not comprehensively explain racial and ethnic tensions in or out of sport, but it goes a long way towards explaining a large variety of conflicts in situations involving prejudice and bitterness invoked by forms of antagonism involving the established and outsiders often in racial or ethnic situations.

In *Race, Sport and British Society*, Carrington and McDonald (2001:13) claim to have challenged racism in sport by providing a powerful rebuttal of the complex and subtle ways in which racial ideologies pervade the world of sport. The original book, while claiming to be about Britain, was in fact about part of Britain, namely England, and yet one of the more important points made in this introduction is the way in which theory and some evidence are in themselves seen as unsatisfactory. The link between theory and policy is viewed as paramount if in this case racial inequality is going to be challenged or creeping forms of social change in this area are going to be brought about. The politics of race, ethnicity and sport are ever changing and have the potential to make a significant contribution to other debates about imperialism, religion and post-colonialism. The dynamics of the contemporary world are such that anti-globalisation protesters now find themselves potentially aligned with al-Muhajiroun, an Islamic movement that exists to fulfil the commands of the Koran. While C. L. R. James denounced European colonialism, it is worth remembering that he had a profound respect for Western civilisation that today would probably be dismissed as Eurocentric or even racist.

The following are indicative questions that might arise out of an anti-racist or ethnic approach to sport.

- To what extent has racism and ethnicity in sport contributed to the politics of exclusion?
- What does an ethnic or multi-racial or anti-racial sports policy entail?
- How has institutional racism affected sportsmen and sportswomen of colour?
- How has sport helped to reproduce and challenge stereotypes, myths and prejudices about ethnic minority groups?
- In what ways has sport contributed to the cultural politics of imperialism and Eurocentrism?

It should be added that much of what is commented upon under the section on post-colonialism would connect with the politics of sport, racism and ethnicity.

Globalisation

Globalisation theories in relation to sport have tended to focus upon the spread of sport across the globe in economic, cultural and political terms. A particular strand of this process has been to argue that the nation-state and the national are no longer as important as the global or the European or indeed broader configurations such as the Celtic. There are two competing concepts of globalisation. One encompasses a community of human citizens for which a group of environmentalists might work, who talk in terms of thinking global and acting local. The other is of an unregulated free market where capital is king or queen and the poor are left to struggle with the consequences of deregulation, privatisation, and the international plundering by international corporations. Proponents of globalisation typically argue that we live in an age in which a new kind of international world has emerged, one that is characteristic of global competition for markets, consumers and culture. A facet of the free-market driven form of globalisation has been that markets have decided whether we will have pensions in our old age; whether people suffering from ill-health in Africa will be treated and what forms of games and sports will be supported or even whether certain regions will have football clubs or not.

Critics of globalisation insist that the process and development of global sport has neither been created completely nor produced a world that may be defined by rampant free markets or passive nation-states. While globalisation may exist as a process it has not been achieved as an end point. The movement for global change is often referred to as an anti-globalisation or anti-capitalist movement. There are two competing concepts of anti-globalisation, one termed radical and one moderate. The radical wing views globalisation as a process largely designed to ensure that wealthy elites become wealthier at the expense of poorer countries. The moderate wing, although more difficult to define, tends to share the view that globalisation has the potential to be good or bad. It has the potential to provide for a sharing of cultures paid for out of the economic growth provided by free trade. However because the institutions and rules that govern the world are currently controlled by wealthy elites, inequality, instability and injustice are inevitable. In a sporting context a corollary of this might be to argue that traditional cultural rights and sporting traditions need to be at least equally recognised as socially and culturally, if not economic-ally, as important as market-supported forms of commercialised sport.

The following are indicative questions that might arise out of an approach to sport informed by globalisation theory:

- What processes have led to the development of global sport?
- To what extent are peripheral sporting nations in the world dependent upon or devalued by virtue of their relationship to core sporting nations?
- Have national and local forms of sport been marginalised as a result of globalisation?
- To what extent is global sport a euphemism for Western or American or colonial forms of sport?
- Are sporting organisations such as FIFA and the IOC global sporting organisations?

Post-modernism

The belief that society is no longer governed by history or progress is one of the central tenets of post-modernism. Post-modern epistemology is highly pluralistic and diverse with no grand narrative directing its development. Although the history of the concept of post-modernism might be traced back to the 1960s, the post-modernist and subsequent post-structural influence on sport, culture and society emerged in the late 1980s and 1990s. It has hardly touched the Islamic countries, Asia or Latin America. The post-modern perspective is characterised by the rejection of grand theory and an emphasis on human difference. This potentially distances post-modernism from structuralism with its base in grand theory and a potential emphasis on the capitalist mode of production. Post-modern work on the body demonstrates that commodities do not necessarily have to be consumed, you merely have to gaze at them and be seduced into desiring them. Hence the post-modern body becomes a signifier of desire and you get bodies for aerobics, bodies for fashion, bodies for vacations, bodies for everything in the sense that the body can be seen to be an all-consuming metaphysical object of signs and desires. It signifies an unreal world of commodity signs rather than the real world of capital, production, consumption and exploitation.

The centrality of the symbolic value of post-modernism or post-structuralism is evident in Wynsberghe and Ritchie's (1998) analysis of the five-ring logo associated with the Olympic Games. Rather than being appropriated with the pseudo-sacred symbols and ideals associated with the modern Olympics signification, they argue that the logo has become a hyper commercial signifier used to signify virtually any product around which advertisers want to construct a story. They also argue that it signifies something for diverse groups of different people. In the same way Slowikowski's (1993) studies of sporting mascots, in particular those referred to as Native American mascots, are discussed or framed as a nostalgic, hyper, real, post-modern American culture that is absolutely fake.

Post-modernist writers tend to distance themselves from grand narratives or universal law-like statements. This emphasis on the need to study sport, culture and society from a number of viewpoints of diverse individuals and groups has been reflected in studies of gender differences as well as in studies of spaces of exclusion from and in sport occupied by minority groups defined by class, marital status, sexuality, race, age and disability. A major criticism directed at the post-modern approach to sport, culture and society is its unlimited approach to relativism. Because it privileges the views of all individuals, it appears that there is no limit to the range of possible interpretations to any given situation. In other words, there is no real world because everything is a signifier. This in particular has attracted concern from socially committed sports researchers and activists who decry post-modernism's inability to add anything to the real problem of sport's contribution to alleviating poverty and disadvantage.

The following are indicative questions that might arise out of an approach to sport informed by post-modernism:

- What are the characteristics of post-modern sport that suggest that the boundaries of sport have moved beyond modernity?
- To what extent do children of the bourgeoisie dominate the discussion of post-modern sport?
- If modern sport has failed, what promise does a post-sport world hold?
- Is the athletic body, or the sporting body or the healthy body a source of discipline and pleasure?
- To what extent has sport become a pure event devoid of any reference to nature and susceptible to imagined or synthetic images?

Perhaps the real value of post-modernist and post-structuralist thinking about sport is that it has shaken and challenged previous authoritative bodies of knowledge about sport but the extent to which it has brought about social change in the real world, if such a thing can exist, is open to question.

Post-democracy

Democracy in many parts of the world, not just the Western world, thrives when the mass of ordinary people actively participates in shaping the agenda of public life. Almost fifty years ago the Canadian political scientist C. B. Macpherson reminded us that there was a great deal of muddle about the term democracy and that at least three different types of democracy existed within the late twentieth century, these being the liberal democracy of most of the advanced capitalist countries, the underdeveloped variant of democracy that existed in many African countries and the then non-liberal form of democracy that characterised the now deceased communist eastern bloc countries (Macpherson, 1965). Much of this might be irrelevant to contemporary ways of being, but in conclusion Macpherson suggested

> societies that can best meet the demands of their own people for equal human rights and equal freedom for their members to realise their essential humanity will be the ones that survive and . . . if the West continues to rely upon market morality alone then it will decline in power.
>
> (Macpherson, 1965:66)

The idea of post-democracy describes situations in which boredom, frustration and disillusion with late twentieth-century forms of democracy exist. Such situations reflect the fact that in some places powerful minority interests have become far more influential than the wishes of ordinary people. Furthermore we live in a world in which many people have to be persuaded to exercise their vote because of a lack of trust and suspicion of political elites or oligarchies manipulating the system. Post-democracy is in part characterised by shifting patterns of irreverence and deference in which politicians anxiously seek to discover what their customers want in order to stay in business. It is part of the family of post-worlds in which it is increasingly difficult to distinguish appearance from reality because appearance is the only reality and the alleged end of ideology politics means that there are big ideas to hold on to. The disengagement of ordinary people from politics, which is developing across the world, is a further characteristic of a shift to a post-democratic period. The global or international firm has become the key institution in the post-democratic world. Social class is no longer a driving force behind democracy while the gap between rich and poor remains. The geography of anti-globalisation protests signals that a new world political landscape and international social forums have replaced national civil societies as the political ground for questioning neoliberal globalisation.

The questions that are facing a post-democratic world are not irrelevant to study of sport, culture and society. The following are indicative questions that might arise out of an approach to sport informed by post-democracy.

- How should sport be organised in a post-democratic world?
- To what extent has the rise in corruption within sport reflected a post-democratic world?
- What is the significance of global sports firms in influencing sport today?
- Is the nature of sport different between democratic and post-democratic worlds, and if so how?
- What should be done to promote trust in a post-democratic sports world?

Historical sociology

Historical sociological studies of sport have in some cases attempted to fill the middle ground between overtly theoretical sociological accounts of sport and dense micro-empirical historical accounts of sport. Such an approach is self-evident in Dunning and Sheard's (1979) study of the development of rugby; Gruneau (1999) on Canadian sport; Jarvie (1991) on the Scottish Highland Games; Maguire (1999) on global sport; Hill (2002) on sport, leisure and culture in twentieth-century Britain, and Hwang (2001) on sport in modern China. At least three types of concern constitute the focus of historical sociological studies of sport, namely a specific concern with explaining how sport has been affected by transition of one form of society to another; a further concern with tracing patterns of freedom and constraint in the life-histories of sports personnel and the relationship between these and broader public issues, and, finally, an insistence that historical studies of sport which are insensitive to sociological concerns are just as inadequate as those sociological studies of sport that do not pay due attention to historical or developmental concerns.

The following are indicative questions that might arise out of a historical sociological approach to sport:

■　How has sport been affected by the historical period in which it is located?
■　What is the role of the sports person in producing change?
■　To what extent have contemporary sporting problems and issues been inadequately resolved as a result of a tendency for sports journalists, politicians, writers and academics to retreat into the present?
■　What is the relationship between personal sporting biographies and broader public issues?
■　To what extent has sport had a part to play in the formation of different forms of identity and/or social division?

It might be useful to elaborate upon the term *problematic* at this point. Each of the approaches outlined above and all other forms of analysis are *problematic*, not in the sense that they are wrong or unethical, but that at various levels of sophistication they have provided the basis for the organisation of a field of knowledge or research about sport. In this sense this book speaks of a problematic as a definite structuring of knowledge about sport which organises a particular research enquiry into making certain kinds of questions about sport possible or permissible, and making other questions suppressed or marginalised. In other words, the problematic in which one chooses to operate as a student or researcher will in part determine the sorts of questions that are asked about sport. At the same time it will also highlight what questions are not being asked and why.

SUMMARY: IN SEARCH OF COMMON GROUND AND SOCIAL CHANGE

Each of the major approaches mentioned, and many others, can claim to illuminate some part of the complexity that is sport, culture and society. Writing better histories and more inclusive progressive theory means the pursuit of complexity rather than totality. Whatever position or story that the student of sport, culture and society wants to tell about the changing nature of sport in different cultures or societies, they can always be more complex and always partial. The student of sport needs to provide more reality-congruent bodies of knowledge by continually evaluating the continual inter-play between theory, evidence and the broader context.

In reality just as sociology needs history (and geography) so does theory need evidence. Purely theoretical accounts of sport, culture and society are just as unsatisfactory as those empirical accounts of sport that exude findings without any theoretical grounding or explanation. The constant interaction between theory and evidence remains one of the best defences against the imposition of grand theory or dogma or empiricism without explanation. The student of sport, culture and society should never be value-free or far less value-neutral. It is impossible to develop theoretical or problematic frameworks by which one can understand sport, culture and society in contemporary life by adopting a value-free position.

Students, like researchers, carry with them domain assumptions that inform their ontological existence and not just the approach to sport, culture and society. It might be suggested in the first instance that the student of sport, culture and society has at least three strategies (Bauman and May, 2001:170–173). The first strategy might be to reproduce or replicate the conventional scientific enterprise laid down by certain domain assumptions or epistemological rationale. The second strategy might be to produce scientific status in one's work without necessarily replicating existing practices or studies of sport, culture and society, but adding meaning to the object of enquiry. However thoroughly explored the world of sport described by science might be, it remains meaningless if the student or researcher of sport, culture and society does not attempt to recover the meaning of reality. This might be simply deemed as a more reflective position. Finally, it might be that the strategy option is neither replication nor reflection, but one of effect. The aim here is to demonstrate how the knowledge one has accumulated and the values one believes in can be demonstrably effective in pursuing practical ends in the analysis of sport, culture and society. To put this very simply, all the above approaches to sport, culture and society might be thought of in terms of epistemology, ontology and intervention. All the above approaches help equip the student to cope with the future role of the intellectual as public servant and destroyer of myths.

The object of the exercise does not rest solely with explanation, but with a sustained effort to produce social change, and challenge inequalities and myths. Understanding lies in the linkage between personal values, the interpretation of evidence and the epistemological vantage point from which to arrive at the conclusions or recommendations made by any particular piece of work, essay or research project. Simply stated, it lies in the reflexivity and critical consciousness inherent within a much more inclusive form of sociological imagination introduced by C. Wright Mills more than half a century ago.

In a sensitive and socially committed conclusion to *Sport, Leisure and Culture in Twentieth Century Britain*, Hill (2002:183–185) comments that there is an immense chasm between the grand all-consuming narrative informing sport and studies of sport that offer a smaller focus that might be traditionally empirical in their orientation. The search for whatever the truth might be perhaps lies somewhere in between these two polarities, but there is no escaping the idea that sport, culture and society is an important popular ideological battle-ground over values and therefore can never be neutral. Ultimately, the student of sport, culture and society needs to decide upon an entry point into the battleground over the particular issue, debate or social phenomena being studied. In all of this, critical social and historical analysts should acknowledge the socially situated nature of their work. The process of producing social change necessitates the need for multi-layered committed perspectives that move beyond just an explanation of what is going on in sport, culture and society.

KEY CONCEPTS

Culture	Ontology
Epistemology	Political economy
Ethnicity	Post-colonialism
Feminism	Post-modernism
Figurational sociology	Power
Functionalism	Problematic
Globalisation	Racism
Historical sociology	Symbolic interactionism
Ideology	Theory
Interpretative sociology	Values

KEY READING

Books

Coakley, J. and Dunning, E. (eds) (2002). *Handbook of Sports Studies*. London: Sage.

Donnelly, P. (2003). 'Sport and Social Theory'. In Houlihan, B. (ed.) *Sport and Society: A Student Introduction*. London: Sage, 1–28.

Hargreaves, J. A. (2000). *Heroines of Sports: The Politics of Difference and Identity*. London: Routledge.

Jarvie, G. and Maguire, J. (1994). *Sport and Leisure in Social Thought*. London: Routledge.

Gruneau, R. (1999). *Class, Sports and Social Development*. Illinois: Human Kinetics.

Journal articles

Blackshaw, T. (2002). 'The Sociology of Sport Reassessed in the Light of the Phenomenon of Zygmunt Bauman'. *International Review of the Sociology of Sport*, 37(2): 199–218.

Nash, K. (2001). 'The Cultural Turn in Social Theory: Towards a Theory of Cultural Politics'. *Sociology*, 35(1): 77–92.

Sugden, J. and Tomlinson, A. (1999). 'Digging the Dirt and Staying Clean: Retrieving the Investigative Tradition for a Critical Sociology of Sport'. *International Review for the Sociology of Sport*, 34(4): 385–397.

Therborn, G. (2001). 'Into the 21st Century'. *New Left Review*, 10 (May): 87–111.

Vaugrand, H. (2001). 'Pierre Bourdieu and Jean-Marie Brohm: The Schemes of Intelligibility and Issues towards a Theory of Knowledge in the Sociology of Sport'. *International Review of the Sociology of Sport*, 36(2): 183–220.

Further reading

Bale, J. and Philo, C. (eds) (1998). *Body Cultures: Essays on Sport, Space and Identity: Henning Eichberg*. London: Routledge.

Bale, J. (2003). *Sports Geography*. London: Routledge.

Giulianotti, R. (ed.) (2004). *Sport and Modern Social Theorists*. Basingstoke: Palgrave Macmillan.

Henry, I. (2002). *The Politics of Leisure Policy*. Basingstoke: Palgrave.

Sugden, J. and Tomlinson, A. (eds) (2002). *Power Games: A Critical Sociology of Sport*. London: Routledge.

Wearing, B. (1998). *Leisure and Feminist Theory*. London: Sage.

REVISION QUESTIONS

1. Explain the role of theory in the investigation of sport, culture and society.

2. Compare and contrast any three approaches to social thought that have informed our understanding of sport.

3. Explain ways in which a commitment to any particular problematic or epistemology might bring about social change.

4. In searching for common ground what three strategies are open to the student of sport, culture and society?

5. To what extent do values influence the study of sport, culture and society?

PRACTICAL PROJECTS

1. Through discussing sport with your friends link five personal sporting troubles they may identify to broader public issues about sport.

2. Write down five policy directives that would be at the heart of any policy aimed at tackling racism or sexist behaviour.

3. Chose any five sports clubs and ask members of the club what badges, flags and songs are associated with supporters or club members. Use the evidence to write a short report on what the club stands for and what values or symbols are associated with the club.

4. Design and implement a small survey aimed at gathering empirical information about the voting patterns of (a) fans or (b) sports club members or (c) any other specific sport or exercise population. What does the information gathered tell you about sport and political values?

5. Investigate the committee or executive membership of any sports club or organisation over a five-year period and explain the process of election or appointment to the committee or executive board.

WEBSITES

British Sociological Association
   www.bsa.co.uk

Fabian Global Forum
   www.fabianglobalforum.net

Mathare Youth Sports Project
   www.mysakenya.org

University of Stirling sport sites
   www.sport.stir.ac.uk/NewSite/SportSites.htm

The First Tee Project
   www.thefirstee.org

Chapter 2

Sport, history and social change

Women's football is not a new phenomenon. The picture above, showing Leith Ladies, is evidence of organised women's football being played in Scotland as early as 1938. Trustees of the National Museums of Scotland

PREVIEW

Why sports history matters • Dangers of contemporary sport • Change and continuity in sport • Comparative physical cultures • Sporting plausibility and complexity • Change and the meaning of sport • Sporting past, heritage and mythology • Making sporting heritage and golden sporting moments • Sporting tradition and invention • Historical and sporting forces • Sport and post-feminism • Sport and post-modernism and sport and post-colonialism.

OBJECTIVES

This chapter will:

■ answer the question why sports history matters;

■ evaluate the historical contribution to sport, culture and society;

■ consider the value of historical sociology, popular memory, heritage and tradition to the study of sports history;

■ critically discuss some of the major forces which have influenced modern sports historiography;

■ explain why the historical contribution to the study of sport and social change cannot be left to questions about identity history.

INTRODUCTION

Social historians ask questions about the nature and place of sports in given times among given peoples and about how and why people constructed particular forms of sport, where these sports have travelled to around the world and what they mean to different groups of people. The socio-historical development of sport tells us where and when particular sporting practices emerged. It owes as much to acknowledging cross-comparative contexts as it does to contemporary social history. The stories of people's sporting experiences located and understood within the context of their time and place are a valuable part of the story of sport, but they also help to shed light on many if not all of the core themes in this book and more. This chapter introduces some of the core historical forces and rationales that are used to explain why, when and how sport has changed. As mentioned in Chapter 1, the process of producing social change itself entails the need for multi-layered committed perspectives that move beyond explanation of what is going on in sport, culture and society. History is an important part of this committed perspective. To paraphrase Sugden and Tomlinson (1999:387), 'it is vital to give research into contemporary phenomena a dynamic historical dimension'; or Struna (2002:197), 'we need to begin to attend to continuities as well as to discontinuities, over time rather than focusing on what appears to be new in time. In so doing we might understand better what if anything is ever new in the world of sport'; or Holt (2000:54), 'sports history has been overwhelmingly concerned with establishing the context under which sports could develop'; or Mason (1988:7), 'the notion that sport has nothing to do with anything else has a strong and revered history as well as an extremely energetic present'; or Polley (2003:59), 'while sports historians recognise the value of looking at sport in the past as a way of understanding sport in the present, their work shows that sport in the past needs to be understood on its terms'; or finally Southgate (1996:137), 'historical study can provide one route in the required direction, one focus from which to try to make sense of ourselves and most importantly, history can therefore help to determine the future that we want'.

By enabling us to know about other centuries and other cultures, an understanding of the social-historical development of sport provides one of the best antidotes against both a temporal sporting parochialism that assumes that the only time is now and a geographical parochialism that assumes that the only place is here. There is not only here and now, there is also there and then. In sport one of the best defences against retreating into the present is sports historiography, in part because it helps us understand how other sporting worlds have developed. The impact of historical interventions and ideas upon the study of sport has been one of the richest and most enduring. As with other areas it has had to answer post-modern debates about facts, objectivity and truth, post-colonial debates about the non-Western worlds, colonialism and other histories and representations of sport, while at the same time adding plausibility and complexity to what we know about sport in the past and present.

WHY SPORTS HISTORY MATTERS

While the following list is not exhaustive, it is perhaps illustrative of the areas in which the historiography of sport has helped to illuminate what we know about sport, culture and society. The following are not in any order, rather they form the bulk of what have been key areas of investigation or topics or questions over the past ten or fifteen years. The historiography of sport is still being constructed and the areas listed below will not necessarily be the agendas of the future. On the other hand, any attempt to construct a synthesis of what we know about the contribution of sport to past and present cultures and society would have to acknowledge some or all of the following general bodies of sporting history or themes:

■ the roots of sport in ancient societies;
■ sport in the middle ages;
■ sport in colonial and post-colonial societies;
■ women's sporting experiences from at least the nineteenth century;
■ nineteenth- and twentieth-century working-class sport;
■ rich internal sporting histories of clubs or events;
■ sport in the lives of different racial, ethnic and indigenous groups;
■ the social formation and transformation of sport within the historiography of various nations;
■ sporting tradition and the making of heritage and mythology;
■ post-sporting histories, such as post-modernism, post-colonialism and post-feminism;
■ comparative and cross-cultural histories of sport and physical cultures;
■ oral histories and biographies of sporting heroes and heroines.

The history of sport teaches students and researchers many things not least of which is that it instils a sense of caution with regard to dogmatic generalisation and theorising. Many of the above themes have provided rich, detailed, micro-histories of sport that have stressed the continual interplay between change and continuity. It makes little sense to argue that women have more power in sport today without acknowledging the power and influence of women in sport in the past. To argue that sport has become increasingly global implies that sport today is being compared with sport in a previous period. The *process* of globalisation or urbanisation or commercialisation or professionalisation implies that some sort of change has taken place over time and therefore to talk of commercialisation in sport is to suggest that the levels of commerce associated with sport have increased or decreased. When governments insist that participation rates in sport have improved it is necessary to compare rates of participation in sport over a period of time. History teaches students that social surveys upon which much policy information on sport depends, only really provide a snapshot or moment in time and cannot really be understood without acknowledging or exploring further what went on before.

You cannot begin to understand the significance of rugby union in Wales without knowing about the social, cultural and economic history of Wales. Similarly, the symbolic relationship between the Grey Cup (ice-hockey) and Canada, or the World Superbowl (American football) and the United States of America, or the All-Ireland Gaelic Football Final and Ireland, or Wimbledon (tennis) and Great Britain, cannot be fully explained without substantiating and acknowledging that such sporting occasions are also social institutions that have increasing or decreasing levels of importance to various nations because of the historical association between these events and the cultural and national historiography of the respective nations. Indeed, all of the ways in which sport contributes to the making of nations (see Chapter 5) have histories, as do colonial and post-colonial sporting traditions and indigenous forms of sport that offer challenges to mainstream forms of sport and culture. It is crucial to acknowledge that sport has been played differently at different times in different nations and places.

Dangers of contemporary sport

Perhaps the historiography of sport's unique contribution lies in its potential to unshackle minds from the constraints of the present. An important role for the history of sport is to liberate students from the chronological aridity and constraint of the present, or what others have termed a retreat into the present (Elias, 1983). Contemporary sport at times may seem more accessible to the sporting enthusiast or student of sport, but contemporary 'tunnel vision' fails to acknowledge the fact that the history of sport can tell us a great deal about contemporary sport.

It is often assumed that the popular involvement of women in sport is relatively modern and yet the historiography of women's sport has done much to alter our views about sport in society. Box 2.1 is an *illustrative* history of the development of women's sport. Much of this body of work has moved beyond identifying particular women as sporting heroines or victims of patriarchy. Helen Lenskyj (1990) has explored the once taboo subjects of sex and sexualisation and how they provided boundaries that impacted upon women's sport; Jennifer Hargreaves' (2000) painstaking oral histories of Muslim, Aboriginal and Black women have crucially intervened to provide a far less Eurocentric picture of world sport (this body of work is one of the few which is sensitive to the way in which the story of women's experiences of sport over time has been overlaid by class and race); Patricia Vertinsky (1994) has explored the changing nature of women's control over their own bodies at given points in time; Todd Crosset's (1995) oral testimonies from US women professional golfers not only illuminate and describe an evolving process within a world of sport where what is required to achieve success as a golfer is clearly at odds with wider expectations of what it takes to make it as a woman; while Vicky Paraschak (1990, 1995) has documented and explored the strategies adopted by native Inuit peoples, including women, who have historically struggled to maintain the values, often utilitarian, of traditional sports and pastimes threatened by the march of modern sport.

BOX 2.1 A SELECTED HISTORY OF SOME MILESTONES IN WOMEN'S SPORT

1500 BC	Female bull jumpers in Crete defy death.
1000 BC	Atalanta out-wrestles Peleus; the women-only Herean Games take place in Greece.
440 BC	Kallipateira sneaks into the Olympic Games and men devise the first sex test to keep women out.
396 BC	Princess Kyniska of Sparta is the first female Olympic champion, winning the chariot race.
1424	Madame Margot outplays Parisian men at *jeu de paume*, an early version of tennis.
1900	Women are included on the programme of the modern Olympic Games competing in golf and tennis; tennis player Charlotte Cooper of Great Britain becomes the first woman Olympic champion.
1922	Suzanne Lenglen makes her Wimbledon debut.
1924	The Fédération Sportive Féminine Internationale organises the first Women's Olympic Games in Paris; in one day alone, 20,000 spectators watch 18 world records broken in track and field.
1926	Alexandrine Gibb spearheads the formation of the Women's Amateur Athletic Federation of Canada (WAAF) to initiate international competition for Canadian women; the second Women's Games are held in Gothenburg, Sweden, with entries from 10 nations.
1928	Staging the only feminist boycott in Olympic history, the British women stay away from the Games to protest against the lack of women's Olympic events.
1930	The third Women's Games are held in Prague.
1934	The fourth and last Women's Games are held in London.
1936	The Women's Games are cancelled in exchange for a nine-event Olympic programme for women.
1948	Fanny Blankers-Koen of the Netherlands is the first mother to be an Olympic gold medallist.

continued

1968   Enrigueta Basilio becomes the first woman in Olympic history to set alight the modern Olympic flame.

2002   Vonetta Flowers becomes the first black American athlete to compete at the Winter Olympic Games.

No women took part in the first modern Games in 1896. Today the balance remains weighted in favour of men, but it is tilting. At the XXVIth Games in Atlanta, for example, 97 of the 271 events were open to women, with 11 contested by both genders; 3,626 of the 10,629 athletes were women.

For a more detailed history of women in sport with specific reference to one country see http://www.caaws.ca/milestones

Accounts of women and sport in the nineteenth century emphasise participation in terms of patrons, spectators and players. In Scotland wealthy women presented sporting prizes, such as the miniature silver curling stone that Mrs Houison-Crawford of Craufurdland gave for competition between the curlers of Fenwick and Kilmarnock. The number of women who had access to sport at the start of the nineteenth century was small, but not as small as the number of women who boxed, as two did on Glasgow Green in 1828. The first Ladies Golf Club was established at St Andrews in 1867, shortly followed by Ladies Golf Clubs at Musselburgh (1872), at Carnoustie (1873), Panmure (1874) and Perth (1879). Almost two-thirds of the 42 founder members of the Avon Lawn Tennis Club at Linlithgow in 1880 were female; in some cases the number of females equalled and exceeded the number of males in the Tennis Club Championships, as happened in the Braid Club in Edinburgh in 1895. The point that is being illustrated here is that sports historiography can help to qualify, complement and add to present-centred approaches to the study of sport, culture and society.

The danger of thinking solely in contemporaneous terms is that of remaining blinkered to the past and the extent to which contemporary oral histories and testimonies, past newspaper accounts of sport, government archives, photographs, club histories, minutes and other forms of historical knowledge are all sources of evidence which potentially stop researchers from retreating into the present. They are important in evaluating trends and rates of development and critically evaluating whether change has taken place or not. They also serve as a reminder of the necessary evidence-based nature of sports historiography. The history of sport helps to define and answer sporting problems, provide evidence and to illuminate the context in which sport has developed or could develop.

Change and continuity in sport

In his history of sport and society since 1945, Polley (1998) demonstrates ways in which sport has figured in the post-war British historical experience. The argument is that sport has literally given physical form to debates about gender, class, ethnicity, the nation, the state and commerce in Britain since 1945. This succinct conclusion is worth commenting upon in some detail since it serves as an illustration and reminder of one of the crucial facets of historical work, namely evaluating and mapping out the extent to which change and continuity have or have not occurred. Polley (1998:161) notes that while continuity and change may be relative concepts and that problems may exist with various interest groups contesting whether change has been good or bad for sport, nonetheless it is one of the challenges and duties of the historian to analyse and chart such developments.

In his summation of the development of British sport Polley (1998) mentions some of the changes that have taken place since 1945 as being that: the state has a more structured relationship with sport; sport has become less insular through embracing international developments; a transition from amateur to professional management structures emerged; rates of commercialisation associated with sport have changed; women have more access to sport than in 1945; social mobility has altered the class appearance of British sport; sport has also become more ethnically diverse; there has been a certain degree of hybridisation in sport itself with combined rules sports emerging in certain contexts (i.e. combined rules for shinty/hurling international matches between Scotland and Ireland) and there is a greater diversity of sport available for people to participate in.

On the other hand, there has been a great deal of continuity since 1945 and many of the changes, asserts Polley (1998:162), may have been quantitative rather than qualititative differences. The structure of British sport with the emergence of governing bodies of sport, enforcement of standardised rules and regulations and the development of regular competition remains intact; voluntarism and amateurism continue to inform in part the way in which mass sport is administered and played; the maintenance of club colours, names and cultures reinforces notions of continuity and sport continues to be part of the debate about inequality and opportunity. That is, as Holt and Mason (2000:ix) put it, 'Post-war sport had its own agenda which has to be understood in its own terms.'

Comparative physical cultures

The uses of historiography in exploring comparative physical cultures, as Holt (2000) reminds us, can help with defining comparative sporting problems and, more importantly, understanding the context because, for Holt (2000:54), 'sport history has been overwhelmingly concerned with establishing the context under which sports could develop'. Comparative work on sport has illuminated links between the making of identity and nationalism. Students and researchers of sport, culture and society may want to take up some of Holt's challenges: to develop comparative analysis of the way sporting heroes and heroines in different cultures are produced and projected; to compare sport and physical culture in any two great cities or capitals of the world, Edinburgh and Paris; Madrid and Moscow; Beijing and Calcutta; London and Washington; Nairobi and Glasgow; or Tokyo and Seoul, to name but a few; to examine how sporting excellence has been produced in two different regions; or to compare the values associated with body cultures in nineteenth-century Germany and Britain or Denmark and Pakistan or Italy and Kenya. While historically processes such as urbanisation, industrialisation and colonialisation have profoundly influenced the development of sport and physical culture it is doubtful whether such experiences have been the same for any two nations, regions or continents. Thus, some of the best comparative cross-cultural work needs history to properly understand the totality of the underlying forces that have impacted upon the development of sport and physical culture in different places.

The fundamental purpose of comparative cross-cultural work applies to both historiography and other areas of investigation, notably anthropology and sociology, but as a component of critical reflection upon sport, culture and society the comparative lessons include understanding more about 'others' both in terms of sports geography (place and space) and sports historiography, understanding the subtleties and nuances of sport in terms of time and place, and both are different. The work of the archaeologist informs both cultural and historical knowledge about sport and physical culture. Cave dwellers placed pictographs of sporting and physical pursuits on cave walls. Perhaps the social and political value of comparative cross-cultural work is that it enhances interpretation and helps to undermine the formation of stereotypical or Eurocentric or insular, parochial, inward-looking thinking about sport. It is invaluable, for example, in thinking about how a particular sport or place stands in relation to general claims about global sport or globalisation. It enhances the complexity of knowledge and understanding about sport and helps to challenge orthodox or complacent claims about core or mainstream sport by arming the student with alternative and residual forms of sport from many places and times.

Sporting plausibility and complexity

Despite the intervention made by various forms of post-history of sport, one of the historical lessons remains embedded within the plausibility and supremacy of the historical evidence collected. Without entering a theoretical debate on issues of dogma, dogmatism and ideology in the history of sport, for some historians the supremacy and plausibility of the research evidence provides the foundation for separating the history of sport from sport as fiction and myth. Like the physiologist or economist the historian of sport aims to increase the sum of our knowledge about sport. Like other areas of investigation that inform our knowledge about sport, culture and society, common issues about the relationship between theory and evidence, description and explanation, and universality and reliability all exist. A large part of the conviction of the story that the historian wants to tell us about sport lies in the accumulative, exhaustive and plausible range of sources that are brought to bear upon any historical problem.

To insist upon the supremacy of the evidence and the centrality of the distinction between verifiable historical fact and fiction is not the holy grail of the professional historian. Within historians of sport, however, there is, one suspects, a consensus on *matters of substance* despite the varied and complex histories of sport that are told. Polley (2003:51) reminds us that generations of historians have been trained to find evidence, interpret it and then come to a plausible conclusion. One of the crucial facets of the making of plausible histories of sport is that the student or researcher of sport, culture and society must at some point answer the question of whether or not the historical evidence is sufficiently complete to provide a solution to the sporting problem or historical question of sport. Good histories of sport, culture and society acquire cumulative plausibility without claiming to be right or wrong

(Holt, 2000:50). Methodology is not a replacement for thinking and interpretation. This can be done without being descriptive or exaggerating any *truth* claims, nor adopting a grand narrative stance.

Sociologists too have recognised the need for complex sporting histories, but the meaning of the word 'complex' varies. The nature and plausibility of the range of sources of evidence is of primary concern to the historian. This is somewhat different from the challenge laid down by Gruneau (1999:127) when it is suggested that the post-modern assault on studies of sport and social development means that writing better history and more inclusive theory involves the pursuit of complexity rather than totality. The challenge, according to Gruneau (1999), is to write theoretically informed histories of sport that are sensitive to multiple and uneven paths of change. The difference between those who write sociological and historical accounts of sport, culture and society is perhaps a matter of emphasis on the nature of the approach that is adopted rather than not recognising the value of sport from a historical sociological point of view.

Change and the meaning of sport

Whether you see the history of sport primarily as an art, as a way of structuring the world through the narrative or stories that you want or have to tell about sport, or whether you conceive of the history of sport as a science, getting as close as possible to the actuality of the past by the rigours of methodologies or accumulation of evidence brought to bear upon it, what cannot be done is to prevent the history of sport from focusing upon social change as part of its *raison d'être*. The history of sport would make little sense in a society that did not change, and equally in a society that did not see change as a fundamental category of existence. Trends, transformations, developments, continuities and changes are perhaps much of the essence and function of the history of sport. How sport has been influenced by the historical epoch in which it moves or is located remains one of the core questions that needs to be addressed by any student or researcher of sport, culture and society.

If answering the above question is one of the reasons why the history of sport matters, then a further core reason is to explore the *meaning* of sport. The degree to which the meaning of sport has paralleled social change is an issue that encompasses some of the most basic questions that might be asked about the changing relationship of sport to processes of globalisation, urbanisation, modernisation, democratisation, bureaucratisation, Americanisation, rationalisation, as well as such issues as social inequality, social division and poverty. The importance of understanding the changing meaning of sport is at the heart of Hill's study of sport, leisure and culture in twentieth-century Britain (Hill, 2002). The sentiments expressed in the conclusions of this study are worth emphasising. Two crucial points are prioritised, first 'if our study of sport and leisure does not attempt to tease out the *meaning* of what we do in our free time and to place it in some context of contestation and negotiation, it seems to me not to be a very significant aspect of our lives' and second, that 'if the study of sport and leisure is not political in the broadest sense of the word, then it isn't worth a damn' (Hill, 2002:187). This sentiment echoes Hobsbawm (1997:140) who

51

insisted that political partisanship together with scholarship and plausibility can often serve to counteract the increasing tendency to look inwards to the academy. It might be that much political partisan scholarship in the history of sport remains trivial, engaged in proving a predetermined truth, doctrine or narrative. But if plausibility, coupled with partisanship, helps to produce new ideas, then the history of sport needs to continue to connect with broader historical and social forces that have brought about social change. This helps in terms of not just thinking about how sport is or has been, but also, and perhaps more importantly, what it can or should be. Thus, the history of sport, for example, has a direct relevance to the contemporary governance of sport because it adds plausible and yet partisan directives for the governance of sport.

SPORTING PAST, HERITAGE AND MYTHOLOGY

The sporting past has been central to issues of tradition and heritage. The heritage industry spends millions on constructing national and local heritages. Sports halls of fame are as important to sporting culture as the laboratory is to the sports scientist. The Manchester United Football Museum, as Vamplew (1998:269) reminds us, attracts in excess of 150,000 paying customers per year. National sporting histories are displayed in museums in Prague, Helsinki, Melbourne and Edinburgh, while specialist sports halls of fame in the United States are to be found for most popular sports. Sports museums and halls of fame are often celebrated as the public face of sports historiography. The celebration of the sporting past, sporting heroes and heroines and inter-generational exchanges over the golden era of a particular sport have all involved issues of selection, nostalgia, myth and romanticism (Vamplew, 1998). Sports museums and halls of fame are useful sites to explore questions about local and national identity while at the same time catering for the commercial and heritage-driven culture of tourism.

There are several specific reasons why sports historians might question the contribution of the sports museum to sports history. Vamplew (1998:297) suggests some of the following: (i) sports museums cater for the nostalgia market and an institutionalised version of the golden age; (ii) errors of fact, myth and interpretation are both perpetuated and problematic; (iii) the sporting artefacts are often displayed without sufficient explanation or context; (iv) the financial imperative often gets in the way of historical objectivity; (v) halls of fame and to a lesser extent sports museums can be shrines to sporting heroes and heroines, they tend to glamorise sporting events and achievements and therefore display an uncritical approach to the material and, following on from this, (vi) the controversial or unsavoury sporting past is often marginalised.

It is possible to be critical of sporting heritage not just because of its association with conservation and a conservative ideology which can be imperialistic, nostalgic, exclusive and part of a nationalistic response to the need to conserve national history and identity, but also because heritage can construct a national fable and glorify and sanitise the past by developing sporting myths. The making of sporting heritage has glorified golden sporting moments and often been part of a reaction or a need to reassert particular values that are often anti-democratic.

Making sporting heritage and golden sporting moments

Heritage is something of a rhapsody on history. The real value of heritage lies in its perennial flexibility and the strength of the emotions it evokes. Celebratory and commemorative reflections on past sporting experiences tend to merge historical sporting incidents, folk memories, selected traditions and often sheer fantasy in order to interpret the sporting past in a way that is meaningful to a contemporary group. The danger is that the bits of the past that seem most significant continually change relative to the present. Heritage representations are often regarded by sports historians as inherently artificial or inauthentic – a sort of staged authenticity involving mythical history to meet commercial and/or tourist demands. The markets, and market values, are viewed as subsuming everything and nothing is valued in itself, only as heritage currency.

Contrasts between idealised pasts and problems of the present are often implicit in celebrations of sporting heritage or golden moments in sports history. The golden era vintage of sports historiography is often underpinned by the notion that sport in the past was better, not just in terms of performance but more regarding conduct and style, than sport in the present and that person x in year w would have run, jumped or fought better than person y in year z. At the turn of this century Muhammed Ali was rightly or wrongly declared to be the athlete of the twentieth century not just because of his athletic ability, but because of the various political stances he took on certain issues and because of his enduring popularity and celebrity status with the public. In other words, he is drawn upon as an inspiration to today's sport and society.

Polley (1998:2) reminds us of two ways in which views of the past are mobilised in relation to the present. The first is to invoke nostalgia and a belief in a golden age. This often takes the form that sport in the past was purer and that contemporary sport has become corrupt: politics, drugs, commercialisation, violence and professionalism are raised as the usual suspects to denounce contemporary sport as not being like it was in the 'good old days' when football crowds regularly exceeded 100,000 in the stadium. Changes in tradition often give rise to puritan conservative defences of the past, as demonstrated by critical responses to the broadening of sports in the Olympic programme to include sports such as beach volleyball. The second way is when the past is mobilised to add weight and authenticity to celebration of the present. Scotland's campaign at the turn of the twentieth century to host the Ryder Golf Cup between Europe and the United States of America was premised upon the ideology of Scotland being 'the home of golf'. A similar 'coming home' theme was raised through the notion of 'football coming home' that accompanied England's 1996 European Championship campaign. Both these types of image, Polley (1998:3) asserts, share some common ground in the sense that nostalgia is used in the first instance in a sentimental, reactionary and backward-looking comparison between past and present sport, while the second attempts to champion the present by drawing upon links to the past.

The mythology of golden age sports historiography is nowhere better encapsulated than in Ramachandra Guha's (2002) *A Corner of a Foreign Field: The Indian History of a British Sport*. Guha (2002:xv) observes that the commercialisation of modern cricket and the corruptions that have come in its wake have led some commentators to speak of a time when this was a 'gentleman's game'. In truth, it is added 'there was no golden age, no uncontaminated past in which the playground was free of social pressure and social influence – cricket has always been a microcosm of the fissures and tensions within Indian society: fissures that it has both reflected and played upon, mitigated as well as intensified' (Guha, 2002:xv). The colonial history of cricket is replaced by an indigenous account of cricket in which the over-arching themes of Indian history, race, caste, religion and nation are to the fore. The history of cricket is located within the context of Indian historiography itself and might be viewed within the notion of the post-colonial because it provides an alternative history to that of the Imperial game variety, in which cricket in India is seen to develop as part of an explicitly colonial environment. It is also *subaltern* in that it develops from some of Guha's earlier work in which the notion of subaltern, originating in Gramsci's notion of the subaltern classes, is used as a perspective to combat the persistence of the colonial perspective (Guha, 2002).

Perhaps the most important conclusion to be drawn from the above illustrations is the way in which the past is continually renegotiated through sporting history, culture, identity and meaning, and nowhere is this more self-evident than in the way in which the celebration of sport in different parts of the world draws upon the selection or invention of tradition to commemorate a lost past or a sense of injustice or to assert a particular set of identities.

THE INVENTION OF TRADITION AND SPORT'S POPULAR MEMORY

Sporting traditions, like traditions in general, may be seen as a set of social practices which seek to celebrate and inculcate certain behavioural norms and values, implying continuity with a real or imagined past and usually associated with widely accepted rituals or other forms of symbolic behaviour. Signs, symbols and artefacts play a central role in the development of sporting culture, traditions and myths. Here there is a potential overlap with anthropological or ethnological contributions to the study of sport, culture and society. Some of the most common sporting traditions would involve sporting festivals, the display of flags, the way in which ceremonies associated with sporting occasions are conducted, and the singing of songs or ritual chanting at sporting events, all of which evolve over time. The following elements seem to be contained within the idea of a sporting tradition: (i) traditions are essentially shared, there are solitary sporting habits but no solitary sporting traditions, and are understood as such; (ii) they denote a class or form of intentional actions along with the thoughts, beliefs, perceptions and associations that motivate them; (iii) they are often associated with certain forms of conservatism in order to assert the validity of respect for the past; (iv) they create a background of shared expectations against which deviance and originality may be evaluated – hence the phrase 'deviating from the norm', implying deviating from tradition or the way things are usually done and (v) they are often associated with theories of the state and its institutions since they themselves are offshoots of tradition, invented or otherwise. The term traditionalism may be used in reference to any policy or practice founded in the defence of tradition.

Many traditions may be fabrication, and those that are perceived to be relatively long-standing may in fact be relatively recent inventions or selections of tradition. The standard example of an identity culture that anchors itself in the past by means of invented tradition or myths dressed up as history is nationalism. The past is continually re-created to explain and give meaning to the present. Imagined sporting communities select from history and from tradition that which provides a feeling of connectedness with both those who went before, those present and those separated by time and space. The selection of tradition is an act of identification by which we distil our many statuses and roles into those that we find most meaningful. Selected traditions effectively accomplish what traditions are meant to provide, a coherent sense of self, community and other. The fabrication of sporting tradition often consists of anachronism, omission, decontextualisation and in extreme cases, lies. The following is but an example of invented tradition or myth that has helped to mobilise support for a particular point of view or identity history.

The difference between sporting myth and reality is central to Collins's (1996:33) account of the 1895 split between Rugby Union and Rugby League. Collins argues that a comprehensive mythology has been developed around William Wollen's painting of the 1893 rugby 'Roses Match' between Yorkshire and Lancashire. The original painting hangs at Twickenham, the home of England's national Rugby Union side, while a reproduction of it hangs in the clubhouse of Otley Rugby Union Football Club in Yorkshire. The rivalry between the two codes of Rugby Union and Rugby League was such, contends Collins (1996:33), that those players that went on to play Rugby League and turned professional, have been painted over or at least removed by the artist. Such a story is a myth, but one which Collins (1996:34) contends, has been valuable to rugby union and rugby league for a number of reasons: it signified the alleged power of rugby union over rugby league, it downplayed the importance of the 1895 split which in reality devastated rugby union, and the painting also served rugby league in that it fitted into the popular pattern of belief that rugby union discriminated against rugby league.

Just as the myths surrounding the Wollen painting have become accepted as facts, Collins (1996:40) goes on, so too has mythology affected the explanation for the split between rugby union and rugby league in 1895. The painting, he argues (1996:38), reproduces the myth of amateurism, the North/South divide and the role of the northern businessman as core factors in promoting the split between the two codes of rugby. Alternatively it is suggested that the real cause of the 1895 split between rugby union and rugby league was the coming of the working-class player to rugby in the 1870s and 1880s and the reluctance of the rugby union hierarchy to allow this participation to develop on an equal footing. It is realistic therefore to suggest that the bifurcation of rugby in England into two codes was primarily a symptom of class tension and struggle in Victorian sport and society.

The role of memory in determining social and historical accounts of sport, culture and society is relatively recent, in the sense that only a few but gradually increasing studies have drawn heavily upon oral history. Memory is structured in part by group identities: one remembers one's childhood, one's neighbourhood as part of a local or national community or one's working or non-working life as part of a broader working or non-working group of people. One's memories are shared with others, told in stories and are thus social memories that tell a particular story about the past or how it was. Such memories help to shape people's lives and their association, romantic or otherwise, with places, times and activities. Memories are important in creating an awareness of sports places and sporting pasts. Memory is an important facet of oral sporting history and it helps to

55

facilitate inter-generational interaction about sporting occasions or places or infamous or famous moments.

A sense of shared history and experience is an important part of geographical memory. Hague and Mercer's (1998) study of the role of memory in shaping the relationship between a community and a sports team is evident in their account of the relationship between Raith Rovers Football Club and the Scottish town of Kirkcaldy. Founded in 1883, Raith Rovers first played as a full member of the Scottish Football League in 1902. Arguably the most memorable moment in the club's history was winning the Scottish First Division in the 1994–95 season, obtaining promotion to the Scottish Premier Division and gaining entry to the European UEFA Cup during the 1995–96 season by winning the Scottish Coca-Cola League Cup the year before. Playing the famous German club Bayern Munich and, for a short spell, leading the German champions by 1–0 have become an important part of the club's folklore. An equally important Cup-tie was allegedly played between Raith Rovers and a defunct existing local League Club, St Bernard's, during the 1923–24 season. The infamous St Bernard's Cup-tie is recalled in Hague and Mercer's study (1998:111) as an example of memory passing on historical knowledge from, in this case, a father to his son:

> As far as I can remember, Rovers lost a silly goal and, despite battering the opposing goal nearly all the match, were unable to draw level or indeed take the lead. However, as my Dad used to say, that's what happens in football. I already told you that my father was responsible for introducing me to the Rovers and Stark's Park when I was six.

Sporting memory is therefore a further link to the past and tradition, but tradition, like heritage and oral history, always has to balance historical plausibility with idealised inventions or selections of tradition or the past. Because visions of heritage and tradition most commonly alter and even distort history in appealing ways, what we perceive as heritage and tradition often replaces history and becomes memory (Ray, 2001:xii). When a selected past is remembered it may be a celebration of national unity, such as in Hill and Varsasi's (1997) story of the creation of Wembley Stadium, the twin towers and the English Football Association (FA) Cup Final, but in doing so we also emphasise what divides us from all those with 'other' memories or perhaps a different memory of the same selected past. In Nova Scotia the symbolism and practice of Scottish–American Highland Games and a romanticised and cleansed Scottish heritage can feed racial tensions. In Northern Ireland in 2002, the attitude of nationalist football fans to the Northern Ireland, Catholic Celtic football player Neil Lennon playing for his country in front of a predominantly loyalist crowd is a reminder of ways in which extremists can use heritage in a sporting context as a justification for violence. Thus, it is worth remembering that sporting traditions and sporting heritage can include and exclude, empower and victimise.

HISTORICAL AND SPORTING FORCES

The challenges to more than just the conventional wisdom about how we should think about sport *per se* have been influenced by a number of historical and sporting forces. Substantial bodies of new research have indicated that sports historiography has become more open to different ways of thinking about sport, change and continuity. Sports historiography is not limited to the impact of industrialisation or modernisation or the impact of any particular period upon sport. Any rigid distinction between different forms of sport in the nineteenth or twentieth centuries would fail to acknowledge the possibility of traditional forms of sport surviving and existing today despite the onslaught of history and time.

The idea of various 'post' periods and philosophies of sport is thrown around rather readily within discussions of social change. In one sense the 'post' prefix with reference to historical change can be rather simple. Abstractly it is as if time period 1 is pre-x, and will have certain characteristics associated with lack of x. Time period 2 is the high tide of x, when many things are touched by it and changed from their state in time 1. Time period 3 is post x. This implies that something new has come into existence to reduce the import- ance of x by going beyond it in some sense; some things will therefore look different from both time 1 and time 2. However, x will still have left its mark, there will be strong traces of it still around. More interestingly, the decline of x will mean that some things start to look rather like they did in time 1 again. 'Post periods' are therefore seen as being rather complex, but they need not be.

The following are but three 'post labels', post-feminism, post-modernism and post- colonialism. But what are they? Do they help us understand sport? And what is wrong with the post-history debate?

Sport and post-feminism

Post-feminism has at least two meanings, a popular sentiment that women can have power without losing their femininity and a more academic sentiment that, as a result of the devel- opment of new ideas and knowledge, a label which distances itself from feminist theory as it has been previously understood is required. Post-feminism incorporates a critique of previous assumptions that have been made about the self, the social, the political, the histor- ical, the textual and the West. It is here, for example, that the work of Jennifer Hargreaves (2000) on sport and Muslim women, Vicky Paraschack (2002) on sport in the lives of Inuit women and Fan Hong's (1997) historical account of Chinese women and sport are all valuable in the sense that they collectively and individually have challenged the parochial vision of sport and physical culture as it has been described and championed by Western feminism.

Women's under-representation in sport is a long history in itself. However, one of the major recent points of change in some parts of the world has been the relative political mobilisation of women in sport. Many countries have tried to address women's under- representation in sport by adopting gender equity policies, yet in a review of 24 European countries, Fasting (1989) concluded that a considerable gap still existed between intent and achievement. If we are deemed to have entered a post-feminist world then it would seem logical to assume that the demands of the post-feminist world of sport have superseded the demands of the feminist world of sport. At the beginning of the twenty-first century women still occupy a marginal position in sport in nearly every country of the world (Kay, 2003:102).

It is also worth noting that in *Leisure and Feminist Theory*, not post-feminist theory, Wearing (1998) alludes to the idea of women in a post-modern world as having certain vibrancy and vitality because it allows for the celebration of diversity, difference and self-confidence without the imposition of any all-embracing imposed theory from above. To paraphrase Wearing (1998:145), it may be possible for sports historiography to acknow-ledge ideas from 'post' theories so that sport is resignified as an appropriate space for the diversity of women from all parts of the world. The crucial intervention here is to invoke the notion that sport can provide possibilities for women of colour, as well as working-class and middle-class women to 'rewrite or resignify women's subjectivities so that they are no longer inferiorized' (Wearing 1998:145).

A good deal of post-feminism's attraction comes perhaps from the substantive manifest-ations of 'girl power' and the self-assured displays of confident young sportswomen and the challenge that this poses to old-fashioned, essentialist feminism with its conventional images of feminism as being dowdy, embittered and self-pitying. The differences between women are confidently accentuated within post-feminism and, as such, issues of sporting diversity are perhaps more open in post-feminist sport than they were within feminist sport. It remains to be seen whether a more powerful, younger, energetic post-feminism can obliterate the problems of nature and inequality that older forms of feminism contested. As such it would be important to note both the continuities and changes in sport that have been brought about as a result of post-feminism.

Sport and post-modernism

Adding to the introductory comment upon post-modernism provided in Chapter 1, a number of specific attempts have been made to provide a post-modernist introduction to sports historiography (Jarvie 1994; Hill 1996, 2002). The term post-modernism is a multi-layered concept that directs our attention to a variety of social and cultural changes that took place towards the end of the twentieth century. The philosophy of the Enlightenment in the eighteenth century heralded the notion of modernity within an historical period when industrial production, rationality, positivist science, objectivity and belief in absolute truths, order and stability prevailed. Post-modernity refers to the period following modernity in which all of these certainties were challenged. This critique of modernity has provoked two responses, a conservative one which tries to conserve some or all of the aspects of modernity, and a more radical one which attempts to harness the plurality and freedom of thinking and method which have been released by the post-modern critique and changing historical circumstances.

Championing the cause for a post-modern future in British sports historiography, Hill (1996, 2002) has suggested that issues of identity and meaning may provide historians with fruitful future lines of investigation. Hill (1996:19) skilfully steers a path between the conventional and the radical when he argues that it might be rewarding for sports histor-ians to turn their attention to matters of sport as ideology, symbol and text, while he also argues that the conventional features of the historian's craft provide the equipment to under-take such a task. The importance of uncovering and interrogating the sporting experiences of ordinary people from below, Hill (1996:19) goes on, means that oral history in particular has an important role to play in uncovering accounts of sport which hitherto have been hidden from history. It seems that Hill in one sense is encouraging students and researchers to at least grasp the opportunity provided by post-modern epistemology to tell different stories or narratives about sports historiography while at the same time remembering the craft of the historian in terms of plausibility, reality, evidence and perhaps even the ghost of labour history. The scepticism of modernity's grand theory is coupled with an empirical enthusiasm for uncovering the experiences of sport and of what sport has meant to people hitherto hidden from sports history. In this sense sports historiography provides an important empirical addition to the continuing search for a historiography from below, rather than a history of leaders, personalities and famous sporting institutions.

There is good reason to listen to much of what post-modern sports historiography has to offer and yet much remains to be done if sport is to witness a change as a result of a transition from modernity to post-modernity. At a philosophical level it is doubtful if the assault on truth or the anti-realism inherent within post-modernism will do much to uphold the task of socially committed students or sports historians who are not afraid of clarity, but see their role as explaining complex ideas and problems clearly.

Sport and post-colonialism

As a term post-colonialism may refer to both the effects of colonisation and the efforts being made by various communities to develop anti-colonial strategies. In Chapter 1 the notion of post-colonialism was referred to in three senses (i) as a historical term or stage of development in which post-colonialism has replaced colonial legacies; (ii) as a geographical term which connects those places in the world that have been affected by the imperial process; and (iii) a particular method or epistemology which focuses upon the forces of oppression and coercive domination that operate within the contemporary world, and consequently examines the part played by sport within the politics of anti-colonialism and neo-colonialism. In this sense post-colonial theory's intellectual commitment involves engaging in new forms of theoretical work which is closely linked to activism and social change within the world today and specifically those parts of the world that have been affected by colonialism and imperialism.

In Chapter 7, three important questions are raised. These are simply referred to here as the What, When and How of the relationship between sport and post-colonialism. Post-colonial sport could be said to have arrived when the first 'Third World' sports workers arrived in 'First World' sport. The disadvantages of the term 'Third World' have been generally denounced since it has a negative connotation, suggesting that in a hierarchical sense it comes after the first and second worlds. Alternatively, the term tricontinental or three continents is often used to refer to the land masses of Latin America, Africa and Asia. It presupposes that the history of European expansion and the occupation of most of the available global land mass occurred between 1492 and 1945. Any consideration of the relationship between sport and post-colonialism would necessitate looking at the way in which sport has developed and diffused from these places. As a form of critique of global sport the politics of post-colonial sport necessitates an examination and exposure of Eurocentric or Western forms of dominance in world sport. For instance, does global sport reflect a dominance of the North over the South? One of the general assumptions of post-colonial studies is that many of the wrongs, if not crimes against humanity, are a product of the dominance of the North over the South. If nothing else the study of post-colonial sport provides the opportunity to examine Western ontological assumptions about 'other' sports. Post-colonial sport provides an important point of engagement with Western sport that should warn students and others against accepting any uncritical account of Western sport.

As with all attempts at periodization, objections have been raised about what should be included and excluded from post-colonialism as a historical period. A substantive concern is the inclusion of any countries that did not have a colonial past in the sense that Africa, India and the Caribbean did. All of this simply serves as a reminder that the specifics of the what, when and how of post-colonialism and the study of post-colonial sport are not the same, for example, for Latin America, Australia, Canada, South Korea, Taiwan, Turkey and Iran. Some have argued that the debate about post-colonialism has been superseded by the power of globalisation or a network society and yet the post-colonial era still involves different kinds of anti-colonial struggles which have given rise to changing geographies and have grown out of not theory but activism in the world today.

The selection of the above 'posts' is but a fraction of those influences on the history of sport, culture and society that could have been considered. In 1989, Francis Fukuyama's (1989, 1992) essays on the end of history seemed to symbolise or at least announce that we were living in the aftermath of the historical age in which the big concepts of the nineteenth and twentieth centuries had been or were about to be retired. The end of the history of sport in these terms would have meant that liberal capitalist sport had triumphed universally. It had triumphed over all the concerns and values associated with Marxist, feminist, colonial and modernist accounts of sport that had hitherto been retired as causal historical or social forces that impacted upon sport, culture and society. Beyond the end of history was only boredom with no values to struggle over other than what Fukuyama would have viewed as parochial sporting issues, such as religion or nationalism.

There are a number of shortcomings associated with such developments and it should be no surprise to students of sport, culture and society that many of the facets of sport, which were consigned to retirement, are alive and well. The post-worlds are all worlds without centres. They are worlds without any fixed authority or absolute centre or ideology around which policy or intervention can be organised, not even post-colonialism. National governments or national sports organisations may continue to act as if they have authority, but global capitalism or global sport evades control and can be both *everywhere and nowhere*.

The predicament for the study of sport, culture and society is what to do with the vast number of 'posts' – post-industrialism, post-modernity, post-tradition and even post-history – and what they tell us about sport and the world we live in. Post-isms have proliferated everywhere at a speed that has led to much confusion. They agree only in the view that things are not what they used to be, that we are living in a different world and that the prefix 'post' points us to beyond. But to what remains unclear – new worlds, new sport, new attitudes, new values? Radically varying lists of 'posts' have impacted upon not just sport, culture and society, but upon sports historiography. The post-world is a world in which relativity and discourse rule. There are no absolutes because language, style, image, and so on, are part of a discourse and there is no way of proving or disproving a discourse. The post-world of sport, culture and society is a world in which it is impossible to distinguish reality because everything is allegedly the appearance of reality. We can look at the 'post-worlds' of sport as either a joyous liberation into a free play of 'post' discourses or narratives in which nothing counts and everything is relative, or as a tragedy in which meaning is everything and of no significance, and the latter is probably the hangover resulting from too much of the former. There are no values and the negative thrust of the post-world is not counter-balanced by the positive thrust of progress or social change or a more humanitarian account of world sport.

SUMMARY

What is generally being suggested here is that no informed debate on sport, culture and society can take place without reference to the historical dimensions or processes involved in the making of sport. All aspects of social and cultural life are based upon socio-political and economic events of the past. The past is therefore a permanent dimension of the human consciousness, an inevitable component of the institutions, values, traditions, customs and patterns of human society. The sporting past is much more than just chronology and, as such, the historiography of sport must not be reduced to a simple chronology of events. Rather, sport must be properly located within the social, cultural and historical context in which it moves or is located.

The production and dissemination of sport historiography has many audiences, genres and functions. The main audiences are not mutually exclusive and indeed sports historiography may benefit from a greater rate of exchange between the academic study of sports history that is produced for journals and monographs; popular sports history as part of sporting post-war development that has helped to confirm and mythologise a sense of tradition through sport; the production of sports history through museums and heritage sites; the production of sports history for television and film; and socially committed sports history which seeks out the excluded and fills in gaps to produce a more complete body of knowledge about sport, culture and society. The deconstruction of political or social sporting myths that pass as sports history remains one of the main responsibilities of the sociologist and the sports historian. They and others are responsible both for destruction of myth, despite the onslaught of post-modern sports history, and the production of more reality congruent bodies of knowledge about the historiography of sport.

The history of sport matters for a number of reasons: (i) it helps to avoid a parochial or insular understanding of sport; (ii) it stops research retreating into the present; (iii) it provides the tools by which to evaluate change, whether it be social or otherwise, continuity and meaning; (iv) it helps, like sociology, to destroy sporting myths; (v) it warns against uncritical acceptance of sporting heritage, traditions and identities and (vi) it helps to illuminate past themes, events and changes in their own terms as mattered at the time, and therefore sport in the past is explained on its own terms without necessarily having to call upon whatever vogue theory exists to re-interpret the past.

All human beings, institutions and collectivities need a past and to that end sport is no different. All histories of sport are part of a larger and more complex world and therefore

61

a historiography of sport designed for only a particular section or part of that world cannot on its own be good history. In other words, although identity sports historiography may be comforting to particular groups, left on its own it can be dangerous if it leads or contributes to forms of fundamentalism.

KEY CONCEPTS

Biography	Oral history
Comparative	Popular sporting memory
Continuity and change	Post-colonial sport history
Feminist sport history	Post-modern sport history
Heritage	Social change
Historical sociology	Social history of sport
Historiography	The past
Identity	Time
Meaning	Tradition
Myth	Transformation

KEY READING

Books

Cronin, M. and Bale, J. (2003). *Sport and Post-colonialism*. Oxford: Berg Publishers.

Guha, R. (2002). *A Corner of a Foreign Field*: *The Indian History of a British Sport*. London: Picador.

Hill, J. (2002). *Sport, Leisure and Culture in Twentieth Century Britain*. Basingstoke: Palgrave.

James, C. L. R. (1983). *Beyond a Boundary*. London: Stanley Paul.

Struna, N. (2002). 'Social History and Sport'. In Coakley, J. and Dunning, E. (eds) *Handbook of Sports Studies*. London: Sage, 187–203.

Journal articles

Collins, T. (1996). 'Myth and Reality in the 1895 Rugby Split'. *The Sports Historian*, 16 (May): 33–41.

Hill, J. (1996). 'British Sports History: A Post-Modern Future'? *Journal of Sports History*, 23(1): 1–19.

Parratt, C. (1998). 'About Turns: Reflecting on Sport History in the 1990s'. *Sport, History Review*, 29(1): 4–17.

Paraschak, V. (1990). 'Organised sport for native females on the Six Nations Reserve'. *Canadian Journal of the History of Sport*, 21(2): 70–80.

Pope, S. (1998). 'Sport History: Into the 21st Century'. *Journal of Sports History*, 25(2): i–x.

Vamplew, W. (1998). 'Facts and Artefacts: Sports Historians and Sports Museums'. *Journal of Sports History*, 25(2): 268–283.

Further reading

Hargreaves, J. A. (1994). *Sporting Females*: *Critical Issues in the History and Sociology of Women's Sports*. London: Routledge.

Holt, R. (2000). 'The Uses of History in Comparative Physical Culture'. In Tollener, J. and Renson, R. (eds) *Old Borders, New Borders, No Borders*: *Sport and Physical Education in a Period of Change*. Oxford: Meyer and Meyer Sport, 49–57.

Jones, S. (1988). *Sport, Politics and the Working Class*: *Organised Labour and Sport in Interwar Britain*. Manchester: Manchester University Press.

Polley, M. (2003). 'History and Sport'. In Houlihan, B. (ed) *Sport and Society*. London: Sage, 49–64.

Ray, C. (2001). *Highland Heritage*: *Scottish Americans in the American South*. Tuscaloosa: University of Alabama Press.

REVISION QUESTIONS

1. Explain the dangers of thinking contemporaneously about sport.

2. What does the study of history add to an understanding of sport, culture and society?

3. Outline some of the concerns that historians might have with sporting heritage.

4. Describe a number of invented sporting traditions and explain the ways in which myth, memory and tradition all help to mobilise the past in the present.

5. What is post-modern sports history? Critically evaluate the debate about sports 'post'-histories.

PRACTICAL PROJECTS

1. Visit a sports museum and assess whether it sets its artefacts in context.

2. Interview a parent or older relative about a famous sports incident and produce a short press report.

3. Carry out an Internet search for information in relation to the history of (i) a particular sport; (ii) a sports organisation and (iii) a national sport. Explain how the historical content of each of these is presented.

4. Explore further any one of the many sporting myths that exist. Draw upon a range of primary sources in order to write 1,000 words on the sporting myth.

5. Compare the coverage of sport in one local and one national newspaper of ten and five years ago with today. Write a 1,000-word report on how sport has changed over the past ten years.

WEBSITES

International Society for the History of Physical Education and Sport
     www.umist.ac.jk/sport/ishpes.htm

International Society of Olympic Historians
     www.olykamp.org/isoh

Scholarly sports sites
     www.ucalgary.ca/library/ssportsite/

The British Society for Sports History
     www.umist.ac.uk/sport/index2/htm

The North American Society for Sports History (NASSH)
     www.nassh.org

Chapter 3

Sport, politics and culture

How important has sport been to bringing about change in South Africa? © Telegraph Group Limited (1995)

PREVIEW

Power • Politics of sport • Sport and the politics of culture • Sport, art and elitist culture • Sport and cultural policy • Sport as a site of popular struggle • Sport as anthropology and a particular way of life • Sport, distinction and cultural capital • Sport and cultural identity • Sport and body culture • Politics, culture and cricket • Political successes and failures in world sport • Sport and racism • Sport and the welfare state • Sport and the feminist movement • Sport and human rights • Sport and blood sports • Sport and violence • Sport and individualism • Sport and child labour • Sport and poverty • Sport, personal troubles and public issues • Post-twentieth-century politics of sport.

OBJECTIVES

This chapter will:

■   evaluate the relationship between sport, politics and culture;

■   question certain arguments about sport and culture;

■   consider some of the political successes and failures in world sport;

■   illustrate the connection between personal sporting troubles and public issues;

■   provide examples of some of the future areas of political involvement with sport.

INTRODUCTION

Power refers to the capacity of an individual or group to command or influence the behaviour of others. Power is vested in people who are selected or appointed by a socially approved procedure, is regarded as legitimate and is often referred to as authority. Power may also be exercised through social pressure or persuasion or by use of economic or even physical force. Sport has not generally been central to the issue of determining the outcome of international power struggles, of who gets what, when and how, but it has made a contribution to a number of successes and failures in international politics.

The politics of sport has been given one of the most succinct overviews by Houlihan (2002:212) who suggests that the literature can be divided into two broad schools of thought. These are (i) politics in sport which direct our attention to the use made by governments of sport and the process by which public policy is made and implemented and (ii) politics in sport which lead to a consideration of issues concerned with the way in which sports organisations use power to pursue their own sectional interests at the expense of other social groups. Contained within the former group would be themes relating to the role of the state, including issues of sport and national identity, sport and economic development, sport and foreign policy and the promotion of individual state interests. By contrast, the latter would include an examination of the power of sports organisations in determining the nature of sporting opportunity, an examination of sport both as a source of profit and as a vehicle for the transmission of capitalist values and issues of equality of access to sport.

Whatever definition of the politics/sport axis is used, it is likely to be highly contested because there has been disagreement as to which aspects of social life are political. The content of and approach to the coverage of sport, politics and culture in this chapter emanates from a particular sense of the term politics that eschews and rejects the notion of sport as being separate from the very social forces that influence it. At a bare minimum sport is not unaffected by social, economic and political activity. Hill (2002:150) reminds us that sport can communicate broader political meanings. The politics of sport is no longer about whether sport reflects a particular political system, but whether sport should be viewed as a set of values, or as a social movement or as political practice.

The social character of political struggles over the past 40 years or more has tended to revolve around issues of class, gender and ethnicity. In other words, the conventional social patterning of the politics of sport has been heavily dependent upon categorical notions of class structure, gender and ethnicity as the main drivers of politics of sport in the West. Much of this social intervention within the politics of sport has resulted in part from what Nash (2001:72) has referred to as the cultural turn in social theory and the changing dynamics of national and international politics.

SPORT AND THE POLITICS OF CULTURE

The following discussion of culture expands upon some of the initial remarks made in Chapter 1. The term 'culture' is used in a number of ways within the sports literature and indeed one of the worries is the overuse of the term in the sense that it can be so all-embracing that it means everything. The term has been associated with sport in a number of different ways, ranging from ideas about culture that tended to exclude sport and other forms of popular culture to more inclusive definitions of culture that have recognised sport as an important purveyor of cultural meanings, values and identities. The relationship between sport and the politics of culture has rested upon some or all of the following arguments: the notion of culture as being defined by a particular definition of the arts which excludes sport; sport as a site of popular struggle between different social groups; sport as contributing to a particular way of life of different sub-cultures; sporting involvement and consumption as being viewed as a badge of distinction involving the production and reproduction of cultural capital; sport as contributing to forms of cultural policy; sport as contributing to forms of cultural identity; sport as one form of the broader notion of body culture; and, finally, the evolution of sporting traditions, rituals and meanings being best understood from an anthropological approach to culture. It is worth elaborating upon these in more detail.

Sport, art and elitist culture

It is significant that nearly all the hostility towards the term is associated with elitist definitions of the word culture that historically have been associated with high/low cultural debates, notably in the arts. High art in this sense being associated with the word culture has been separated in some way from popular art or other forms of popular culture. The hostility to the artistic notion of culture stems from its exclusivity and association with some sort of intellectual superiority for those who are seen as cultured. This usage of the word is closely associated with the German notion of *Kultur* which tends to incorporate theatre, music, literature, sculpture, film, media, painting and various forms of scholarship – for example, philosophy, history and areas of intellectual endeavour that make up the arts.

67

At least four points need to be made here: (i) an elitist definition of culture often associated with high culture of the arts is one of many notions of culture that exist, but at times it has been a powerful definition of culture that has done sport no favours despite the fact that sport has contributed to literature, arts and film, (ii) the word culture here is closely associated with a context in which intellectual growth is fostered within a certain narrow range of classical activities; (iii) historically culture, according to this view, would have little or nothing to do with sport, and the only sports that would be allowed into the academy would be the sports of the elite or the leisured classes and (iv) this is an approach to culture which devalues other forms of culture – particularly those which are not included in this particular definition of culture: working-class culture; some traditional forms of culture. More importantly, within the context of this book, it fails to acknowledge the role of sport in terms of social, economic, human or cultural forms of capital. In this sense the word culture is used in an artistic, sometimes elitist, intellectual sense and is, for example, completely different from the anthropological notion of culture. The usage of the term culture as described above is neither neutral, nor value-free.

Sport and cultural policy

The scope of cultural policy in different parts of the world varies; some policies include sport and some do not. The scope of specific policies also reflects divergent political ideologies. Clear statements of principles tend to govern most cultural policies and these might include the following: for citizens to achieve individual creativity; equality of access to cultural life; to safeguard freedom of expression; to promote cultural pluralism and diversity; to promote a flourishing of cultural life; to support cultural renewal and quality; to preserve and use cultural heritage and to promote international cultural exchange. A review of culture in Denmark, Sweden, Norway, the Netherlands and Catalonia noted that all of the aforementioned countries had Ministries of Culture. The same review also showed that there was a growing awareness that cultural policy needed to be owned and implemented by a broad range of government departments (www.scotland.gov.uk/nationalculturalstrategy).

The IOC contract to host the Olympic Games requires host cities to sponsor a cultural festival. A competition of Olympic Arts is not new; since the early Olympics used both art and music to promote prominent educators and public figures. The ancient Greeks valued beauty, intelligence, harmony of body and spirit, as much as physical discipline and strength. Barcelona was the first Olympic city to host a Cultural Olympiad that followed a four-year programme. The Catalans and Spaniards have for a long while championed the relationship between art and sport. Atlanta and Sydney followed the same pattern as that established at the Barcelona Olympic Games of 1992.

The impact of the market upon sport as a facet of cultural festivals is evident in Stevenson's (1997) case study of the cultural festival for sport and the arts associated with the build-up to the 2000 Sydney Olympic Games. The Cultural Olympiad had a budget of 21.5 million Australian dollars. The Sydney Cultural Olympiad, however, tended to reinforce established divisions between high and low culture, providing no opportunity for grass-roots participation, it also made statements from the perspective of Sydney as a world city in financial terms as opposed to its being a centre of artistic and cultural excellence. Stevenson argued that, rather than being a celebration of Australia, the Sydney Cultural Olympiad was a vehicle for celebrating selected aspects/images of Australia. He concluded that the arts programme associated with the Sydney 2000 Cultural Olympiad did not offer a special space for the creative expression of the local and idiosyncratic. It was dominated by a more selective and totalising set of discourses of the national that promoted elite art forms and the work of artists deemed excellent in order to sell Sydney 2000 or, rather, a particular image of Sydney 2000, to a global audience. In terms of long-term community and cultural development and citizenship there seemed little opportunity either to share the spirit or to define the creative and artistic form and content.

Sport as a facet of cultural policy therefore is not neutral, but influenced by values, political perspectives, nationality, attitudes towards the arts, the very definition of culture itself, the issues of access and the place of sports culture in all of the aforementioned.

Sport as a site of popular struggle

One of the major advances brought about by the cultural turn in social theory during the 1980s and 1990s was the fact that due recognition was given to the cultural politics of sport. It became common throughout the latter part of the twentieth century to talk of the transformative or reproductive capacity of sport to bring about change. It was not uncommon for students of sport in society to consider in detail the role of sport as a site of popular struggle. The Gramscian influence upon sports research fired an intellectual and very practical form of intervention that highlighted both the political symbolism and the practical social struggle over sport as a form of popular culture. Put more forcibly, Stuart Hall (1981:239) asserted that 'popular culture is one of the sites where the struggle for and against a culture of the powerful is engaged: it is also the stake to be won or lost in that struggle'. He added that popular culture was partially where hegemony arises and where it is secured. It was not, in Hall's mind, a sphere where socialism or socialist culture could be fully formed, but it was a place where the socialism of the time might be constituted.

The impact of this intervention into the politics of sport was that work on sport, power and culture was undertaken for some or all of the following reasons: (i) to consider the relationship between sport, power and culture; (ii) to demonstrate how a particular form of sport had been consolidated, contested, maintained or reproduced; and, (iii) to highlight the role of sport as a site of popular struggle and resistance. Struggles over the legitimate use of the sporting body, over times to take part in sport and spaces to play in all contributed to ongoing debates about the social and political meanings articulated through sport. The major contribution made by this body of work was the due recognition of and priority given to the sport, power and culture problematic, and that the politics of sport could not be simply limited to analysis of government and policy intervention into sport.

Sport as anthropology and a particular way of life

As mentioned in Chapter 1, the recent appearance of an increasing body of ethnographic field studies has led to resurgence in the anthropological study of sport. Ethnography is at

69

the heart of both a social and cultural anthropology of sport that has moved beyond the traditional cross-cultural study of play, games and sport in non-modern or tribal societies. Anthropological work in particular has tended to unpick the complexity of play, games, athleticism, exercise and sports and the body in different settings. The cultural anthropological influence is at work in, for example, Brownell's (1995) study *Training the Body for China. Sports in the Moral Order of The People's Republic* in which she clears the way for an analysis of the Olympic Movement in China which is critical of the relationship between sport and colonialism, the Olympic Movement and the West.

Traditionally, analysis of culture derived from anthropology has tended to refer to culture as a whole way of life, an all-consuming notion of culture in which anthropologists spoke of the cultures of various peoples, the cultural materialism or etymology associated with people or settings or the evolution of culture in different comparative contexts. Dyck (2000) identifies four specific anthropological themes in his recent overview of the anthropological study of sport: these are, (i) how the game is played in which sociologists *are reminded* that the very terms games, sports and athletic competitions are readily distinguishable by their composition, purpose and complexity; (ii) sport provides a major venue for displaying the body in public, recognising and exploring the bodily dynamics and attractions of wrestling in India, bodybuilding in America or training the body in China or Japan all illustrate the opportunity for cross-cultural fieldwork into different games and sports; (iii) the celebratory and communicative powers of sport are prominent in many ritual or theatrical sporting displays which invoke themes such as nostalgia, memory and the notion of celebrity which are all constructed differently in different cultural settings and (iv) fieldwork on the issue of boundaries and the way in which sports reinforce, redefine, invent and transgress boundaries and identities. This has helped to substantiate the way in which sporting differences and similarities are involved in the making of a multitude of social identities and imagined communities.

Sport, distinction and cultural capital

The notion that sport may contribute to the process of distinction and the acquisition of cultural capital is most closely associated with the work of the late French sociologist Pierre Bourdieu (1990b). The theory of cultural capital sees culture as a system of symbols and meanings and derives its analytical framework from notions of social practice and the social reproduction of symbols and meanings. The result is an internal and durable habitus which gives rise to the reproduction of culture. The dominant group for Bourdieu is not a dominant class as in the Marxist model, since the dominant group remains in the background. Analysis of cultural capital is led by micro rather than macro structures. In his analysis of social behaviour and interactions (practice), Bourdieu suggests that habitus results from a calculation between opportunities and constraints and between what is desirable (subjective) and what is probable (objective).

The distribution of sporting practices amongst and between social classes was determined by three factors, economic capital, spare time and cultural capital. Those sports that required a higher or lower degree of economic capital were separated in part – into those that required property and purpose-built, often private facilities, as opposed to those that were low cost and played in public places. The relationship between available and affordable spare time has historically been associated with the notion of a leisured class. Some sports in the twentieth century, such as golf, racquet sports, sailing, equestrianism, suggested Bourdieu, may be viewed as a mark of distinction by the fact that they were largely confined to the upper and middle classes. The crucial point here is that some sports may have a certain social currency and become a badge or symbol of social class. Knowledge of these sports in France had a higher prestige value than some other sports, such as football or wrestling. Bourdieu also distinguished between privileged and working-class activities by emphasising the relationship of different social groups to one's own body (body habitus). For some social classes participation in sport and physical activity was deemed an important part of their body habitus, whereas for others it was viewed as a waste of time.

Sport and cultural identity

The idea that sport can contribute to different forms of cultural identity has developed alongside the rise of identity politics. In an increasingly impersonal world sport may help different groups of people answer questions like: Who am I? Who is like me? Whom can I trust? In specific discussions of sport and Irish identity, Bradley (1999), and of sport, nationalisms and identities, Reid and Jarvie (2000) have argued that sport helps different ethnic groups or nationalities develop a sense of cultural identity. The argument that tends to underlie such accounts of sport and cultural identity is that sport in a positive way helps with recognition and representation. In my view such accounts fail to recognise that identity politics on its own is not enough. To reduce sport to being simply a contributor to cultural identity is to develop a sort of vulgar culturalism in the same way that early Marxist accounts of sport were criticised as vulgar Marxism.

This can be said without rejecting the idea that sport can provide some genuine insights into understanding aspects of sexism, racism, colonisation and cultural imperialism. It is both theoretically and politically problematic because such accounts of sport and cultural identity tend to reify the notion of identity and stop short of recognising issues of status and the redistribution of wealth. The way in which sport helps different groups with problems of prestige, status and identity cannot be uncoupled from issues of injustice and the redistribution of wealth in sport. Is there any value in countries such as South Korea doing well in the 2000 World Football Championships, or Kenya dominating middle-distance running in the latter part of the twentieth century, or South Africa winning the 1995 Rugby World Cup if the reward for such efforts is simply recognition and enhanced cultural identity? Furthermore, is there not a danger that by contributing to strong forms of cultural identity, sport helps to foster forms of fundamentalism that might take little recognition of the ways in which it might contribute to human rights violations, or as spectacle help to conceal forms of injustice, or poverty, or maldistribution of wealth? The argument that is developed in Part 3 of this book is that the sport and cultural identity model tends to lend itself too much to repressive forms of communitarianism, it displaces the politics of redistribution with the politics of reified group identities and, as such, it is necessary to encourage students to rethink the issue of recognition in sport, culture and society.

Sport and body culture

The relationship between sport, culture and the body has figured in a burgeoning corpus of literature, most notably within feminism and, for example, the notion of body habitus associated with the work of Bourdieu. At least five major reasons might be given as justification for a contemporary interest in the relationship between body, culture and society or bodily studies:

(i) the importance of the body as both a personal project and a cultural project which has given rise to political economies of the body which ask questions about who owns the body and what cultural tastes and patterns of consumption give rise to the body as being marketed in certain ways;

(ii) feminism and women's control over their own bodies;

(iii) the ageing body and what this means and how this is presented in different parts of world;

(iv) the leisured body as opposed to the worked body and how issues of work hard and play hard have impacted upon the body both mentally and physically – the notion of why people 'flog themselves to death' in the gym after a stressful day at work might be given as an illustrative example here;

(v) the post-colonial body and how the body has been framed and thought about in terms of imperialism, colonialism and post-colonialism. This is, of course, related to a core theme which cuts across all of the above themes, namely the issue of embodiment and how the body is used as a source of power in different cultural settings and contexts.

The notion of body has figured not only within sport's place within debates about culture, but more recently in a distinct notion of what Cole (2002) has, in a very useful overview, termed bodily studies in the sociology of sport. Sport has been linked to debates about the body in terms of masculinity, feminism, anthropology, power, desire, consumption, national identity, deviance, celebration, international trade in bodies and distinct national policies on body culture, such as in Denmark. In Denmark the notion of body culture is deliberately used to distance notions of Danish sport and culture from the simple dualistic notion of high performance sport and mass sport that tends to dominate and constrain many other European definitions of sport. Thus, the notion of body culture in Denmark allows policy advisers to consider the place of sports festivals, dance, and broader notions of movement culture within both achievement and social welfare approaches to sport as body culture in Danish policy.

The concept of body culture in the work of Eichberg is traced back to the German notion of *Körperkultur* (literally, body culture). The term as Eichberg (2004) uses it first appeared about 1880 during the free body culture movement of the time that advocated diet and clothing reform, nudism, sport, gymnastics, folk dance and abstinence from alcohol and nicotine. These ideas were adopted by the German Socialist Workers' Movement, noted by Marx, crystallised under the label *fizicheskaya kultura* in Russian, that was in turn translated into English as 'physical culture'. In Germany and Denmark the concepts of *Körperkultur* and *kropskultur* became associated with a perspective on the body that viewed the body as primarily cultural, and therefore differed from American/Scandinavian paradigms that tended to prioritise the notion of society and relegated the notion of the body to the natural sciences.

This introductory comment on the different bodies of work that have utilised the term culture to explain some aspect of sport has been somewhat lengthy although not exhaustive. This has been necessary because of the amount of space allocated to the word culture in the sports literature with which students of sport, culture and society will be confronted in the course of their studies. The term has generated a critical body of thinking that is almost without equal. By way of summary it might be fruitful to paraphrase what Nash (2001) has referred to as the cultural turn in social theory. As illustrated above, there has been a well-documented discussion of culture in both social and political discussions about sport. This has broadly taken two forms of thinking which may be referred to as epistemological and historical bodies of work about sport, culture and society. The first point refers to the fact that there is/has been a theoretical epistemologically driven debate about sport, politics and culture; the second point refers to the fact that sport continues to play an unprecedented role in contemporary cultural politics. International politics and culture may at times seem to be a long way away from the world of sport but, as illustrated above and below, all aspects of social life are considered to be potentially political and sport is no different from other areas where political power is active. The relationship between sport and the state perhaps should not be the sole or even the central focus of any sport, politics and culture, since such an approach could fail to illuminate new forms of politics that traditional models of politics have tended to at best marginalise, at worst ignore.

POLITICS, CULTURE AND CRICKET

One of the enduring examples of the inherent politics of sport remains the early 1960s text on West Indian cricket by the West Indian writer C. L. R. James. *Beyond a Boundary* remains a classic statement of the relationship between cricket and Caribbean society during the 1950s and early 1960s. The book is about the game of cricket, but it is also about the West Indies, poverty, being black and colonialism. Cricket is presented as a sport and a metaphor, the property of the colonisers and the colonised.

James recognised that an almost fanatical obsession with organised games was not merely an innocent social activity, but also a potential signifier of oppression and liberation. It provided a statement about an expanded conception of humanity, as well as the necessity to break from the colonial legacy that had affected the development of the West Indies. In placing the cricketer centre stage, James (1983) attempted to transcend the division between high and popular art. The cricketer in the 1960s was seen as a modern expression of the individual personality pushing against the limits imposed upon his/her full development by society (class/colonial/nationhood/periphery). Non-white cricketers came first to challenge, then to overthrow, the domination of West Indian cricket by members of the white plantocracy. By the 1980s, some have argued, the transformation of West Indian cricket had come full circle – from being a symbol of cultural imperialism to being a symbol of Creole nationalism. In summary it might be suggested that:

73

- The originality of *Beyond a Boundary* was more than just a critical study of cricket in the Caribbean in that it symbolised a new and expanded conception of humanity as black West Indian and formerly colonial peoples burst on to the stage of world history.
- It viewed the contours of Victorian cricket as essentially being the contours of imperial cricket.
- Victorian cricket reversed the process of transporting aristocratic values and allowed the Indians to assess their colonial rulers by Western values and to find the rulers somewhat wanting. It became important to beat the colonisers at their own game.
- Cricket is viewed in the West Indies as more than just cricket, but as a form of art, politics and moral philosophy.
- Cricket is viewed as a privileged site of colonial rule and asks of the colonisers the classic question, what do they know of cricket who only cricket know?
- The cricketer was at the time a modern expression of the individual personality pushing against the limits imposed on his full development by the mentality of an imperial or colonised society.
- Cricket and English literature were complementary in that they were viewed as cultural and ideological expressions of the same social order, a bourgeois order grounded in capitalism.
- The struggle over cricket was a classical struggle over the values associated with the game in a particular context at a particular point in time.
- In short, James's triumph in this book was to reinvigorate the values of cricket with a new political energy, not only by beating the masters at their own game, not by changing the game, but by destroying its values and reinterpreting those very values as a vehicle for political change.

Beyond a Boundary was also the heading of a leading newspaper article on sport and politics that hit the headlines when the English cricket team refused to play a match in Zimbabwe as part of the 2003 Cricket World Cup. Zimbabwe is a former colony to which Britain had clear and stated obligations. In Harare and Bulawayo where the cricket matches involving England were scheduled to be played, the shortage of fuel had in December 2002 almost paralysed the transport system. Famine threatened the lives of seven million people as a result of President Robert Mugabe's policies, which included land seizures and repatriation of land from white farmers to black supporters of Mugabe's political party.

The International Cricket Board wanted England to play in Zimbabwe for fear of loss of revenue from not playing the game. The country that the England cricketers would have been protected from was the Zimbabwe which saw people sprint from their shacks at the noise of an approaching truck carrying maize meal, the staple diet of the impoverished nation. At the time of the tour a chronic fuel shortage existed, but a special reserve supply of fuel was to be used to shuttle the cricketers about Zimbabwe. The patron of the Zimbabwe Cricket Board, President Mugabe, would have been given the opportunity to stage-manage the six international cricket matches scheduled to be played. The politics of cricket in Zimbabwe then was not just about specific issues of lost cricket revenue, but also land seizures, relations between coloniser and colonised, black and white, human rights and poverty. In the end, the players refused to play, forfeited the points from the abandoned matches and eventually failed to progress to the later stages of the tournament.

POLITICAL SUCCESS AND FAILURE IN WORLD SPORT

The social and political forces that have forged post-twentieth-century sport wax and wane within the international arena. This international space itself is relatively weak in the sense that only social actors and actions can influence what can be done in sport. The international political space that is available to sport comprises two broad areas. First, there is the geo-political plane that provides the broad parameters by which governments influence the politics of sport within and between national boundaries and, second, there is the socio/cultural-economic plane which influences the relationship between sport, power and culture. It is necessary to view these two areas or social spaces as being mutually interactive.

Political successes in sport

It is impossible to list all the major or minor political successes and failures in world sport. Sporting activity has been associated historically with political protests that have championed human rights, progressive socialism and social equality. Sport has also been associated with violence, fascism, individualism and strong nation-states. The following might be viewed as some of the most significant successes and failures in which the politics of sport has figured over the past 40 years. These refer to both right and left politics. The discrediting of racism in sport and the recognition that sport has been inextricably associated with colonialism have progressed significantly since the late 1960s when the 1968 Mexico Olympic Games witnessed Black Power protests against the condition of black people primarily, although not solely, in America. The protest drew attention to the denial of black American human and civil rights, but also to the subtle politics of black athletic involvement in world sport. To this might be added the part which sport played in the overthrow of apartheid in South Africa; the role of cricket in the de-colonising of the West Indies; and the part played by baseball in drawing attention to imperialism in Cuba.

The post-war argument that sport could benefit within the then advanced capitalist countries through increased expenditure on the welfare state meant that a social welfare approach to sport was adopted in social reformist countries, such as then West Germany, Sweden, Denmark, Norway, Finland and Holland, to name but a few. The Nordic countries have had a long history of democratic popular sports movements with their independence being protected in legislation. The organisation of sport in Sweden, for example, has often been heralded as being based upon a model of social welfare and as being more democratic in terms of its organisation. For almost five decades Sweden has been known for its social welfare model that has been a hypothetical compromise between communism and capitalism. In practice, it has meant far-reaching government involvement in the private sphere fuelled by a strong conviction that social engineering can achieve the kind of justice that the ruling political party holds to be the ultimate truth. One of the main character-istics is the assumed duty of politicians not only to alleviate poverty, but also to redistribute wealth, including the wealth generated from sport, across Swedish society.

The feminist movement questioned and partially transformed male leadership of movements for liberation and equality in which traditional gender roles remained unchanged. One of the areas of conflict and struggle is funding for women's involvement in sport, exercise and physical activity. Sports policy in Canada during the 1990s in many ways gave a contradictory message to women in that, while supporting the development of a set of structures aimed at addressing and rectifying gender inequality in sport, the federal state also legitimated the ideology of masculine superiority by continuing to provide more funds and sporting opportunities for males than for females (Hall et al., 1991:90). The feminist movement might be viewed as one of the left's successes not just in sport, but also in international social relations, and yet progress has been uneven in that the challenge to west European sport has been more successful than in other parts of the world, such as Africa, China or the Islamic world, but even here sport has made some progress.

The use of sport as a sanction to publicise human rights violations has led to attempts to isolate or draw attention to human rights records, such as those in Iraq, Nigeria and Chile. In the mid-1990s several members of Iraq's national football squad alleged that Uday Hussein, the son of the then Iraqi leader Saddam Hussein, ordered them to be tortured after they lost a World Cup qualifying match 1–0. The players claimed they were locked in cells beneath the headquarters of the Iraqi Olympic Committee and beaten on the soles of their feet. FIFA investigated the allegations, but concluded that Iraq could remain in FIFA. In 1995, Nigeria was subject to sanctions because of its violation of human rights. Between 1974 and 1976 Israel was excluded from the Asian Football Confederation. The politics of Israeli sports remains under-researched. Kidd and Donnelly (2000) have recently explored the contribution which sport has made to the struggle for human rights. They argue that the aspirations for democracy and liberation evoked under the banner of human rights cannot be achieved without human rights in sport. They conclude by drawing attention to the Sports Act in Finland which came into force in 1998 and stated that the purpose of the Act was: (i) to promote equality and tolerance and to support cultural diversity and sustainable development of the environment through sport, (ii) to support recreational, competitive and top level sports and associated civic activity, (iii) to promote the population's welfare and health and (iv) to support the growth and development of children and young people through sport (Kidd and Donnelly, 2000:145).

The struggle over blood sports and the broader relationship between humans and animals has witnessed some successes through the ban on hunting with dogs in some countries. The pro-hunting lobby has often appealed to the civil liberties argument on the basis that the freedom to choose one's recreation may be seen as one of the modern jewels of democracy. Liberty, it is agreed, is a vital principle, but this does not mean *carte blanche* to do as one pleases, for it should always be tempered by respect for others or even the wishes of the majority. Contemporary debates relating to the relationship between animals and humans have raised the issue of the feelings and thoughts of all living beings, not just humans. For example, in the classical English fox-hunt, does the fox's opinion matter? If so, it would surely choose to be somewhere else than at the heart of an ancient recreational pursuit that involves the killing of foxes. Does the fox have a right to a civil liberty as a living being, or is this simply the preserve of the human world?

While the left has been quick to condemn certain blood sports on the grounds of animal rights, it has in part failed to justify policies on angling and other popular sports.

Political failures in sport

If the aforementioned are illustrative of some of the contemporary political successes involving sport, then equally a number of failures need to be mentioned. The capacity for violence has been fatally underestimated by the left and the association between right-wing groups and violence in sport imploded throughout the 1980s as rampaging football hooligans left their mark on the football landscape. Russell (1997) has suggested that football may well have played an important part in popular Tory Britain of the late twentieth century in fashioning middle-class perceptions about working-class Britain. Attempts by soccer clubs to deal with football hooliganism of the 1980s and 1990s were reported with heavy political rhetoric of the right about law and order, social class and the 'English disease' – football hooliganism. Football, according to *The Sunday Times*, was 'a slum sport played in slum stadiums and increasingly watched by slum people who deter decent folk from turning up' (Taylor, 1987:171–191). By the same token, the violence associated with anti-hunt marches aimed at pressurising British political administrations to ban blood sports failed to halt the violence associated with fox-hunting, at least in England, since the Watson Bill (www.scotland.gov.uk/library2/doc16/bhwd-02.asp) which banned hunting with dogs in Scotland. This was one of the first pieces of legislation passed by the Scottish Parliament that came into being in 1999. The violence associated with animals is much more than just the issue of fox-hunting since it may also be associated with many other areas, such as horse-racing on the flat and over jumps, or eventing, show jumping and polo, or greyhounds in coursing, or fishing, to name but a few sports in which animals are viewed as either performers or prey. A succession of left- and right-wing coalition and majority governments in Britain has struggled to contain violence in sport.

The rise of a powerful individualism, which had little or no respect for mutual ownership or co-operation in sport, has led to an extreme individualistic sports culture, but also to the decline in social capital and civic society, what Putnam (1995) called bowling alone. Putnam used the notion of social capital to comment critically upon the process of what he called civic disengagement from American life. By this he referred to the decline in participation, not just in formal political activity, but also in all kinds of social activities, including sport and physical activity. The decline of social capital allegedly included decreasing membership in voluntary organisations, decreased participation in organised activities and a decrease in time spent on informal socialising and visiting. Americans were viewed as becoming less trusting of one another, with a close correlation existing between social trust and membership of civic associations. The late twentieth and early twenty-first-century legacy of the New Right's *Kulturkampf* (cultural battle) has changed the values of the public domain and contributed to the formation of a culture of distrust that has tended at times to corrode the promise of citizenship, equity and accountability in sport. For every volunteer or sports-worker delivering a service, there seem to be numerous administrators, agencies or otherwise looking over their shoulder to check their work.

The implosion of communism in the 1990s may be viewed as a negative turn on an epochal scale for both non-communist as well as communist sport. The planned sports systems collapsed, sporting nations were reconfigured and absorbed into primarily Western, global or American sports configurations. Different forms of corruption mediated sporting practice and, as such, agents' control of athletes, the development of international sports manufacturing on the back of child labour and the sexual exploitation of young high-performance athletes have all continued to be part of an international sporting world that is in need of social if not ethical direction and leadership.

It might be suggested that, while traditionally sport has always been viewed as an avenue of social mobility for some of the world's most talented athletes, the gap between rich and poor throughout the world remains a chasm between the wealthy and the not so wealthy. For example, Hari (2002:24) reminds us that poverty is plainly a factor in the formation of what have become labelled 'feral children', the right-wing press's term referring to some of the most disadvantaged kids in Britain who have been raised without family support or without homes in urban inner-city housing estates. Kids Company is a responsive network set up in many of Britain's inner cities that aims at helping what the right-wing press has dubbed 'feral children'. Talking of these kids Hari (2002:25) reports, 'It's not like these kids want much, they only ever have one pair of trainers, not five, but it is not unreasonable for them to want one pair.'

For poor British kids many areas are desolate, shrinking amounts of public space with no leisure centres, children who might once have played in parks, fields or even streets now have nowhere to go. While middle-class parents may deal with the absence of public space for their children through the consumption of expensive hobbies or clubs or buying houses with gardens, these are not options available to 'feral children'. The relative success of projects in inner cities like Birmingham designed to help 'feral children' lies not in any one social solution, but in a range of social networking by disenfranchised agents working outside the mainstream provision that solely identify with the needs of these children. Sport has effectively failed the poor and as yet the transformative potential of sport in many of the poorest parts of the world has not been fully realised.

Each of these sketches of some of the political successes and failures in world sport is far from exhaustive, but they serve to illustrate that the politics of sport is not just present in and between states, but also in markets and, most importantly, in social patterns or groups.

It is within the triangle of states, markets and social patterns that political ideas about sport gain ascendancy and political action occurs (Fig. 3.1). The following example illustrates the interaction of the state, markets and social patterns in Kenya, notably gender. Lornah Kiplagat and Lina Cheruyiot, two of Kenya's leading women athletes in 2002, have spoken openly about the personal troubles of exploited and mistreated young women athletes in Kenya who have to struggle against not only market exploitation by commercial shoe companies, or state control over the issue of passports which make it difficult for a young girl athlete to travel to international competitions, but also the 'macho' culture or the social patterning of Kenyan society.

C. Wright Mills (1970) identified the sociological imagination as the comprehension of history and personal biography and the relations within the two in any given society. By

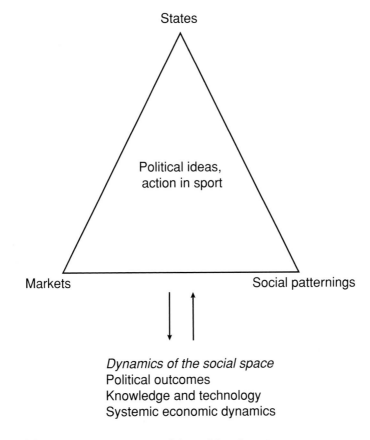

States

Political ideas,
action in sport

Markets   Social patternings

Dynamics of the social space
Political outcomes
Knowledge and technology
Systemic economic dynamics

Figure 3.1 *The social co-ordinates of the politics of sport*

this standard, when one seeks to examine a particular aspect of social life such as sport, it is necessary to make a sustained effort constantly to relate personal biographical concerns in sport to broader public issues in culture and society. The above example from Kenyan athletics illustrates that one of the enduring hallmarks of the politics of sport has been the acknowledgement that many personal sporting concerns may transcend the level of personal sporting biography to become more of a public issue. Maria Isabel Urrutia is another international female athlete, who won a gold medal in weightlifting at the Sydney 2002 Olympic Games. She was not only the first ever South American woman to win an Olympic gold in 100 years, but also the winner of Colombia's first ever gold medal. Urrutia was born into a family where nine of the fourteen children died before she began her athletic career. The town in which she was born was chosen by chance, since it was then the only public hospital in the country that could deliver babies free of charge. Commenting on her Olympic victory, the athlete hoped that her success would reach out to others exactly like her, poor, black and female. She went on, 'as a poor person I hope others see that you can make a living, see the world and get an education through sport and that girls who are now 13 realise that they do not have to become teenage mothers'.

The challenge to students of sport is to be able to recognise their own moral commitment to the normative component of the political perspective and then, through disciplined enquiry, test the evidence against the political or social assumptions to reform or confirm our beliefs as best we can.

POST-TWENTIETH-CENTURY POLITICS OF SPORT

Any speculative forecast about post-twentieth-century politics of sport must acknowledge the enduring dynamics of the capitalist system, and accept that it is inadequate to polarise any debate between left and right political sporting systems. It is crucial to move beyond the polarised debate of left and right in sport since any modern radical politics of sport can no longer be viewed in simple terms, such as socialism versus capitalism or identity politics. It should be noted that newly emerging forms of politics might co-exist with traditional ones rather than replacing them. The old political issues of sport's contribution to issues of employment, inequality, poverty and identity have not disappeared; they have to compete for social and political space with life politics, environmental politics, and fundamental non-Western cultural expressions through sport.

The social space occupied by the politics of sport historically has tended to be associated with distinct social categories or social patterns, such class or gender or ethnicity or the interaction between some or all of these factors. The dynamics involved in the politics of sport, particularly those associated with social categories or patterns might be better thought of in the following continua: irreverence – deference and collectivism – individualism (Figure 3.2).

Irreverence and deference refer to existing inequalities of power, wealth and status in sport, while collectivism and individualism refer to high or low degrees of collective identification and organisation. The twenty-first century is much more irreverent as a result of the declining power of deferential class politics associated with amateur and imperial sport. Traditionally, the sporting left in the West has tended to be driven by the irreverent collectivism of the socialist working-class or anti-imperialist movements, while other radical

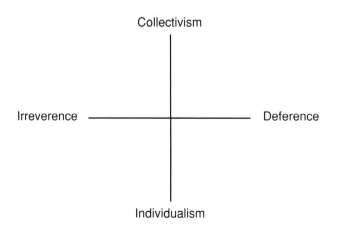

Figure 3.2 The social dimensions of the politics of sport

progressive currents for women's rights or human rights have been by comparison more individualist in character. The traditional sporting right tended to be institutionally collectivist, while liberalism (both old and new) leaned towards deferential individualism – deferring to those of allegedly superior status. In other words, a culture of deference and colonialism was reproduced both within and between sports. One of the major characteristics of any post-twentieth-century politics of sport in the West has been the relative erosion of previously strong forms of traditional deference, religious as well as socio-political.

Deference has eroded in some societies and cultures, while in others it has become more fundamental. The decline of erstwhile authority has given rise to other forms of fundamentalism that are not irrelevant to post-twentieth-century sport, politics and culture. In February 2003, a football team from Baghdad, Al-Nafid, made a trip to opposition-controlled Northern Iraq where they were to take on Irbil, the top Kurdish team in Iraq's national league. To reach Irbil, the Baghdad players had to travel across a reinforced Iraqi frontline, past freshly dug army trenches and up into the mountains of Kurdistan. Prior to the game they expressed their complete support for Saddam Hussein in the war against American and British imperialism and the then impending invasion of Iraq. Baghdad's 20-year-old goalkeeper, Saif Aldin Zaman explained that 'we love President Hussein', while Mista Qalan, a defender, said 'we will fight to the death' (L. Harding, 2003:1). Before running out on to the pitch Al-Nafid players broke into several chants of 'we don't want a war' and 'we give our blood, our blood for our Saddam' (Harding, 2003:1). The Kurdish home crowd appeared at kick off to have forgotten the traditional enemy Saddam Hussein, since they broke into long a series of anti-Turkish songs in protest against an American-backed plan that would involve thousands of Turkish troops pouring into Kurdish Iraq. Most ordinary Kurds now regard the Turks as more of a threat than the Iraqi army. On the other hand, having lost the game 1–0, Zaman was sanguine in defeat: 'we have good relations with the Kurds . . . we are not fighting them anymore' (L. Harding, 2003:2).

The grip of patriarchy too has been significantly loosened as women's rights and questions of gender equality have come on to the sporting agenda virtually everywhere in the world.

What might be termed the social modernisation of sport, resulting from economic change, education and players having more control over their labour, has meant that many different kinds of deference have been eroded, affecting not only women and young people, but also other significant social groups. One element of this erosion of deference has been the struggle over new forms of rebellious collectivism. Indigenous peoples have organised in defence of their rights, including the protection of cultural rights, such as traditional sports and pastimes.

In some senses the challenge to contemporary sport comes not from the West, but from many of the post-colonial re-evaluations of sport. Some of this work has already begun with Bale's (2002b) critical examination of the legacy and the challenge of rewriting the cultural history and geography of sport in Africa, and Hwang's (2001) study of the dynamics between Western and Chinese imperialism in the development of sport in modern China. Perhaps the political field of the future will contain more elements of life politics in sport around issues of health, exercise, extreme sports, ageing or environmental issues or the impact of sporting tourism in different parts of the world or, alternatively, the impact of technology. The latter and, in particular, the power of the media have raised questions about public order controls and public service communications, as well as control over sporting outcomes.

The study of sport, politics and culture is not an exact science and it must be remembered that post-twentieth-century politics of sport has just begun. That being said, in the immediate future, say the next 5 to 15 years, the following concerns are likely to impact upon any sporting politics:

- sport and poverty;
- human rights in sport;
- sporting irreverence and identity;
- post-colonial sport;
- sport and the environment;
- lifestyle politics.

SUMMARY

Sport in certain parts of the world might not be defined as a social democratic system, but the promise of sport might be that it can be an inspiration, a way of being, a manner of acting based upon both democratic and social values. The politics of sport then is all that bears on the attempt to order sporting relations and is not simply limited to the conventional approach that encompasses the everyday processes of involvement in sport by politicians, parties and parliaments – important as this may be. The value of such an approach is that it helps individuals understand that the social and political dimensions of sporting activity can reveal how personal troubles within sport are in fact related to broader public issues. The basic idea is that sporting involvement and practice is not value-free, but involves complex interactions, not least of which are the dynamic relations of power between states, markets and social patterns. Sport has always been an arena in which various social actors and groups can actively rework their relationships and respond to changing conditions as a whole. The resources to do this have invariably been uneven both between and within different groups and sports. There is no single agent, group or movement that, as Marx's proletariat was supposed to do, can carry the hopes of humanity; but there are many points of entry or engagement into a debate about sport that offer good causes for optimism that things can get better. It is crucial that current and future students and researchers of sport, culture and society recognise the socially situated nature of their work and engage with the future politics of sport.

KEY CONCEPTS

Body culture   Personal troubles
Cultural capital   Politics

Cultural identity	Popular struggles
Cultural policy	Power
Cultural turn	Public issues
Culture	Racism
Elitist culture	Social capital
Feminist movement	Social control
Kultur	Social patterning
Market exploitation	Welfare state

KEY READING

Books

Hargreaves, J. A. (2000). *Heroines of Sports*: *The Politics of Difference and Identity*. London: Routledge.

Henry, I. (2001). *The Politics of Leisure Policy*. London: Macmillan.

Houlihan, B. (2003). *Sport & Society*: *An Introduction*. London: Sage.

James, C. L. R. (1983). *Beyond a Boundary*. London: Stanley Paul.

Maguire, J., Jarvie, G., Mansfield, L. and Bradley, J. (2002). *Sport Worlds*: *A Sociological Perspective*. Illinois: Human Kinetics.

Journal articles

Harris, J. (1998). 'Civil Society, Physical Activity and the Involvement of Sport Sociologists in the Preparation of Physical Activity Professionals'. *Sociology of Sport*, 15: 138–153.

Mertes, Tom. (2002). 'Grass-Roots Globalism'. *New Left Review*, 17 (October): 101–112.

Sader, E. (2002). 'Beyond Civil Society'. *New Left Review*, 17 (September/October): 87–101.

Stevenson, D. (1997). 'Olympic Arts: Sydney 2000 and the Cultural Olympiad'. *International Review of the Sociology of Sport*, 32(3): 227–238.

Therborn, G. (2001). 'Into the 21st Century'. *New Left Review*, 10 (May): 87–111.

Further reading

Bale, J. and Philo, C. (eds) (1998). *Body Cultures*: *Essays on Sport, Space and Identity*. Henning Eichberg. London: Routledge.

Fabian Review (2003). 'Non-economic Boycotts'. Spring: 8–10.

Gourley, B. (2002). 'In Defence of the Intellectual'. Stirling: Stirling University Robbins Papers.

Leader, P. (2003). 'Why Boycott Zimbabwe but not China?' *New Statesman*, 6 January, 4–5.

Marqusee, M. (2000). 'Sydney and the Olympics: Corruption and Corporatism Versus a Positive Social Role for the Olympics'. In Workers' Liberty Australia Newsletter, October at http://archive.workersliberty.org/Australia/Newsletter/Oct00/olympics.html

Ouellet, J. G. and Donnelly, P. (2003). 'Sport Policy, Citizenship and Social Inclusion' at http://policyresearch.gc.ca/page.asp?pagenm=horsunset_06_01

REVISION QUESTIONS

1. What have been the key political successes and failures in twentieth-century sport?

2. Compare and contrast anthropological, sociological and policy approaches to sports culture.

3. Explain the politics of West Indian cricket.

4. What forces make aspects of sport political? Answer using two illustrative case studies.

5. Are personal troubles linked to public issues and if so to what extent might these relationships influence any future politics of sport?

PRACTICAL PROJECTS

1. Carry out a content analysis of the political party manifestos in your country of residence. Explain the importance of sport to the political parties and where possible compare the different political approaches to sport.

2. Design a strategy or 10-point policy aimed at increasing the involvement of one of the following in sport (i) women; (ii) a specific minority group of your choice; (iii) the poor; or (iv) the elderly.

3. Find out how much money is spent on sport in your country and the rationale for spending that money on certain sports and activities.

4. Examine the process by which any four presidents of any four national sporting bodies get appointed or elected and write a 1,000 word report on sport and democracy based upon the evidence.

5. Listen to the content of the opening addresses of any major world-sporting event and compare this with the coverage of main reasons for hosting the event in the national newspapers. Write a short 1,000 word report on the politics of the event.

WEBSITES

Bill of Rights for Young Athletes
    http://ed-web3.educ.msu.edu/ysi/bill.html

Building Social Capital and Growing Civil Society
    www.pendlehill.org/von_til.htm

Canadian Policy Research Institute Papers
http://policyresearch.gc.ca

Council of Europe (Committee for the Development of Sport)
www.culture.coe.fr/sp/splist.html

European Football Players Union
www.fifpronet.com/

Scottish Executive Cultural Strategy
www.scotland.gov.uk/nationalculturalstrategy

The Protection of Wild Mammals Bill
www.scotland.gov.uk/library2/doc16/bhwd-02.asp

Part 2

Sport, globalisation and other communities

INTRODUCTION

The five chapters that form the second part of this book examine the notion of global sport and in particular, the national, international or global and post-colonial contexts and debates about sport, culture and society. The first theme at the heart of this section is whether we should think of the world as one place or many and, consequently, one global sports product or process or many sports products or processes, including the national, international, local and global. The second important theme within this section is the issue of power and governance and who is or should be involved in influencing the world of sport today.

Sport and globalisation

When did global sport emerge and has it ended? The study of global sport has been examined from the point of view of the processes involved in the move towards something called global sport. The characteristics of global sport have included the changing rates of migration of sports personnel; the transfer of sports finance on a global scale; the delivery of sport through the media on an international scale; the exchange of ideas about sport throughout the world; the emergence of trans-national sports organisations and the extent to which sporting tastes and cultures have moved across national boundaries to be consumed in different corners of the earth. An understanding of globalisation is central to an understanding of the changing nature of contemporary sport, culture and society. While global sport has been documented and discussed at length, less has been said about sport and anti-globalisation. To what extent is sport part of the challenge to global sport? The coverage of global sport in Chapter 4 therefore is inclusive of these two core questions: what and when is global sport? and what contribution has sport made to the movement for radical or moderate anti-globalisation?

An important dilemma is the extent to which sport is viewed primarily in global terms or international terms and this provides the focus of attention in Chapter 5.

Internationalism and sport in the making of nations

Has the emergence of global sport weakened national and international sport? Does sport have a role to play in developing national identity or is it a substitute for political nationalism? It has often been assumed that this latter has in fact been the case, and that the increasing influence of global sport has meant that national sport has been affected. The increasing international or cosmopolitan nature of sport brought about by, for example, the migration of athletes across national boundaries has resulted from the realisation that the contemporary sports world is a smaller place, but also from the focus of sport having in part shifted from the national to the international and global arena. Perhaps it is more appropriate to talk of international sport and not global sport? Chapter 5 critically assesses the notion of global sport and rejects the idea that sport should simply be thought of in global or local terms. One of the major power players in sport today has been the media and, in particular, television and the changing rates of commercialisation associated with mediated sport.

Sport, media and television

Sporting spectacles dominate television in many parts of the world. The timing of major world sports events is influenced by peak viewing times for different countries around the world. Terms such as old and new media are now readily used in relation to their specific influence upon sports, culture and society. But what do the terms mean and what exactly is the scope of their influence? The media in many ways have colonised sport and, as a result, sport at various levels has become dependent upon media rules, but without completely losing its separate identity. Perhaps one of the greatest challenges facing sport today is the extent to which sport participates, obtains a stake within the media and is not simply the passive recipient of media politics and policy. Indeed, society needs to exercise oversight and control over the media system and its mode of communication, for the dangers of one-dimensional politics, society, football or any other sport are all too evident.

Sports law and governance

Is there a crisis of confidence in global sport and what possibilities are there for adopting a more inclusive approach to corporate sporting governance? How can and should sport be regulated? Is sport above the law and to what extent should sporting governance be influenced by sport's own court of arbitration? In relation to the debate about global sport the challenge facing the world of sport is whether such a notion can be sustained given (i) the influence of corruption which has influenced the development of international sport, (ii) that sporting governance occurs at so many different levels that it is rarely co-ordinated or seen to be committed to international justice or social reform and (iii) the power of European and American models of professional sport and the issue of whether non-Western forms of sport can modernise and become powerful players in the international arena while at the same time holding on to values, beliefs, traditions which are perhaps not governed by Western values. To what extent can the law help to embrace those other communities discussed in Chapter 7?

Other sporting communities

The extent to which Western sport, power and influence have been challenged and indeed viewed as part of the problem within many non-Western nations has raised a substantial post-colonial critique of sport, culture and society. Non-Western sporting concerns are raised throughout this book, but are the particular focus of Chapter 8.

If colonial sports history was the history of sports involvement within the imperial appropriation of the world, then post-colonial sports history must be concerned with certain peoples of the world appropriating sport for themselves. This chapter initially focuses upon the relationship between sport and post-colonialism by considering three questions; what, when and how is post-colonialism associated with sport? It is generally acknowledged within this chapter that historians and geographers have carried out much substantive work that has uncovered and re-interpreted the colonial influence upon sport. Post-colonial sport is not Third World sport. The disadvantages of the term 'Third World' have been well documented in terms of its hierarchical relation to other worlds. The International Amateur Athletics Federation has stated that its aim is to remove cultural and traditional barriers to participation in athletics, which may imply that indigenous practices and culture may be viewed as something that have to be removed in order that Western forms of athletics and sport might take their place (Bale and Cronin, 2003:55).

The post-colonial critique draws upon a broad range of areas as a basis of effective political intervention. If the role of the student or scholar is to uncover the contest, to challenge and defeat an imposed silence and the normalised quiet of unseen power, then post-colonial sport and the role of sport in humanitarian terms must have a much louder voice in the world today. At the very least the orthodoxy of global sport must be more progressive and humanitarian in terms of its governance and mode of arbitration.

Chapter 4

Sport and globalisation

Is sport truly a global phenomenon and what values are associated with global sport?
© Nan Fang Sports (2005)

PREVIEW

Global sport • Globalisation • Sport processes • Global media coverage • Nike sport • What is globalisation? Characteristics of global sport • Political, economic and cultural globalisation • When did global sport start and end? Sportisation • Phases of development of global sport • Figurational sociology • Sporting ethnoscapes • Sporting technoscapes • Sporting financescapes • Sporting mediascapes • Sporting ideoscapes • Values • Global or international sport • Sport and anti-globalisation • Radical and moderate anti-globalisation • Sporting intervention • Summary.

OBJECTIVES

This chapter will:

■ explore the notion of global and international sport;

■ critically evaluate the impact of globalisation on sport;

■ consider when global sport came into being;

■ ask whether the global era has come to an end;

■ consider forms of resistance to globalisation and global sport;

■ question the notion of globalisation as being an appropriate term to describe the development of international sport.

INTRODUCTION

The term global sport and the associated processes of globalisation are not uncommon within discussions of contemporary sport, culture and society. This has tended to take place at two levels, the extent to which the globalisation of sport itself has occurred, and the extent to which sport makes a contribution to other globalisation processes. The existence of world satellite information systems, global patterns of sports consumption and consumerism, the emergence of global sports competitions, such as international tennis matches or the Olympic Games or other international sports tournaments, have all contributed to the idea that the world of sport is more of a single entity. Such a notion tends to overlook the complexity of international sport that is in itself both historically variable and multi-dimensional. It is one thing to say that sport x is the most popular sport in the world and has increased its international presence, and another to say that sport x is global. Can you think of a truly global sport or product that exists in every country of the world?

It is difficult to deny or challenge the fact that the world has become a smaller place or that the sports clothes people wear or the relentless coverage of sport on television has helped to evoke the idea of global sporting products or experiences. However, it is meaningless to equate the sporting experiences of young women in Cuba or Afghanistan with that of a teenage American or German. The experiences are as similar as they are different. In other words in order to understand the sporting world of these young people it is necessary to resist the temptation to treat sporting experiences as if they were even or universal or equal. Bairner (2001:14) reminds us that even the most powerful nation in the world, the USA, has only been partially successful in the export of American games to other parts of the world, with basketball and volleyball being more international than baseball, which has only really established itself in certain Caribbean islands and in countries such as Japan. Ice-hockey is popular in many parts of Europe, but there is little evidence to suggest that even American sporting forms have become global. On the other hand, one of the world's most popular international sports, football, is of secondary importance to other sports inside America.

The notion of global sport therefore is difficult to define as a product since it is not homogenous or universal, and consequently those who have attempted to explain the emergence of global sport have tended to refer to the process or development of global sport.

The term globalisation itself has been poorly defined, often meaning different things to different people. In particular it is often unclear whether people are dealing with globalisation in all its forms or whether they are referring to economic or political or cultural or all three aspects of it. Globalisation is the process by which interaction between humans, and the effect of that interaction, occurs across global distances with increasing regularity, intensity and speed. Much of the debate about globalisation gives the impression that the process is relatively new and yet most analysts tend to agree that globalisation has in fact been underway for centuries. With specific reference to global sport, some have argued that the development of global sport has in fact emerged as a result of a long-term process emerging out of eighteenth-century English sport. Possibly the central argument has been whether globalisation actually promotes or produces economic well-being throughout the world. Its critics argue that its emergence is one of the key causes of increases in poverty and inequality.

There are a number of themes that have contributed to the debate over globalisation and sport and in some senses Maguire (1999:15) has succinctly summarised these for us when he raises the following questions: Are globalisation processes one-dimensional or multi-dimensional? What is the main dynamic behind globalisation in terms of mono-causal or multicausal factors? Does globalisation lead to unity, a perception of unity or fragmentation? Are globalisation processes intended or unintended? To these we might add to what extent does global sport actually exist and what effect does it have on indigenous sports? Maguire (1999, 2002) in particular has added much to our understanding of the relationship between globalisation and sport and even he is cautious of making too many grand claims relating to the relationship between globalisation and modern sport. It is clear, Maguire (2002:357) asserts, that globalisation processes have gathered momentum, with some of the main features being the increase in the number of international sports agencies; the growth of global forms of communication; the development of international sports competitions and prizes; the increasingly international acceptance of rules governing primarily Western sport forms. Even the speed, scale and volume of each of these developments have been uneven.

One of the most popular arguments supporting the notion of global sport has been the increasing global media coverage of international sports events, such as the Olympic Games. But a closer examination of the content of television coverage of events may suggest that the commentary is based upon not so much internationality as nationality and forms of subtle cultural nationalism. Television companies such as the American networks traditionally have attracted viewers to their Olympic coverage by stressing political controversies along with asserting national interests and symbols. The theme of the coverage between 1960 and 1988, writes Coakley (2003:395) was not focused so much on international friendship, more of 'us versus them' and 'this nation versus that nation'. The television networks justified this approach by claiming that the home viewers preferred nationalist themes that promoted American values and American international superiority.

The globalisation of sport has often been closely associated with economic interests, and the differences between national interests and identities and corporate interests and identities are often blurred and contradictory. Nike's use of a sports-based marketing strategy to sell an international assortment of athletic shoes and clothing has been well documented, notably by Robert Goldman and Stephen Papson (1998) in *Nike Culture*. In 1993 Nike sold an estimated 100 million pairs of shoes, one in five of its shoe sales was outside of the United States, mostly in Europe. Company officials expected foreign revenues to exceed US revenue by 1996. Nike gave Brazil's national football team $200 million to market Nike products throughout the world up until 2005. The power of Nike allegedly influenced the team selection for the 1998 World Cup Final in which Brazil lost 3–0 to the host nation France but Brazil's star forward Ronaldho allegedly played while injured as a result of commercial pressure placed upon the Brazilian team manager to pick his injured celebrity striker. Nike Chairman Phil Knight has always had a keen sense of the linkages between sport, consumers and profit. The relationship between patriotism, team loyalty and global profit is complex. The same Phil Knight in 1994 explained the basis for his team loyalty during the 1994 Football World Cup. The American Chief Executive of the then US-based Nike organisation reported that when America played Brazil in the 1994 competition, 'I rooted for Brazil because it was a Nike team. America was Adidas' (Coakley, 2002:399). Knight sees logo loyalty as being more important than national loyalty and consumerism replacing patriotism when it comes to international sporting teams.

It would be misleading to suggest that the notion of globalisation remains unchallenged although it remains one of the defining issues of the early twenty-first century. For those on the left the sharing and cross-fertilisation of different sporting cultures is something to be celebrated. Sporting culture is richer, more diverse and caters for different lifestyles and tastes. Those on the right tend to argue that globalisation poses a threat to traditional, in particular national, sporting heritage, and it has weakened the position of national or even local sporting traditions that have been marginalised at best and eradicated at worst. There has also been opposition from other parts of the world; they argue that the notion of global sport in terms of the governance of world sport tends to conceal traditional Western, or even colonial power bases that need to be replaced by representatives of a post-colonial world of sport. At this stage it is appropriate to examine some of the issues further and in more depth.

GLOBALISATION: WHAT IS IT?

At a very general level globalisation is an increasingly criticised term used to describe a set of related processes that have served to increase the interconnectedness of social life. The term has been used to reflect the compression of the world and the intensification of the world's consciousness as a whole. The term has become ubiquitous because there is no agreed definition of its meaning. This in part explains the extent to which it has figured within many international public debates, including debates about the nature and ethics of international sporting organisations and the power of international sporting finance to determine sporting practices, such as the timing of Olympic competitions or World Cup Finals. There is little point in seeking to deny the fact that global capitalism has affected the way sport is administered, packaged and watched, but this has not been an even process. For some, globalisation and global sport is nothing more than neo-liberalism and equates to market forces controlling sport, minimising the role of the state in terms of sports provision and inequality within sport being non-problematic. Critics of this agenda denounce global sport and globalisation as being a vehicle of global exploitation which has produced sports goods on the back of cheap labour, helped to maintain global poverty levels and maintained different levels of inequality in sport, particularly in terms of access of women and ethnic minority groups to positions of power in global sport.

There are primarily two competing approaches to globalisation. One encompasses a community of human citizens and is worked for, for instance, by environmentalists who talk in terms of thinking global and acting local. The other is of an unregulated free market where capital is king or queen and international corporations leave the poor to struggle with the consequences of deregulation, privatisation and international plundering. Proponents of globalisation typically argue that we live in an age in which a new kind of international world has emerged, one that is characteristic of global competition for markets, consumers and culture. A facet of the free-market driven form of globalisation has been that markets have decided whether we will have pensions in our old age; whether people suffering from ill-health in Africa will be treated and what forms of games and sports will be supported or even whether certain regions will have football clubs or not.

It is worth asserting at this point that globalisation is a highly uneven set of processes whose impact varies over space, time and between groups. Global forces and many international sports bypass many people and places. In many localised parts of the world the development of sport is for local or national consumption and not for global or international consumption. Even within many international sporting cities or places where mega sporting events are held, certain neighbourhoods within these cities or places where poverty or disadvantage prevail will, at one level, remain peripheral to the event itself and, at another level, to the working of the international sporting economy. It should be recognised that the current situation of social and economic disadvantage in many parts of the world has been triggered on a macro scale by the actions of trans-national corporations based in a city or place often on the other side of the world. The uneven penetration of global sporting markets and sports is not simply a question of which sporting institutions, industries, people and places are affected, but how they are affected. The unevenness of globalisation and global sport is therefore apparent at all levels of society and culture.

95

BOX 4.1 SOME CHARACTERISTICS OF GLOBALISATION AND SPORT

■ Globalisation and sport is not a new phenomenon. The processes of sports globalisation have been ongoing throughout human history, but the rate of progress and effects have accelerated since at least the 'early modern' period of the late sixteenth century.

■ Globalisation involves both an intensification of *worldwide* sporting relations through time–space compression of the globe, and local sporting transformations involving enhancement of local sporting identities as well as of *local* consciousness of the world of sport.

■ In the global–local sporting nexus, global forces are generally held to be most powerful and their control more spatially extensive.

■ Global sporting forces are mediated by locally and historically contingent forces as they penetrate downwards, coming to ground in particular places.

■ A number of 'trigger forces' underlie sporting globalisation but the dominant force is generally regarded to be economic.

■ Globalisation reduces the influence of national governing bodies of sport.

■ Globalisation through sport operates unevenly, bypassing certain institutions, people and places. This is evident at the global scale in the disparities between booming cities of sport and declining sporting regions.

■ The differing interests of actors means that global sporting forces are sometimes embraced, resisted or exploited at lower levels.

■ The mobility of capital diminishes the significance of particular sports places, although it may also strengthen local sports identity by occasionally engendering a defensive response by local actors.

Functional descriptions of global sport have a tendency to isolate particular elements of globalisation processes without relating them to one another. In what follows the relationship between sport and globalisation is articulated at a number of different levels, but very rarely do these levels operate in isolation from one another. Ultimately any strategy that is aimed at producing change needs to be unitary and totalising in nature rather than being fragmentary and locked into a form of dualism that views globalisation as simply good or bad, monocausal, deterministic, or in terms of the relationship between core and peripheral nations within the global economy. At a minimal illustrative level globalisation can be articulated at the level of politics, culture, economics, technology and society.

Political globalisation

Political globalisation might refer to the increasing number and power of international sporting organisations that influence or govern international sport. Prime amongst these bodies would be the International Olympic Committee (IOC) or the Fédération Internationale de Football Association (FIFA). Alongside these increasingly genuine world sporting organisations might be the establishment of a number of national or continental sports organisations, such as the European Traditional Sports and Games Association or the American Baseball Association. The very spread of international sports organisations can also be seen as a response to the process of political globalisation whereby the types of problems confronting national sports organisations can no longer be addressed locally or nationally. Political globalisation is seen in arrangements for the concentration and application of power in sport.

In discussions of globalisation at the political level, one question that has tended to predominate has been that of the nation-state. What kind of national autonomy do nations and national sporting organisations or cultures lose under this new world order? Is it really not merely a new kind of domination or colonisation? In particular, when the term globalisation is used contemporaneously, are we not really referring to the spreading political and economic power of the United States of America? Are we not really discussing the subordination of nation-states indirectly or directly to American power?

Economic globalisation

Economic globalisation refers to the increasing occurrence, speed and intensity or production of trading and financial exchange across national boundaries. This includes the trading of sports personnel and, for example, increasing rates of labour migration within and across national boundaries. Indeed, economic globalisation might be taken to refer to a series of linked phenomena that have emerged over the last 30 years or more. The increasing flow of sporting finances would include the international flow of finance brought about as a result of trading of players, prize-money and sporting endorsements. Economic globalisation is seen in arrangements for the production, exchange, distribution and consumption of sport.

Cultural globalisation

Cultural globalisation refers to the growth and exchange of cultural practices between nations and peoples. Many researchers point to the way in which new technologies, such as commercial television, the Internet and other forms of mass communications, have created a world that increasingly consumes identical products. The Internet is central to democratic international cultural exchange in that shared sporting interests and enquiries can be accessed internationally between people involved in sport. Thus, there are now specific sports websites and email networks which individuals from different cultural backgrounds share. Sport itself has been viewed as a cultural product that lies at the heart of the telecommunications attempt to attract international audiences. Cultural globalisation is also seen in arrangements for the production, exchange and expression of sporting symbols that represent facts, meanings, beliefs, preferences, tastes and values.

GLOBAL SPORTING PROCESSES: WHEN DID GLOBAL SPORT START AND END?

Globalisation is not a new phenomenon. The process of globalisation has been ongoing throughout human history but the rate of progress and effects of certain actions have accelerated and decreased the process at various periods in its development. Critics of globalisation insist that the process and development of global sport has neither been created completely, nor has it produced a world that may be defined by rampant free markets or passive nation-states. Some have suggested that although the global era may not have been completely created, it has come to an end as the more local, fundamental and international forces such as the United Nations or religious fundamentalist groups increasingly assert their influence in the early part of the twenty-first century. Trends towards greater global sporting interaction have, in fact, ebbed and flowed quite radically as they have developed alongside the rise of local, national and continental interaction and power.

The different phases of sportisation outlined by Maguire draw upon the work of Robertson (1992; 1995). Maguire's (1999:75–94) discussion of the complex process of development of global sport identifies five stages in what is more specifically referred to as phases of global sportisation, none of which are historically concealed periods of time. They rather refer to phases of development, some of which may overlap at the edges of the beginning and ending of certain phases. This simply asserts that processes of development do not suddenly stop at one period and begin at a certain date, but are more fluid in the transition from one phase to the next.

Phase one refers to an initial sportisation phase from about the 1550s to the 1750s, during which many of the antecedent folk origins of modern sport emerged alongside the incipient growth of national communities. The initial sportisation process involved the emergence of sport as a form of physical combat, primarily in England, not Great Britain or Alba or Ancient Caledonia, according to Maguire. England is viewed as the cradle and focus of modern sporting life. Sport and parliament as they emerged in the eighteenth century were viewed as both being characteristic of the changing power structure in England and resulted in diminishing levels of violence as the aristocrats and gentlemen of England found more civilised ways of enjoying their leisure time.

Phase two refers to the period from about the 1750s to the 1870s when the processual nature of sportisation involved the formation of voluntary associations or sports clubs. The patronage bestowed upon sports, such as cricket, boxing, folk football, fox-hunting, Association football, rugby and boxing, led to a calming down of violence compared to the previous period, as well as a spurt in the shift towards modern male achievement sport. Folk games became less widely practised.

Phase three refers to the period from about the 1870s to the 1920s, when the diffusion of English sports and pastimes to continental Europe also involved the export of the amateur ethos and notions of fair play. These co-mingled with other European forms of achievement sport. The last quarter of the nineteenth century witnessed the international spread of sport, the growth of competitions between national teams, the establishment of international sports organisations and the international acceptance of rules. Phase three in essence entailed the differential diffusion of sport and the emergence of inter-state competition between nations.

Phase four from 1920 to 1960 is when, according to Maguire (2002:365), sport can be seen to have become a global idiom. Anglo-American speaking peoples dominated international sporting governing bodies. Non-Western peoples not only resisted and re-invented forms of Western sport, but increasingly challenged the Western domination of global and/or male sport. This period witnessed the early stages of what Bale has referred to as the Kenyan running phenomenon and the emergence of sumo wrestling onto a world stage. While Western missionary sporting forms had penetrated mainland China, it should not be forgotten that traditional Chinese sport has a heritage that predates many English sporting pastimes. Local, traditional and international sport from many parts of the world all struggled and competed for recognition, power and influence within the dynamic that was world sport. The reflexive relationship between the global and the local should not lead to the assumption that global sport automatically leads to the disintegration of local or national sport or that globalisation automatically leads to the disintegration of local or national life. More generally in the place-bound daily lives of ordinary sportspeople, particularly those outside the mainstream of global sport or advanced capitalism, global sport may promote a search for local identity in a mobilised international world.

The final phase Maguire refers to as a period from about 1960 to 1990, is a time when Cold War Olympic politics between capitalist sport and communist sport diminished with the collapse of the Berlin Wall and the fragmentation of the former Union of Soviet Socialist Republics (USSR); women secured further changes and recognition in world sport; former colonial nations defeated the former colonial masters at their own game, as evidenced by the West Indian dominance of world cricket in the 1960s and 1970s; Anglo/Euro and American control of global sport was challenged, with African and Asian countries securing more power in FIFA and the IOC; a resurgence of European traditional sports and games served as a reminder that residual forms of sport in different parts of Europe have a strong traditional base – in Catalonia, France, Germany, Belgium, Switzerland, Ireland, Spain and Switzerland, to name but a few places where there is a strong regional/national affinity for indigenous forms of sport. All this can be alluded to without forgetting the global power of the media and the mass consumption of international and local sporting tastes and preferences.

It is important to realise that there is no single globalisation theory upon which to pin any one understanding of contemporary sport. Maguire's ongoing contribution to the analysis of global sport is one of the most consistently researched approaches. For students of sport, culture and society Maguire's analysis cannot be fully understood without a rudimentary understanding of developmental or figurational sociology. That is to say, the body of knowledge that informs the work of Maguire (1999) and others is epistemologically driven or informed by a framework or perspective that may be relatively detached, but not value-free. A greater understanding of *Global Sport: Identities, Societies, Civilizations* (1999) can only be fully realised by reading the text alongside others that provide an introduction to process sociology. For example, Maguire has identified a number of global flows that, he points out, are neither evolutionary, nor linear in terms of their progress. Use of the term 'process' is very specific in that it implies that sporting processes develop at different rates, and consequently different sporting developments do not necessarily occur at the same time, speed or rate of development. Put simply, the association between money and sport or the process of monetisation implies that money has been associated with sport at greater or lesser amounts at different points in the development of monetisation. In such a tradition of social thought, 'isation' terms are common, and they imply a process or developments over time. The emphasis in Maguire's work is on a particular historical sociological understanding coupled with technically specific terms, such as process, development, figurations, a rejection of evolutionary or linear thinking and false dualisms, power balances, insider and outsider relations, and other terms associated with the language of figurational or process sociology. (See Chapter 1 for a brief comment on figurational or process sociology). There are many conceptualisations of globalisation and global sport; the above approach has been prioritised because of the major contribution it has made to our understanding of global sport.

The following points are illustrative of five different cultural flows that may help to characterise the development of globalisation processes: ethnoscapes; technoscapes; financescapes; mediascapes and ideoscapes. All these processes develop at different speeds.

- Sporting ethnoscapes might involve the migration of professional or non-professional sports personnel through player, manager or coach transfers;
- Sporting technoscapes would include sports goods, equipment, landscape-building golf courses and transporting of sports technology which is now a multi-million pound business;
- Sporting financescapes refer to the global flow of finance brought about through the international trade of players, prize-money, endorsements and sporting goods;
- Sporting mediascapes refer to the sports-media complex which transports sport across the globe at different times in different countries and delays events and recordings to suit viewing times of international and national audiences;
- Sporting ideoscapes are bound up with the ideologies or philosophies expressed by, in and through sport; professionalism; amateurism; sport for all; liberal notions of integration and critical notions of exploitation. All these different ideologies compete in the battle for how world sport is, should or could be.

One final point in terms of the development of globalisation needs to be made. While global sport as illustrated in this chapter may have developed as a result of different stages of development, it has also been suggested, by Gray (2001:25), that the era of globalisation has come to an end. The dozen years between the collapse of the Berlin Wall and the al Qu'eda attack on the twin towers of the World Trade Center in New York on 11 September 2001 might have marked the end of an era. The West greeted the collapse of communism – though it was itself a Western utopian ideology – as a triumph of Western values. The end of a way of life was welcomed as an opportunity to further develop a global free market. This part of the world was to be made over in an image of Western modernity – an image deformed by a market ideology that was as far removed from any human reality as Marxism had been.

Following the attacks on New York and Washington the conventional view of globalisation as an irresistible historical trend seems to have changed. It may be that we are back on the classical terrain of history, where international conflict is waged not over ideologies but over religion, ethnicity, territory and the control of natural resources. The attempt to force life everywhere into a single mould was bound to fuel conflict and insecurity. Perhaps if sport is to develop a greater degree of social currency then the notion of international sport should be considered in place of global sport not least because the values associated with global sport and globalisation in the late twentieth century seem to have melted down as sporting markets as well as financial markets went into free-fall in the early part of the twenty-first century.

GLOBAL OR INTERNATIONAL SPORT?

Some have argued that it is important to distinguish between international and global sport. Are the Scottish Highland Games and Gatherings that take place in different parts of the world examples of global sport or international sport or something else altogether? There is the international and/or North American image that is presented through magazines such as *Celtic World*, which continues to report and carry stories of the Scottish Highland Games to all corners of the Celtic world and beyond. It is in many senses an image that contributes to an international or Celtic image of the Scottish Highland Games. If you visit the Scottish Highland Games 2000 website (http://www.albagames.co.uk/Highland_games2000.htm), you will be promptly transported to Scottish Highland Games in Waipu New Zealand (1871); The Auckland Highland Games and Gathering (1980); Turakina Highland Games (1856); Highland Games Sychrov – near Prague (2001); The Tri-Annual Highland Gathering at Leeuwarden (1998); the Hengelo Scottish Games – Netherlands (2002) and the Highland Games Association of Western Australia. The language and appeal of these activities now extends around the world. The web pages of the Highland Games Association of Western Australia receive daily hits from many corners of the globe in a way that would have been unthinkable 10, 20 or 30 years ago. All of these developments are testament to the place of traditional and non-traditional Highland Games as perhaps being international, although not a global form of culture.

Is FIFA (http://www.fifa.com/index.html) a global organisation? FIFA is undoubtedly one of the most powerful sporting organisations in the world. It controls world football and is comparable with the IOC as one of the most influential world sporting organisations. The growth of the game is such that it is estimated that globally the football industry is worth US $250 billion annually, which means that it has a higher financial turnover than companies such as Mitsubishi or General Motors. If you look at the FIFA web page, the organisation talks of FIFA as being the governing body of the world's most popular sport, a game played by some 200 million people throughout the world. It has more than 200 member organisations, more than any other sports organisation including the International Olympic Committee. It talks of football moving millions on all continents; its emblem is two stylised footballs in the shape of the globe – the symbol quotation 'of a global fraternity united in sport'. FIFA is supported by a world-wide spread of confederations that include the AFC in Asia, CONCAF in North and Central America and the Caribbean, CONMEBOL in South America, UEFA in Europe and OFC in Oceania. Contracts for the rights to televise the 2002 and 2006 World Football Cups are such that television viewing in poorer regions such as parts of Africa and Asia, is distributed free of charge, whereas special fees are charged to the wealthier nations of the world.

McGovern's (2002:28) study of the migration of footballers into the English League between 1946 and 1995 prefers to use the terms 'Celtic' and 'International' rather than globalisation when talking of the labour migration of footballers into and within Britain. As such it is concluded that the migration of professional footballers is clearly becoming more international in nature and that this is a trend that is developing along regional rather than global lines. Thus, it is suggested that as far as one sport that claims to be global is concerned the notion that globalisation has been achieved is fundamentally flawed. It might be suggested that, in terms of the spread of traditional games and sport, terms such as international, local and/or Celtic, for example, might be more appropriate than the all-consuming notion of globalisation.

By way of summary what is being suggested here is that much of the debate about global sport has tended to accept the idea of globalisation as at least an inexorable free-market process, which is best characterised through use of the term globalisation. It might be suggested that the term internationalisation is equally appropriate, if not more so, given that patterns of labour migration in sport have become increasingly international without specific trends developing along regional rather than global lines. As such, the terms global sport and globalisation needs to be employed very carefully because of their analytical value in helping to portray a more reality-congruent picture of sport today.

SPORT, ANTI-GLOBALISATION AND ANTI-CAPITALISM

We should acknowledge that the values associated with globalisation and global sport have been subject to pressures for change. The movement for global change is most commonly referred to as an anti-globalisation or anti-capitalist movement. Other terms that are sometimes associated with oppositional threads to globalisation are anti-free trade and anti-imperialist. Some have argued that this movement emerged in Seattle in the mid-1990s as a result of protests against the World Trade Organization and the International Monetary Fund. Others maintain that it began more than 500 years ago when colonists first told indigenous peoples that they were going to have to do things differently if they were to develop or be eligible for trade. Whatever the point of origin, the privatisation of every aspect of life and, in particular, the transformation of every activity and value into a commodity has resulted in a number of oppositional threads which have taken the form of many different campaigns and movements.

Sport has not been immune from these campaigns for change. Landless Thai peasants have taken over and planted organic vegetables on over-irrigated golf courses, and the power of Nike has been challenged on several American university campuses. Students facing a corporate take-over of their campuses by Nike linked up with workers producing Nike clothing, parents who were concerned at the commercialisation of youth, and church-goers campaigning against child labour in the production of sports goods. *Red Card to Child Labour* was a world-wide campaign against the use of child labour in football. The *Red Card to Child Labour* campaign is symbolised by the red card handed out by referees for serious violations of rules on the soccer field. The then International Labour Organisation (ILO) Director,

General Juan Somavia, said, 'Working hand in hand with the world's most popular sport, we hope to galvanise the global campaign against child labour with this potent symbol – the red card means you're out of the game' (www.un.org/pubs/chronicle/2002/p19). The Portugal and then Real Madrid star Luis Figo, who was voted World Footballer of the Year in 2001, supported the campaign. The ILO, in conjunction with FIFA and UNICEF, launched the campaign to coincide with the 2002 Africa Football Cup of Nations. The initiative was aimed at highlighting the harsh reality of child labour in sport.

There are two competing concepts of anti-globalisation, one termed radical and one termed moderate. The radical wing views globalisation as a process largely designed to ensure that wealthy elites become wealthier at the expense of poorer countries. It would argue for instance that globalisation undermines the working conditions and pay of sports personnel in wealthy countries, while at the same time exploiting cheap sports labour in other parts of the world. The radical wing sees trans-national corporations as the main cause of the problem in that they have so much power that international sporting organisations undermine the power and decisionmaking of national governing bodies of sport. Furthermore, it is suggested that indigenous sporting cultures have been threatened as a result of global sport or capitalist sport that has tended to market uniform sports products across the globe. Whereas 20 years ago children in local communities might have worn the sports gear of local sports teams, children today tend to wear more uniform sports brands such as Nike. The view expressed here is that globalisation as a process is fundamentally flawed and immoral.

Solutions to these problems offered by the radical wing are various, depending upon the situation. In a sporting context, the solutions to combating global intervention in sport might include some or all of the following strategies:

1. a re-assertion of the power of national and local sports organisations;
2. the return of economic, political and cultural power to localities;
3. quotas on the migration of sports talent into the country;
4. re-evaluation and redistribution of wealth derived from sport to alleviate poverty;
5. support for campaigns such as sport relief and critical evaluation of the role of companies such as Nike.

The moderate wing, although more difficult to define, tends to share the view that globalisation has the potential to be good or bad. It has the potential to provide for a sharing of cultures paid for out of the economic growth provided by free trade, but because the institutions and rules that govern the world are currently controlled by wealthy elites, then inequality, instability and injustice are inevitable. In a sporting context a corollary of this might be to argue that traditional cultural rights and sporting traditions need to be at least equally recognised as socially and culturally, if not economically, as important as market-supported forms of commercialised sport. For the moderate wing the solution to many of the above problems lies with reforming the institutions that govern world sport. The proposed reforms are multiple, but they might include some or all of the following:

1. a tax on international transfers of sports labour, the revenue of which could be used to promote sports development in poorer countries;

103

2. a total reformulation of rules and remits of international sporting bodies to allow for greater representation on the boards from poorer and essentially non-Western countries;
3. a greater role of the international court of sports arbitration in promoting the role that sport can play in the promotion of justice, the environment, human rights, and loss of work through, for example, doping scandals;
4. recognition of the emergence of individual or extreme sports as alternative forms of leisure to more global sporting forms such as football. It might be argued that the rise of extreme sports in itself is a form of protest against global or capitalist forms of sport.

The National Sporting Goods Association claims that skateboarding was the number one sport in America during 1999, and that mainstream sports participation is falling as extreme sports participation is up by 65 per cent. The argument that is being presented here is that the world today is more individualistic and that changing trends in the consumption of sport support the argument that team sports, co-operation and solidarity have been replaced by increasing individualism, including the individualism associated with individual choices in extreme sports. Are people looking for different values through sport today? Has the rise in popularity of extreme sports been a reaction against globalisation as children seek individual and not team identity? Are extreme sports a form of rebellion against capitalism or globalisation's impact upon contemporary sport? Are the forces or values that are changing the world reflected in the choice of sports that people participate in? These issues are explored further in Chapter 13 where lifestyle and alternative cultures are discussed.

Globalism is an all-consuming term which by definition does not recognise the possible existence of those outside. Although post-modern intellectuals such as Fukuyama, Baudrillard, Lyotard and Foucault have encouraged the extinction of words like opposition, resistance and critical vocabulary, the role of the student as future public intellectual in the field of sport, culture and society necessitates a re-examining of the world of sport outside the gaze of the trans-national corporation or globalism. The global Nike economy is only global in the sense that giant corporations have free access to every space in the world, if they so choose. To the extent that the money and production flow is beneficial to the privileged few and inaccessible to many, resistance is perhaps inevitable. The baggage of national sport and the nation-state has never been adequate because the issues of nationalism and ethnocentrism tend to travel with it and yet the state and internationalism are but some of the areas which will not halt the march to global sport. However, they illustrate that there is another world of sport, or at least a world of sport outside the zone of the trans-national corporation.

SUMMARY

There is no single theory of globalisation or global sport. The idea of globalisation and global sport has become the source of intense political dispute. Perhaps the central argument in terms of globalisation has been the extent to which it promotes economic well-being throughout the world. For its proponents the spread of free trade encourages enterprise, economic growth, jobs and wealth creation. For its critics globalisation is seen as a key cause of rises in poverty and inequality. Global sport like globalisation operates unevenly, bypassing certain institutions, people and places.

The impact of globalisation processes upon sport is one of the core areas of investigation and reflection in sport, culture and society. The way in which global sport seems to be changing has been the subject of heated debate. For its proponents the sharing and cross-fertilisation of different sporting cultures and tastes is something to be celebrated. For its critics global sport is seen to undermine traditional sporting heritages of nations which are key to people's sense of their belonging and these have been undermined by the co-mingling of diverse sporting tastes and forms. Indigenous sporting cultures have been replaced by market-driven sport that can be sold in the market-place or prove to be popular to television viewers.

The term anti-globalisation has been associated with a movement for global change which is an extremely loose network of individuals and campaigning organisations seeking to transform the way in which globalisation is proceeding. If a summary were possible of the basic differences between radical and moderate approaches to global sport, it might be along the following lines: while the radical wing sees fundamental flaws in the whole process of global sport, the moderate wing is more open to the potential good that may be derived from all forms of globalisation. The true potential of global sport for moderates is undermined by globalisation's domination by a neoliberal agenda and undemocratic sporting structures.

Some have suggested that the term international sport might be a more reality-congruent term than global sport given the debate on whether the global era has ended or not. The ideas associated with internationalism, cosmopolitanism and sport's dynamic role in the making of nations are examined in the next chapter.

KEY CONCEPTS

Anti-globalisation	Process sociology
Child labour	Radical anti-globalisation
Cultural globalisation	Sporting ethnoscapes
Economic globalisation	Sporting financescapes
Globalisation	Sporting ideoscapes
International sport	Sporting mediascapes
Labour migration	Sporting technoscapes
Moderate anti-globalisation	Sports migration
National sport	Sportisation
Political globalisation	Trans-national corporations

KEY READING

Books

Bairner, A. (2001). *Sport, Nationalism and Globalization.* Albany: State University of New York Press.

105

Baylis, J. and Smith, S. (2001). *The Globalization of World Politics*: *An Introduction to International Relations*. Oxford: Oxford University Press.

Lafeber, W. (1999). *Michael Jordan and the New Global Capitalism*. New York: W.W. Norton and Company.

Morrow, S. (2003). *The People's Game? Football, Finance and Society*. Basingstoke: Palgrave.

Maguire, J. (1999). *Global Sport*: *Identities, Societies, Civilizations*. Cambridge: Polity Press.

Journal articles

McGovern, P. (2002). 'Globalization or Internationalization? Foreign Footballers in the English League, 1946–95'. *Sociology*, 36(1): 23–42.

Mertes, T. (2002). 'Grass-Roots Globalism'. *New Left Review*, 17 (October): 101–112.

Chiba, N., Ebihara, O. and Morino, S. (2001). 'Globalization, Naturalization and Identity: The Case of Borderless Elite Athletes in Japan'. *International Review for the Sociology of Sport*, 36(2): 203–221.

Rowe, D. (2003). 'Sport and the Repudiation of the Global'. *International Review for the Sociology of Sport*, 38(3): 281–295.

Further reading

Bentley, T. and Stedman-Jones, D. (2001). *The Moral Universe*. London: Demos.

Gray, J. (2001). 'The Era of Globalisation is Over'. *New Statesman*, 24 September, 25–27.

Leadbeater, C. (2002). 'Globalisation: want the good news?'. *New Statesman*, 1 July, 29–31.

Miyoshi, M. (1997). 'Sites of resistance in the global economy'. In Pearson, K., Parry, B. and Squires, J. (eds) *Cultural Readings of Imperialism*. London: Lawrence and Wishart, 49–66.

REVISION QUESTIONS

1. What are the implications of globalisation for local, national and international sport?

2. Describe and evaluate any four themes that have contributed to the debate about global sport.

3. When did global sport come into being and how has it progressed to date?

4. The values associated with global sport have been the object of criticism and protest. Critically analyse the radical and moderate approaches to anti-globalisation and the role of sport within such policies.

5. The debate about global sport has been dominated in the late twentieth century by figurational or process sociology. Does this approach offer an adequate framework for analysing global sport?

PRACTICAL PROJECTS

1. Empirically calculate the migration of players from different countries into any sport of your choice over the period of one season. Describe and interpret the pattern of sports labour migration.

2. Map out the names of the different countries that have participated in the Olympic Games since 1948. Use this data to argue for or against the Olympic Games becoming truly global or simply international.

3. Using the Google search engine develop five detailed case studies of sport that might be used to substantiate sport as a facet of anti-globalisation.

4. Consult the web pages of any major international sports organisation to obtain information on the nature and scale of their presence in different parts of the world. Use the data as a basis for finding out more about the organisation, its objectives, its investments in different countries and its policies towards all or some parts of the world.

5. Write a short report of about 1500 words based upon a web-based investigation into child labour in sport.

WEBSITES

Focus on the Global South
    www.focusweb.org/

One World
    www.oneworld.net

Open Democracy
    www.opendemocracy.net

The Globalisation Guide
    www.globilisationguide.org

The Global Site
    www.theglobalsite.ac.uk

Football Against Child Labour
    www.un.org/pubs/chronicle/2002/p19

Chapter 5

Internationalism, reconciliation and sport in the making of nations

Can sport help to bring about reconciliation between warring or troubled countries or nations? Getty Images

PREVIEW

Sport and nationalism • Sport's role in the making of nations • Sport, nationality and globalisation • Sport, nationalism and their futures • International sport and internationalism • International sport • Past and present examples of sport and internationalism • International sports labour migration • Dispersal of power in sport • Sporting governance and states of denial in world sport • Sport as reconciliation • Olympic truces, diplomacy and international relations • Global or local sport: A false choice.

OBJECTIVES

This chapter will:

■ evaluate some of the ways in which sport has contributed to nation building;

■ suggest that sport and its relationship to nationalism and internationalism can provide a particular qualification of the global–local thinking about sport;

■ illustrate the part played by sport in processes of reconciliation within nations;

■ look at the emergence of new nationalisms in relation to sport;

■ introduce the notions of internationalism and cosmopolitanism as part of the global–local continuum of sport.

INTRODUCTION

It has often been suggested that nationalism is becoming obsolete as a result of globalisation and that the relationship between sport and nationalism is weakening. Fukuyama (1992:12) has championed the cause of a globalised culture within which the nation-state is viewed as anachronistic. Alternatively, Hirst and Thompson (1999) argue that the role of the nation-state remains pivotal in terms of international governance. Nation-states may no longer be viewed as absolute governing powers able to impose outcomes on all dimensions of policy, including sporting policy. They none the less remain an influential locus of power because of their relationship to both territory and populations. Populations remain territorial and subject to the citizenship of a national state, not in the sense that they are all-powerful, but because they still have a central role to police the borders of a territory and, to the extent that they are potentially legitimately democratic, they remain representative of the citizens within fluid border territories. The corollary is that national governing bodies of sport and national sports agencies continue to be vital to the governance of sport within certain countries. At the same time, international decisions and forces also influence the governance of national sport.

The nationalism that is connected to sport may be constructed by many different forces, be manifested within and between different types of nationalism, be real and imagined, be a creative or reflective force, be both positive and negative, transient and temporary, multifaceted and multi-layered and/or evolutionary in its format (Cronin, 1999:55). Drawing on some specific examples, Cronin asks a number of pertinent questions concerning the ways in which sport is inextricably linked to the forces of nationalism. Are countries in the search for a new national identity appropriating sport? How has the relationship between sport and nationalism developed? Why is it so important in contemporary society and what should we do with it or about it? While it is increasingly difficult to sustain the argument that a single sport represents any one nation, nonetheless certain 'nation-specific' games, such as Gaelic games,

American football, shinty, Aussie rules football, or pelota, still thrive despite the advances of global sport and continue to play a central part within various national cultures. To use an engendered Swedish example quoted by Cronin:

> Nothing awakens Swedish national feeling so easily and strongly (at least among men) as sporting success. Glorious history, royalty, a splendid army, democracy and the welfare system, ancient ideals and traditions, Volvo and other great companies – none of these things can measure up to sport in providing bonds of national solidarity or in creating collective consciousness of one's country.
>
> (1999:59)

Initially the points that need to be made here relate to the changing geography of the world. It is also crucial to recognise that the content of the relationship between sport, nationalism and national identities is fluid in terms of time and place. The potential weakness in thinking of the nation as only a place, or linking a particular sport to a particular nation, is that these cases run the danger of becoming fixed in content, time and space. This is a view that fails to acknowledge the nation or territory as a process that is neither fixed nor immutable. Territorial expansion or contraction is one of many ways in which the nation as a place changes over time. But the idea of what the nation is or which sports represent the nation also changes in relation to the social, cultural and political contexts.

The content, timing and symbolism of sport, nationalisms and identities in South Africa today are completely different from the content, timing and symbolism of sport, nationalisms and identities that existed during the apartheid era. Both sets of experiences are part of the process of South African sport and South Africa. In this sense it might be suggested that there is no single essential nation, only a South Africa that embraces different territorial spaces and times. South African sportsmen and women, like Nelson Mandela, Zola Budd, Hassan Howa, Sam Ramsamy, Jasmat Dhiraj, Basil d'Olivera and Justin Fortune, all express the idea of belonging to a South African nation or solid community moving up or down history.

Similarly, Australian sportswomen like Cathie Freeman, Evonne Cawley and Dawn Fraser, all of whom have represented Australia, might all be deemed to be patriotic sportswomen. Yet they represented Australia at different points in the history of Australia. Therefore, the twenty-first-century Australia represented by Cathie Freeman as she won the gold medal at the Sydney 2000 Olympic Games was a different Australia from the 1970s Australia experienced by Evonne Cawley, the first Aboriginal woman to play tennis at Wimbledon. This in turn was different from the Australia experienced by Dawn Fraser. The Australia of the 2000 Sydney Olympics seemed to be more tolerant and celebratory about its Aboriginal sporting history than the Australia of the 1970s experienced by Evonne Goolagong (Cawley).

111

Vamplew and Stoddart's (1994) examination of Australian sport acknowledges that in the twentieth century Aborigines were vastly under-represented in most sports and virtually non-participants in many others. In only three sports were Aboriginal men disproportionately successful, namely Australian Rules football, boxing and rugby league football. Hargreaves's (2000:85) discussion of Aboriginal sportswomen notes that these sporting heroines are part of two worlds of sport and two forms of nation-building, namely the imperial culture of Australia's mainstream sport and the indigenous sporting culture of the indigenous nations within the nation-state that is Australia. Aboriginal women have forged sporting opportunities in both mainstream sport and Aboriginal sport and yet Australian sport cannot be properly understood outside the contexts of discussions about racism, colonisation, post-colonialism and how Aboriginal sportspeople have been portrayed, represented and empowered within Australia.

These examples illustrate that sports men and women were all embroiled at different times in the process of forging what it meant to be a South African or an Australian. The point being emphasised here is that a specific understanding of the relationship between sport nationalisms and national identities needs to be analysed in terms of time and place. The above-mentioned sporting women and men may all express a sense of belonging to the idea of a nation or solid community and have contributed to the process of helping to define what it meant to be a twentieth or twenty-first-century South African or Australian. At the same time, any nominal sense of unity or agreed notion of what exactly the nation was amongst these people would be hard to find.

In an earlier discussion of the role of sport in the making of nations it was concluded that the word nation might be used to describe a human community that has acquired national consciousness, since it is clear that national consciousness is different from other forms of collective consciousness (Maguire et al., 2002:160). The same authors went on to examine the issue of globalisation and its relationship to sport and the nation-state and suggested that if one accepted the notion that nation-states are no longer viewed as absolute governing powers, but are simply one class of powers, then sport must reflect the changing system of world power that operates from global to local levels. What was missing from this earlier discussion on sport in the making of nations was any recognition of the notion of internationalism.

The social benefits of internationalism as a reality-congruent form of globalisation are strong. The challenge for sport is for it to cross the boundaries of prejudice and parochialism and recognise that sporting loyalties to local, regional and national sporting forms also need to co-exist alongside internationalism. In this sense sport and globalisation emerge as the natural enemy of bigotry and inward-looking varieties of sporting patriotism and nationalism. Thinking globally and acting locally was one of the many slogans of the 1960s. The debate about global sport has tended to dismiss the debate about international sport and internationalism as socialist utopias of the nineteenth and twentieth centuries. Internationalism is associated almost uncritically with the creation of a specific international working-class culture, beginning with songs and the celebration of May Day and reaching its most advanced forms within the Socialist and Communist Internationals of the inter-war period. There were certainly international worker organisations for sport, theatre, youth, students, film, photo, nature-lovers and tourism. The vitality of the international women's movement, environmental and ecological groups, peace and human rights protests tell us that any understanding of globalisation and global sport needs to account for internationalism and international sport in new ways.

The discussion that follows is developed around four themes. What is the relationship between sport and nationalism? What is the future of sport and nationalism? What is the relationship between sport and internationalism? To what extent might the notions of internationalism and cosmopolitanism add to our understanding of the complexity of global sports processes? As an extension of the arguments developed in the previous chapter, this chapter suggests that sport has not been at the forefront of global or international change. Neither has it been dormant or unaffected by changing boundaries. The advance of globalisation does not make the state redundant; many would argue that it makes the state more necessary as a guarantor of civil and human rights. Internationalism has made and continues to make small contribution to these and other sporting developments.

SPORT AND NATIONALISM

General discussions of nationalism and sport are often problematic because of the 'slipperiness' of the term. Writers such as Low (2000:357) have suggested that nationalism is more complex than the conceptual tools we have at our disposal. The value of Cronin's (1999) typology of nationalisms is that it highlights a much broader set of ideas than simply that of civic or ethnic nationalism. Four approaches to the historical origins of nationalism are presented. First there is the *primordialist* view on nationalism which asserts that nationalism is rooted in the land. Primordialists champion the dangerous notion that nationalism is a product of ethnicity that can be rooted in history. Second there is the *modernist* view that nationalism is a product of the modern age. Thus, the origins of the formation of nationalism are specifically tied to a particular historical epoch. Third there is the *statist* view which suggests that nationalism itself more than anything else is associated with the idea of the state. Statists argue that the state uses sport to manage forms of state identity and allegiance. Finally, there are the *political mythologists* who locate the ideology of nationalism within the imagined or mythical symbols of national representation. The objective of this form of nationalism is to suggest that nations share a sense of community.

There are many different concepts associated with nationalism and any cursory discussion is illustrative of the fact that different types of national communities and identities exist in different parts of the world. There are many different notions of the nation or nationalism or identity and to reduce the terms to some form of rational universalism simplifies the concepts and the reality of sport in the making of nations. Whatever the nation in question, the quest for identity inevitably involves questions of representation, nostalgia, mythology and tradition. Many nations themselves are fabrications or constructions, many states are not nations and indeed many nations are not states. Modern states and stateless nations have often required an explicit sense of loyalty and identification that has at times been mobilised through identification with certain symbols, icons, hymns and prayers, all of which are continually changing over time.

The implications of specific comparisons, contrasts and distinctions used to define nationalism are, like different viewpoints on its origins, rarely value-free. Nationalism can at times be seen to be positive in relation to narrow local attachments or feudal loyalties while at the same time being viewed as a negative social force in relation to ideologies of civic community. It can seem positive in the context of combating forms of imperialism and yet negative in relation to other supra-national phenomena, such as humanity or international class or gender solidarity. The issue of the values associated with nationalism or nationhood depends on what one is comparing it against and as such the specifics of any situation will often prove to have a greater explanatory potential than broad generalisations.

Much of the debate has centred upon distinctions between civic forms of nationalism and ethnic forms of nationalism. The former is often closely associated with citizenship and territory, while the latter is often associated with ties of blood. A significant problem with notions such as ethnic and civic nationalism is that they are used to describe certain types of abstract social relationships. Yet what is crucial is not the level of abstraction or meaning, but the underlying relationship to the reality within which the experience is lived out. Ethnic forms of nationalism cannot be freely chosen. They imply, for example, that you are a Hutu, a Croat, a Catalan, a Basque, a Scot, a Welsh or English person or you are not. You cannot opt out because within this framework ethnicity is conveyed at birth. Within the ever-changing twenty-first century multiplicities of identity are the norm.

This distinction between absolutist civic and ethnic nationalism can be criticised on a number of grounds, not least the forms of racism embedded within either absolute definition of nationalism. In absolute cases it is impossible to keep blood and soil apart and, despite modern attempts at ethnic cleansing in territories such as Croatia and Serbia or between ethnic groups such as Hutus and Tamils in Tanzania and Ethiopia, in practice such forms of nationalism can never be absolute. Multi-culturalism and hybridity are embedded nearly every place, and any claim that the state or stateless nation has to a single culture, a single identity or single form of nationalism becomes almost impossible to sustain. When the English Conservative politician, Norman Tebbit, sought to apply his racist cricket test rule – if you live in England, you should support the national English cricket team, even if it is playing against your country of origin – he failed to acknowledge this very point. People have many complex allegiances and it might be suggested that both ethnic-nationalist absolutism and civic state absolutism are untenable in a post-nationalist world. Both diminish active personal choice, one more so than the other, and hence are fundamentally illiberal.

Politicians from various political parties, including nationalist political parties, have used the emotions associated with different sports to rally support for the nation. In the 1960s the then Labour Prime Minister, Harold Wilson, made great political mileage out of England's football victory in the 1966 World Cup. Throughout the 1970s Julius Nyerere of Tanzania often remarked that in developing nations sport helped bridge the gap between national and global recognition. Immanuel Wallerstein suggested that African citizens could feel affection for the victorious athlete and the nation (Jarvie, 1993). He suggested that this affection might not have existed in the first instance given the social and ethnic divisions within African nation-states. The process necessary to develop this affection depended on athletes accepting the politics of the nation and working with the party structures. During the 1980s a key element of African National Congress (ANC) policy in South Africa was 'One Can Not Play Normal Sport in an Abnormal Society'. By the 1990s, President Mandela argued that sport had become part of the new glue that held the nation together. This was exemplified by South Africa's victory in the 1995 Rugby World Cup, a victory viewed as being symbolic of a new post-apartheid era. Jim Sillars, the then Deputy Leader of the Scottish Nationalist Party (SNP), following his defeat in the 1992 General Election, chastised the Scottish electorate for not voting for the nationalist cause, maligning them for being '90-minute patriots' and saving their nationalist fervour for major sporting occasions (*Herald*, 24 April 1992:1). In other words sport as a form of cultural nationalism served as a substitute for voting for the political nationalism of the Scottish Nationalist Party in that patriots could show an affinity for the nation on various sporting occasions without necessarily voting for nationalist parties.

The symbolism of sport has also helped to promote national identity and sentiment at major sporting events. Sport has helped provide a sense of cultural autonomy to such places as Catalonia in Spain, Brittany in France, or Taiwan. Specific sporting success has helped to foster a close symbolic link between specific sports and specific places, such as athletics and Kenya; football and Brazil; ice hockey and Canada or Sweden; golf and Scotland; sumo wrestling and Japan; cycling and France; baseball and Cuba; and hurling and Ireland. The idea that sport and sporting achievements contribute to a nation's greatness and national identity, and at times help to transcend internal strife and social deference, is but one argument that has been dressed up in a number of guises and commented upon extensively over the last decade or more.

Sport at times has also been implemented in the politics of imperialism and national reconciliation. In the build-up to the 2002 football World Cup, jointly hosted by Japan and the Republic of Korea (ROK), Emperor Akihito of Japan acknowledged that Japan's imperial family was descended from the Kingdom of Paeckche, an ancient Korean civilization. Following Japan's annexation of Korea in 1910 and the subsequent 35 years of colonial rule, Emperor Akihito used the then imminent sporting event to break the ice between the two nations. The co-hosting of the World Cup was the first time since World War II that Japan and Korea had co-operated over an event. The two countries made attempts to normalise relations in the run-up to the event. Japan dropped its visa requirements for ROK short-stay visitors while Seoul removed a ban on broadcasting Japanese music. In reality any reconciliation over the colonial past, remarked one of Japan's first Korean residents, would not come about through football but through ordinary Korean and Japanese people being brave enough to acknowledge the past and move on (*The Financial Times Weekend*, 25 May 2002:10). At times, football travels beyond the confines of national identity, reconciliation and national politics. In the first match of the 2002 football World Cup in Japan and ROK, Senegal defeated its former colonial rulers, and the then World Champions, France. The country's President praised the success of the team in terms of defending the honour of *Africa* (*The Times Higher*, 14 June 2002:19).

The relationship between sport and nationalism and the role that sport has played in the making of nations have tended to rely upon some or all of the arguments listed in Box 5.1.

BOX 5.1 ARGUMENTS RELATING TO SPORT IN THE MAKING OF NATIONS

- Sport acts as a form of cultural nationalism
- Sport acts as a substitute for political nationalism
- Sport can contribute to both ethnic and civic forms of nationality, many of which may be mythical, invented or selected
- Sport helps with the process of national reconciliation
- Sport provides a safety valve or outlet of emotional energy for frustrated peoples or nations
- Sport helps to build national identity and patriotism
- Nations denied national sports representation have at times vested great national sentiment in specific clubs or sports such as 'Barça' (Barcelona, capital of Catalan Spain)
- Nationalist support for sport has been a natural reaction against the pressures arising out of the development of global or international sport
- Sport contributes to the building of national consciousness
- Sport has contributed to the politics of cultural imperialism and colonialism.

Sport, nationality and globalisation

One particular theme is worthy of further discussion before considering the future relationship between sport and nationalism – the assertion that the relationship between sport and nationality has diminished in importance as sport has become more global. As mentioned earlier, it has been suggested that nationalism is becoming obsolete as a result of globalisation. This seems doubtful and on those occasions when the perceived global imagined community comes into view – the millennium, concerts to raise money for world hunger or Aids victims, the Olympic Games, the football World Cup, the World Athletic Championships, or Princess Diana's funeral – these are but occasional and *rarely total* global events. Saying that there has been an increased rate or occurrence of globalisation or inter-nationalisation of sport over the past 20 years is entirely different from saying that sport is global or that the end point of the global era has arrived.

In a review of national responses to globalisation in sport, Allison (2002:353) maintains that the degree of globalisation impacting upon different cultural, political and economic areas is not only complex but also different from sector to sector. Thus, while the global governance of sport may be advanced, this is only relative to other less advanced areas, such as the global or international governance of environmental regulation or human rights. It is argued that in sport the alleged global governance results from a combination of factors, many of which are international by nature. Three examples are provided: (i) international organisations involved in the governance of sport whose leaders and authority are often virtually unaccountable; (ii) trans-national corporations, particularly in the media, that sponsor sport and (iii) the growth of an effective system of international law which has influenced elements of sport, such as the 1995 Bosman ruling which outlawed certain aspects of the football transfer system to bring it, at the time, more in line with European legislation on the freedom of workers to travel within Europe. Moreover, in 1999 the Monopolies and Mergers Commission of the UK government intervened to stop the media mogul Robert Murdoch – through his ownership of British Sky Broadcasting – from taking over Manchester United Football Club.

A subtle version of these arguments has been to suggest that, as a result of globalisation and the diminishing power of nationalism, sport and society have become increasingly homogenous. Bairner is unequivocal that any analysis of the above should stop short of arguing that global forces have resulted in greater homogenisation or Americanisation. To speak of Americanisation in such terms is to distort reality and, in agreement with Maguire, Bairner concedes that any assessment of global sport should accommodate the idea that globalisation has resulted in increasing varieties and diminishing contrasts. In other words while various societies have become increasingly similar to one another, each country also has afforded its inhabitants a far greater choice of sports to play and watch (Bairner, 2001:176).

The term *glocalisation* is coined to refer to the extent to which sport and nationality have resisted globalisation. Yet global capitalism through the sponsoring of international sporting competition has ensured that national sporting identities remain to the fore, indeed are the 'flagships of the global sporting economy' (Bairner, 2001:176). It is for this reason, the author goes on to say,

> that we can talk of nationalism having successfully resisted the encroachment of globalisation's homogenising tendencies . . . sport and globalisation have become accomplices in the process whereby the importance of national identity has been ensured.
>
> (Bairner, 2001:176)

Thus, it is concluded that sport will continue to play a part in allowing nations to resist global homogenisation.

All of the above serves to illustrate that in terms of world sport today the issues are perhaps not so much about the question of national democracy versus global governance of sport, more about the complex interaction between local, national, international, post-colonial and global forces, all of which are potential points of entry into any analysis of the changing nature of contemporary sport.

SPORT, NATIONALISMS AND THEIR FUTURES

It is perhaps misguided to forget the power of nationalism and its relationship to sport. The idea that sport and sporting achievements contribute to a nation's greatness and transcend internal strife and social deference remains as potent in the twenty-first century as it has been in the past. Following the war in Afghanistan, the former Tottenham Hotspur football captain Terry Mabbutt was involved in the organising of football matches between peacekeeping forces in the area and Afghan citizens in Kabul during February 2003. A spokesperson for the Ministry of Defence suggested that football was a global language and that more matches in the future would be played between peacekeeping forces and local people. During the American and British invasion of Iraq in the early part of 2003 it was suggested that, when the fighting was over, the Football Association and, in particular, the then England Football Captain David Beckham, should play a role in restoring normality and peace to Iraq. Indeed, during the early part of the war British forces played a football match against local people in Umm Khayyal and more than 1,000 spectators turned out to watch the home side win (*Sunday Express*, 5 April 2003:11).

Despite the momentous events of the twentieth century the nation-state remains a unit of political currency and it is perhaps helpful to outline several ways in which the relationship between sport and nationalism may have a future. The changing configuration of nation-states is such that it would be a brave person who would predict the future make-up of international sports competitions, such as the Football, Rugby or Cricket World Cups or the Olympic Games or the Asian or Pan-American Games or any other international sporting event. The effect of proliferation of nationalisms and nation-states over recent decades only serves to confirm this point. The complex relationship between sport and nationalisms, rather than waning, seems to be waxing and certainly shows no signs of dying.

For example, sport continues to play an important role in the construction of national consciousness in modern China. The complexity of sport in post-Maoist China is evident in the fact that Chinese leaders in the build-up to and subsequent gaining of the right to host the 2008 Olympic Games in Beijing used sport and in particular Western sports in what Hwang (2000) describes as an attempt to break out of Asia and advance further into the international arena. At the same time, specific attempts to modernise traditional forms of sport and exercise are resisted for fear of enhancing Western ideas of democracy. Following the bombing of the Chinese Embassy in Belgrade on 8 May 1999, the immediate response of the Chinese government was to ban the broadcasting of American National League Basketball (NBA) games on national television. NBA teams were popular amongst 79 per cent of Chinese teenage television viewers at the time. On the other hand, the traditional form of exercise known as *quigong* featured in a public protest staged by more than 10,000 members of the Falun Gong in Beijing on 25 April 1999. The government responded by saying that 'this kind of gathering affected public order and it was completely wrong to damage social stability under the pretext of practising martial arts and traditional sports' (*Central Daily News*, 29 June 1999:7).

There are at least four immediate arguments that may initially be put forward to assert that the relationship between sport and nationalism is likely to have a future. First, in a sovereign sense the nature of the nation-state may change, but the existence of sports teams representing territorially defined nations or regions aspiring to be nations is likely to continue. Second, nationalist-orientated governments or organisations such as the African National Congress or the Palestinian liberation movement, or forms of national sovereignty such as Great Britain (however fragile the Union may be) are likely to promote distinctive sporting policies. Third, distinctive nationalist sporting organisations such as the Gaelic Athletic Association will continue to provide a national focus for traditional national sports. Finally, whether these be sporting or otherwise, an international society as an association of states cannot totally rely upon supra-national bodies to make and enforce laws since these require states to accept legal and constitutional limitations above and below. In this sense the nation-state or new forms of sovereignty involving national factions remain central to any proposed international economy, society or culture. Sport as an entity is managed both nationally and internationally – it is not a question of either or.

Nationalisms have continued to rise in regions and territories that have expressed a wish to break away from existing states. In some senses McCrone (2000:129) is correct to point out that the contemporary relationship between nationalism and the nation-state is at best contradictory, if not illusory. Just as nationalism is growing in importance, nation-states appear to be losing their powers as they are in part challenged by global or international powers such as those exercised by the International Monetary Fund, the Court of Arbitration for Sport, the World Bank, the European Union and the International Olympic Committee. All these forces would seem to have eroded the power of the independent state or national sports organisation. So why has there been an increase in national movements wanting a state of their own? One answer is that a homogenous view of the viable nation-state is over, if it ever existed, and national vision must be redefined. Sport could be viewed as a good indicator of modern nationality and internationality in the sense that international sports teams are less dependent upon players being born in the country which they play for. Indeed many international athletes have played for different countries and they are national, by definition, if they play for the national side.

In a rapidly global or internationalising world many of the traditional things that helped us with a sense of belonging – nation-states with relatively homogenous populations, sports teams of home-grown nationals, well-established local communities, allegiance to local teams or to history and tradition – are all being challenged. To know thyself is a fundamental human need. Having some idea of who we are helps us to define how we ought to live and conduct our daily affairs. In other words, who or what we are either as an individual or nation or international community helps determine how we may conduct or live out our lives. Sport through allegiance to all of the above can help different configurations or groups to know themselves.

SPORT AND INTERNATIONALISM

While past and present commentaries upon sport, culture and society have mapped out the complex relationships between sport and nationalism and sport and globalisation, less has been said about notions such as internationalism and to a lesser extent cosmopolitanism. It is not as if such notions have not been relevant to the history of sport, but discussions of global sport and sport in the making of nations have tended to marginalise the very vivid role that sport has had in terms of internationalism.

Undoubtedly the world is changing rapidly and much of what has been advocated about sport diminishing contrasts and increasing varieties of nationalism and globalisation remains crucial to our understanding of sport, culture and society today. As the examples in Box 5.2 illustrate, this is not at the expense of the role that sport has played in terms of internationalism, or at least particular versions of it. It is important, therefore, to remember the complexity of the global–local axis and for students of sport, culture and society to appreciate that notions such as internationalism and cosmopolitanism, as well as orientalism, are pertinent to understanding the dynamic processes that are impacting upon the post-millennium world of sport. Few political notions are at once so normative and so equivocal as internationalism. Whatever sense is given to the term internationalism logically it depends upon some prior conception of nationalism. At the turn of the millennium, while nationalisms as a force have proved to be alive and well, it has been within certain limits. Paradoxically, internationalism and internationality may be viewed as having positive values *both* as a defence against, for example, American unilateralism, and as a form of American hegemony.

On the one hand, American unilateralism itself may be viewed as a creeping notion of internationalism that needs a series of checks and balances to be put in place. On the other

BOX 5.2 PAST AND PRESENT EXAMPLES OF SPORT AND INTERNATIONALISM

1928　The entry of women into Olympic athletics after being excluded for 32 years

1931　The worker Olympics held in Vienna, involving 8,000 worker athletes from 23 countries held under the banner of internationalism and peace

1936　Jesse Owens winning four gold Medals at the 'Nazi' Olympic Games held in Berlin

1964　The expulsion of South Africa from the Olympic Games, thus heralding the official international anti-racist campaign against apartheid

1984　The Algerian athlete Hassiba Bourghiba winning an Olympic gold medal and screaming as she crossed the line on behalf of all oppressed women

1988　The Seoul Olympic Games which were the first Olympic Games for years not to be affected by more than a token boycott

1995　Nelson Mandela wearing a baseball cap and Springbok shirt following South Africa's victory in the Rugby World Cup held in South Africa, so demonstrating the need for the new 'Rainbow' nation to work together and respect one another

1998　France's victory in the football World Cup held in France with an international team which proclaimed its representation of the new ethnically-integrated France

2003　Liverpool and Celtic football fans during the quarter final of the UEFA Cup competition singing the same songs together and wearing scarves with Liverpool and Celtic printed on the same scarf

hand, the international community also needs to assert itself, not least over the issue of human rights for all people and not just those conforming to American internationalism. Internationally, Islamic fundamentalism and orthodox Catholicism muster as residual places for an alternative form of life that is equally international, but also less captive to the world of consumption. It has been suggested (Anderson, 2002:25) that the dangers of Americanism and Britishness as forms of Western internationalism under the banner of human rights are problematic. For instance, they provide in the name of the international community the forces to blockade, bomb or invade peoples or states that displease them (Cuba, Yugoslavia, Afghanistan, Iraq), while at the same time nourishing, financing and arming states that appeal to them (Turkey, Israel, Saudi Arabia, Pakistan). As for the Chechens, Palestinians, Tutsi, Sahrawi, Nuer and other peoples, some without a state, they are left to a world of charity that cannot after all be ubiquitous.

Sport is not exempt from the uneven gaze of human rights as the last part of this book illustrates. Some or all of the following arguments may be associated with sport and internationalisms: (i) the international governance of sport is relatively advanced in the twenty-first century and the relationship between sport and specific national territories cannot be fully understood without recognising the part played by trans-national organisations and international forces of development; (ii) sport in specific times and at specific places has contributed to specific forms of internationalism. Sport at times may be a catalyst in reviving or sustaining international sentiment and in this sense sport has reflected rather than led political sentiment; (iii) sport can help with the process of reconciliation; (iv) the hybridity associated with post-modern international sport has meant that sport operates in both a post-nationalist and post-colonial phase of development and yet, at the same time, it is important to recognise that post-colonial sport has impacted upon sport's historical role as an agent of both imperialism and colonialism and (v) the nation-state and forms of internationalism provide potential sites of hope for the 'other' worlds of sport outside the gaze of the trans-national sports corporation.

Examples of sport and internationalism

There are a number of ways in which sport might be thought of being actively international rather than national. All of these in turn serve as a qualification and warning *vis-à-vis* accepting too uncritically the notion of global sport. First, historically international contacts through sport have provided opportunities for European workers to understand those factors that divided nations with a view to attempting to overcome them. The available evidence from the stories of worker sports movements throughout Europe and beyond suggests above all that worker sportsmen and women were internationalists and supported causes such as anti-fascism which tended to circumvent national boundaries (Jones, 1988; Kruger and Riordan, 1996).

By 1930 worker sport united well over four million people, making it by far the most popular working-class cultural movement. Certainly one of the most interesting aspects of worker sport in Britain was the way in which sport was used to forge links with the continental worker sports movement in Germany, France, Austria, Italy, Finland, Israel, Canada, Czechoslovakia and the former Soviet Union. The principle of internationalism flowed over into the sports arena with sport festivals, and Workers Olympiads became popular forums for continental socialists. If international peace was to be advanced by bringing together workers, then sports events had to be organised effectively and in such a way as to develop political awareness as well as sporting progress. The provision for worker sports events spread throughout Europe to the extent that, between 1926 and 1934, as many as 966 national and international sporting events had been organised under the auspices of the Socialist Worker Sports International (SWSI), which had 1.3 million members by 1927 from eighteen different countries (Jones, 1988:170). If nothing else, the worker sports movement strengthened a rather weak internationalistic ethic among continental workers during the first half of the twentieth century. Despite political difficulties worker sport helped to stimulate some form of common European ethos or internationalism through sporting contact.

Second, at an empirical level contemporary studies have concluded that certain aspects of sport today may be more international, regional and local rather than global. Therefore, a second way in which international sport might be thought of as a critique of globalism is empirically. A particular critique of globalisation is borne out in McGovern's (2002) study of the migration patterns of foreign football players into the English football league between 1946 and 1995. McGovern writes that the idea of globalisation producing a global football market is naive. The study presents a case study of the football labour market where global-isation might reasonably have been expected. The empirical evidence provided lends support to the idea that international labour migration might reasonably have been expected to be one of the defining features of globalisation as far as football is concerned. Within the football industry the employers – the clubs – tend to be permanently fixed to specific geographical locations while the employees – footballers – can move within certain limits between cities, continents and countries. Towards the end of the twentieth century the increased mobility of footballers led to the popular view that the football industry was undergoing a process of globalisation mostly because of the increasing numbers of European clubs importing players from a wide range of countries. Because of the social embedded-ness and historical patterns of recruitment involved in football migration, McGovern concluded that labour market migration in football was characterised by a process of inter-nationalisation and that the recruitment of players was influenced by a range of social, economic and political factors that were national and international in origin, if not British. Thus, it is important to distinguish between the terms globalisation and internationalisation, where internationalisation refers to the extension of activities across national boundaries, whereas globalisation refers to the geographical extension of economic activity across national boundaries, as well as the functional integration of such internationally dispersed activities. There was no evidence in the study to suggest that international sources of recruit-ment had been functionally integrated into the labour market practices of English football clubs between 1946 and 1995. While the market for professional football players was clearly becoming more international in nature, this trend (McGovern, 2000:38) was developing along regional rather than global lines.

Third, at a relational level sport may influence new generational attitudes towards past conflicts across national boundaries. Following the 2002 FIFA World Cup, co-hosted by Japan and the Republic of Korea (ROK), a new Japanese internationalism may have been encouraged through football. In an editorial entitled, 'A Key Role for the World Cup Generation', *Chosun Iibo*, a leading South Korean newspaper, stated that the World Cup had awakened young people's pride in the Republic of Korea and that the performance of its football team, which reached the semi-finals of the tournament, seemed to have left young Japanese with the impression that South Korea was 'cool' (www.fpcj.jp/e/shiryo/jb/0223.html). Japan's relations with the ROK, as indicated previously, have been tense, the two nations have been close but hostile neighbours, and yet some feel that the co-hosting of the World Cup, together with the performance of the ROK team, laid the groundwork for future internationalism between Japan and the Republic of Korea. A leading Japanese paper, *Asahi*, referred to this as a new easy-going nationalism that transcended borders; it suggested that the relations between Japan and the ROK were entering a new international era (www.fpcj.jp/e/shiryo/jb/2003.html).

Fourth, sport today might be thought of as being cosmopolitan and providing a popular basis for internationalism. The terms cosmopolitan and internationalism are neither historically dead, nor irrelevant to the debate on sport. The changing composition of sports teams, even national teams, is more cosmopolitan than it has been in previous decades and supporters are being asked to associate with a range of identities rather than with any one national team defined in only territorial terms. This factor may merely add to its complexity. Historically, cosmopolitanism has combined two distinct ways of thinking about sport. On the one hand, it designates an enthusiasm for different sporting customs and rituals. The combined rules of shinty/hurling matches, which take place every year between Ireland and Scotland, allow for a merging of their two sets of rules, enabling a completely different form of game to take place. The term cosmopolitan allows for the blending or merging of customary differences that may emerge from multiple local sporting customs.

On the other hand, cosmopolitan sport projects a theory of world sporting governance and corresponding citizenship. In other words, the structure of the hypothetical underlying unity of the cultural meaning of the term cosmopolitan is also carried over to the political meaning of the term – cosmopolitan sporting structures or events would also imply more cosmopolitan sporting citizens. The cosmopolitan ideal (and it is an ideal) envisages a federation or coalition of sporting bodies and states rather than an all-encompassing representative sporting structure in which members can deliberate about sport on a global scale. That is to say that cosmopolitan sport is neither local nor global and is closer to the term international. The transformation of local sport into 'glocal' sport may at some point require recognition of cosmopolitanism. This may include (i) elements of sporting mobility in which people have the means, opportunity and right to travel to and experience other places through sport; (ii) an openness to other peoples and cultures and a recognition of 'other' sporting traditions and customs as being of value and (iii) a commitment to voluntary sports activity involving communities outside one's own locality. It might be that sporting coverage through international TV coverage has contributed to an awareness of a shrinking sporting world and a more cosmopolitan awareness of the world of sport.

By contrast, internationalism seeks to establish global relations of respect and co-operation based upon acceptances of differences in polity as well as culture. Internationalism is not necessarily at odds with national sporting sovereignty. Internationalism allows for multinational sporting forums, for there are few other ways to secure the support of weaker peoples, societies or sporting groups. However, this is not globalisation nor is it cosmopolitan sport. Forms of cosmopolitan sport may spring from the comfortable culture of middle-class sporting tastes and choices. Internationalism may be said to be more inclusive of an ideology of the domestically restricted, recently relocated, the provisionally exiled and the temporarily weak. Cosmopolitan sport is not a new modern form of internationalism but rather the two are incompatible. They both serve to warn the student of sport, culture and society that the choice between local or global sport is not that simple and in many ways is a false choice. The following are four arguments that should be kept mind when reflecting upon the debate about global/local sport.

The dispersal of power in international sport

The dispersal of power in world sport means that the control, management and organisation of sport do not simply occur at local or global levels. In pre-devolution times, UK sport remained a centrally controlled function of government, directed by Westminster government through the respective national offices and agencies. After 1999, within a devolved Great Britain, power in sport has been dispersed to the respective parliaments in Scotland and Wales although a UK sports cabinet and Sports Council still exists. An examination of the calculus of power in sport today, by comparison with say the 1950s, would partially conclude that power in world and national sport has been increasingly dispersed as sport has become more irreverent. The control of sport through deference to the old establishment world order or amateur class ideals of due deference and respect has been eroded. In 1904, membership of FIFA was limited to seven countries, France, Belgium, Denmark, the Netherlands, Spain, Sweden and Switzerland. By 2003, membership of this same organisation has been extended to 204 members spreading across all continents. The staging of international tournaments, such as the African Nations Cup, affects European football clubs, such as Chelsea, Glasgow Rangers, Celtic, Manchester United, Barcelona, A. C. Milan etc., in a way that was unthinkable 20 years ago. Power in world sport is increasingly international, although national sports organisations are not powerless.

Sporting governance and states of denial in world sport

The dispersal of power in world sport might have diminished the power of national governing bodies in certain sports, but it has also meant the development of a crisis of confidence in global sport. Many major sports have been shaken by issues ranging from bribery and corruption, to strike action amongst the players, to international bureaucracy out of control, to a lack of trust in sporting governance. The headline controversies may feed into wider debates about whether sporting bodies have the capacity to deal with contemporary challenges, change and the world of agents, player power, the growing role of the courts, the needs of sponsors, new media rights and technological advances both fair and foul. Added to this is the fact that the old structures of loyalty and identity have been losing their authority as sport has become more irreverent; a healthy distrust of authority has encouraged a more egalitarian commitment. So the need for transparency, accountability and movement to a state of trust rather than official denial in sport is needed today.

It is about putting in place structures that can give those who play and follow sport more confidence that those in charge are doing the right thing. The global era has presented fundamental challenges for sporting governance, but it has also created the opportunity for sport to be a force for internationalism. At very least it should create a reflex suspicion of official denials.

Sport as reconciliation

The role of sport in terms of reconciliation is perhaps one of the most important humanitarian ways in which sport can contribute to the world today. The twentieth century was one in which the world witnessed more great wars than in the previous century. The beginning of the twenty-first century has shown no early signs of national conflict decreasing between or within nations. In Northern Ireland different community groups have generally recognised the cultural importance of sport in reconciling civil, national and religious tensions in a divided Ireland as set out under the Good Friday Agreement between the British and Irish Governments. In South Africa, shortly after the collapse of the apartheid government, the Head of the Department of Sport and Recreation within the Governments of National Unity's Ministry of Sport stated in 1997 that mutual recognition would be given to the critical role that sport was destined to play as a catalyst for change and reconciliation within the new South Africa.

Olympic truce, diplomacy and international relations

International sporting organisations, such as the IOC, are in many senses contradictory when it comes to internationalism and humanitarian causes. The International Olympic Committee, in support of the 2000 Sydney Olympic Games, spent US $230 million on a series of advertisements around the theme 'Celebrate Humanity'. This exercise was designed to encourage viewers and those attending the Olympic Games to see the event as a celebration of the best that humanity had to offer in terms of health, internationalism and sport. At the same time, the Sydney Olympic Games Committee assembled a security apparatus to prevent protesters using the Olympic Games as a vehicle for highlighting Australia's record on human rights. Thirty thousand private security guards, 4,000 state military personnel and thousands of state police were charged with ensuring that the Sydney Olympic Games was a peaceful Olympic Games.

Acknowledging the contradictory messages given by international sporting organisations does not necessarily negate the way in which international sporting organisations and sport are implicated within international relations. Following the break-up of the Federal Republic of Yugoslavia in 1992, the IOC revived the notion of 'Olympic Truce'. The original stated objective of the IOC was to defend the interests of athletes, protect the Olympic Games and consolidate unity within the Olympic movement. However, UN Security Council Resolution 757 of 1992 listed sport as a recognised element within any sanctions policy, so a compromise was reached permitting the athletes of Yugoslavia to participate in the Barcelona 1992 Olympic Games as individuals.

125

The support for the concept of an Olympic Truce is noteworthy in terms of recognising the role of international non-governmental organisations (NGOs) in influencing and brokering international relations (Beacom, 2000). A further Olympic Truce was launched on 24 January 1994 to cover the period of the Lillehammer Winter Games given the continuing conflict in Yugoslavia. This Olympic Truce involved representations from the World Health Organization (WHO), UNICEF, the Red Cross, the UN High Commissioner for Refugees and the Norwegian Government who had to resolve the issue of evacuating National Olympic Committee (NOC) leaders and athletes from Sarajevo so that they could compete in the Winter Olympic Games. Thereafter any potential Olympic Truces arising out of any global, local, national or international situations is an item permanently on the agenda of the UN General Assembly in the year prior to an Olympic Games. The UN flag also flies at all Olympic Games competition sites. The examples above do not reflect internationalism *per se*, but they do help to illustrate that a straightforward choice between global and local sport is too simplistic, if not false.

Local or global sport: a false choice

As indicated above and in Chapter 4 the assertion is often made that global sport has eroded local sport. The corollary is that globalisation has reduced the power of national sporting agencies to be self-sufficient. Those who support local and national sporting traditions and forms often romanticise a lost world of traditional, local and national sporting forms. The argument is that global sport, and in particular global market capitalism and the multi-nationals, including sports firms such as Nike and Adidas, and international sporting organisations should be restricted or regulated or even reduced. If that is done, a return to the golden age of local sporting self-sufficiency will be assured. This characterisation may be somewhat unfair, but it represents a view about sport, culture and society advocating the protection of the local, regional and national against the global. A further contemporary facet of this argument is that within an increasingly global sporting community in which diversity of choice is dictated by the marketplace, there is a need to protect and value the diversity of our sporting communities and traditional sporting cultures.

The question that faces students of sport, culture and society is to what extent can global sporting events assist in influencing cosmopolitanism, internationalism and global solidarity? It may be suggested that the development and discussion of global sport is not simply a question of thinking globally and acting locally, but of recognising that the actual transformation of local sport and the role of sport in the making of nations involve issues of internationalism and cosmopolitanism.

SUMMARY

Sport in the future will continue to play an important part in response to the questions who are we and who do we wish to become? The foundations of identities in different parts of the world are crumbling and many segmented sporting communities are changing from traditional local forms of sporting identity to those of a more international nature. The idea that identity history and identity politics are not enough has been one of the common themes throughout this book. Sporting identities, such as allegiances to national sports teams, often invoke a desire to be patriotic, nationalist and different. Sport can also evince a desire to be similar.

While sport at times reproduces the politics of contested national and other identities it should not be at the expense of an acceptance of the possibility of internationality or focus upon common humanity. Living sporting identities are in constant flux, producing an ever-changing international balance of similarities and differences that may contribute to what it is that makes life worth living, and what connects us with the rest of the changing world. If we are to come to terms with the contemporary crisis of sporting identities then we need to transcend the nationalist or global–local simplicities and celebrate difference without demonising it. Increasing similarity of sporting tastes, choices and aspirations can exist without implying homogeneity. As such, the notion of international sport and new forms of internationality must remain part of the vocabulary of global and regional sporting debates not just because it is a more reality-congruent way of explaining the governance of sport today, but because it tempers the all-consuming notion of globalisation and provides grounds for explaining the 'other' worlds of sport outside the trans-national corporation. The notion of other sporting worlds is developed further in Chapter 8.

KEY CONCEPTS

American unilateralism
Civic nationalism
Cosmopolitanism
Denial
Diplomacy
Ethnic nationalism
Glocalisation
Hybridity
Imperialism
Internationalism

International relations
Modernism
Nationalism
National identity
Orientalism
Political mythology
Primordialism
Reconciliation
Statism
Symbolism

KEY READING

Books

Bairner, A. (2001). *Sport, Nationalism and Globalization*. Albany: State University of New York Press.

Allison, L. (2002). 'Sport and Nationalism'. In Coakley, J. and Dunning, E. (eds) *Handbook of Sports Studies*. London: Sage, 344–356.

Cohen, S. (2001). *States of Denial*: *Knowing About Atrocities and Suffering*. Cambridge: Polity Press.

Cronin, M. (1999). *Sport and Nationalism in Ireland*: *Gaelic Games, Soccer and Irish Identity since 1884*. Dublin: Four Courts Press.

Polley, M. (1998). *Moving the Goalposts*: *A History of Sport and Society since 1945*. London: Routledge, 35–62.

127

Journal articles

Anderson, P. (2002). 'Internationalism: A Breviary'. *New Left Review*, 14 (March/April): 5–25.

Beacom, A. (2000). 'Sport in International Relations: The Case for Cross-disciplinary Investigation'. *The Sports Historian*, 20(2): 1–25.

Brennan, T. (2001). 'Rooted Cosmopolitan v International'. *New Left Review*, 7 February, 75–85.

Jarvie, G. (2003a). 'Internationalism and Sport in the Making of Nations'. *Identities: Studies in Global Culture and Power*, 10(4): 537–551.

Kidd, B. and Donnelly, P. (2000). 'Human Rights in Sport'. *International Review for the Sociology of Sport*, 35(2): 131–148.

Further reading

Begg, Z. (2000). 'What the Olympics Really Celebrate', at www.greenleft.org.au/back/2000/417/417p14/htm

Eichberg, H. (2004). *The People of Democracy: Understanding Self-Determination on the Basis of Body and Movement*. Arhus: Klim.

Katwala, S. (2000). 'The Crisis of Confidence in Global Sport', at www.observer.co.uk.

Marqusee, M. (2000) 'Sydney and the Olympics: Corruption and Corporation Versus a Positive Social Role for the Olympics', in Workers Liberty Australia Newsletter, October at archive.workersliberty.org/australia/Newsletter/Oct00/olympics/html.

'World Cup Influences Japanese in Variety of Ways' 5 July 2002 at www.fpcj.jp/e/shiryo/jb/0223.html

Kruger, Arnd and Riordan, James (1996). *The Story of Worker Sport*. Champaign, IL: Human Kinetics.

Ramsamy, S. (2002). 'Olympic Values in Shaping Social Bonds and Nation Building at Schools' at www.gov.za/Conf_Wshops_Events/Values/Sam_ramsamy.htm

REVISION QUESTIONS

1. Explain how sport is associated with nationalism.

2. Discuss and critically evaluate Cronin's typology of nationalisms.

3. Consider whether sport is governed by global or international factors.

4. Outline the ways in which sport can help with internationalism and reconciliation.

5. Critically evaluate the notion that sport is either global or local.

PRACTICAL PROJECTS

1. Observe the national opening ceremonies of the last four Olympic Games and explain how the sporting world has changed over the 16-year period.

2. Examine the nationalist policies of four national parties of your choice that have used sport as a vehicle for promoting nationalism and nationhood. Write a critical report describing and contrasting the four case studies you have chosen.

3. Use the Internet to collect information about the way in which sport has assisted with reconciliation and international diplomacy. Write a short report based upon four case studies that you have developed as a result of your search for information.

4. Interview ten people at any international sporting setting and collect their views on the importance of the role of sport to the cultural and/or political identity of the country.

5. Examine the FIFA website and explain the ways in which this international sporting organisation attemps to contribute to solidarity, internationalism and peace.

WEBSITES

Foreign Policy Centre
www.fpc.org.uk see discussion on Democratising Global Sport

International Olympic Committee
www.olympic.org/

Scholarly sports sites
www.ucalgary.ca/library/ssportsite

'Sport: A Commonwealth Bond to Inspire and Unite'
http://www.youngcommonwealth.org/htm/green/sgeneralcont98.htm

Sport: nationalism/internationalism
wais.stanford.edu/sports_soccer102500.html

World Football Governing Body
www.fifa.com

Workers Liberty Australia
archive.workersliberty.org/australia/Newsletter/Oct00/olympics/html

Chapter 6

Sport, media and television

Does television sport truly reflect sport today or is it just a false image of reality?
WILLIAM WEST/AFP/Getty Images

PREVIEW

Television viewing hours of sport • Key trends in sport and the media • Television sport and imperialism • Top 17 sports-related media companies in 2004 • Sports messages • Sport and the media • Sport and the press • Space devoted to sport in the British press • Sport and television • Sports production • Sports content • Sports audiences • The filtering of sport into media-sport • Visual content • An alternative sports media • Sports, online and the Internet • The promise of the Internet • Online sports gambling • Virtual horses and virtual races • Major league baseball on the Internet • Private and public infrastructure • Sport in the information age • Sports information and the Fourth World.

OBJECTIVES

This chapter will:

■   illustrate the importance of sport to both the old and new media;

■   consider ways in which the media mediates sport;

■   explain the ways in which sport has developed a relationship with the Internet;

■   introduce and critically discuss the notion of an information age;

■   provide illustrative examples and sources for further information.

INTRODUCTION

The media have come to play a fundamental role in the consumption, ownership and delivery of sport. The number of television viewing hours of Davis Cup tennis matches between different tennis nations stood at 839 hours in 1989, 1,219 hours in 1993, 1,460 hours in 1998 and 1,660 hours in 2000. The 2000 UEFA Champions League football final was viewed in more than 200 countries, involved more than 300 hours of coverage world-wide, using 80 broadcasters and more than 100 television channels. Media coverage is central to the hosting of the Olympic Games. In March 2004 the IOC began the bidding process for the European TV rights to cover the 2010 and 2012 Olympic Games. The United States bidding process had already been completed with NBC securing the rights as a result of a $2.2 billion package. Today the means by which the mass media communicate information and messages has moved beyond that of newspapers, magazines, television, radio, cinema, videos and compact discs to include new media platforms of delivery such as digital interactive television, pay-per-view sport on television, broadband and the Internet. The Internet is allowing unprecedented levels of interconnectedness and interactivity. The number of world-wide Internet users has grown rapidly and the range of activities that can be completed online continues to expand. Visitors to the Wimbledon Tennis Championship official website rose from 100,000 in 1995 to 9.04 million in 2000; while Internet hits stood at 2 million in 1995 they had risen to 2,340 million by 2000. While the Internet provides new possibilities for sport some worry that Internet usage in general may undermine human relationships and communities by contributing to rising levels of social isolation and anonymity.

The general perception is that the media industry has become increasingly globalised over the past three decades with the following being some of the key trends: (i) the ownership of the sports media is increasingly concentrated in the hands of the larger media conglomerates; private ownership of the media is threatening if not eclipsing public service provision and ownership; (ii) media companies purveying sports coverage operate across national borders (for example the Europe TV Olympic bidding process makes it possible for a broadcaster to deliver a Turkish service in Germany, which has a large Turkish population, which reflects Turkish Olympic sports interests delivered to a Turkish community because Turkey would otherwise be disenfranchised unless full EU membership is ratified by 2010); and (iii) that the sports media industry is dominated by a small number of multinational corporations. The illusion of inhabiting one world of sports coverage is in part a result of the international scope of sports media and communications. An international world of sports information and an international system of sports production, distribution and consumption has come into being. Writing in the introduction to Coakley's essay on sports and the media, Real comments that ignoring media-sport today would be like ignoring the role of the church in the Middle Ages or ignoring the role of art in the Renaissance; large parts of society are immersed in media-sport and virtually no aspect of life is untouched by it (Coakley, 2003:404).

Given the positioning of the major European and American media companies in the world sports media-complex, many believe that the developing countries have been subject to a new form of media imperialism. Whannel (2002) regards international television sport as a form of Western cultural imperialism. On a bigger scale critics worry that the concentration of media power in the hands of the few companies or powerful individuals, such as Rupert Murdoch or Italy's President Berlusconi, is undermining the workings of democracy.

Resolutions, meetings and manifestos calling for a new world order in international information structures and policies have been a feature of the international media scene since at least the 1970s. The original impulse came from the non-aligned nations, many of which gained independence in the post-war years. These same years witnessed the rapid development of what was then the new communications media and the era was constantly characterised as the Information Age – one in which information would be the key to power and affluence. To many developing countries it was clear that multinational companies that were based in the most powerful nations dominated the flow of information, including sports information. As Table 6.1 indicates, in 2004, all of the top 17 sports-media related companies were based in either Europe or America, with 10 of these 17 companies registered in either New York or London. Political independence had not been matched by independence in the economic and socio-cultural spheres. A number of non-aligned countries saw themselves as victims of cultural colonialism and sport was viewed as a contributor to this process. In 2000 sport contributed to 7 per cent of the broadcasting genres around the world with the others being news and special events 18 per cent; entertainment 30 per cent, fiction 44 per cent and others 1 per cent (*SportsBusiness*, May 2001:55).

The strong symbiotic relationship between sport and the media often suggests that they are one and the same thing but it is crucial to point out that sport and the media is not sport *per se*, but sport that has been mediated for the sports media complex. Many if not all aspects of media-sports are social, economic and political constructions that carry messages, are controlled by human beings, and provide selected representations of reality. Sports through the media carry messages about gender, race, class, nationhood, violence and what is good and what is bad sport. Much of the research into media-sport has concentrated upon an examination of the meanings, messages and representations provided through the process of producing media-sport. Critics of multinational capitalism's control of the sports-media frequently complain of the tendency towards a cultural convergence and homogenisation of, for example, sports television coverage across the globe. This is also a major criticism of the discourse on cultural imperialism that takes sport and capitalism as its target. Is the Fourth World excluded from the new sports information age of the twenty-first century? Indeed it is astonishing that we see so little of sport in Asia or sport in Africa or sport in Latin America on European TV and yet key American sporting dates such as the super-bowl final or the final of the US Open Tennis Championships or US PGA

Table 6.1 *Sports-related media companies*

Company	Exchange	Symbol	MC (millions)	1yr %change	3mnth %change
Sports-related media					
AOL Time Warner	NYSE	AOL	$81,834.04	61	23
British Sky Broadcasting Plc	LSE	BSY	£14,670.58	28	18
Cablevision Systems Corp	NYSE	CVC	$7,568.98	−4	7
Carlton Communications Plc	LSE	CCM	£1,824.35	143	26
Clear Channel Communications Inc	Nasdaq	CCU	$27,799.65	13	11
Comcast Corp	Nasdaq	CMCSK	$332.54	32	4
Eckoh Technologies Plc	LSE	ECK	£49.33	N/A	−20
Fox Entertainment Group Inc	NYSE	FOX	$27,781.04	12	11
Granada Plc	LSE	GAA	£3,744.02	111	15
Interpublic Group of Companies Inc	NYSE	IPG	$6,541.39	30	12
News Corporation Ltd	ASX	NCP	A$64,751.63	9	−2
Seven Network Ltd	ASX	SEV	A$1,483.23	31	−1
SportsLine.com Inc	Nasdaq	SPLN	$68,295.82	60	37
Television Corp Plc	LSE	TCP	£26.45	−42	9
Vivendi Universal	Paris	EAUG	€23,177.04	39	20
Walt Disney Co	NYSE	DIS	$48,641.33	38	7
Wireless Group	LSE	TWG	£102.76	73	38

Source: *SportsBusiness*, No. 89, March 2004:40.

golf championships regularly appear as major productions in the annual sports television coverage of major world sporting events.

The social and cultural implications of the reconfiguring of the new sports media landscape relate to issues of democracy and access and the creation or not of new public spheres of media-sport. Developments such as pay-per-view television sport and subscription are seen to introduce an increased element of consumer responsiveness into programming whilst the more developed forms of sports interactivity associated with video, digitalisation and the Internet allow the sports fan and other consumers to organise their own way through particular sports media experiences. Theoretically the Internet can provide each of us with the ability to create our own spectator sport realities and experiences. The Internet is also seen to offer positive possibilities for groups previously marginalised. Alternatively, critics have pointed to the increasing gap between the so-called information rich and the information poor in a new or evolving media-sport universe. Novick (2004:24) points out that to 'free marketeers and sports fans alike the new world of television sport is a joy' but the same author goes on to point out that not only do many not have access, but that the 'free market was not set up for the benefit of the poor'.

SPORT AND THE MEDIA

Live sport and the sports media are in one sense two different entities in that the experience of live sport for the sports fan in the stadium is a different experience from sitting in front of the computer or standing at the sports bar, even the last two forms of media-sport are different. By its very definition the sports media is sport mediated by the media and as a result students, teachers and researchers need to question the influence of such processes, the stories told, the impact of technology on what we think about sport and the extent to which world-wide exposure to Internet sport exists in reality and the price of its development not just in economic but also in social terms. The coverage of sport and the media in this section is divided into two discussions, the first providing a brief history of the relationship between sport and media while the second is more thematic and gives a more topical and theoretical synopsis of sport and the media.

The development of a match made in heaven?

The influence of the mass media and sport has contributed to a significant body of research in the area of sport, culture and society not just in terms of television but all forms of media communication that have provided sports information and entertainment. The study of media-sport in the conventional sense might be approached by analysing the part played by the different forms of media that have contributed to sports information and sports entertainment. The domination of the sports–media relationship by television and new media styles should obscure the fact that sport has sustained a relationship with the press and radio in some cases for more than a century. Boyle and Haynes (2000:25) note that sport was marginal to the news agenda of the respectable press of the nineteenth century, sport could not compete for space in the restricted copy-space environment and yet as early as 1751 a specific sporting press existed in the form of *The Racing Calendar* which helped the Jockey Club publicise the rules of racing. The growth of popular gambling was a second and more economic rationale for the growth of an early sporting press.

Modern sport and the modern press, argues Mason (1993:3), grew up together. The newspapers provided free publicity, described the main events, published the results and in the early years of the nineteenth century they provided prizes, management, commitment and even judges and referees. Newspapers and the sporting press, Mason (1993:4) goes on, helped in the formation of specific sporting sub-cultures that grew up around particular sports and particular events. The early coverage of sport in the British press might broadly be divided into three categories; the evening and the Saturday sports specials; the national daily papers; and the Sundays and the specialist sporting press. In 1890 Britain could boast of the existence of *Sporting Life*, *The Sporting Chronicle* and *Bell's Life in London*. Racing coverage was the staple diet for all three but they also covered sports such as quoits, football, pedestrianism and golf. By 1900 the Sunday papers were selling up to 2 million copies; the *News of the World* gave 14 per cent of its space to sport, especially racing, cricket, football and athletics. By 1905, 15.75 per cent of an enlarged paper was reserved for sporting coverage. By the 1930s the *People* devoted 10 per cent to sport, a figure that rose to 20 per cent in the 1950s (Mason, 1993:8).

A simple content analysis of the national British daily papers in 2004 illustrated that the national dailies devoted over 200,000 words to football. Horse-racing was the next most popular sport after football in terms of coverage in column inches. The raw data from the coverage of some of the major national newspapers for Monday 6 December 2004 is presented in Table 6.2. It illustrates the amount of space devoted to sport as a percentage of the total number of pages.

Some of the contemporary issues about the relationship between sport, the press and radio are not new. How close should sport be to the press? Is the media's role to celebrate the present or sit in critical judgement? How far should the press be prepared to criticise the role of sport in society or to what extent does the price of investment in sport mean an increased stake in the decision-making process about how sport is organised, presented, when it is played, who is displayed and what sort of commentary or interpretation should be placed around the story or the visual pictures of sport? The close relationship between sports editors and boxing promoters in America during the inter-war years meant that sports journalists expected big payoffs in return for favourable publicity. To what extent have things changed in the twenty-first century? Boyle and Haynes (2000:29) conclude that the press rarely question the politics of sport and only when corruption or scandal arise does the notion of questioning the values associated with sport or the press ever shake the conventional framework or the parameters for thinking about the symbiotic relationship between sport and the media – a relationship that in the contemporary era is dominated by sport, television and new media forms.

Sport first appeared on British screens in June 1937 when the British Broadcasting Corporation (BBC) transmitted pictures of the Wimbledon Tennis Championships to about 2,000 households. Ten years earlier, having secured its charter in 1927, the BBC used its service to carry commentaries and reports on a wide range of sports with the Football

Association Cup Final (the FA), the Cambridge and Oxford University boat race and the Derby horse race all recording popularity with listeners during the 1920s and 1930s. Radio was something of a forerunner to television but until the middle of the 1950s the BBC had a broadcasting monopoly of both radio and television. It should be remembered that audiences for television sport before World War II were insignificant by today's standards with *viewing* figures for both the 1938 and 1939 FA Cup Finals being approximately 12,000 each.

During the 1940s and 1950s particular individual sporting bodies and rights owners offered resistance to the televising of events. The British Boxing Board of Control was particularly vociferous about its resistance to television, noting at the time that in the USA

Table 6.2 *Coverage of sport in the British press*

NATIONAL DAILIES, MONDAY 6 DECEMBER 2004

Newspaper	Total no. of pages	No. of sports pages	% of total devoted to sport	No. of football match reports	% of sports coverage devoted to football	2nd most covered sport	3rd most covered sport
Guardian	126	32	25	17	51	Racing (13%)	Rugby union (11%)
Daily Star	72	27	38	39	70	Racing (12%)	Grey-hounds (7%)
Daily Mail	88	23	26	17	58	Rugby union (12%)	Athletics (10%)
Sun	88	41	47	38	85	Racing (4%)	Cricket (4%)
Daily Mirror	80	36	45	40	85	Racing (6%)	Rugby union (3%)
The Times	120	40	33	44	60	Rugby union (8%)	Cricket (3%)
Daily Express	80	20	25	23	59	Racing (10%)	Rugby union (9%)
Independent	108	22	20	12	60	Rugby union (13%)	Racing (11%)
Daily Telegraph	44	12	27	19	40	Rugby union (20%)	Racing (10%)

television had a detrimental effect on boxing audiences with reductions of as much as 80 per cent in some cases. Yet as a major purveyor of national culture the BBC in the 1950s viewed the coverage of sport as one of its statutory obligations. Whannel (1992:21) points out that the corporation believed it had a function analogous to the press, possessing an obligation to report and broadcast on all relevant areas of social activity such as football which showed record attendance figures of 41 million during the 1948/49 season. By 1964 the BBC had extended its coverage by providing its first football highlights programme *Match of the Day* and during the last 40 years of the twentieth century various television companies have been in competition for the right to broadcast sport.

Initially, the BBC and ITV in Britain acted as a cartel, thus limiting how much would be paid for the right to broadcast live sport. However, during the 1980s and 1990s the advent of Rupert Murdoch and his company British Sky Broadcasting (BSkyB) meant that an initial price war for the battle to show live sport emerged with the advent of satellite television. In 1991 Murdoch reportedly paid £191.5 millon for the rights to show sixty English premier league football matches per season between 1992 and 1997. BSkyB's monopoly of Premier League football coverage was challenged in 2003 when the European Commission raised two key objections (i) to the monopoly coverage of broadcasting rights which limited consumer access to live football coverage and (ii) to the way in which the football league was acting as a cartel in the selling of football coverage. The lack of exclusivity has meant the fall in rights fees and consequently the drop in money available to football clubs who in turn are looking to the new media as possible outlets for football content as a way of balancing the loss of revenue from television fees. In 1998 Manchester United became the first club to brand its own channel with MUTV broadcasting on a national and international basis.

Themes and issues: A brief overview

The study of the media in relation to sport, culture and society has tended to be dominated by television rather than the print media. Within this form of communication, research has distinguished between at least three aspects, namely production, content and audience (Whannel, 2002). The production of media messages through sport involves the study of the structures and finances of the institutions that frame the production of the sports media. Media organisations exist within legal frameworks that in part determine their activity. In Britain, for example, the BBC for the time being remains a public corporation while media super-companies regularly try to influence large sections of the media market and create the situation where a few large companies cover global sports media production. The increasing control of sports production by United States firms has had an inevitable impact upon sports coverage in terms of which sports are covered, when TV viewing times of major sporting events are scheduled and the impact of advertising during the coverage of the sports event. The vision of sport through the Internet, for example, in the hands of a few media conglomerates stands in stark contrast to the idea of a free and unrestricted electronic realm in which individual sports choice is relatively free from corporate messages.

The production of the media message invariably involves hierarchisation, personalisation, narrativising and framing of events for a particular audience. The production of sport for television involves all four of these processes. As such it is crucial that students, teachers and researchers to continually consider how television and other forms of media-sport production are represented and organised for public consumption. What production practices and professional and political ideologies inform the representation of sport on television and what is the cultural, social and economic relationship between a sports event and a mediated sports event? How will a producer frame and edit coverage of a particular sports event, what narratives will be attached to sports stars and celebrities and will the coverage of sport in the twenty-first century be dominated by sports performance or a more critical coverage of the sporting world?

The second part of the communication process involves a consideration of content. In attempting to maintain and maximise television viewing figures for sport what strategies should be used in terms of determining balance between commentary and visual effect? Does the excitement generated in the commentary serve to camouflage the lack of excitement in a sports event or do particular visual shots and styles help to create rather than report a particular sporting event? In the early 1980s Clarke and Critcher (1982) argued that the transformation of sport to televised sport was a form of ideological production in which competitive individualism, local, regional and national identities and male superiority were all presented as natural rather than the specific selection of content. Feminist scholarship has also been concerned with the documentation and presentation of gender differences through sport in the media. The reproduction of the sports media gaze, it may be suggested, continues to associate women with appearance rather than performance and consequently feminist scholars have pointed out that the content of sports media production at times places women athletes as the object of this sports gaze rather than the subject.

A third part of the communication process concerns the audience and in particular audience reception. The consumption of mediated sport by the sports fan often requires locating and understanding sports fandom within its broader social context. Is sports fandom a male ritual? How does the media cater for the female or ethnic sports audiences? To what extent should public service television viewing have a strict regulatory policy on sports violence or should, as in some Scandinavian countries, sports violence be banned from peak viewing hours? Boyle and Haynes (2000:202) point out that even mediated football consumption is experienced differently by sports fans who have their own sense of tradition, community and place. To some extent the challenge for the new sports media is how to capture that sense of belonging to class and community, and in some cases gender, that is important to the sports fan. The pleasures involved in sports viewing are complex while the experience of viewing is often ritualised and communal as opposed to the more individual or solitary experience of viewing television. Whannel (2002:295) is right to assert that it is the distinctiveness of sport and its uncertainty that make it an elusive product to package for an audience. The notion of the global sports fan or audience is in many ways a myth because the level of intensity with which different audiences, in different countries, interact with different sports is far from homogenous.

Despite the advent of the new media and the suggestion that we live in a new information age the media still have an extremely limited range of topics or themes with sport being but one form of production. The media have only a limited capacity to transmit a full and complete picture of sport and therefore they have to continue to pick and choose what will feature and how to present it. Thus at least two main filters operate in translating sport into a sports media product. The first filter of selection is that of general news or audience value and the higher the value the more likelihood that the media will cover it. The second filter consists of the rules of presentation which are picked up from the codes of theatre performance and the discourses of popular culture such as story-telling, personification, conflicts between mythical heroes and heroines, drama, archetypal narratives, verbal duels, actions with symbolic overtones and reporting rituals, all of which transform the logic of sport into the logic of the media. The media stage as pre-structured by these twin filters has a capacity to handle sport in a number of different ways. It can create a celebratory sporting spectacle or it can destroy sporting careers. It can transform the aesthetics of sport beyond that which is real sport.

The logic of the media is closely interwoven with its economic structure. In the case of the privately owned media the products are first and foremost commodities since sales figures, sports ratings in the case of the sports media, are a primary justification for activity. Heightened private sector competition has led to an intensification of the rules that are inherent in the production of the sports media and as with other areas of production the pressure for ratings that afflicts commercial sports coverage is also being felt within public broadcasting systems. There is a sharp tension between media logic and sports logic and between the uncompromising filters inherent in media production time and the time required to cover sport.

As the sphere of sport falls under the influence of the media logic it changes to the extent that sport becomes dependent upon media rules but without completely losing the reality of real sport. The term colonisation is justified in the sense that the almost unconditional surrender of sport, at least in all its visible publicly accessible aspects, involves the colonisation of sport by the media systems. At least three forms of entertainment are provided by the sports media event, pseudo sports events, image projection events and pseudo sports actions. All of these modes of media-sport are used with increasing professionalism and frequency. The mass media-sports stage, particularly that of television, is subject to a complex and highly selective set of conditions for producing or covering sports material which limits access and cannot be easily circumvented. The logic of selection and presentation of sports coverage affects who and what gets on centre stage and for how long. At a very simple level the commentary and the visual presentation of sport is not neutral in that texts and images are organised to tell a particular story.

At least five conventions for analysing the visual content might be mentioned: (i) the transformation of the sports event into a TV, film or media event; (ii) the balance between the impulse to produce realism and/or entertainment is different but the two distinct approaches are tensions that are ever-present; (iii) the ideal pursuit of providing maximum action in a minimum amount of time; (iv) while visual framing through the camera lens produces a presence for some action and people it also produces absences with the tendency, for example, to focus on winners rather than losers, men rather than women, the sport of the Western world as opposed to other worlds and popular rather than minor cultural sports; and (v) time itself is manipulated as a result of the editing process. Five types of visual effects that are available to television sports audiences that are not available to the live audience might include, changing the size of the image, manipulating time to drama-tise action through slow motion or instant replays, collapsing the actual time of an event through edited highlights, a specific focus on isolated action within the event and the provi-sion of comparative statistical information.

Given that significant parts of the world of sport have bought into the logic of the sports media complex it is perhaps difficult to consider what an alternative sports media complex might entail. However it is also relevant to remember that the relationship between sport and the media is not only economic, but also social and cultural, and while it might not be of equal parts it is one of inter-dependency. The politics of an alternative sports media needs to remember that any audience is not passive but active and as potential consumers of both real sport and mediated sport, strategies for change might include those of sports media criticism, internal reform within the sports media industry, the development of a sports media reform league, audience resistance, with all of the aforementioned strategies not being mutually exclusive but to some extent mutually supportive. The object is for viewers, sports fans, sports readers and others to publicly resist the ready-made incorporation into the sports audience commodity. The object of viewers is to point out the silences or absences within world sports coverage. Perhaps fundamental change will only occur when sports audiences change their orientation towards sports coverage to one of seeking real informa-tion about sport and its progressive potential rather than simply seeking to be entertained through the production of a spectacle.

It is not only the major sports that have the attention of the public but also those outside of the limelight. Potential sponsors may consider the notion that, for example, in the USA coverage of skating is one of the best vehicles for reaching women aged 25–54 as a target audience. Bowling as a participatory sport has 50 million Americans a year playing the game, mainly for social reasons (Wilner, 2004:14). The challenge even in the new media age is to strike a balance between real sport and entertainment, between commerce and culture, between economic and social motives and between coverage of the local and the global. An ongoing struggle continues in terms of directing the sports media gaze and resources to the silent parts of the world that receive little coverage or attention and yet have indigenous vibrant sporting heritages. The larger project of truly democratising the media will also demand a transformation of audience expectations and uses of the media. The task of democ-ratising the rules of sports media selection and presentation may be one of the single biggest challenges that a more progressively-orientated form of sports coverage will face in the future, despite the advent of sport on the Internet and the advent of broadband.

SPORT, ONLINE AND THE INTERNET

Many see the Internet as exemplifying an image of the new global order. Users of the Internet live in cyberspace, meaning the space of interaction formed by a global network of computers that compose the Internet. It has been suggested that in cyberspace we are no longer people but messages on one another's screens (Giddens, 2001:470). At least two broad categories of opinion exist. On the one hand are those observers who view the online world as fostering new forms of electronic relationships, often anonymous, but supplementing existing face-to-face interaction. Distance and separation allegedly become more tolerable. Others critically view the time interacting through the Internet as a threat to interaction in the physical world which leads to social exclusion, isolation, less quality time for families, with the lines between work and home life becoming blurred as many employees seek to work from home. An analogy would be that people spend more time watching sport than going to sport and participating in sport, and therefore some of the fabric of social life for some groups is weakened.

The Internet is but one new form of communication that is associated with a new media age, others being digital television and mobile telephony. The impact of the new media has brought into question the extent to which television may continue to be the main platform for viewing sport in the twenty-first century. The promise of the Internet as a platform for communication lies in the possibility of a global, boundary-less audience for sport coupled with a direct threat to future coverage of sport through national broadcasting corporations or indeed the old media. With specific reference to the football industry Boyle and Haynes (2004:166) remind us that the new media age has seen two related media systems develop a new relationship of co-existence – namely the global Internet and the nation-centred television service. They go on to suggest that the digital age is increasingly one driven by commercial values and the wider economic climate in which the market remains the central driver of the digital economy. The new media have become increasingly concentrated and commercialised and they continue to encroach upon the functioning of what Habermas (1989) refers to as the public sphere – the places or arenas where the public congregate to debate or discuss issues of general concern and where opinions are formed, places where individuals in principle, could come together as equals in a forum for public debate and sociability. The question remains to what extent is real sport as a facet of the public sphere influenced or eroded by the development of new media forms?

The Internet has proved to be an effective medium for expanding an online sports gambling industry. A report from investment bank Merrill Lynch predicts that the online gambling industry will turn over £123 billion ($177 billion) by 2015 with online sports betting worth £100 billion ($144 billion). By 2001 the growth of the market had reached such a stage that more than 1,800 online sports betting and casino operations operated world-wide, all looking for part of the estimated $4.6 billion revenue generated through the e-gambling industry. It is estimated that interactive television betting will account for almost half of the income generated. Sports betting channels are a potential source of high revenue for sports rights holders but a danger exists if any sport becomes too dependent on this sole source of revenue. A deal between Go Racing and the British Horse Racing Board in 2001 means that the future of UK horse-racing in this area now hangs in the balance because of the inability to resell the intellectual property rights associated with the sport. At the same time there is little to prevent bookmakers who are unwilling to pay the licence fee for those rights from creating their own organic betting properties. Given the existing marketing, advertising and different legal restrictions governing world online international gambling services it seems inevitable that an affiliation with the broadcaster or sports rights holder will prove key to future customer acquisition. This will become a compelling reason for bookmakers to seek mergers with established media brands whether these are established sports clubs who own their own sports rights or TV broadcasters.

News-corporation owned BSkyB has already demonstrated the possibilities of such a merger strategy by paying £250 million in 2000 to forge an alliance with Sports Internet Group. Wap Integrators, a technology company with a UK betting licence recently signed a revenue share deal with Leeds United Football Club to enable Leeds fans to access unique mobile content from the official Leeds site on a Leeds United branded phone, with the means to place a bet on their team. The I-Race is a horse-racing product launched at the end of 2003 that allows betting to take place on virtual horses running in virtual races. The line between the betting industry and the entertainment industry in this case provides for a chain of live virtual races every ten minutes. The consumer is offered three options, one to watch the race passively, two to press the interactive red button, log on and play for fun with a fictional pot of money and three, the full version that provides the option to register, deposit real money and place real wagers on the races (Britcher, 2004a).

Major League Baseball (MLB) views the advent of the Internet as the key to providing compelling global baseball content to fans as a result of web-based technology. It provides an increased opportunity for fans outside of the USA and Japan to tune into live games. The MLB.com figures for 2004 suggest that more than 65 million people visited the site during the 26 days of the Division Series, League Championship Series and the World Series – more than double the 29 million who visited in 2002. It is estimated that 750 million visitors will log on to MLB.com during 2005, with the link between Internet and mobile phone technology viewed as a future growth area that will provide a quicker return on the investment in improved technology. The logic of capitalism is self-evident in the words of the Chief Executive of MLB who points out that

> we will try to take anyone who does not have an economic relationship with us and turn it into one. We estimate about 95 percent of our traffic does not spend money and our goal is not to shift the percentage but shift the numbers so that so instead of 750 million this year we want to do 1.5 billion in two years. Undeniably, across all sectors, the acceptance and the comfort the consumer now has with spending online has helped enormously with paying for better sports content.
>
> (Britcher, 2004b:27)

For many of the major US sports the Holy Grail of global expansion continues to be the attraction of the new media-sports platforms but few have been able to achieve it. The Far East is becoming a hub of interest for both NBA and MLB web offerings.

Despite the surge in uptake of broadband Internet usage for sport in 2004 the development across cities and nations remains uneven. The mix between private and public supported infrastructures plus the new media mix available to sports audiences is diverse. More than 12 million people used the BBC interactive button service during the 2004 Athens Olympic Games but the level of infrastructure support for new media public service broadcasting in Britain remains lower than, for example, Stockholm in Sweden. Different cities cater for the development of a new media infrastructure in different ways. The Stockholm model reflects the more general Swedish belief in the public provision of fundamental infrastructure. There is a very clear vision in Stockholm that the building of a knowledge economy, the attraction of inward investment and the provision of better public services will all be facilitated by a fibre-based communication infrastructure that wishes to turn Stockholm and Sweden into a wireless hot spot. In Milan the driver was not the knowledge economy or the desire to put e-learning into schools or do health consultations in people's living rooms, but the demand for video telephony and entertainment provided mainly through private provision by e-Bisom. In places such as Warsaw in Poland the provision of electronic cabling and connections was based upon a private/public partnership mix.

Sport in the new information age is keen to provide further sporting experiences for the sports fan and connect cities around the world through new media-sports opportunities. Ellen MacArthur's 2005 race around the world may be cited as an example of the way high-speed Internet connection has revolutionised offshore racing in at least two ways. The sea in parts of the world might be viewed as one of the most remote places on earth, but modern technology facilitated scenes of this offshore round the world boat race that were beamed into people's homes all over the world. From the audiences' point of view through TV quality footage and webcams, e-mail and photos, the world was able to communicate with the sailor, and experience the swells of the world's oceans from the comfort of home. For the sailor, tactical and security points of view were informed by up-to-date, high quality weather images and thus routes could be planned more accurately and safely. In short, the performance of media projects, sailing speed and sailor safety took a big step forward due to high speed connections.

SPORT IN THE INFORMATION AGE

In one of the most sustained attempts to map out and evaluate the impact of the information age, Castells (1998) argues that the emergence of such an age is marked by the rise of networks and the network economy, a new economy that depends on the connections made possible by a global communications network. Telecommunications and computers form the new basis of production. The effects of this production impinge upon personal identity and everyday life to such an extent that Castells (1998:354) asserts that we no longer control the world we have created. As Castells (1998:56) puts it, 'humankind's nightmare of seeing machines take control of the world seems on the edge of becoming a reality – not in the form of robots that eliminate jobs or government computers that police our lives but as a world-wide electronically based system of financial transactions'. Yet, the argument goes on, the same power of information technology can serve as a means of local empowerment and community renewal. He thinks it is possible and important to regain more effective control of the global market-place and that the route to this salvation is through international organisations and countries that have a common interest in regulating and re-distributing global capital. The collective efforts of international organisations must, it is asserted (1998:379) have a common interest in regulating international capitalism.

The information age is certainly characterised by the international use of technology but it is also part of a society in which networking appears to be an important organising form of social life in certain parts of the world. It may be more appropriate to say that we live in a networked society rather than an information or knowledge society. Networks theoretically know no boundaries, they exist on an international, if not global scale. Networked organisations, including sports organisations, out-compete all other forms of organisations, particularly the rigid, vertical command and control sports bureaucracies. Sports organisations are part of the world of mergers and conglomerates but the successful ones are those based upon flexible networked partnerships that can react and change quickly in response to given information. Since a whole range of social practices both global and local communicate through the media space, this space is an important public space of our time, through which sports organisations, activists, fans, chief executives and volunteers can plan, organise and share experiences and information about the sporting landscape that exists or could exist in the twenty-first century. The flexibility, elasticity and interactivity of the media-sports text provides the sports media space with an infinite capacity to exchange information, to integrate, to exclude but also influence the boundaries of sport in society and how we think about sport and how we the audience are represented and represent sport through the media-sports complex. The networked sports media complex continues to be a fundamental structuring force in the worlds of sport today. Networks therefore matter because they are an increasingly underlying structure of not just society and culture but sport, culture and society.

Sports information and the Fourth World

Castells did not comment on the role of sport, culture and society in the new information age or the role of sport as a vehicle for global financial transactions although he did suggest that the power of technology and information might provide the promise of and opportunity to experience spirituality through leisure. Yet the idea of the creation of an information age Fourth World in an unequal world order applies as much to sport, culture and society as it does to other spheres of life. The promise of new technology is intended to provide great benefits in the information age. The promise of unprecedented productivity, taking care of needs and the promise of affluence for all is reminiscent of the sorts of debate that heralded the promise of a post-industrial leisure society of the 1970s. The history of such promises tells us that social polarisation may also have increased substantially throughout the world during the last two decades – a theme we shall return to in the last chapter of this book. There are various dimensions of inequality, such as inequality between countries, inequality between peoples, and inequality between different social groups, but no matter how social inequality is defined a substantial gap between rich and poor is maintained. Societies change, explanations change, governments and policies change but somehow the needs and conditions of those at the bottom of society are systematically denied. Consequently it is vital not to forget that extremism and polarisation are as much a part of sport in the new information age as they were in the era of the old media-sport relationship. In truth, in the transformation from the twentieth century to the twenty-first century, we have also witnessed an extraordinary intensification of social exclusion both between countries and within countries, between and within regions and between and within metropolitan areas. This may include a Fourth World made up of much of Africa, rural Asia and rural Latin America but also territories and segments that can be found in many parts of the planet.

There are clear exceptions to such a broad generalisations. Appadurai (1995) refers to the decolonisation of sport in India as a process of indigenisation, changing the way sport is managed, patronised and publicised away from its colonial past as a tool of socialisation that spread Victorian upper-middle-class values. He claims the media have played a crucial role in the indigenisation of cricket in India, with radio and television broadcasting in the vernacular languages, and the arrival of television deepening national passion for the game along with the star status of players. Sports fans in the information age may be more distant geographically in the future. The impact of the information age may mean that clusters of virtual fans will be built around hubs of virtual sports activity. Writers such as Smith and Westerbeek (2004:199) claim that sports organisations must be a virtual place of social experience, a hub of activity and tribal identity. They go on to suggest that communities are about tribal values and that the virtual online providers of new community sport must provide the opportunities for these values to be exposed and encouraged.

Yet despite such an aspiration, access to the Internet, for example, is highly uneven. In 1998, 88 per cent of the world's Internet users lived in the developed world. North America accounted for more than 50 per cent of all users, although it only contained at the time 5 per cent of the total world population. The United States is the country with the highest levels of computer ownership and online access. More than 100 million Americans use the Internet while Germany and Britain both boast more than 10 million users each. In Japan, a country where the Internet craze arrived late, more than 14 per cent of the population, some 18 million people, used the Internet in 1999. Variations in technology and affluence around the world preclude a truly global market for sports technology and sports access through the new and old media forms.

The Fourth World does not often relate to the First World except under extreme circumstances. Castells (1998) argues that in the emergence of an information age and a networked society access to education, information, science and technology becomes critical for countries, firms and peoples in the network society. It might be suggested that access to these resources but also sport in the new media whether it be access to online sporting gambling opportunities or sport on channel TV stations also becomes increasingly unevenly distributed despite the fact that new technology in the First World is often viewed as the saviour of isolated places and spaces. True there is more and more sports technology in the world but at the same time there is also a growing unevenness in people's capacity to properly access and use technology. So there are growing links between globalisation, information, networking, rising inequality and social exclusion if not isolation. The links are asymmetrical and power-laden; the globalised, informationalised First World countries exploit the devalued, disconnected Fourth World countries. The new media may provide new media forms of sports experience but it is questionable whether this is new informationalism or just old style capitalism. The new information age may provide new possibilities for the sports fan or consumer but it is also an age that is profoundly unjust.

One final point is that while the power, the promise and the reach of new media-sport is undeniable there are forces within countries that resist and question the onslaught of new media forms primarily produced from and for Western audiences. The rise of international electronic information empires that operate across state borders is often perceived as a threat to cultural and national identity in, for example, many Islamic countries. Reactions have ranged from muted criticism to outright banning of Western satellites. Programmes that offend traditionalism are sometimes prone to being censored. The BBC and consequently

146

BBC sports coverage is no longer supported in Saudi Arabia. At least three Islamic states have banned satellite access to Western television – seeing it as a form of cultural pollution supportive of the promotion of Western consumer values.

SUMMARY

From the sports daily, to television to film and the Internet we live in a world in which the media and networks have a profound influence upon sport and the way it is shaped, represented, presented, consumed and challenged. Sporting heroes and heroines are created and destroyed by the influence of the sports media. The way in which particular sporting events are covered influences what people think about particular sporting action or events. The logic of the media as a form of capitalism continues to permeate sport economically, socially and culturally to such an extent that it remains one of the most powerful influences upon sport and social life in different parts of the world. The First World and the Fourth World are provided for and experience mediated sports opportunities differently. The media promises sport much but the sports media relationship is one that is both facilitating and problematic. This chapter has set out to explain the impact of both the old and new media upon sport and the way in which the relationship between sport, media and television in particular influences the way we think about sport, culture and society.

This chapter has linked developments of the sports-media complex to that of the possibilities and limits brought about by the advent of an information age and increasingly networked sports world. Understanding and mapping out the changing nature of power in a networked society is one of the immediate tasks facing any student, teacher or researcher interested in explaining and influencing the relationship between sport and the media. Power no longer simply resides in individual sports institutions but through what Castells (1998) refers to as the switchers through which networks regulate terms of entry and privilege or exclude interests or positions. As such it is vital not to lose sight of the fact that just as sport in the new information age affords new opportunities for the control, ownership and structuring of sport so too does it afford new opportunities for networked campaigning, providing an increased voice from different parts of the world. The role of the sporting celebrity in promoting and facilitating messages and resources of hope for and by different parts of the world may have a part to play in a new reconstructed civil society. The Internet certainly provides the promise of not just increased gambling opportunities but also the development of numerous social forums and discussion groups about sporting issues and problems. The media itself faces significant challenges but some of the immediate challenges for sport and the media include those of transparency, knowledge, innovation, regulation, accountability, ownership, citizenship, access and the use of power.

KEY CONCEPTS

Audience	Monopoly
Colonisation	Narrative

147

Democracy	Network society
First World	New media
Fourth World	Old media
Framing	Online gambling
Information age	Ownership and control
Internet	Sports-media complex
Knowledge economy	Sports spectacle
Mass media	Visual techniques/effects

KEY READING

Books

Boyle, R. and Haynes, R. (2004). *Football in the New Media Age*. London: Routledge.

Boyle, R. and Haynes, R. (2000). *Power Play*: *Sport, the Media and Popular Culture*. Essex: Longman.

Castells, M. (1998). *The Information Age*: *Economy, Society and Culture*, Vol. 111. Oxford: Blackwell Publishers.

Moller, J. and Andersen, J. (1998). *Society's Watchdog – Or Showbiz' Pet? Inspiration for a Better Sports Journalism*. Vingsted: Danish Gymnastics and Sports Association.

Whannel, G. (1992). *Fields of Vision*: *Television Sport and Cultural Transformation*. London: Routledge.

Journal articles

Billings, A. and Tambosi, F. (2004). 'Portraying the United States vs. Portraying a Champion: US Network Bias in the 2002 World Cup'. *International Review for the Sociology of Sport*, 39(2): 157–167.

Chisari, F. (2004). 'Shouting Housewives!: The 1966 World Cup and British Television'. *Sport in History*, 24(1): 94–109.

Knoppers, A. and Elling, A. (2004). 'We do not engage in Promotional Journalism: Discursive Strategies Used by Sports Journalists to Describe the Selection Process'. *International Review for the Sociology of Sport*, 39(1): 57–75.

McCarthy, H., Miller, P. and Skidmore, P. (2004) 'Network Logic'. Special Edition, *Demos* 20: 7–219.

Mason, T. (1993). 'All the Winners and the Half Times'. *The Sports Historian*, 13 (May): 3–11.

Further reading

Britcher, C. (2004a). 'Virtual Horses for Virtual Courses'. *Sport Business International*, 88 (February): 28–30.

Britcher, C. (2004b). 'MLB Upwardly Mobile': *Sport Business International*, 86 (January): 25–28.

Davies, H. (2005). 'The Fan'. *New Statesman*. 14 February: 59–60.

Meyer, T. (2002). 'Towards a New Political Regime'. *Fabian Review*, Winter: 16–19.

New Statesman (2004). 'After Switch Over: What Next for Public Service Television?' 15 November: i–xv.

Novick, J. (2004). 'World of Sport'. *Herald,* 15 October: 24.

Whannel, G. (2002). 'Sport and the Media'. In Coakley, J. and Dunning, E. (eds) *Handbook of Sports Studies.* London: Sage, 291–308.

REVISION QUESTIONS

1. Explain the relationship between sport and the press in both the pre- and post-1900s.

2. Describe and critically comment upon the ways in which the media filters sport to produce media-sport. You may want to consider how visual and auditory techniques are used to frame a sports story.

3. Does the advent of the new media enhance or reduce the possibility of open debate about sport?

4. What are the advantages and disadvantages of the Internet and how has it developed sports content?

5. Describe what the information age is and its implications for sport. You may want to consider how sport has become part of a networked society and what the implication of this is for different people in different parts of the world.

PRACTICAL PROJECTS

1. Using newspaper reports of one of the major international tennis championships, compare and contrast the ways in which women players were portrayed in selected years from each of the following: 1965, 1985, 1995, 2005.

2. Videotape or access a recording of the opening ceremony of a major international sports spectacle such as the Olympic Games, the rugby or football World Cup, the Asian or African Games. Using a method of content analysis, describe and explain the themes that have been selected to create a spectacle.

3. Arrange for two similar groups to watch a recording of a major sports event at the same time in two separate rooms. Group A watches the programme with the sound as normal and Group B watches the programme with the sound turned off. Ask the two groups to write up an independent report of the action and what they saw. Compare and contrast the two reports and use the evidence to write 2,000 words on how the commentary influences the views of the audience.

4. In a sport of your choice use the Internet as a source of information to produce a diagram that traces the network of media interests, marketing, advertising and sponsorship interests in your chosen sport. What does the diagram tell you about media interests and influences upon your chosen sport.

5. Choose ten separate days, perhaps Mondays, as a basis for carrying out a content analysis of the sports that are covered in your daily newspapers. In what ways are certain sports prioritised and others marginalised? Use the empirical evidence gathered to write 2,000 words on the uneven coverage of sport in a nation of your choice.

WEBSITES

Latest information on TV sponsorship deals with football
    www.footballjob.com/newsletter.htm

Museum Television Archives
    www.museum.tv/archives/etv/index/html

Official site of UK Sports Journalists Association
    www.sportsjournalist.co.uk/home.html

TV Sports Rights information
    www.media.guardian.co.uk/sport/0,14629,1224331,00.html

Chapter 7

Sport, law and governance

Should violence, corruption, and/or the taking of drugs in sport be dealt with within the international sporting community or outside the jurisdiction of sport itself? Getty Images

PREVIEW

The Bosman ruling • Democratic sport • Sport as a symbol of meritocracy • Sport and the law • What is the law? • Should sport be regulated? Models of professional sport • Pure market model • Defective market model • Consumer welfare model • Natural monopoly model • Socio-cultural model • Is sport above or below the law? • Court of Arbitration for Sport • International Council of Arbitration for Sport • The myth of sporting autonomy • Is global sport sustainable? Sporting governance in question • International sporting organisations • The deep challenge of global sporting democracy • Children in sport • Zimbabwe and the 2003 Cricket World Cup • Ten challenges for global sport.

OBJECTIVES

This chapter will:

■ look at the relationship between sport and the law;

■ examine the role of sport's independent Court of Arbitration;

■ evaluate the allegation that corruption is an identifiable feature of sport;

■ answer the question what is democracy in relation to sport;

■ consider broader questions of sporting governance and the need for regulation.

INTRODUCTION

This chapter provides a critical comment upon law and governance within international sport. The issues of sports governance and sports law have been freely used in contemporary discussions about the sporting world. The theme of governance has a prominent place in discussions about global sport and whether or not it is possible or even desirable to develop a more progressive approach towards the reform of sporting structures, regulations, practices and laws. We know, as Eitzen (2003) has recently reminded us, that the duality of sport means that it unites and divides, is fair and foul, healthy and destructive, expressive and controlled, myth and reality, and both public and private in terms of team ownership. Living with an increasingly international entity that is sport today involves a mutual responsibility for all that comes with twenty-first-century sport. Arguably the enduring moral problem of global sport is the vast gap between and within different sporting worlds. One thing that so far has escaped global sport has been the collective ability to act globally.

At the same time as there has been a resurgence of interest in issues relating to sports governance so too there has been a specialist development in sport and the law. The implicit notion that sport is above the law or has separate mechanisms for dealing with sporting problems and issues has produced not only a burgeoning body of case study material, but also a body of literature which has begun to add to our knowledge about sport, law and society; the governance of sport; commercial regulation of sport; regulation of the sports workplace and comparative directives such as European Community law. For example, the Bosman case and ruling has had a significant impact upon the organisation of professional sports in the European Union. It resulted from a private right strategy of regulation under the EC Treaty (see Box 7.1).

At the heart of this chapter then are some straightforward questions: If global sport exists should a system of global sporting governance exist? Is sport above or subject to the law and, if so, what law, national, international and/or a specific sports judiciary?

The term governance as it has been used in sport has tended to be closely related to organisational theory, management and the governance of sport *per se* (Henry and

BOX 7.1 SUMMARY OF THE BOSMAN RULING

The judgment passed in the Bosman case

The Bosman case – the first one of its kind in the legal history of football – made it necessary to reconsider the transfer of players and the restrictions foreign athletes face in EU countries.

The Bosman judgment refers to transfer fees on the one hand and to nationality clauses in sport on the other. The principles in this decision apply to all sports federations and not just to football. As far as transfer fees are concerned, the decision refers to the professional and semi-professional athletes of a sports federation, athletes who are being sponsored and athletes who generate an income from advertising.

Limitation: the decision refers to solely to situations after a contract has run out.

The facts of the case

Mr Jean-Marc Bosman agreed to switch to the French club US Dunkerque shortly after his contract with the Belgian club RC Liege had run out, but was unable to do so because the two clubs failed to reach agreement on the transfer fee. The Belgian Football Federation then refused to grant the required transfer approval to the French club. Because of the delay caused, US Dunkerque withdrew the contract with Bosman. He brought an action for compensation before the Belgian courts for loss of income, requesting that the case be referred to the European Court of Justice.

Summary of the legal basis

The judgment passed by the European Court of Justice addressed two totally different problems, although the legal basis is the same in both cases: Article 48 of the Treaty Establishing the European Community.

No transfer fees are paid if a player moves from one Member State to another after their contracts have expired (special regulations apply to nationals of third countries and to countries that have concluded an association agreement).

As far as the nationality clause is concerned, it is generally invalid to restrict the number of EU nationals in a club/team.

The consequences of the judgment passed in the Bosman case

The consequences the Bosman judgment has had for sport are far-reaching. The example of professional footballers in England shows that the quota of foreigners in English football leagues has risen sharply. The sums paid by English clubs for international transfers has also risen since the Bosman case, as more and more football clubs are looking further afield to foreign countries in their efforts to find new players. This revival in the transfer market has led, among other things, to football clubs attempting to tie their players to their clubs by having them sign long-term contracts.

Thedoraki, 2002). The concept of governance is intrinsically bound up with that of globalisation. It remains imprecise as a term but might loosely be referred to as consisting of self-organising inter-organisational networks. It is essential to stipulate that governance is much more than government. This chapter begins at another level: that is that any progressive notion of global sport necessitates paying attention to a system of governance at both national and international levels. It is tempting to suggest that a system of global sporting governance is already evolving, based on various relationships between the sporting organisations of nation-states; supranational feder-ations such as UEFA; international sporting institutions, such as the International Athletics Association or the International Olympic Association or FIFA, multinational corporations, such as those which finance major sporting events; non-governmental sporting organisations, quasi-autonomous government quangos and others. The most difficult, perhaps impossible, task is to ground these institutions in forms of democratic accountability.

One final point needs to be made by way of introduction and that is, as Maguire and colleagues (2002:76) have alluded to, contemporary ideas relating to the demo-cratic nature of sport are both mixed and evolving. Many sports organisations at an ideological level think of themselves as being democratic despite operating exclusive sport for *some* policies. In this sense democracy remains one of the key ideologies for sport, governance and society in the early twenty-first century. It could be suggested that contemporary liberal democracy as practised throughout Western sport is lacking in a number of fundamental ways. Notably, it is lacking in its inability to control the way in which global sports companies such as Nike exploit world labour markets, or the way in which certain sports fail to recognise individual differences of, for example, age, ethnicity, gender and even class. Sport in the West tends to be undemocratic in at least one sense, in that large sections of the population remain disenfranchised when it comes to voting for positions of power and influence within sporting clubs and organ-isations. For example, the football authorities in Great Britain and even governments view sceptically the setting up of supporter-owned football trusts or an increased community stake in the sports Public Limited Company model of governance. There have been few opportunities in Britain or the United States of America to develop the sort of ownership pattern practised within Barcelona Football Club or to develop a system of free associations that characterise the very essence of democratic sport in certain Scandinavian countries, such as Sweden or Denmark.

The issue of democracy has been one that has been readily debated within sport, culture and society. There are various national sports organisations that claim to be more democratic by the fact that they operate at arm's length from government and yet the notion and future of democracy is rarely in itself questioned. Today, the conno-tations of the word are so favourable that organisations and forms of state control that have no claim to being referred to as being democratic still use the term. As a descrip-tive term, democracy is closely associated with majority rule and yet there is no real consensus as to what majority rule really means. For example, do issues relating to majority rule or the democratic nature of sport include: (i) who are to count as the people and what is a 'majority of them'? (ii) why, if at all, should majorities rule minorities? (iii) which system of democracy should be preferred, a direct or representative system of democracy? Or (iv) what are the dangers of majority rule for minority rights?

Sport has long been viewed as a graphic symbol of meritocracy despite the fact that sociologists and others have been questioning the substantive basis for such a claim for more than half a century. Writing almost 30 years ago, the Canadian sociologist and cultural critic Richard Gruneau questioned the extent to which taken for granted claims about sport's meritocratic basis could be substantiated (Gruneau, 1976). Thus, the popular image of sport as an unquestioned democracy of ability and practice, it might be suggested, is somewhat exaggerated, if not mythical. Generally speaking, the term democratisation tends to imply a widening degree of opportunity or a diminishing degree of separatism in varying forms of sports involvement. The term has also been used to describe the process whereby employees or clients have more control over sporting decisions and sporting bodies. The expansion of opportunities in sport over the last quarter of the twentieth century might be used at one level to argue that sport, at least in the West, has become more open. Moffat (2000:33) suggests that the reality in Britain, at least, is that the extremes of privilege and poverty remain sharply drawn.

Nowhere is this better illustrated than in the case of access to private golf clubs in Britain. The secretary of the Honourable Company of Edinburgh Golfers resides at Muirfield, host to the 2000 Open Golf Championship and one of the most difficult clubs to gain membership of. Despite the popular currency of the image that Scotland is somehow a more egalitarian society than a class-cleaved England, in golfing terms the assertion could be challenged. Hiding behind the façade of the Honourable Company is an important segment of Scottish society, mainly the privileged, who have particular attitudes towards open participation and club membership. The secretary of the Club, remarking upon the exclusivity of the membership, tells the story 'of a distinguished group of visitors who approached the secretary to ask if they might be permitted to play a round as guests; the official looked over the near deserted 18 holes to see three foursomes playing and replied that the course was busy' (Jarvie and Burnett, 2000:45). The Muirfield Golf Club and, more particularly, the Honourable Company of Golfers continue to practise a closed-door policy in terms of membership. The secretive and mysterious nature of the inner workings of the Scottish establishment are hard to track and yet it is evidenced on the public face of a place such as Muirfield, which shows scant regard for the simple goals of equality of regard and equality of sporting opportunity, which are values allegedly held dear by the Scottish electorate.

The above is one of many possible examples that could be given from the world of sport in relation to sporting governance and whether private sports clubs are above

155

certain aspects of law or subject to certain aspects of the law. Should golf clubs that are in receipt of public monies be allowed to operate exclusive policies? Just as progressive globalisation needs a system of democratic governance at both a national and international level, so too does sport. Sport, law and governance are therefore linked to other notions, such as democracy, ownership and power. The danger is that in a world of global sporting interdependencies, with no corresponding global or international sporting polity and few tools of global sporting justice, the rich of the sporting world are free to pursue their own interests, while paying little attention to the rest.

SPORT AND LAW

The contemporary relationship between sport and the law can be partially gleaned from the topics covered by the magazine *Sportsbusiness* over the two-year period, 2001–2003, listed in Box 7.2. The last few years have witnessed growth in litigation involving sports matters. The threat of players' strikes in Britain and America has illustrated the growing influence of players' unions in disputes over earnings and players' rights. The part played by sport and Internet gambling has raised questions over whether specific laws concerning data protection stop at the state or national border or are, in fact, subject to international laws. The celebrity status of sportsmen and women enables them to cash in on their fame through endorsements and merchandising, yet many sport stars have instigated legal action in order to own their own name for the purposes of using it as a domain name on the Internet. The employment contracts of football managers and players have often appeared to be 'unique' in character when compared to those of executives in other sectors of employment. The difference between a violent tackle in some sports and that which amounts to an act of violence is sometimes hard to define and varies within and between sporting codes – for example ice-hockey, water-polo, wrestling, boxing, rugby union and rugby league.

Terrorist attacks in different parts of the world have meant that contracts to host mega-sporting events now have to cover the possibility of event cancellation, and so insurance companies consider the extent to which insurance coverage operates in such circumstances. The matches of the 34th Ryder Cup golf tournament between Europe and the United States of America were postponed following the events of 11 September 2001 in New York. It has been suggested by many that in terms of regulating the use of drugs in sport there cannot be one system of doping regulation that applies equally to all sports because the nature of sporting activity varies. As the genetic code is unravelled, the issue for sport will be the extent to which genetic manipulation is used to enhance prowess and performance. It seems clear from this very superficial glance at some legal issues that sport is likely to provide plenty of employment for lawyers in the present and the future.

It might be fruitful at this point to answer the question – what is the law? For practical purposes the law, for example, in Scotland, is according to Stewart (2000:1), what the Queen in Parliament says it is, although it must be acknowledged that customary law is the body of decisions of the courts of law. The basic form of law making or legislation is the Act of Parliament that may produce specific sports legislation. It is interesting to note that certain Scandinavian countries, such as Finland, have the equivalent of a Sports Act that

BOX 7.2 SPORT AND THE LAW

The following topics formed the basis of sport and the law articles in *Sportsbusiness* between 2000 and 2003.

- The impact of anti-trust law upon US professional sport
- The ways in which sport is affected by the Human Rights Act of 1998
- The regulatory framework surrounding the selling of TV sports rights
- The impact of insolvency upon sports rights transactions
- The harmonisation of sports doping rules and regulations
- The movement of professional players internationally
- The licensing laws relating to online sports gambling
- The separation of image rights from playing contracts
- The impact of collective bargaining as a mechanism to resolve player disputes
- The effects of competition law upon the setting up of sports leagues

ensures a statutory minimal level of provision for sport in Finland (see Chapter 20 for further comment upon sports legislation). The law for many sports administrators remains the rulebooks of their governing bodies and such internal laws often rightly or wrongly provide a mini legal system for those subscribing to it.

At another level, European law is viewed as superior to both Scots law and the laws of the United Kingdom parliament. European Community law is the body of law created by the founding Treaties of the European Community, the Treaty of Paris (1951) and the Treaties of Rome (1957). The European Commission has applied European Community law to the sports sector and has probably had the biggest impact since, as Middleton (2000:86) asserts, 18 out of the 23 Directorates in the European Commission have impacted directly or indirectly upon European sport. A number of legal cases have been brought before the European Commission, covering such issues as broadcasting rights, the freedom of movement of players across Europe, the employment of foreign players, nationality clauses and quotas and community competition rules covering concerns such as the regulation and monitoring of ticket sales by agencies. The European Convention on Human Rights has recently been incorporated into UK law by virtue of the Human Rights Act of 1998, which means that sport is now subject to this legislation.

How can and should sport be regulated?

In a relatively recent examination of the regulation of professional team sports it was concluded that considerable confusion exists over exactly what stance should be taken towards professional team sports and competition law (Sloane, 2002:64). Should professional sports team leagues be treated as natural monopolies, cartels or joint ventures? What is the appropriate definition of the market? How should sports law cater for global sport in which at least two completely different models of professional sport operate – namely, the US model and the European model? The special features of professional team sports mean that treating them like other industries would seem an unlikely way to maximise consumer welfare, while a *carte blanche* exemption from competition law would leave open the route to monopoly abuse of power. If a US-style player draft system were to operate in Europe, it would likely fall foul of the freedom of mobility of labour legislation guaranteed by the Treaty of Rome. Salary cap provision would at present be difficult to implement within the context of European sport, although it has been operationalised within both rugby league and rugby union (Sloane, 2002:64). In terms of promoting a redistribution of wealth in professional sport a more equal revenue sharing policy would add to both the uncertainty of outcome of matches, but would also help to control labour costs. Yet it is likely that such a scheme would be resisted by the G14 group of European football clubs because it would reduce their ability to compete in the cash-rich European club competitions.

It is necessary to comment briefly upon US and European models of professional sport before turning to the question of regulation (Barros et al., 2002). The dominant model of sport in America is a professional sport model that celebrates profit maximisation and commercial objectives. Teams are organised into leagues that operate as sealed cartels. Player contracts are organised on a collective bargaining basis between players' unions and team owners. Teams enter into collective agreements that restrict the scope of economic competition. The three central general internal laws of the US model are (i) a sporting contest is uninteresting unless its outcome is uncertain; (ii) in team sports a contest is made more uncertain by establishing an equal distribution of economic resources among the teams and, (iii) an equal distribution of economic resources is best achieved either by limiting the role of economic power in hiring players or equalising economic power through income redistribution (Barros et al., 2002:3).

Generally, the European model of professional sport is dominated by football and by and large European soccer or football leagues engage in far fewer restrictive practices, while revenue-sharing is almost unknown, as is joint merchandising. No attempts have been made to equalise the redistribution of player talent that exists in the sense that there is no draft system, no team roster limits other than those determined by income, and no salary caps. Players' trading for cash is the norm within the European model. Larger differences in income exist between the top and bottom clubs than in the North American model, while a system of relegation and promotion is a distinctive feature of European professional football. It has been suggested that European team owners and managers are motivated by goals other than profit maximisation, although the trend of placing more and more football teams on the stock exchange would seem to contradict such a hypothesis. The major difference is that the leagues in Europe are not effectively sealed and therefore European competition exists. Finally, sporting competition within the European model is more complex and is generally inconsistent with balance-enhancing measures. Thus, the ability of players to move to the highest bidder is greater than in the US where collective bargaining and strong anti-trust laws exist as the norm. Player unions are fragmented across Europe, while a limit of one per country means that employers have almost been able to bypass the unions. Even if a single European Union for players became established, there is still no equivalent of antitrust exemption from the collective bargaining agreements that dominate the US professional sport model. In Europe, the European competition authorities give teams almost no incentives to write long-term contracts and the market for players is much more individualistic and liberal.

The issue of regulation cannot be seen in isolation from different market models of sport and, as Foster (2000) acknowledges, at least five different market models for sport might be suggested in relation to the legal regulation of sport. These might be summarised as shown in Table 7.1. The *pure market model* tends to view sport purely in terms of business. Money comes before sporting success and unregulated economic competition is a means to this end (Foster, 2000). The dominant ideology is that competition is the best regulator. Within this model, governing bodies of sport have broad functions, but they mainly provide a loose regulatory framework in which profit maximisation occurs. The public interest is generally ignored and sports fans have limited powers in terms of resisting exploitation. There is a network of contracts between economic units with individualistic ideologies. Within this model the normal form of regulation is the market, with the normal means being the contract as the legally binding authority. In stark contrast to this view the *defective market model* exposes the limitations of the pure market model, the main one being that within the free market model the weakest economic units are usually eliminated. Sporting competition tends to need equal economic strength and monopolies of success are bad for sporting business. Unpredictable values are a key facet or value of this model. Governing bodies of sport and the competitions that they license are often the monopoly controllers of sport. They can use this power to restore sporting balance by reallocating resources. The main legal method of regulation in a defective market is competition policy. Thus if the market fails, competition law can be used to counter-balance monopolies or abuse of power.

Table 7.1 *Sports regulation and the market*

Model	Values	Form of regulation	Governing bodies
Pure market	Profit/private interest (shareholders)	Contract/intellectual property	Maximise commercial opportunities
Defective market	Equal sporting competition (teams and players)	Competition law	Reallocate
Consumer welfare	Fans and viewers	Protective legislation	Widen democracy and accountability
Natural monopoly	Public interest	Independent regulator	Overcome rival organisations
Socio-cultural (traditional)	Private club	Immunity/voluntarism	Preserve sporting values
Socio-cultural (modern)	Fairness, internal constitutionism and rule of law	Supervised self-government	Preserve sporting values with due process

Source: This table has been adapted from Foster's (2000) insightful article on sports regulation.

Note: There has been increasing concern about the ineffectiveness of sports administrators in the modern world of international sport. It has been suggested that a solution may lie in increased regulation. The alternative view is that legal intervention disrupts good administration of sport.

159

The *consumer welfare model* provides a critique of the pure market model (Foster, 2000). Different interests may be linked through contracts, but there can be very unequal economic power between respective contracting parties. The fan or consumer has weak market power against the sports club. Players have historically had weak or limited economic power against their employers. Players and clubs at times need protection against federations that can take decisions over them with major economic consequences. The legal form of regulation is protective legislation to protect the weaker party, or to allow a greater protection of the wider public interest. The fourth model alluded to by Foster (2000) is the *natural monopoly model*. One of the arguments to support statutory-backed regulation is that the regulated industry is a natural monopoly and therefore market competition is absent. A natural monopoly is characterised by a single seller, a unique product and barriers to ease entry to the market. Sport, it is claimed, has these characteristics and therefore needs a regulatory structure that assumes it is a private monopoly likely to ignore the interests of the public. Competition law is an inappropriate mechanism of regulation because the market cannot be freed if there is a natural monopoly; an alternative regulatory strategy is therefore needed.

During the summer of 2003, the European, if not the world, financial football market was shaken as a result of the Russian businessman Roman Abramovich securing a majority stake in the ownership of London-based Chelsea Football Club (*Herald*, 15 July 2003:30). Overnight, the Club literally became the wealthiest club in the world as a result of the £140 million initial investment. The alleged link between sport, governance and corruption has a further case study as a result of this development. The source of Abramovich's wealth has been linked to a number of oil companies within the former Soviet Union. The oil magnate's wealth flourished under the patronage of the former Russian President, Boris Yeltsin. Abramovich assumed control of the Sibnyeft oil company, among others, and was appointed Governor of the Chukotka region of northern Russia which he declared bankrupt, leaving many public sector workers unpaid. It is this money that has allegedly become the new money behind Chelsea Football Club. From virtually sliding into liquidation in the late 1990s, Chelsea has assumed the mantle of the richest club in the world, seemingly prepared to outbid anyone for many of the world's available football stars. Within two weeks of assuming control, £13 million had been released for two players, £100 million was reported to have been made available to sign the French internationals Patrick Vieira and Thierry Henry from Arsenal Football Club, while a bidding war was started with Manchester United through a further £20 million being put aside for the services of the Brazilian Ronaldinho. At a time when this self-regulating football business had been hit by deflation, the notion of such wealth being made available to one club may yet have alarming consequences for other clubs struggling to stay afloat within the financial footballing climate since 2003. A handful of clubs in each country has contested the major honours each year, but if the alleged people's game still harbours any slim ambition of being a responsible meritocracy rather than a plutocracy then the impact of such a development may be problematic, and it is unlikely to be benign. As mentioned above, the football market is unlikely to be freed if a natural unregulated monopoly of domestic or European football emerges.

Finally, there is the *socio-cultural model* that promotes the notion that sporting values are dominant and profit is ancillary. The autonomy of sport is valued, with the historical governance of sport taking a number of forms, such as the private club with voluntary administrators, or supervised self-government through, for example, undemocratically elected British sports quangos. This allows governing bodies to be autonomous and regulate the sport without too much external intervention. This requires internal constitutionalism, due process and good governance. In short, the socio-cultural model outlined by Foster (2000) argues for autonomous self-government with constitutional safeguards to protect sporting values. The problem with such a model is that it is often difficult to define exactly what values are being protected and promoted since global sport has been increasingly linked with corruption, vested interests and a distinct lack of democracy, if not at the level of participation, certainly at the levels of power, governance and privilege.

Is sport above or below the law?

Given the above, it is tempting to suggest that Western sport in terms of both the US and European models of professional sport enjoys a certain degree of autonomy and internal policing. Perhaps the most vivid international example of this is the Court of Arbitration for Sport (CAS), originally created by the International Olympic Committee in 1983. The funding of CAS is now shared between the different groups that constitute the International Council of Arbitration for Sport (ICAS). These are the IOC, the Association of National Olympic Committees (ANOC), the Association of Summer Olympics International Sports Federations (ASOIF) and the Association of Winter Olympics International Sports Federations (AWOIF). CAS also receives funding from UEFA and other international sports federations. The business of CAS has been dominated by Western sports problems with few if any cases coming from Asia or Africa. CAS has two divisions: the ordinary division that deals with commercial disputes and the appeals division that deals with the facts and the law in relation to sporting matters, such as doping, voting mechanisms and cruelty to horses. At the 1996 Olympic Games in Atlanta, CAS developed an ad hoc division (AHD) that facilitated a 24-hour resolution to a dispute (Morris and Spink, 2000:67).

A decision or award rendered under CAS is final and binding on the parties concerned and can be enforced through the rules of Private International Law. Horse rider Elmar Gundel, whose horse had tested positive for a banned substance, challenged a CAS award in February 1992 and consequently horse and rider were banned from international competition and from the International Equestrian Federation. The grounds for the appeal were that CAS was funded by the IOC and was therefore not an independent tribunal. On 15 March, the Swiss Federal Tribunal rendered the judgment safe and ruled that CAS, according to Swiss Law, as an arbitral body can enforce awards. The Swiss Federal Tribunal also noted that where the IOC was part of any dispute then CAS was not a sufficiently independent body. This led to the establishment of the International Council for Arbitration in Sport (ICAS).

Morris and Spink (2000:75) suggest that there are at least four issues or challenges in relation to the power of CAS: (i) the enduring perception that CAS is owned or influenced by the federations that fund it and that it is second best but cheaper than the law courts; (ii) major sporting organisations such as FIFA and IAAF have still to subscribe or submit to the jurisdiction of the tribunal; (iii) with regard to the institutional structures that make up CAS, the interests of the athletes are not necessarily given a fair hearing in terms of athlete

161

representation on the boards, and (iv) significant room exists for closer collaboration between CAS and other sporting arbitration schemes within different national and international frameworks, sporting or otherwise. It may be that such a development would curtail or at least limit the number of cases reaching CAS to those of a particularly contentious or novel dispute.

The development of CAS is but one contemporary example of the juridification of sport that simply adds to the paradox about sporting autonomy. Sport would appear to have a diminishing degree of freedom as it becomes more commercialised and, in a simple sense as sport becomes more commercial, the need for law and forms of regulation increase. The myth of sporting autonomy has historically been used as an argument against legal intervention in sport. It has appeared in various forms and disguises: (i) that sport and the law are separate realms and that the relationships within the world of sport operate differently from the legal norms of fixed rules, rights and duties; (ii) that a degree of relative autonomy from the law should exist because sport may also be viewed as a leisure pursuit and that sport is therefore for pleasure not profit; (iii) that in this area of activity sport is a private activity, pre-eminently within civil society and outside the confines of the state; and (iv) that sport should create its own internal law which negates the need for external regulation and intervention.

The establishment of CAS may be viewed as an attempt by sport to forestall further intervention from the external law, and yet nationally and internationally the trend would appear to be one of increasing rates of juridification in sport. CAS merely helps to facilitate this process in terms of sport itself.

There seems to be a further paradox at the centre of the debate about sport, law and governance that merely adds to the question as to whether global sport is myth or reality. Global sport is not a panacea for a world of sport that is borderless, prosperous, even, democratic and accountable. Globalisation cannot be understood as a single driving force. We do not have a simple form of global sporting governance which one might expect if the notion of global sport was a possibility or reality. The regulation of sport usually portrays or reflects the triumph of market-led values. Even the most cursory examination of sport and the law would suggest that while sport is regulated both internally and externally, perhaps the more important challenge facing world sport is whether the notion of global sport can be sustained given (i) that there have been clear indications that it is in crisis in terms of various forms of corruption, and (ii) that sporting governance occurs at a multitude of different levels and is rarely co-ordinated or committed to international justice or social reform, and (iii) that while transatlantic forms of sport in both Europe and America may continue to modernise, it is hard for non-Western forms of sport modernise, become powerful players in the international sports forums while at the same time holding on to values which are perhaps not governed by Western laws, beliefs, values or traditions. If non-Western countries continue to follow their own road towards economic and social modernisation through sport, then it is only to be expected that future disputes between, for example, Western and Asian values over issues such as human rights, gender and religion in sport will persist. It is only reasonable to expect resistance and expressions of disappointment from the countries of the Southern hemisphere that perceive international or global sport to be following a Northern sporting agenda.

162

Somehow the translation of the moral impulse into universal globally binding standards of honesty, fairness, justice and responsibility has gone astray in global sport. What the hidden artificial hands of the morally sensitive controllers of international sport do bears little resemblance to any sustained social commitment to the power of sport when tough choices have to be made between profit and more socially committed forms of international governance in sport. Arguably the true function of our incipient global sporting institutions is the perpetuation and reinforcement of a polarising trend that merely reproduces and extends the gap between rich and poor sporting nations. In a world of global dependencies with no corresponding global polity and few tools of global justice, the rich of the sporting world are free to pursue their own interests while paying little attention to the rest. To cite one contemporary example, plans to increase the number of non-European players in European football during 2003 have been met with divergent responses from different countries within Europe which see the emergence of cheaper footballers coming into the European game from Africa, Asia and the Americas as a threat to local pools of football talent, current salary levels, perhaps leading to the downgrading of emphasis placed on youth development by many local clubs. The average monthly wage of Brazilian footballers in Brazil is equivalent to £99. The prospect of the influx of younger, cheaper talent from Africa, Asia and South America has raised objections internally within British football, while externally the Department of Employment is considering revising the criteria for work permits allowing non-European footballers entry into the British football leagues. It would seem that the global game is only global until it threatens national interests and then an international and external legal approach to the free trade of footballers becomes problematic. The potential for a more social and less economic approach to football is undeniable but it is not pre-ordained. Trade, including trade in footballers, is a vital tool to lift people out of poverty, but it will only be effective if the rules of the game are radically changed.

SPORTING GOVERNANCE IN QUESTION

The accelerated spread of global sporting relations has had a number of important implications for patterns of governance in world sport. Any notion of progressive globalisation through sport requires a system of democratic governance at both national and international levels and yet the increasing level of corporate sporting involvement has brought into question the relevance of corporate governance to sport today. The challenges for sport are immense and have led some commentators to argue that global sport is in a state of crisis and that international sporting agencies and trans-national corporations are more famous for corruption and corporatism rather than for a positive social role (Katwala, 2001, 2000a, 2000b). Katwala (2000a) insists that the global era presents fundamental challenges for sporting governance, but also the opportunity for sport to become more of a force for internationalism. The path of transformation from the traditional amateur association to a socially responsible global sports industry is far from complete. Katwala (2000a) goes on to suggest a series of guidelines for modernising sporting governance, emphasising stakeholder participation, greater transparency, and co-operation between governments, the European Union and the governing bodies of sport.

The problems of world sports organisations are similar to other organisations with visions that are primarily concerned with money, material wealth and unregulated profit. In free-market sport accountability often means the boardroom's responsibility to shareholders and the company's responsibility to the customer. Yet until relatively recently shareholders had rarely challenged or effected principled changes in corporate policies, and sporting consumers had been often captives of an oligopoly. Mechanisms for access and participation in market-based governance of sport are often determined by wealth and income. One needs capital to become a shareholder. One needs power to influence and participate in FIFA or UEFA decisions. Very few people receive invitations to attend meetings of bodies like Nike or other major sponsors of international sport and almost all of the participants come from a narrow and highly privileged circle. Shareholder owned companies or organisations are arguably far more accountable than bodies such as the IOC, FIFA and UEFA.

Some of the most important sociological questions concerning global sport relate to issues of accountability. How can sporting organisations, such as the IOC, that seek to speak for the whole world and especially the youth of the world, represent peace and harmony between nations, justify the ways in which they conduct their business? Lenskyj's (2000) study of the internal workings of the Olympic industry examines the rationale, the processes and outcomes of the Olympic bidding process, the efforts made by cities and countries to win IOC votes, and the responses of communities and citizens who are left with the after-math of an Olympic Games when the show has left town and country. The study portrays a culture of corruption and collusion in a body consistently purporting to speak for universal human values. It is often forgotten that anti-Olympic protest groups in cities such as Nagano, Toronto, Sydney, Berlin and Atlanta have often portrayed a different interpretation of the work of the IOC.

The role of international sporting organisations within world sport may be viewed from at least three different positions. Table 7.2 outlines three divergent views about international sporting institutions and the extent to which they can or cannot affect change. Institutionalists regard the world as an arena of inter-state co-operation. Institutionalists argue that international sporting organisations will play an increasingly important and positive role in the governance of global sport and will ensure that the benefits of global sport are spread widely throughout the world. However, several pre-conditions are necessary for this to occur. These conditions include: the existence of mutual interests that make joint gains from co-operation between sporting nations; rational choices and a long-term relationship between a relatively small number of sporting organisations, such as FIFA and UEFA; and reciprocity according to agreed standards of behaviour. Under these conditions institutionalists argue that national sporting organisations will agree to be bound by the rules, norms and decisions of the international sporting organisation or institution. Institutionalists are optimistic about the possibility of progressive steps towards increased rates of international governance within world sport based upon co-operation, mutuality and negotiation.

Realists disagree with institutionalists and reject the notion that international sporting organisations are the primary solution to universal sporting problems and issues. They argue that the institutionalist model does not account for the unwillingness of powerful sporting organisations to sacrifice power relative to other sporting organisations. The position adopted is that the governance of international sporting bodies will always reflect the

Table 7.2 A debate about sporting institutions

	Institutionalist (or 'neo-liberal institutionalist')	Realist (or 'neo-realist')	Constructivist
Under what conditions will states create international sporting institutions?	For mutual gains (rationally calculated by states).	Only where relative position vis-à-vis other states is not adversely affected.	Sporting institutions arise as a reflection of the identities and interests of states and groups which are themselves forged through interaction.
What impact do sporting institutions have on international relations?	Expands the possible gains to be made from co-operation between sporting organisations.	Facilitate the co-ordination of policies and actions but only insofar as this does not alter the balance of power among states.	Reinforce particular patterns of interaction, and reflect new ones.
The implications for globalisation and aspects of global sport.	Sporting institutions can manage globalisation to ensure a transition to a more 'liberal' sporting world.	Institutions will 'manage' globalisation in the interests of dominant and powerful states.	Changing patterns of interaction and discourse will reflect in sports' responses to global sport.

interests of the dominant governing bodies of sport. When these powerful sporting bodies wish to co-ordinate international sports policy with others they will create appropriate institutions, which will be effective only for as long as they do not diminish the power of the dominant sporting nations vis-à-vis other states. For realists, co-operation and institutions are heavily constrained by underlying calculations about power and vested interests. From a realist perspective it follows that anti-global sports campaigners are right to argue that international sporting organisations do not work for the interests of poor sporting nations.

Finally, constructivists pay more attention to how institutions, states and other forces construct their preferences, thus emphasising the part that identities, dominant beliefs and contested values have to play in the process of negotiation. They argue that the interests, normative ideas and beliefs of, for example, the organisation, sporting body or national association, influence the identities of sporting institutions. They reject the realist position on the grounds that it is wrong to assume that sporting bodies can only be mere reflections of power politics whether it is the government of the day or institutions at a more micro level. In other words, sporting identities and interests are more fluid and turbulent than the realists realise. A constructivist approach to global sporting institutions would highlight the actors and processes involved in globalisation that are neglected within realist or institutionalist approaches. For example, the protesters who are active within anti-global sporting campaigns would be part of the construction of an ongoing dialogue about sporting

165

institutions that affects state, national and international facets of sport in several ways. The globalisation of sport is thus viewed not just as a process affecting and managed by states, but rather the governance of global sport and indeed globalisation are shaped by a mixture of interests, beliefs and values about what sport is and what sport should be and can be. The existing sporting institutions doubtless reflect many of the interests of powerful states; however, these interests are the products of how sporting organisations and companies and people interact and are therefore always subject to reinterpretation and change.

Finally a brief comment upon one of the many practical strategies in the move towards a more equitable approach to international sporting governance is the need to closely regulate trans-national corporations (TNCs). There are at least two factors that explain how trans-national sporting corporations have managed to escape genuine regulation of their behaviour. These are (i) *legal limitations* in terms of regulating corporate accountability and, in particular, the fact that international law is still largely focused upon state-to-state legal frameworks, and (ii) *power imbalances between powerful TNCs and comparatively weaker states* that result from governments globally courting the economic wealth of TNCs, and collectively the TNCs lobbying governments for preferential terms and conditions with regard to bidding for mega-events or contracts to build capital-intensive sports facilities. Yet on an international scale this leads to a potential imbalance of investment in certain countries that does little to help sustain a sporting infrastructure in the poorer parts of the world. Trans-national corporations have invaluable resources that, if harnessed correctly, could bring many sporting benefits to all of the countries in which they operate.

THE DEEP CHALLENGE OF GLOBAL SPORTING DEMOCRACY

Perhaps the emergence of a more socially committed approach to global sport has to start from actively acknowledging the huge differences of opportunities, wealth, democracy, sporting tastes and models of professional sport that divide the world. The deep challenge facing global sport is to outline the mechanisms by which sport can be seen to contribute to social and economic welfare on an international scale. At the international level the more powerful sporting nations would seem to have the power to enforce many of the rules and decisions affecting world sport and yet there are perhaps unprecedented opportunities at the beginning of the twenty-first century in that sport is free from the Cold War politics of the twentieth century. Perhaps the most obvious and disturbing concern is the extent to which the core institutions of sport are trusted and sensitive to ways of addressing the interests of the majority in the non-Western world. The chief causes of inequality in global sport remain twofold: the transformation of global sport by financial capital and the displacement of democratic political power in sport by unaccountable market power.

Sport historically has always been viewed as a pathway to social mobility or an avenue out of poverty for talented sportspeople. The marketability of sportswear has contributed to the situation where children as young as 13 are now effectively sold to the highest bidder. In May 2003, Freddy Adu, a 13-year-old American schoolboy, signed a $1 million deal with Nike. Why should Nike spend that amount of money on a schoolboy who plays soccer in a country in which soccer is a minority sport? The answer lies in Nike's desire to gain an even bigger share of the £10 billion global market in sports shoes. Freddy Adu had only been playing soccer for five years when he arrived from Ghana with his mother Emilia, who had won a Green Card lottery to live in the USA. He is tipped to become a future world soccer star and to that end, in Nike's view, they cannot afford not to sign him up, or let rival companies such as Reebok or Adidas secure Adu's signature, in case he turns out to be a superstar. In an increasingly youth obsessed sports world, Freddy Adu is not particularly well paid in comparison to other child sport stars. Only days before Freddy signed his contract Nike signed a contract for $90 million with 18-year-old Lebron James, a high school basketball player who had never appeared in a professional match. The merest hint that a young sportsperson may become a star is enough to spark a bidding war between multi-national companies (*Observer*, 1 June 2003:21).

The example is insightful for a number of reasons, not least of which is that it is one of many millions of examples of sporting talent moving from relatively poor countries to rich countries with little if any compensation or redistribution of monies from the rich part of the world to the poorer parts. The example of Freddy Adu is merely illustrative, but in this one example there are issues of child labour, the power of unregulated financial capital, the seduction of living the American dream and the migration of football talent to the football cities of the sporting world without any recognition in financial terms of the part played by the periphery or the Ghanaian Football Association. The consequences of such a view of sporting progress for global sport are simply that the rich sporting nations stay rich and the poor but talented sporting nations are mined for sporting excellence without any recourse to the redistribution of wealth. The production of wealth derived from global sport could be geared towards human aims. Western liberalism needs to strive for honesty about the implications of lifestyle preferences, not just for its own societies, but also for other members of the global or international community.

Zimbabwe and the 2003 Cricket World Cup

Examples at this point might be drawn from situations arising out of the involvement of Zimbabwe in both the 2003 Cricket World Cup and the subsequent cricket tour of England in May 2003. England's progress to the last four of the 2003 Cricket World Cup was ultimately ended when the International Cricket Council ruled that England should forfeit points for not playing their first match in Harare against Zimbabwe. The English captain, Nasser Hussain, pleaded with both the UK Labour government, the international cricket authorities and the English Cricket Board (ECB) to rule on the issue of whether England should play Zimbabwe, given that Zimbabwe was ruled by an illegitimate regime whose head of state, Robert Mugabe, was patron of the Zimbabwe Cricket Union. More than half the country's 13 million people were suffering from starvation, and yet the players would have been put up in the best hotels, the cricket team would have been shuttled around in special cars using petrol from a special reserve supply (given that the average motorist at the time had to queue for two days for petrol). The Libyan government had stopped oil deliveries to Zimbabwe because the government had not made its payments. Human rights groups, such as the Amani Trust, which used to monitor and publicise human rights violations in Zimbabwe, folded because of state-sanctioned harassment and intimidation. Both the US and UK governments at the time refused to use any sanctions or enforce international human rights laws. In the end, the English cricketers themselves made a decision not to play, and their progress in the Cricket World Cup was ultimately affected by this decision, a decision that the sporting authorities and British government felt they could not make.

The Cricket World Cup in South Africa was followed by a test series against Zimbabwe that took place in May 2003 (Tatchell, 2003:16). Only players and officials uncritical of President Robert Mugabe were eligible for selection. Earlier in the year two team members, Andy Flower and Henry Olonga, wore black armbands to mourn the death of democracy in Zimbabwe. They failed to make the team to travel to England and were subject to death threats. Other critics of Zimbabwe had also been removed, including the coach Kevin Curran, the trainer Malcolm Jarvis, the former captain Alistair Campbell and the all-rounder Guy Whittal. Gagging orders were written into the contracts of the players who made the trip. Most of the officials who make up the Zimbabwe Cricket Union are also members of Robert Mugabe's political party Zanu-PF. The President's authority was required before the tour could go ahead. The ECB not only agreed to play two test matches against Zimbabwe in 2003, but also signed a commercial contract with the Zimbabwe Cricket Union to play a return series in Harare in 2004 with the promise of financial compensation made for England's withdrawal from its World Cup fixture in 2003.

The challenge to sporting democracy in Zimbabwe is, to paraphrase C. L. R. James, beyond a boundary. The paradox of the 2003 Cricket World Cup involving Zimbabwe in a tournament hosted by South Africa was that during the apartheid era the African National Congress urged the international community to exert economic and cultural pressure on the governments of P. W. Botha and F. W. De Klerk. The demise of the apartheid regime was aided by international sporting sanctions invoked against South Africa under the slogan 'You cannot have normal sport in an abnormal society'. Perhaps President Thabo Mbeki's South African government should have supported the struggle for democracy in Zimbabwe by exercising authority upon the cricket authorities and others to impose similar sanctions against Zimbabwe during the 2003 Cricket World Cup. Furthermore, if the English cricket authorities were interested in supporting not only sporting democracy, but also a more social sporting agenda, it would have to answer at least two questions. Why is England playing cricket against a Zimbabwe squad whose members have had to pass a political loyalty test? Are there times when the values associated with sport should not be purely economic ones? The example above has been used simply as a short case study in relation to the challenge facing global sporting democracy. Zimbabwe versus England cricket relations would have benefited from a degree of international support that, rather than upholding the amateur adage of 'Keep politics out of sport', might have been better served by acknowledging that here sport was all about politics. That was certainly how President Mugabe saw it, and the opposition who failed to turn up.

Challenges for global sport

At first glance the notion of global sport would seem to provide possibilities and opportunities for regulating sporting governance and finance to ensure a more equitable re-distribution of sporting wealth. Any clear template for how sport in the world should be governed has not accompanied the transition towards a more global notion of sport. The governance of global sport is multi-layered, complex, national, local and international, but in all of these, states, sporting agencies, the sports market, civil societies and governing bodies of sport have all suffered from shortfalls with respect to popular participation and access, consultation and debate, inclusion and representation, transparency and account-ability. Forms of global sporting governance through market-driven channels would seem to imply deep inequalities and the rule of efficiency overriding democracy. Suprastate sports organisations would appear to suffer from severe democratic deficiencies. At the moment it is unclear whether and how democracy can be adequately realised in a more global sporting world. Above all, Western sport embedded within national and increasingly European sporting governance, as well as the continuing dominance of American sporting capital, seems incapable of showing the historical imagination needed to grasp the radical challenges facing world sport. If global sport means recognising common situations, sharing a single world of sport, then the gaps between West and non-West, rich and poor, demo-cratic and democratising, or even England and Zimbabwe, will need a different kind of consciousness.

Global sport cannot make a significant difference to globalisation, but it can make a contribution, as Part 4 of this book attempts to explain. However, in the meantime, it is sufficient to suggest here that the enduring deep challenge for forms of global sporting democracy might involve some or all of the ideas outlined in Box 7.3.

BOX 7.3 CHALLENGES FOR GLOBAL SPORT

- Global sport must advocate a distinctive social agenda for sport
- Social democracy must become a distinctive feature of global sporting reform
- Global sporting institutions must be active in publicising human rights violations in sport and, linked to this, the places and cities chosen to host mega-sporting events must undergo a human rights audit as part of the selection process
- Global sport should institutionalise a global framework for sporting mobility and migration
- Sport needs to monitor child labour violations in sport and production of sport merchandising
- Sport may be seen as a popular vehicle for debating and promoting global politics
- Models of sporting governance need further to embrace local communities as stake-holders in the mutual governance of sport
- Given popular support for sport, then international sporting and/or other sanctions are options that may be used to help further sporting democracy

SUMMARY

Just as globalisation is very uneven in its effects so too is global sport. The notion of a level playing field is of course a sporting metaphor but even the most superficial glimpse at sport in the twenty-first century would suggest that international finances, global markets and forms of governance are far from progressive in terms of their impact upon sport itself. The concentrations of wealth and power in world sport have the capacity to sustain and develop new inequalities within sports, between sports and among sporting nations. According to the rich list compiled by Deloitte-Touche all of the top 20 wealthy clubs are based in Europe. During 1999 global expenditure on sport sponsorship trebled but its distribution was unbalanced with 37.8 per cent of the sum being spent in North America; 36.4 per cent being spent in Europe and 20.8 per cent in Europe with South America way behind and Africa virtually out of the reckoning. (Callaghan and Mullin, 2000:43). As mentioned at the beginning of this chapter the enduring moral problem of global sport remains that of the vast gap between different sporting worlds, organisations and peoples. It is tempting to suggest that while international sporting politics during the Cold War era was the political divide between East and West the crucial divide in the twenty-first century is that of the North versus South divide. A sporting paradox exists in the sense that world sport, while striving to be more inclusive, is so expensive that only certain parts of the world can afford to compete for hosting mega-events such as the various sporting World Cups or the Olympics.

This chapter has reviewed different potential forms of regulation and governance which may or may not impact upon sport. It is perhaps inevitable that as sport becomes more and more enmeshed with the world of finance then the law and lawyers in different parts of the world are sure to benefit first and foremost. Yet if the management of global or international sport is going to progress then it needs to adopt certain forms of structural reform and common rules which have the potential to lead not so much to recognition of sporting power and wealth but to the re-distribution and regulation of sporting power and wealth. At very least sporting organisations have to be increasingly accountable, transparent, be aggressive about representing key community or local stakeholders in the governance of sports organisations. This chapter has suggested some of the ways in which this might progress while the next chapter illustrates just how unjust and different the nature of sport is in other communities. It is crucial that students and researchers read these two chapters together, and not in isolation from one another.

KEY CONCEPTS

Accountability	Institutionalist
Arbitration	Juridification
Cartel	Justice
Constructivist	Meritocracy
Consumer welfare model	Natural monopoly model
Defective market model	North/South divide

Democracy	Pure market model
Governance	Realist
Global sport	Regulation
Human rights	Socio-cultural model

KEY READING

Books

Barros, C., Ibrahimo, M. and Szymanski, S. (2002). *Transatlantic Sport*: *The Comparative Economics of North American and European Sport*. Northampton: Edward Elgar.

Baylis, J. and Smith, S. (2001). *The Globalization of World Politics*: *An Introduction to International Relations*. Oxford: Oxford University Press.

Chaker, A. N. (2004). *Good Governance in Sport*. Strasbourg: Council of Europe.

Gardiner, S., James, M., O'Leary J., Welch, R., Blackshaw, I., Boyes, S. and Caiger, A. (eds) (2001). *Sports Law*. London: Cavendish Publishing.

Katwala, S. (2000a). *Democratising Global Sport*. London: The Foreign Policy Centre.

Stewart, W. (ed.) (2000). *Sport and the Law*: *The Scots Perspective*. Edinburgh: T&T Clark.

Parrish, R. (2003). *Sports Law and Policy in the European Union*. Manchester: Manchester University Press.

Journal articles

Brackenridge, C. (2004). 'Women and Children First? Child Abuse and Child Protection in Sport'. *Sport in Society*, 7(3), 322–337.

Chung, H. (2003). 'Sport Star Vs Rock Star in Globalizing Popular Culture: Similarities, Difference and Paradox in Discussion of Celebrities'. *International Review for the Sociology of Sport*, 38(1): 99–108.

Donnelly, P. and Petherick, L. (2004). 'Workers Playtime? Child Labour at the Extremes of the Sporting Spectrum'. *Sport in Society*, 7(3): 301–321.

Kidd, B. and Donnelly, P. (2000). 'Human Rights in Sport'. *International Review for the Sociology of Sport*, 35(2): 131–148.

Further reading

Armstrong, G. (2004). 'The Lords of Misrule: Football and the Rights of the Child in Liberia, West Africa'. *Sport in Society*, 7(3): 473–502.

Foster, K. (2000). 'How can sport be regulated?' In Greenfield, S. and Osborn, G. (eds) *Law and Sport in Contemporary Society*. London: Frank Cass, 268–285.

Lenskyj, H. (2000). *Inside the Olympic Industry*: *Power, Politics and Activism*. New York. New York University Press.

Katwala, S. (2000b). 'The Crisis of Confidence in Global Sport' at www.observer.co.uk/ Print0,3858,4421203,00.html

Morrow, S. (2003). *The People's Game*? *Football, Finance and Society*. Basingstoke. Palgrave.

Tatchell, P. (2003). 'Ambassadors of Tyranny: Zimbabwe Cricket Tour'. *New Statesman*, 19 May: 16.

REVISION QUESTIONS

1. Describe and compare at least four different models of sports regulation.

2. Argue for and against the idea that sport is above the law.

3. Describe the work of the work of the International Council for Arbitration in sport.

4. Critically evaluate the debate about different approaches to thinking about international sporting institutions.

5. What are the key challenges facing global sport in terms of democracy, governance and the law?

PRACTICAL PROJECTS

1. Investigate the websites of any two sports arbitration agencies and list the cases that have been brought before the court/agency in the last three years.

2. Prepare a portfolio including at least ten legal case studies involving sport.

3. Review the constitution of ten local sports clubs in your area and determine whether the club is governed in a democratic way. You may want to consider asking how elections to the committees are made or how decisions by the committee are operationalised.

4. Examine the constitution of one professional sports club in your area and identify what the club pledges to do for the players, shareholders and the community. Design a community stakeholder model of governance for the club.

5. Identify legal companies who specialise in sports law and see if you can arrange an interview with a lawyer to discuss how the law is influencing sport today.

WEBSITES

European Football Players Union
www.fifpronet.com

Governance in sport website
www.governance-in-sport.com/Koss.pdf

Soccer Review
www.supporters-direct.org/docs/SoccerReview.pdf

 172

Sportbusiness
www.sportbusiness.com

World Football Governing Body
www.fifa.com/

Chapter 8

'Other' sporting communities

Do the Olympic Games need to further recognise other sporting traditions? PANAPRESS/
Getty Images

PREVIEW

Justice and charity in sport • Western sport as dogma • Northern and southern hemispheres
• Other sporting communities • Trobriand Island cricket • Wushu • Globalisation and 'other'
state forms • Post-colonialism – what is it? • Sumo wrestling • Post-colonialism and sport
• How, what and when was post-colonial sport? • Sport in Australia • Sport in India
• Football in Africa • Not yet global or post-colonial sport • Sport, power and the South
• All-African Games • The Asian Games • The Pan-American Games • Social dimensions
of global sport.

OBJECTIVES

This chapter will:

■ explain what is meant by 'other' sporting communities;

■ explore the notion of post-colonialism and post-colonial Sport;

■ consider the utility of post-colonialism in relation to sport;

■ discuss other ways of highlighting sport in other parts of the world;

■ comment upon sport in Africa, Asia and the South.

INTRODUCTION

Sport has the potential for good in all parts of the world, but not if the forms of sport are preordained and governed solely by the fundamentalism of the free market or Western sport. Global sport on its current commercially driven path risks the re-colonisation of the world by Western commercial sporting values and dogma that fail to recognise other rich sporting cultures, societies and peoples. Protecting and empowering social and cultural diversity through sport must therefore be seen as a crucial part of any progressive approach towards sport in the world. The poorest countries in the world must be given improved access to world sport in a way that respects the values of the 'other'. In a vindication of the rights of women more than two hundred years ago, the activist Mary Wollstonecraft expressed the idea that it was justice and not charity that was wanting in the world (Kinnock, 2003:1). In many ways the same might be said of global sport. Development is itself a matter of justice, and global sport, if it is to be truly global, has to respond to the fundamental aspirations of sport in all parts of the world, to be recognised on mutual terms and not simply through the dogma or values of the major power brokers in world sport who tend to be located in the Northern hemisphere.

To view global and Western sport as a corpus of dogma allows us to question the values in the idea of an aspirant global sport rather differently. All major dogmatic systems, whether or not they are dogmatic about the free market or religion or world sport, need to avoid the twin pitfalls of absolutist and relativist attitudes towards sport, both of which are forms of fundamentalism. Absolutist standpoints run the risk of regarding Western sport as a sacred set of commandments brought to the developing South by the developed North. Those who lag behind are pressurised or compelled to convert to the faith of sport and modernity, thus raising barriers to encouraging a greater participation in international sporting festivals staged in or by the West from, for example, Islamic women or Trobriand Island cricket or sumo wrestlers or wushu, which may never be represented at the Olympic Games.

The relativist view, on the other hand, considers that Northern or Western sport is designed to suit only the Northern or Western sporting hemispheres and need have no meaning for 'other' places or communities. To assume that there can be no communication between major sporting doctrines from different parts of the world is in itself a form of fundamentalism that treats indigenous or local belief systems as closed and inflexible. Both variants of Western sporting dogma present countries of the South with a simple alternative, either to transform their sporting practices by denying who they are, or remain who they are, but give up any idea of transforming sport and them. Perhaps it is impossible for humanity to arrive at an understanding of the values that unite it, but if the countries of the North cease automatically to impose their own ideas on the rest of the sporting world and start to take due cognisance of other sporting cultures in a common exercise of critical self-examination, the aspirations of global sport may become more just and less charitable.

OTHER SPORTING COMMUNITIES

The term 'other' sporting communities as it is used in this chapter is drawn from the post-colonial critique of the colonial or imperial worlds and consequently the way in which sport developed in many countries. The term at one level refers to something separate from oneself, but as it is used in this chapter it primarily refers to the articulation of differences between and within imperial, colonial and often European stereotypes and actions associated with people, sports and places. Bhabha (1983) has talked about the 'other' in terms of the regimes of truth that are produced by colonialism or imperialism. Such truths invariably view indigenous, non-European or non-Western forms of sport as inferior.

The term 'other' can refer to colonised 'others' who are marginalised by imperial thinking, values and actions. Those 'others' are identifiable by their difference from the centre, the colonial; the mainstream has perhaps become the subject and focus of anticipated mastery and domination by the imperial ego. Post-colonial and subaltern studies of sport seek to uncover 'other' material accounts of sport in colonised countries such as Africa, India, China and Australia. The 'other' is often the marginalised or the forgotten or viewed as less important within the overall notion of global sport.

Different bodies of research into sport, culture and society have attempted to ensure that 'other' sporting worlds are forever present. Anthropologists have brought to our attention the significance of the Mayan ball game Pok-ta pok, Karuta in Japan, Bachama wrestling, sports of the Samoans, dart matches in Tikopia, cockfighting in Bali, ritual rural games in Libya, Aboriginal sport, the structure of Trobriand Island cricket, Indian running, Kalenjin runners in Kenya, Tarahumaras runners in Mexico, Sumo in Japan, the role of sports among the Maori, the training of the body in China, the alleged use of *juju* in football in Tanzania, the role of football for Palestinians in Jordan, or football amongst the Baga of Guinea.

Geographers have contributed to the opening up of sport in 'other' places, locations and landscapes, while at the same time calling for imaginative geographies of sport (Bale, 1994, 2002a, 2003). The spatial dynamics of sports has contributed to a greater understanding of the geographical diffusion of sport, talent migration, the relocation of sports clubs and the changing content of the sporting landscape. This work has included analysis of running in Kenya, sports stadia in Scandinavia, the way in which African footballers are reported in the Western press, images of Rwandan high-jumpers, memory and identity in one local Scottish football community, women athletes and Islam, a geography of baseball and athletic representation in the colonial world. Perhaps it is useful at this point to consider two examples in more detail.

Trobriand Island cricket and wushu are illustrative of 'other' sports. European mission-aries introduced cricket to the Trobriand Islands in the 1920s and 1930s as part of an overall colonising mission that included the usual requisite changes in dress, tradition, social prac-tices and values. Very quickly the Trobriand Islanders refashioned the game to meet local needs. The number of players in the team was not restricted, as long as they were even, bowling actions were replaced by spear-throwing actions that in turn, because of their accuracy, led to shortening the stumps. The ball was made from local materials and the fall of each wicket was accompanied by dance celebrations while teams practised elaborate celebratory rituals. Games were invariably accompanied by feasting and became part of the inter-village political activities. The 'other' cricket in the case of the Trobriand Islanders was not inferior or marginal, but an essential part of Trobriand culture with deep ritual significance (Stoddart and Sandiford, 1998:139).

Wushu, the collective phrase for Chinese martial arts, is one of the most widespread traditional sports in China. Many other Asian martial arts have originated from its wide variety of fighting techniques. Within China, wushu has displayed a number of local vari-ations, and collectively the All-China Federation of Trade Unions has estimated that almost three million Chinese people practise wushu on a daily basis for both physical and spiritual needs (Theeboom and De Knop, 1997:267). At one and the same time, wushu represents a traditional Chinese sport and a modern form of Chinese culture, looking to acquire Olympic status and recognition. It none the less runs the risk of being influenced or re-invented by American-Chinese culture, given the significant place that martial arts have found in the American imagination. The American and potential Olympic fascination with the 'other' therefore gazes at wushu through Western eyes, while looking to re-invent or colonise the tradition within the American imagination, thus potentially reducing its oppos-itional potential to Western culture. Since the 1980s, both the Chinese Wushu Association and the International Wushu Federation have lobbied for wushu to be included as an official Olympic sport. In post-colonial terms the inculcation into 'modern sport' of traditional Chinese wushu by Olympic, American and Western forces would most likely lead to hybridity, which commonly refers to the creation of new transcultural sports forms by contact between the colony and the 'other'.

While the above is illustrative of some of the 'other' worlds of sport, what follows is illustrative of the changing dynamics of state development in different parts of the world. One of the most serious flaws of conventional discussions about globalisation is its blind-ness to strongly differentiated state forms that have developed over the past 40 years. These serve as a reminder of the increasingly diverse and deferential world in which we live. Social modernisation resulting from economic change, education, mass communication, calls for formal democratic rights, and trans-national migration has impacted upon different parts of the world in a very uneven way. Successful state forms have included the welfare statism that has been deployed and consolidated in much of western Europe. The more outward developmental model adopted by East Asia, characterised by state planning, control of banks and credit, and aggressive world market export-orientated structures, has also been successful. The Asian development states have been more concerned with political and cultural protection against unwanted foreign influences, with Japan and South Korea both being tenacious about incoming foreign investment. If the East Asian models of state development have been relatively successful, there have been less successful state models that have been more inward looking. With the exception of North Korea and China in Asia, the former communist state models have disintegrated. China, Vietnam, Cambodia and Laos have all staked out new courses of development. China, the largest country on the planet, has become history's most successful development state with a 20-year growth rate per capita of almost 10 per cent per year. Tourism has helped Cuba to survive, while in the post-colonial African states, government-encouraged socialist ambitions have struggled to overcome administrative chaos, ethnic tensions and rising poverty.

In the same way as globalisation has been blind to the uneven and differentiated models of state formation emerging in the twenty-first century, the same might be said about our current knowledge of global sport. It is impossible at this stage to draw up a balance sheet of the combined effects of globalisation and other social forces with their many contradictions, exceptions and unevenness. By the same token, it is also impossible to map out the changing patterns of global sport. But it is essential that any contemporary understanding of sport, culture and society must actively listen to and engage with other sporting communities, places and voices. If nothing else, the dynamic body of work, which contributes to what we know about sport and post-colonialism, is helping with this sensitivity. In the same way that dependency theory of the 1960s and 1970s provided a means of explaining the development of Latin American sport on its own terms, or the way in which Said's work on orientalism and cultural imperialism has influenced different ways of looking at Japanese sport, or Henning Eichberg's work on body cultures has insisted on at least three ways of thinking about sport as a trialectic, the post-colonial critique of colonial sport serves as a reminder that 'other' sporting communities contribute to and influence global sport. Its overall value lies in it being a safeguard against inward-looking parochialism and the conscience of cosmopolitan sport, lest it forgets 'other' traditions of sport, the poor or the use of cheap labour in sporting production, or the humanitarian power of sport in 'other' parts of the world.

POST-COLONIALISM – WHAT IS IT?

Post-colonialism along with a number of 'posts' has become increasingly active in accounts of sport, culture and society. The prefix 'post' aligns 'post-colonialism' with a series of other 'posts' – 'post-structuralism', 'post-modernism', 'post-Marxism', 'post-feminism', 'post-deconstructionism' – all sharing the notion of a moment beyond a particular period. In this sense the prefix 'post' aligns the 'post-colonial' with another genre of 'posts' – 'postwar', 'post-Cold War', 'post-independence', 'post-revolution' – all of which underline a passage into a new period and a closure of a certain historical event or age.

If colonialism exists in support of Western powers, it is debatable whether colonialism has declined at all. Post-colonialism may signify changes in the official power structure after a period of de-colonisation, as well as colonialism's enduring effects, particularly as they

179

are manifested interpretatively. Post-colonial theory is an umbrella term which covers different critical approaches, and is particularly critical of European thought in areas as wide-ranging as philosophy, history, literary studies, anthropology, sociology, political science and sport, culture and society. Within this perspective, the term post-colonial refers not to a simple periodisation, rather a radical methodological revisionism and wholesale critique of Western structures of knowledge and power.

As mentioned in Chapter 1, at a general level post-colonialism presents a challenge to previously accepted values and criteria for ways of looking at and thinking about the world. The need to re-write sport, culture and society arises in part from forms of intervention, such as post-colonialism, which assert that our past knowledge of sport has been dispro-portionately influenced by specific ideologies of the dominating powers, usually European and invariably colonial, and that 'other' sporting communities are not sufficiently repre-sented in that which currently accounts for the literature on global sport. The history of global sport has been disproportionately influenced by the ideas or ideals of nineteenth- and twentieth-century imperialism. These include an assumed superiority of Western, often white, sporting cultures that have promoted historically questionable ideologies of sport relating to fair play, amateurism, athleticism, the role of sport in the civilising process, the marginalisation of indigenous sporting forms as inferior to Western, often European, sporting forms, and sport's particular links with forms of religion that gave rise to phrases such as 'muscular Christianity'. In the latter, a fundamental clash of cultures is exposed in the very words that prioritise particular sports and a particular religion.

'Other' sports have in some cases aligned themselves with aspects of religion and athleticism, but have had to develop a certain level of hybridity. Sumo is a traditional Japanese wrestling sport that has always included a strong element of religion and ritual. A fundamental clash of cultures and values is evident in Guttmann and Thompson's (2001:139) account of sumo wrestling in Japan in which they write that from the 1890s onwards many Japanese intellectuals have struggled with the problem of understanding Japanese society and the place of sumo as a modern and a traditional sport. Some of sumo's traditions pre-date the nineteenth century but, as Guttmann (1996:380) concludes, the elders who traditionalised twentieth-century sumo were quite successful in that sumo flourishes today as baseball's most serious rival amongst spectator sports in Japan. Together the two sports symbolise Japan's desire to be simultaneously a traditional and a modern society.

Sumo also encapsulates the clash between a sport that has at least a 2,000-year-old history and the struggle to survive against the inroads being made by sports such as soccer, following the success of the national soccer team in the 2002 FIFA World Cup. Traditionally the number one sport in Japan, sumo wrestling has been hit by reduced sponsorship, falling attendances and TV viewing figures. At the same time soccer is fast capturing the minds of a new generation. Corporate sponsors have fallen away as Japanese companies such as Mitsubishi, Nissan, Posco and SK Corporation have looked to support more international sports, such as golf and soccer. Ticket sales to tournaments fell by 15 per cent between 2000 and 2002 while television ratings were, at the end of 2002, 50 per cent down on the 1998 figures. There is also the alleged problem that match fixing has become common in the sport. Japanese gangs, known as the Yakuzza, are said to control betting on fights. The

Japanese Sumo Association (JSA) has responded by cutting seat prices, selling tickets at convenience stores, claiming to have solved the problem of match-fixing and attempting to add internationality by luring foreign wrestlers to fight Japanese sumo wrestlers.

In 1998 the IOC provisionally recognised the Tokyo-based International Sumo Federation (ISF), thus boosting the sport's chances of making it into the Olympic Games. By 2001 sumo's amateur world championship featured women for the first time. At the 2005 World Games men's and women's sumo will make their debut for the first time at this high-profile event for non-Olympic sports. The view of the ISF is that the rise of women's sumo should only strengthen the case for the sport to be represented at the Olympic Games. The official Japanese argument on this issue is that judo is an Olympic sport, but that sumo is older and better (www.amateursumo.com). In 2002, IOC President Jacques Rogge however, had condemned the sport's gargantuan competitors as presenting the wrong image, claiming that it was ugly and bad for one's health (*Sunday Herald*, 15 June 2003:18).

The problem may be approached in two ways. One is to stress the difference between Japan and the West, since the West invariably characterises or invents Japan as it wants to see it in terms of being rational, progressive, scientific, individualistic, meritocratic, lacking material wealth but having spiritual qualities. The other possible way is to differentiate Japan and Japaneseness from the West, while at the same time maintaining and constructing Japan's own definition of Japaneseness. Both these approaches can be seen in Japanese assessments of the relative merits of imported Western sports and indigenous traditional martial arts and sumo. If the West in this case is viewed as the 'other', it is the interaction between Japan and the other that makes it possible for Japan to differentiate itself from other nations. In other words, Japaneseness has to be imagined by the other as well as by its own members. Japan constructs its images of Western sports just as the West constructs its images of Japanese sport and Japaneseness. Western sport can be viewed as individualistic, secular, involving modern forms, players' rights and labour unionism, whereas something as traditional as sumo can still be viewed as spiritual, hierarchical, ritualistic and yet struggling equally with twenty-first-century professional sporting problems.

POST-COLONIALISM AND SPORT

Normally, three meanings are given to the term post-colonial. First, it is the end of a period of time in the sense that the old colonial control has diminished. Second, post-colonial refers to a stage of development in which post-colonialism has replaced colonialism. This may be viewed as a goal or aspiration that necessitates a critical examination of today's sporting content and representation. In this sense post-colonialism might refer not so much to a state of being after colonialism, but the process by which we might reach that particular aspiration or state of being. Finally, the term post-colonial might be viewed as a method that adopts a post-colonial approach to sport.

The following are questions that might arise out of a post-colonial approach to sport:

- To what extent has the process of external imperialism and/or colonialism influenced the development of sport?

- How has Western sport controlled the development of sport in non-Western parts of the world?
- To what extent has the history of sport been written or challenged by non-Western perspectives?
- Is the nature of sport different in Western and non-Western parts of the world and, if so, how?
- Do the notions of hybridity or orientalism help us to explain sport?

In one of the most comprehensive introductions to sport and post-colonialism, Bale and Cronin (2003) raise three crucial questions, which we need to elaborate upon before considering whether the term is reality-congruent, for example, in places where a United States of America has moved offensively in both sport and society in general (Ali, 2003). Two of the questions raised by Bale and Cronin (2003) refer to the how and the what of post-colonial sports, in which the 'how' refers to methodology and 'what' refers to some illustrative forms of post-colonial enquiries into sport. As mentioned in the introduction to this book, one of the potential roles of a student, researcher or intellectual working in the field of sport, culture and society is to uncover, contest, challenge and ultimately defeat both imposed silences and the normalised quiet of unseen power. In terms of doing post-colonial sport this refers to the general goal of opening up the injustices or the silences within global sport in relation to 'other' sporting communities. It means a challenge to the values of Western sport so that what might first appear as odd and out of 'place' no longer becomes out of 'place'. More specifically, Bale and Cronin (2003:9) see in the context of sports and body cultures post-colonial method, involving emphasising aspects of sport in the relations between coloniser and colonised; re-interpreting and providing alternative understandings of sport; displaying an awareness of the way in which sport and body culture have resisted colonisation and the removal of post-colonial sport from universal or general metropolitan ideas or policies about sport. In a very practical sense if it is generally accepted that sporting festivals and world championships are too big, then in any downsizing we must ask which sports will go, which countries will go and in whose interest it is that such a downsizing policy is accepted? As Bale more than anybody else has done over the past decade, this means challenging, for example, the European construction of athleticism of various groups of 'other' people in the colonized world. It means giving a voice to 'other' sporting communities in terms of their own values.

What then are post-colonial sports? Several illustrative types of post-colonial sports are provided by Bale and Cronin (2003:5):

- forms of body culture which have survived colonialism, such as Rwandan high jumping;
- indigenous local forms of body culture which have been transformed into modern sports, such as lacrosse, ice-hockey and shinty;
- body cultures which were re-invented by a former colonising power, such as baseball and basketball in the USA;
- colonial sports which have been modified by former colonies into national sports, such as Gaelic and Australian football;

- sports which have travelled with the colonising powers and have adopted 'other' styles, such as Brazilian football and Kenyan running;
- sports that have developed a degree of hybridity such as Trobriand Island cricket or combined rules shinty/hurling matches.

The final question posed by Bale and Cronin (2003) is: When was post-colonial sport? – and it is worth discussing this in more detail?

When are sports post-colonial?

Although the term post-colonial has a clear chronological meaning, designating the period after which independence had been secured from colonial governance, from the late 1970s, the term has been used in a variety of different ways, not least of which has been a denouncing of the literary impact of colonialism. Originally used by historians to refer to periods after the World War II, in which post-colonial states emerged, it is clear that there is no one fixed starting date for post-colonialism or post-colonial sport, but a number of post-colonial sports. Post-colonial sport is not a term that can be precisely pinned down. Rather it can be articulated in different ways in different places at different times, while still maintaining the common core problematic thrust of attempting to develop a healthy degree of suspicion and self-consciousness about what has passed as colonial, imperial and even neo-colonial sports. The hyphenated term 'post-colonial sports' denotes a particular historical period or epoch, after colonialism. But the plurality of the term 'sports' also indicates not just the number of sports, but also a number of epochs or historical periods in which sport in different places may have taken on different post-colonial politics. Post-colonial sports are not contained by tidy common categories of historical periods or dates, although they remain firmly bound up with historical experiences, particularly after independence from colonial governance.

In attempting to answer the 'when' of post-colonialism and sport, Bale and Cronin (2003) offer the following suggestions (i) when the first 'third world sports workers' arrived in the 'First World'; (ii) the period following independence from nineteenth-century imperialism when sport played such an important part in transmitting values and/or (iii) the present and future attempts to challenge international sports organisations that continue to promote a colonising policy towards sport in an attempt to achieve global expansion for any particular sport. Many of the specific studies of sport and the body contained within *Sport and Post-colonialism* also struggle with the 'when' issue of post-colonial sports. In Hay's (2003) analysis of Australia as a post-colonial sporting society, he specifically refers to the evolution of Australian sport within a post-imperial context. This draws upon Australia's ambivalent relationship to the sporting metropolis or centre, by which Hay means British and American sport, and also Australia's own attitude and actions towards ethnic minority and Aboriginal Australian sport. For Mills and Dimeo (2003), the body is a central and unique way to inform the relationship between sporting activities in both colonial and post-colonial South Asia. The 'when' of this research refers to post-colonial India and in particular the way in which football has acted for the colonisers as an 'idiom and as a technology for imagining and transforming the Indian body' (Mills and Dimeo, 2003:157). Given that India

183

and Pakistan gained independence in 1947, the framework for this particular contribution to sport and post-colonialism revolves around pre- and post-1947 reflections upon sport and the Indian body.

Finally for Vidacs' Africa (2003) the post-colonial refers to post-colonial states in particular parts of Africa and thus the issue of 'when' relates to the period following the ending of colonial rule in Africa, not the lingering effects of colonialism; this refers to the lingering lived experiences of Africans inhabiting this post-colonial Africa. Specifically drawing upon this second meaning, Vidacs' account of Cameroon football is set against the context of the 1998 Football World Cup in France in which the ideal world of football and justice outside of Cameroon was deemed to be lacking. Cameroonians, like other Africans (Vidacs 2003:237), create outside models of great nations to make sense of their own lives. The football ideal of the level playing field was smashed in 1998 and this gave rise to bitterness and despair among many Cameroonians. Following the defeat of the Cameroon football team, the problems of football in a post-colonial Africa were hidden or explained by an anti-FIFA, anti-white and anti-European account for the failure of the Cameroon football team to live up to the ideal of post-colonial football.

Attending to the cultural, historical, social, political and geographical differences of post-colonial sports is crucial. But as the above examples illustrate, the specific 'when' of post-colonial sports cannot be answered in the singular. The specifics of 'when' in regard to post-colonial sport would need to take cognisance of the fact that India and Pakistan gained independence in 1947, Ceylon (now Sri Lanka) in 1948, Ghana, the first majority rule independent African country, in 1957, followed by Nigeria in 1960. Jamaica and Trinidad and Tobago followed suit in the Caribbean in 1962 and, more recently, Hong Kong passed from Britain to China in July 1997.

The post-colonial sporting world would also need to take cognisance of the way in which sport has or could contribute to anti-colonial struggles in those countries recently occupied. Should China's human rights record in Tibet, for example, have influenced the awarding of the 2008 Olympic Games to Beijing or should the awarding of the 2002 World Cup to Japan and South Korea have recognised those Koreans who cannot return to their own country at this time? Perhaps at this point in development of research into post-colonial sports it is wise to suggest that detailed historical work on aspects of local post-colonial sports should serve as a defence against simplistic historical or geographical generalisations. Post-colonial sport should not be a generalising term, but students and researchers of sport, culture and society may inevitably link differences and think comparatively across differences as well as between 'other' sporting communities.

Not yet global or post-colonial sport

The power of sport to make money has been one of the key drivers behind the expansion of sport. Three of the main drivers behind the aspiration of global sport have been money, technology and the quest for cultural recognition on the international playing field. The impact of new technology has meant that the world itself has seemingly become a smaller place. Television and new media have contributed to new home-centred forms of entertainment. Telecommunications in general have also brought a richer diversity of world sports into people's homes. At the same time, developments in communications technology have made it more difficult to shield a state population from impressions of the outside world.

While the breakdown of selected economic frontiers may have allowed sport to become more international, part of the problem facing northern-dominated professional sports organisations has been their assumptions concerning the rest of the world. These assumptions have in part been born out of a colonial or Western mentality. There are at least two modes of contemporary thinking about contemporary sport that display such a mentality. First, there is the notion that the professional sports market is dominated by professional sports that have been propagated in the West and that professional sports enterprises around the world have followed this model. Part of this assumption has been to suggest that international trends emerging in sport have been examples of Americanisation rather than of globalisation. The argument is supported as a result of the outcome, power and explosion of sports on television, particularly on pay and cable platforms, such as Fox in the United States, Star TV in Asia, BSkyB in Britain and Foxtel in Australia. Television will continue to expand its markets throughout Asia and Africa and yet such vast warehouses of sports entertainment are also accompanied by the not-so-subtle reinforcement of the consumption experiences that have become commonplace in the United States, but not in perhaps 'other' parts of the world.

The core problem, however, remains one of cultural compatibility and recognition that the professional Western sports model is not the only way to deliver sport. The Western model seems to want to continue to reinvent sport in the rest of the world in its own image, a universal approach that does not recognise or value the fundamentally different value systems that operate in different parts of the world. It is incomprehensible to imagine such a model of professional sport prospering in parts of the Middle East, simply because the values of professional sport are incompatible with the wider cultures. Sport in the above form will struggle to make significant inroads into the Middle East and other Islamic nations until sport managers abandon the need to inculcate Western values. It is doubtful if in the early part of the twenty-first century the promise or aspiration of global sport is worth dilution of the distinctive national ethnic and religious cultures. Attempts to represent sport both in and from 'other' sporting worlds have involved issues of hybridity, mimicry, Orientalism, myth and invented sporting traditions. Sport might have become increasingly international, but not yet global or post-colonial.

SPORT, POWER AND THE SOUTH

In terms of terminology there are several problems associated with notions such as First World sport or Third World sport, not just in terms of the very language reproducing a hierarchical stereotype, but the terms themselves have changed over time. The term Third World was first used in 1952 to designate those countries that were aligned with neither the United States, nor the former Soviet Union during the so-called Cold War period. Third World sports by definition followed the same geographical demarcation as those sports associated with the local indigenous Third World. The term First World was widely used to refer to the dominant economic and political powers of the West, while the term

Second World was used to refer to the Soviet Union and its allies. The term tricontinental has often replaced the term Third World as a geographical and cultural description of the three continents of Latin America, Africa and Asia, while the North and South divide refers to countries in the Northern hemisphere or the Southern hemisphere.

Yet there needs to be a word of caution here in accepting too readily a definition or process of globalisation that acts purely against the interests of the Southern hemisphere. It has been relatively easy for Islamic countries and those countries of the South to denounce imperialism, globalisation and global sport as unjust. It is necessary, however, to guard against seeing global sport and globalisation as simply imperialism or yet another form of unequal exchange between the North and the South. To dismiss globalisation and global sport purely in terms of imperialism obscures the extent to which some Arab countries have different stakes in globalisation in that they provide oil and, by continuing to feed the West, such countries actively feed globalisation. It also fails to acknowledge the power of the Asian economy or the way in which sport in Japan may synthesise Western and traditional cultures. Alternatively, a significant body of research into baseball in the Dominican Republic during the 1980s and 1990s suggested that the development of Latin baseball was conditioned in part by a dependency upon the power of the American baseball leagues to attract the best players and undermine baseball at 'home'. However, in the early part of the twenty-first century, such an argument would fail to acknowledge the extent to which Latino baseball players might play in Japanese or American leagues and therefore reduce the power of the American hold on baseball by playing the interests of Japanese baseball off against the power of US baseball.

As examples of the development, background and symbolism of sports in 'other' communities, the All-African Games, the African Nations Cup, the Asian Games and the Pan-American Games are a particularly fertile soil for thinking more internationally about sport, culture and society in places other than Europe.

All-African Games

Attempts had been made to hold African Games in Algiers as early as 1925 and in Alexandria in 1928, but they failed owing to, amongst other reasons, colonial politics and economic difficulties. The impact of colonialism was such that in the early 1960s the Friendship Games were held amongst French-speaking countries in Africa. At the conference of African Ministers for Youth and Sport held in Paris in 1962, it was decided that the Games would thereafter be called the Pan-African Games, as they would include countries other than those colonised by the French. The All-African Games eventually emerged in 1965 as a force for African solidarity and as a means of uniting the continent against South Africa's apartheid regime. That same year the Games were granted official recognition by the IOC. Some 2,500 athletes from 30 independent African states attended the 1965 All-African Games held in Brazzaville, Congo. The sixth All-African Games were held in 1995 with the inclusion of (post-apartheid) South Africa for the first time (Levinson and Christensen, 1996:4). The 2003 eighth All-African Games were hosted in Abuja, Nigeria with the specific mission to act 'as a wake-up call for an African continent threatened by war, disease, hunger and poverty, to respond positively to the challenge by using sports as a strong weapon' in this struggle (www.8allafricagames.org). As the world has viewed the images and cries for help highlighted by the international singer and songwriter Bob Geldof in parts of Africa such as Ethiopia, it is often forgotten that humanitarian political leaders, such as Nelson Mandela, the former South African President, have repeatedly stated that football is a force that mobilises the sentiments of a people in a way that nothing else can (*Observer*, 13 July 2003:14).

The promise that football holds out in Africa may be illustrated by two recent examples of the complexity, difference and possibilities that are part of African football. The first example is drawn from the 2003 African Nations Cup match between Rwanda and Uganda. The match was characterised by scenes of violence between players, and between the players and police (Carlin, 2003:14). A couple of early saves by the Rwandan keeper Mohammed Mossi incited the 60,000 crowd to claim that the Rwandan goalkeeper was using supernatural powers. Abubaker Tabula of Uganda started digging behind the Rwandan goal to find the offending *juju* – a witchcraft doll placed by the Rwandans behind their goal. Mayhem followed with the referee ordering the players to leave the pitch. Half an hour later, the game resumed and Rwanda went on to win 1–0. Celebrations across a united Rwanda followed in a country which less than ten years earlier in 1994 had endured the government-incited massacre of 800,000 Tutsis and as many people murdered in any one day for 100 days, as died in the 11 September attack on the World Trade Center in New York. Following the match, Hutus and Tutsis, genocide killers and genocide survivors danced in the streets of Rwanda together, while the then Tutsi President Paul Kagame was joined at the airport by almost half the country's eight million people to meet the Hutu captain and the victorious football team (*The Observer*, 13 July 2003:14). The President announced there and then that new Presidential elections would be held the following month, the first since his coming to power. It was generally acknowledged that only football could have had such a huge impact upon the task of national reconciliation in one of the world's most ethnically divided and damaged countries.

In June of 2003, the Cameroon footballer Marc Vivien Foé died during a semi-final of the Confederations Cup match in which Cameroon was aiming to become the first African nation to qualify for the final of a major World Cup football tournament. The death of the football star was front-page news across Europe and Africa, with the *Cameroon Tribune* summing up the loss to the nation in the phrase 'a giant is killed in combat' (*Herald*, 28 June 2003:4). One of the poorest nations in the world, Cameroon has a life expectancy of well below 50, an average annual wage of £350 and at the time was on the brink of war with Nigeria over contested oil territories. It is the home to around 130 different ethnic groups and several languages. There are few things with the potential to unite and reconcile the nation that is Cameroon, but since 1990 the footballing 'Lions' of the national team have succeeded in bringing peoples together in a way that few other aspects of life can. It is viewed as an opportunity for Cameroon to compete and succeed on an equal footing with the rest of the world. The final against France went ahead despite the death of the player. This led to criticism of the President of FIFA, Sepp Blatter, from the French Captain Patrick Vieira.

187

The Asian Games

The Asian Games are held for the purpose of developing inter-cultural knowledge and friendship within Asia. The Games are intended as a forum for cultural exchange with the official programme including both sport and the arts. The roots of the current Games date back to 1913 when the Far East Championships were held, involving China, Japan and the Philippines. The modern Asian Games, the invention of tradition, were re-established at India's suggestion following the World War II and were first held in New Delhi in 1951. Eleven nations and some 489 athletes competed in the first Games. Israel attended, but Syria did not; Pakistan, only recently separated from India, refused to attend, while communist China and Vietnam boycotted because India refused to recognise either government. The fourth Asian Games held in Jakarta, Indonesia, in 1962 witnessed a move to establish a separate structure termed the Games of the Newly Emerging Forces (GANEFO). Such a move was in clear opposition to the Western powers. Both China and the then Soviet Union supplied money and sent athletes. GANEFO survived long enough to show the West that the Asian nations could organise alternative games.

The Olympic Council of Asia was formed in 1982 with 43 countries and regions affiliating by 2003. The traditional Asian game of kabbadi was featured at the Beijing Games of 1990, but most of the events remained modern and Western. In 1994 the Asian Games were hosted by Hiroshima, Japan, and symbolised the regeneration of the city, Kazakhstan became the first ex-Soviet Asian Republic to attend the Games and was another illustration of the dynamic changing geography of world sport (Levinson and Christensen, 1996:22). The emblem for the 1994 Asian Games depicted a dove, the symbol of peace and the 'H' of Hiroshima, reflecting Hiroshima's desire for peace. The slogan accompanying the emblem expressed the wish that the Games would foster mutual respect among the Asian peoples as they worked to build an attractive dynamic Asia for the twenty-first century.

The 2002 games were hosted by Busan in South Korea. North Korea participated for the first time in games held in South Korea; North Korea's national anthem was played for the first time in South Korea, the law banning the display of North Korean flags being set aside for the Games although it was still illegal for individual South Koreans to fly North Korean flags. Internal Chinese colonialism meant that Taiwan was represented as Chinese Taipei and athletes from Taiwan were forced to march behind the Chinese banner. Afghanistan participated in the 2002 Asian Games, the first since the Taliban came to power, despite the lack of facilities or sporting infrastructure in Afghanistan.

The 2006 Games are to be hosted in Doha, Qatar (www.internationalgames.net/asian.htm). Qatar is a state of only 600,000 inhabitants and one of the issues to be resolved is the demand made by some Muslim states with regard to sportswear worn by some Muslim women athletes. As a result, Western-dominated sportswear manufacturing companies have been accused by some Islamic nations of exploiting women athletes and not developing suitable sportswear for women in Islamic countries. There is also the issue of various interpretations of the Koran, which raises issues of modest dress worn by women, but is in fact interpreted by some Islamic sections as the obligatory covering up of limbs and even the face and raises questions as to whether the issue is one of faith and religion or a mixture of faith and patriarchy. Qatar sent a team of women athletes to Busan in 2002 in preparation for 2006. Women of Qatar are expected to compete in a number of events with the official website explaining that Qatar 'intends to train women volunteers, referees, technicians, officials and athletes so that they can attain international standards while still respecting Islamic values' (www.internationalgames.net/asian.htm p. 17). While Islamic fundamentalism might be viewed in the West as problematic, it is no more so than one of the other forceful ideologies of the twenty-first century, namely global and domestic free markets extending as widely and as rapidly as possible.

The Pan-American Games

At the 1932 Los Angeles Olympic Games representatives from Latin American countries proposed a regional games for all the Americas. A Pan-American Sports Congress was proposed for 1942, but it was not until 1948 in London that such an event took place. The founding Pan-American Games took place in Buenos Aires in 1951, in what was termed a festival of sport and international friendship. Twenty-two countries and 2,500 athletes competed in 19 events. The organisation governing the Games was renamed in 1955 as the Pan-American Sports Organization (PASO). In 1979 Puerto Rico spent US $60 million on new facilities for the Games. Cuba hosted the 1991 games and set new records in the numbers of athletes and countries participating. The USA's economic embargo on Cuba meant that only $1.2 million of the original agreed figure of $9 million from television rights reached Cuba. The Games returned to Argentina in 1995 with more than 5,000 athletes from 42 countries competing in 37 sports. The Games' slogan 'América: Espírito, Sport, Fraternité' uses the principal languages of the hemisphere, but is also in itself a symbol of various forms of colonialism (Levinson and Christensen, 1996:288). The phrase loosely translated means 'the American spirit of friendship through sports' (www.aafla.org/8saa/PanAm.htm). PASO, currently made up of the 42 nations of North, Central and South America and the Caribbean, continues to govern the Games.

The three examples given above illustrate the cultural politics of sport in other worlds. The dialogue about Southern sport, and in particular Latin American sport, often starts from the position that the power structures of global sport have not materially shifted since the end of the imperial era. Such an argument runs the risk of passing over the differences within and between sports in other communities in the Southern hemisphere. It is important that the cultural politics of sport presents neither a homogenous picture of the West, nor sport on the three continents. None the less, a substantive body of work relating to the relationship between sport in Africa, Asia and the Americas, particularly those countries south of the United States of America, might be further enhanced by linking the politics of sport in anti-colonial or post-colonial struggles with the politics of sport and anti-globalisation. The geography of the current anti-globalisation protests signals a new world political landscape, and the seeds of what have been sown in Chiapas or Porto Alegre or Seattle or Genoa or Barcelona point towards an entirely new ideological, political and geographical shift.

It is not necessary to see this as irrelevant to sport, culture and society and indeed such issues are explored further in Parts 3 and 4 of this book, but the potential emergence of a global three-way split in the values associated with contemporary sport and other sporting

189

communities is as serious as the ideological differences that divided sport in the twentieth century. The following are but three contemporary developments that mark the return of ideology into world sport: (i) aggressive American expansionism with American sports and television companies seeking a greater share of global sport – American-dominated trans-national sports companies are able to come and go as they please in many of the poorer countries of the world; (ii) sport and progressive globalisation or internationalisation, in which the pursuit of a genuine multilateral effort in sport is leading to greater economic, political and social equality in and through sport and (iii) sport and physical culture within Islamic fundamentalism either allowing for the opening up of or mutual respect for the place and presence of Islamic sport and body culture or conflict, in which the values associated with sport and physical culture are positioned as an alternative to American neo-liberal expansionism or progressive globalisation. Only one of these three ideologies has the potential for contributing to the reality of global sport.

Finally, it might be suggested that the social dimension of global sport is destined to remain an empty slogan as long as there exists a relative imbalance between the means for the peoples of the South to propose to the North their own interpretation of global sport and the common ground between the different worlds of sport, values and societies. There is much more to this than the production of a post-colonial understanding of sport in other communities, or the proliferation of hybrid sporting alternatives, or a redistribution of some of the wealth brought about through international sport. Yet if nothing else the value of a post-colonial understanding of sport is that it serves as a constant reminder that attending to the cultural, historical, social, political, economic and geographical differences of other sports is paramount to an understanding of sport, culture and society. Comparative modes of thought about sport remain a valuable means of critique, and need not lead to generality and universalism, but are also a safeguard against fundamentalism or identity sporting politics.

SUMMARY

At the heart of all of these divisions is the issue of inequality of opportunity in sport that is clearly linked to unequal distribution of power. Inequality is a complex issue and varies both within and between other communities. One of the historical causes of division between rich and poor parts of the world has been linked to the legacy of colonialism and imperialism, which extracted resources from the countries in the Southern hemisphere, including sporting resources in terms of athletes, for the benefit of those in the North. More recently attention has been turned to the way in which trans-national corporations contribute to this uneven divide and distribution of sporting commodities. A recent and growing body of work on sport has focused on an evaluation of colonial and post-colonial sport.

Post-colonialism is not the only idea that has drawn attention to sport in other communities. This chapter has considered the strengths and weaknesses of post-colonialism as an idea that draws attention to the dynamics of sport in other communities. There are many under-studied regions, places and peoples of the world that are not included within the umbrella terms of post-colonialism or indeed global sport. There is a greater danger in global sport or free-market sport being adopted as a euphemism for Western sport. None the less, the social and political dynamics of contemporary sport necessitate not only an understanding of 'other' sporting communities; the value of sensitivity to other sporting communities is one of the best defences against inward looking parochialism, nationalism and a sole concentration upon identity sporting politics.

A related issue might be the right of all people to have access to sport, to participate in sport and to be represented through sport. A sensitivity to the expanding world of sporting communities has, at least at the time of writing this book, begun to present itself through a number of significant and sustained bodies of sporting work that have opened up particular avenues into 'other' sporting communities. Yet, as alluded to earlier in this chapter, perhaps the overall value lies in its method as a safeguard against inward-looking parochialism and as the conscience of cosmopolitan sport, in case it forgets 'other' traditions of sport, the poor or the use of cheap labour in sporting production, or the humanitarian power of sport in 'other' parts of the world.

KEY CONCEPTS

All-African Games	North/South divide
Asian Games	Orientalism
Colonialism	Other
Core	Pan-American Games
First World	Periphery
Globalisation	Power
Hybridity	Post-colonialism
Imperialism	Second World
Inequality	Third World
Internationalism	World power

KEY READING

Books

Bale, J. (2003). *Sports Geography*. London: Routledge.
Bale, J. and Cronin, M. (2003). *Sport and Post-colonialism*. Oxford: Berg.
Guha, R. (2002). *A Corner of a Foreign Field*: *The Indian History of a British Sport*. London: Picador.
Pacione, M. (2001). *Urban Geography*: *A Global Perspective*. London: Routledge.
Wearing, B. (1998). *Leisure and Feminist Theory*. London: Sage, 162–176.

Journal articles

Ali, T. (2003). 'Re-Colonizing Iraq'. *New Left Review*, Vol. 21 (May): 5–20.

Bale, J. (1998). 'Capturing the African Body? Visual Images and Imaginative Sports.' *Journal of Sports History*, 25(2): 234–252.

Gen Doy, A. (1996). 'Out of Africa: Orientalism, Race and the Female Body'. *Body and Society*, 2(4): 17–45.

Henry, I., Amara, M. and Al-Tauqui, M. (2003). 'Sport, Arab Nationalism and the Pan-Arab Games'. *International Review for the Sociology of Sport*, 38(3): 295–311.

Walseth, K. and Fasting, K. (2003). 'Islam's View on Physical Activity and Sport: Egyptian Women Interpreting Islam'. *International Review for the Sociology of Sport*, 38(1): 45–61.

Further reading

Bale, J. (2002b). 'Human Geography and the Study of Sport'. In Coakley, J. and Dunning, E. *Handbook of Sports Studies*. London: Sage, 170–186.

Carlin, J. (2003). 'Rwanda's Magic Moment'. *Observer*, 13 July: 14.

Guttmann, A. and Thompson, L. (2001). *Japanese Sports*: *A History*. Honolulu: University of Hawaii Press.

Levinson, M. and Christensen, K. (1996). *Encyclopaedia of World Sport*. Oxford: ABC-CLIO.

Stoddart, B. (1998). 'Other Cultures'. In Stoddart, B. and Sandiford, K. (eds) *The Imperial Game*. Manchester: Manchester University Press, 135–149.

Van Ingen, C. (2003). 'Geographies of Gender, Sexuality and Race: Reframing the Focus on Space in Sport Sociology'. *International Review for the Sociology of Sport*, 38(2): 201–216.

REVISION QUESTIONS

1. Having read the introduction to Bale and Cronin (2003) explain the what, when and how of the relationship between sport and post-colonialism.

2. Explain what is meant by other sporting communities.

3. Critically evaluate the notion of First World sport making due reference to the notion of power.

4. Provide a short but detailed history of the Asian Games, the Pan-American Games or the All-African Games.

5. How might the notion of post-colonial sport be used as a critique of global sport?

PRACTICAL PROJECTS

1. Alongside the huge disparities in wealth between rich countries and poor countries is also the idea that sport in the world is unequal and unfair. Examine the sports that are represented at the Olympic Games and make a list of those traditional sports in non-Western countries that are not represented.

2. Explore further one of the websites provided in this chapter with a view to finding out about the All-African or Asian Games and provide a short history of this event.

3. Carry out a Google search on sport+postcolonialism and write a 2,000-word report on the topic.

4. Identify four sports in your own country which are not given a great deal of coverage. Carry out a number of interviews with people from these sports and comment upon sport on the margins in your country. Finish your investigation with a brief comment on how your findings might be related to a broader analysis of sport on the margins in different parts of the world.

5. You are charged with the task of developing the programme of events at the next Olympic Games. You have to prioritise sports that are not represented in the Olympic Games. What criteria would you use to ensure that sports from Africa and Asia are given greater prominence?

WEBSITES

All-Africa Games
    http://www.internationalgames.net/african.htm

Asian Games
    www.internationalgames.net/asian.htm

Pan-American Games
    www.aafla.org/8saa/PanAm.htm

Sport and peace
    www.un.org/sport2005/index.html

Sport and reconciliation
    www.austkii.edu.au/au/other/IndigLRes/car/1994/5/1.html

Part 3

Sport, identities and alternative lifestyles

INTRODUCTION

The six chapters that form the third part of this book critically examine the quest for recognition. The character and the scale of the struggle for recognition in and through sport have changed dramatically. Many of the world's social conflicts are driven by more than just struggles over gender, race, religion, class and other multiple forms of social division and identity. Part 3 attempts to develop an account of recognition through sport that accommodates the full complexity of social identities instead of one that promotes reification and separatism. This section builds upon some of the issues raised in Chapter 3 which identified aspects of identity and lifestyle as key aspects of any post-twentieth-century analysis of sport, culture and politics. Part 3 of this book is divided into six chapters that may be briefly introduced through the following summaries of the areas covered in each chapter.

Sport, violence and deviance

How do we know that our neighbour is not a serial football hooligan or staunch supporter of blood sports? Football and blood sports are only two sports which have been associated with different forms of violence. The whole question of identities is far more complex than these questions imply. It is very unusual for a person to have just one identity since we live in societies in which sport and related activities help to sustain, confer and challenge multiple identities that are both conformist and deviant depending on the context and the time. The duality of sport is such that sport is seen as both a source of violence and crime but also a partial cure to a perceived problem of violence and youth crime in particular. Within liberal accounts of sports policy in the West, sport is continually linked to forms of intervention aimed at ameliorating or changing crime rates among certain groups. The terrain of sport, violence and deviance is fluid with player violence, spectator violence, bodily violence including drug abuse, blood sports and other forms of violence in sports being only some of the rich substantive areas which can open up an investigation or critical enquiry. There are a number of liberal and non-liberal explanations of the relationship between sport and violence. The economic argument against sports violence centres on the risk of injury and loss of livelihood as a result of foul play. The issue of violence in women's sport has been brought to the fore in relation to current gender relations in sport. Chapter 9 draws upon some of these areas while exploring sport, violence and deviance in relation to some people's identities and quest for recognition and excitement. How should we think about the changing relationship between sport, violence and deviance?

Sport, body and society

The body has been the focal point for many new research streams in sport, culture and society. Four main reasons for this have been (i) the importance of the body as a personal project and cultural object; (ii) the impact of feminisms and other forms of intervention upon the engendered nature of the body in sport; (iii) the development of the ageing process on sporting bodies and (iv) the way in which the body in sport is thought of differently within and between different cultures and societies. How should we think about sporting bodies in the twenty-first century? Should sporting bodies be thought of in terms of being constrained, symbolic, liberated and/or naturalistic? Body culture has been central to the framing of policies involving sport in many of the Scandinavian countries. Does sport continue to be a vehicle for controlling, regulating, disciplining and punishing the human body? Does high performance sport have an impact upon the way athletes in later life think about the body? Chapter 10 provides the basis for students and researchers acquiring a sound grasp of some of the fundamental ways in which sports bodies and societies are inextricably linked to issues of identity and recognition.

Sport and the environment

The environment, environmental movements and environmental policies have impacted upon our knowledge and thinking about sport, culture and society. The historical and systematic relationship between sport and the weather has only recently been the subject of enquiry while the determining impact of the environment has been regularly commented upon in relation to a number of sporting phenomena. The emergence of Kenyan and Ethiopian dominance in athletics is misleadingly often attributed to single factor explanations such as high altitude and even here it is often the high altitude factor that is stressed or prioritised over other environmental-social factors such as lifestyle. The 2000 Sydney Olympic Games in Australia were seen to be the first Green

Olympic Games. Environmental movements such as Greenpeace were ambivalent about such a claim, arguing that the 2000 Sydney Olympic Games were both a success and failure environmentally. The Global Anti-Golf Movement rooted in Asia has been critical of the financial, environmental and societal impact of golf tourism. In particular parts of the world golf tourism is viewed as problematic since its expansion has created problems for many indigenous populations who seem removed from the profits associated with the promotion of golf as a green and environmentally friendly sport. Does sport contribute to a sustainable environment? What would a radical environmental approach to sport entail? What does the term environmentalism mean and how recent is the debate about sport, the environment and society? Chapter 11 introduces and critically examines the ways in which sport, the environment and society have been thought about in the past and the present.

Sport and religion

In August 2004 an article in a leading British newspaper started with the heading 'Lewis hands surfers never on a Sunday warning'. The article referred to a clash of cultures between those who viewed Sunday as sacred and those who wanted to develop a remote Outer Hebridean island of the west coast of Scotland as one of the major professional world surfing centres. The evolution of Jewish Maccabi Olympic Games serves as a reminder that faith provides a basis for not only separatist forms of provision in education, religion and welfare but also in sport. The aims and objectives of these games are broad but include that of cultivating a deeper understanding and instilling an appreciation of Jewish values within Jewish youth; promoting and encouraging the health, physical fitness and well-being of Jewish youth through participation in recreational and athletic activities; and introducing Jewish youth to the international Maccabi Movement, which presents athletic, cultural, and social opportunities for Jews from around the world. The aforementioned are but two substantive examples of the relationship between two sports and two faiths. At a more general level, does religion help sport cope with the uncertainty of competition (i) by providing a platform for the display of religious symbols and rituals; (ii) by providing a psychological edge in the quest for success or coping with failure and (iii) by establishing team solidarity or (iv) does sport competition reflect religious divisions and conflict in the world today? Chapter 12 looks at the different ways in which sport and religion have come together while at the same time providing a critical overview of the relationship between sport and religion. This relationship is not new, but how and why do various faiths influence sport in the world today? Religious faiths carry a premium in the contemporary world and while some suggest that faith can provide an ethical underpinning for involvement in sport, others may suggest that being in possession of a divinely-prescribed rulebook does not provide the basis for any moral high ground in sport.

Sport, lifestyles and alternative cultures

Sport, lifestyles and alternative cultures have often been associated with the language of opposition, resistance, alienation and exclusion from mainstream sport. The history of alternative sports cultures has to date included a spectrum of studies examining activities such as windsurfing, snowboarding, skateboarding, surfing and a rapid growth in extreme sports. Alternative sports are invariably defined as offering ideological and practical alternatives to mainstream sport and sport values and yet the process by which alternative lifestyles become mainstream activities is not uncommon. Alternative choices to mainstream sport may also involve choices over sexuality, risk and uncertainty, freedom, expression, universalism and life politics. Life politics is not the politics of life chances but lifestyle, identity and in this chapter the consumption of alternative sports. In the more fragmented, uncertain world of the early twenty-first century, are the future alternative choices primarily associated with Western sporting cultures or are the alternatives to mainstream sports arriving from other worlds and communities? Chapter 13 interrogates the social issues that have emerged from research into sport, lifestyles and alternative cultures and questions whether the promise and possibilities of freedom carried with these sports are indeed alternative or extreme or primarily Western fads and fashions.

Sport identities and recognition

In the last quarter of the twentieth century struggles for the recognition of difference in and through sport seemed to have been charged with emancipatory potential. Jackie Robinson broke the colour barrier in baseball in 1946–47 and is generally held up as a pioneer of racial equality, especially by African–American athletes who followed him to riches. In the 1970s Billy-Jean King's aspirations for sexual equality and increased recognition for women on the international professional tennis circuit paved the way for a redistribution of wealth within the world of international professional tennis. According to Eitzen (2003:21) women's professional tennis in 2002 had at least as much fan support as men's tennis, as measured by attendance and television viewing in the USA. With the turn of the century issues of recognition and identity have become even more central and yet the character and scale of these campaigns in sport and other areas have changed. Chapter 14 seeks to re-think the social dimensions of identity politics in and through sport. While individual sporting identities may reflect the complexity of multiple positioning, issues of social inequality in and through sport must include both demands for recognition and economic redistribution of wealth within world sport. This chapter concludes by suggesting that recognition in the world of sport is not best served by being premised upon models of identity politics.

Chapter 9

Sport, violence and crime

Is sport more or less violent today than it was in the nineteenth century? Getty Images

PREVIEW

Violence, sport and the law • European football club championship and violence • Violence in sport and society • Child jockeys and human rights abuse • Anti-slavery campaigners • World Health Organization and violence • Deviance, crime and sport • Deviance and criminal behaviour • Sport as social control • Sport and physical activity as crime prevention • The Twic Olympic Games • Oil violence in Sudan • Risk and violence in sport and society • Deviance, sport and risk • A risk society • Children at risk in sport • Sexual violence in sport • States of denial and world sport.

OBJECTIVES

This chapter will:

■   introduce the reader to previous work linking sport to violence in society;

■   evaluate ways in which sport is used to tackle deviance and crime prevention;

■   comment upon sport as a facet of risk in society and of a risk society;

■   provide illustrative examples of sport, violence and crime;

■   explain the significance of and main ways in which the notion of denial might be considered as a useful analytical tool in the area of sport, violence and crime.

INTRODUCTION

On 2 February 2000 in Vancouver during a National Hockey League (NHL) match a player took a swing, from behind, at another player's head with his hockey stick. The NHL disciplinary body instigated an enquiry while the federal law courts decided to bring formal charges for assault with a weapon against Marty McSorley. The NHL fought the court action on the grounds that the concussion was sustained during an organised game. The court decided that the actions of the player exceeded the limits of the NHL rulebook. The player was suspended from the NHL for a year and, as of the time of writing this book, has still to return. The example is just one of many which has brought the issue of on-field violence through sport to the attention of the criminal law courts and has been used to substantiate a number of assertions relating to changing rates of violence in sport and society. Lawyers will testify that the legal landscape in respect of violent sports participants has changed in parts of the UK such as England. The court has determined that liability will be judged in accordance with the game as it is actually played by the participants of the sport. Participants are therefore open to cases of negligence with respect to individual conduct and behaviour (James and McArdle, 2004). It is important to listen to sociologists such as Dunning and Elias who have constantly reminded us that before accepting uncritically the notion that sport is more or less violent in relation to other sports in other times and places, it is important to establish rates of change over time, and the precise nature of the violence and the different levels of causality that may or may not give rise to intended or unintended acts of violence. Violence in sport is certainly not a new phenomenon.

Throughout the last quarter of the twentieth century the winners of the European Football Club Championship played the winners of the South American Club Championship for the right to call themselves world football club champions or simply the best club football team in the world. The matches between Glasgow Celtic Football Club and Racing Club of Buenos Aires in 1967 and Manchester United Football Club and Estudiantes La Plata in 1968 were reported at the time as being amongst the most brutal and violent matches ever played. In November 1967 the then Celtic goalkeeper, Simpson, was carried from the ground barely conscious having been hit on the back of the head by a brick thrown from the crowd as his team came out to start the second leg of the World Cup Club Final. Celtic lost 1–0 to Racing Club, to force a playoff three days later in Montevideo, Uruguay. Simpson was not fit to play in the match, a game that saw four Glasgow Celtic players being sent off along with two Racing Club players while armed riot police came on to the field, not to protect the players from angry spectators, but from each other (Russo, 2004:5).

One year later, much the same happened when the Argentinian club Estudiantes La Plata met Manchester United. The United team contained England internationals such as Bobby Charlton and Nobby Stiles, who had both played in the 1966 ill-tempered quarter-final World Cup match between Argentina and England, in which the Argentinean captain had been sent off and the England football manager, Sir Alf Ramsay called the Argentinean players 'animals'. Before the game with Manchester United the local Argentinean press had dubbed Nobby Stiles 'The Assassin' while the official match programme described him as a brute. In the match itself Stiles was head-butted and then sent off for dissent, Bobby Charlton needed several stitches in a gashed leg, while in the return leg George Best was sent off for fighting. Throughout the 1970s the World Club Cup (at the time the unofficial world championship decider played between the winners of the South Americas Cup and the European Champions) was neglected by the European Champions and the Japanese Football Association, eager to build the game in Japan, offered to stage the game in 1980. In the 24 years since the match was moved to Japan there has been no hint of the levels of violence that had threatened the existence of the competition during the previous decade. In 2005 the competition has been reformatted to involve the best team from each of the six FIFA confederations, Africa, Asia, the Confederation of North and Central American Football (CONCAF), Europe, Oceania and South America. In the end it was not violence that brought an end to the old competition but commercialisation and the growth of the world game, something that did not seem likely back in the summer of 1967.

VIOLENCE IN SPORT AND SOCIETY

Violence in sport in society has a robust body of literature in that different forms of violence, rates of violence and varying solutions involving sport in relation to violence and deviance have generated a vast amount of research. The above examples are both illustrative and reflective of the fact that a critical contribution to what has been produced to date has evolved out of an interest by sociologists, historians, psychologists and anthropologists in the study of, for example, football hooliganism or other forms of sports violence in different cultures and societies.

Young's (2002) overview of the field of sport and violence directs attention to: (i) different explanations and manifestations of *crowd violence* associated with sports events including but also beyond football; (ii) social and legal contributions resulting from the analysis of *player violence*. These include brutal body contact, borderline violence viewed as part of the culture of the game but prohibited by the official rules of the game; quasi-criminal violence which violates the rules of the game, the law of the given land and the norm accepted by players and criminal violence involving players in which the incidents are so serious that they are deemed to fall outside the boundaries of acceptability and are therefore handed over to the criminal courts; (iii) *other forms of violence related to sport* such as sexual assault and harassment, employment violations of young athletes and the stabbing and stalking of sports heroes and heroines; and (iv) *sports violence and the mass media* and in particular the role of the mass media in producing, legitimating and reinforcing violent forms of behaviour associated with sport.

Human rights abuse

Violence in sport is a phenomenon that is not limited to the West. Regular press briefings from the United Arab Emirates have reported child abuse and human rights violations (Beaumont, 2001:27). Child jockeys as young as 4 years old are regularly sought after for camel races in the Gulf because of their light weight and skill in manoeuvring the animals. The Karachi-based Ansar Burney Welfare Trust (founded by Ansar Burney, a human rights lawyer) claimed in 2001 that as many as 2,000 boys had been smuggled to camps since 1999 despite laws introduced in the UAE in 1998 forbidding the use of young boys in this dangerous sport. The rules of the Emirates Camel Racing Federation forbid the use of riders under the age of 14, or weighing less than 45 kilograms. The trade in boys for camel racing has been the subject of campaigns by both the United Nations (UN) and Anti-Slavery International. Children are sold for up to $3,000 (£2,100) each (Beaumont, 2001:27).

Anti-slavery campaigners have had some success in returning camel slaves. In 1999 the authorities repatriated an 8-year-old Pakistani boy who had been kidnapped to work as a camel jockey. In August 1999, a 4-year-old jockey from Bangladesh was found abandoned and close to death in the desert. In 2000 Anti-Slavery International reported the case of another 4-year-old jockey from Bangladesh whose employer had burnt him on his legs for under-performing. The boy was left crippled. Although some of the children are taken as indentured labourers with the parents' consent, in other cases children are drugged and abducted. In November 2001 UAE police rescued two Pakistani brothers aged 6 and 4 who had been kidnapped to work as jockeys (Beaumont, 2001:27).

In the second half of 2001, the Committee on the Rights of the Child monitored the situation of child rights in Oman, Qatar and the UAE. It expressed serious concern that sometimes very young children are involved, are trafficked, particularly from Africa and South Asia, are denied education and healthcare and that such an involvement in sport produces serious injuries and fatalities. When questioned about the camel races, members of the delegation from Oman explained that 'camel riding was considered a sport, not a job and that participation of children in it was a source of pride for both children and their parents' (David, 2005:178). The delegates from Qatar stated that addressing the issue of the involvement of children in camel racing was a priority for the government.

At this stage it is appropriate to examine some key themes that have been associated or related to the notion of sport, violence and crime. In the technical sense of the word the World Health Organization (WHO, 2002:5) defines violence as

> The intentional use of physical force or power, threatened or actual, against another person or against oneself or a group of people, that results in or has a high likelihood or resulting in injury, death, psychological harm, mal-development or deprivation.

This chapter develops at least three themes by means of providing a critical evaluation of the broad field of sport, violence and crime. At the heart of this is the concerted attempt to emphasise the changing nature of sport, violence and crime and to draw attention to the fact that teachers and researchers in the field of sport, culture and society have moved the study of sport, violence and crime some way beyond the areas of football hooliganism, sport and deviant youth sub-cultures, violence in sport and changing rates of violence in sport and society through the ages. The aim is simply to prompt thinking about the nature of sport, violence and crime by broadening the horizons of understanding in the hope that a questioning attitude to understanding others might enable us to better understand ourselves with others.

DEVIANCE, CRIME AND SPORT

Giddens (2001:237) suggests that it would be a mistake to regard crime and deviance wholly in a negative light. Any society that recognises that human beings have diverse values and concerns must find a space for individuals who do not always conform to the norm followed by the majority. Academics who develop new ideas in politics, science, sports studies, art or other fields are often viewed with hostility at first by those who hold on to orthodox ideas. The introduction of the wearing of seat belts in cars was met with hostility and scepticism when it was first introduced in the United Kingdom. The emergence of rule changes in different sports has often been initially met with hostility. People fiercely resisted ideas such as freedom of the individual and equality of opportunity at the time they were introduced and yet they are viewed to day as being accepted ideals in many parts of the world. To deviate from the dominant norms of any society or sport takes courage and conviction and is often a key part of the process of change. In this sense deviance may be viewed as behaviour that transgresses commonly held norms in any culture or society but it need not necessarily be viewed in a negative way.

One general comment might be to think about the relationship between criminal violence and societies that experience higher rates of individual liberties. Are crimes of violence inevitable in societies where rigid definitions of conformity are applied? In some societies such as Holland or the Scandinavian countries, where a wide range of individual freedoms and progressive toleration of activities are deemed to exist, rates of violent crime are low. Conversely in countries where individual freedoms are restricted are the levels of violence higher? Giddens (2001) asserts that a society that is tolerant towards deviant behaviour need not necessarily suffer social disruption. Perhaps it is utopian to suggest that a good outcome might be to work towards the norm where individual liberties are joined to social justice in a social order in which inequalities are not so glaringly large and in which everyone has a chance to lead a fulfilling and satisfying life. If freedom is not balanced with equality and if a lack of self-fulfilment is the norm then it is likely that deviant behaviour would be channelled towards socially destructive ends. Sport within this context has historically often been viewed as a means of social control, a means of curbing or deflecting deviant behaviour and yet as Bauman (2001) and others have pointed out, no other form of social control is more efficient than the spectre of insecurity that hangs over the heads of the controlled. The pragmatic key to any strategy that involves sport as a mechanism for either increasing rates of violence or controlling rates of deviant behaviour lies with knowing what is appropriate and what is not and when and where certain interventions should be taken forward.

According to Coakley (2003:197), the study of deviance in sports presents at least four interesting challenges. First, the forms and causes of deviance in sports are so diverse that no single theory can explain all of them. Second, actions, ideas and characteristics accepted in sports may be defined as deviant in the rest of society. Third, deviance in sports often involves an uncritical acceptance of norms, rather than a rejection of them. Finally, that training in sports has become medicalised to the point that athletes use medical technology in ways that push normative limits. While it may not be necessary to provide a wholly convincing theorisation of deviance through sport it is possible to provide more of a sense of what deviance means in sport. Thinking about deviance in sport has for sometime moved beyond the notion of deviance as being attributed to forms of behaviour, or that deviance in sport should be measured against patterns of norm violation in sport, or that deviance is a social construct, a stigma or label bestowed upon participants in sport who breach the changing norms of behaviour in sport at any given time. One of the central tensions inherent within evaluations of deviance in sport or whether sport may be used as an instrument of social control is whether or not deviance is associated with behaviour of a particular person or whether deviance is a feature of certain kinds of social structure, or social formation. It is a sympathy for the latter that has in part characterised one of the most recent and fluid contributions to the study of sport which draws attention to the fact that deviance through sport may be contingent upon a particular type of society in which it is important for individuals to have a heightened sense of awareness of who they are, an identity that is the object of an individual reflexive self-activity (Bauman, 2000b).

In one of the most refreshing and recent contributions to an understanding of specific aspects of the broad field of violence and related areas in sport, Blackshaw and Crabbe (2004) seek to suggest that what is required today is to recast the sociology of deviance as the sociology of 'deviance' – the emphasis here being on the last word. It is suggested that we need a better interpretation in order to understand the complexity of the social world of sport while at the same time recognising that notions of deviance will always be contested and influenced by the events of the time (Blackshaw and Crabbe 2004:14). In many ways they play the popular sociology of sport game of the 1970s, 1980s and 1990s by attempting to claim that particular aspects of sport in society should be thought of in a different way and they do this by systematically critiquing and engaging with approaches to the sociology of deviance that have hitherto got in the way of what they want to say.

The strategy involves the following steps: (i) arguing that attempts to explain deviance in sport to date have been useful but none the less lacking in some aspect and are at the very least problematic for understanding deviance in sport today; (ii) substantiating the case that the everyday make-up of contemporary sport is increasingly characterised by the experiences of deviance and that we need new ways of re-imagining deviance and sport through the notion of performativity and (iii) arguing that an examination of the uses of the categorisation of 'deviance' may help to provide for an understanding of how power and social control continue to be exercised in today's world of sport and broader society. It is in many ways a critical synthesis of the sociology of deviance as applied to sport and has the hallmarks of much of the strategy adopted by those who used classical sociology in previous decades to stake a claim and direction for certain aspects of sport. Instead of the driving force being a Marx, a Weber, an Elias or Durkheim the guru behind the mask is very much to be located in the work of Zygmunt Bauman. In a critical statement Blackshaw and Crabbe (2004:15) reveal, drawing on Bauman, that if sociology in its twentieth-century format was too preoccupied with the circumstances of conformity, obedience and consensus making, the challenge facing sociology today is the matter of choice between taking responsibility as its focus or by asserting that responsibility for one's actions need not be taken. In their own words 'their approach then is to create a disorderly inquietude out of what has already been written about the sociology of deviance and provide a new beginning' (Blackshaw and Crabbe (2004:15)) – rather than an end in itself.

Just as approaches about sport and deviance need rigorous critical scrutiny so too do questions about sport and physical activity as strategies in crime prevention. Crime prevention may not be the primary objective of sport and associated activities but it is often, sometimes mistakenly, argued that such activities may be a positive strategy in crime prevention. The conclusions from one such approach are presented in Box 9.1. Many of the arguments about the positive role that sport can play in the area of crime prevention tend to draw upon some or all of the arguments presented in this box.

The role of organised sports and cultural activities for young people in many countries is often linked to the expectation that investment in deprived areas in this way will help to reduce street crime and rates of robbery. In January 2002 Tessa Jowell, the UK Culture Secretary, hailed the success of 'Splash Extra Schemes' in that through publicly funded investment in sport and the arts it claimed to have brought about a 5.2 per cent fall in local crime (Jowell, 2002). The five main crimes commonly associated with youth offending are motor crime, domestic burglary, robbery, criminal damage and drug offences. This cross-government street crime initiative in England during the summer of 2001 received £8.8 million of public funds attached to deprived neighbourhoods and city centres and involved some 91,000 young people between the ages of 13 and 17. The male/female split was approximately 62 per cent to 38 per cent, marking a slight increase in the number of females participating when compared with the previous year. Around 2.5 million hours of activity were delivered at the cost of around £2.60 per hour. The results suggested that street crime and robbery fell by 31 per cent in those parts of the country in which the

BOX 9.1 CRIME PREVENTION THROUGH SPORT AND PHYSICAL ACTIVITY

An Australian study by Cameron and MacDougall (2000) through the Australian Institute of Criminology concluded that in relation to young people:

- It appears that sport and physical activity can reduce crime by providing accessible, appropriate activities in a supportive social context. In other words, sport and physical activity must be connected positively within the social fabric of groups and communities.
- Sport and physical activity-based interventions must be conducted in collaboration with a range of other strategies and sectors.
- Elite sporting bodies can be involved in programmes directly aimed at particular crimes or communities.
- It is essential to consider how the design, location and funding of sporting and recreational infrastructure contributes to social cohesion, and avoids taking sport and physical activity out of its social context.
- The cases do not suggest 'one size fits all' strategies; instead, they represent the value of community development approaches to tailor programmes to particular needs. Nevertheless, this should not prevent us from suggesting common strategies and processes, and collecting examples of good practice.
- Recreation and sport programmes established for the explicit purpose of crime prevention should be subject to rigorous evaluation.
- Programmes should be based on evidence that a problem exists, and that the solution works.
- Programmes should be sustainable.
- Evaluations should aim to identify the factors that influence crime reduction and change in the young person.

Source: 'Trends and Issues in Crime and Criminal Justice: Crime Prevention through Sport and Physical Activity' at 2004 Australian Institute of Criminology – http://www.aic.gov.au/publications/tandi/tandi165.html

schemes ran compared to an increase of 56 per cent in areas where the schemes did not run (Jowell, 2002). Similarly, in other parts of the UK twilight basketball schemes have been partially aimed at diverting young people from crime and anti-social behaviour while combating drug, alcohol and other physical abuse by young people (www.scottishrocks.co.uk). In an evaluation of the role of sport in preventing crime in areas of deprivation the Scottish Executive (2000:2), drawing on the work of Coalter, Allison and Taylor, suggest that sport is most effective when combined with programmes addressing wider issues of personal and social development and that short-term funding often means that such interventionist projects rarely last long enough to achieve meaningful, sustainable impacts.

The Twic Olympic Games

Sport is a powerful seductive force in drawing people beyond their immediate circumstances rather than ensuring submission to them. By 2002 Sudan had been at war for the worst part of 50 years. Its peoples have endured bombing, slave traders and pillaging troops. Life had been shattered and through the staging of the Twic Olympics sport ensured not a level of normality, but a moment of tolerance and compassion, with the important fact being not the winning or taking part but that the contest had taken place at all (Harris, 2002). The Twic Olympics was the beginning of an aspiration for a Games for Southern Sudan. Currently only the people of the Twic County, one of the border regions that lies adjacent to the Arab land of the North, compete. Twic is divided into six districts, or payams, and each January a team of athletes from each district gather to compete at football, volleyball, dancesport athletics and tug of war. The competitors are lots of people like James who was drafted into the army at the age of 11, 'does not smile and in playing sport points out that nothing is normal for us' (Harris, 2002:28). James fought the Nuer as a child soldier but as an almost teenage athlete at the Twic Olympics he races with them and against them while commenting that there is now peace between the Dinka and the Nuer (Harris, 2002:31).

Oil is the reason why tribes such as the Nuer have become displaced in Sudan. It is perhaps the last thing that at the time Southern Sudan needed because oil in the south means that the north will not let go of the south while there are riches to be wrestled from the ground. Implicit in the conflict are the multinational energy companies such as Canada's Tailsman Energy, Malaysia's Petronas and Sweden's Lundin Oil and there is little that local people, even rebels, can do to get in the way of the oil companies. The oil violence that is at the heart of the troubles takes place despite the fact that before any oil can be exploited there has to be peace but in Sudan there are worse atrocities than the oil wars and the thousands of child soldiers. Each dry season, columns of horsemen made up of the nomadic Arab tribes burn villages, kill the men and take women and children back north as slaves. Slaves such as Mowien Akway, whose 15 years of life include four spent captive in the north, was branded with a hot iron across his legs with his crime being to complain of long days spent herding his master's cattle. He played volleyball in the Twic Olympics along-side Aguek Athie who was taken from her home by mounted raiders and would not speak of the suffering she had received at the hands of her Arab master (Harris, 2002:31). At the end of these Twic Olympic Games the district with the most medals will be declared the winner with the prize being a mechanised flour grinding mill. In a country with few roads or even brick buildings, or little of that which is deemed the norm by other standards and values, this is worth competing for.

For nations used to the extravagance of the modern Olympic Games or even the £8.8 million investment in sporting initiatives to help reduce crime in the UK, the Twic Olympics offer a surreal parallel. At the opening ceremony, each district had a flag bearer at its head, carrying a homemade banner with stars, or leopards or bulls crayoned on. Behind them marched the athletes and an effort was made to keep colours uniform within each district. Few in Sudan can afford to choose their clothes with care, none of the athletes wore shoes and yet the significance was not the dress of the athletes but that it was taking

207

place at all. It is also a reminder that living in an international or even globalised world means being aware of the pain, misery and suffering of countless people whom we will never meet through sport or otherwise. It raises a relative perspective upon questions of both crime and violence. In a world of global dependencies with no corresponding global polity and few tools of global justice, the rich are free to pursue their own interests while paying little attention to the rest – is not this too a crime or violence of another order?

RISK AND SEXUAL VIOLENCE IN SPORT AND SOCIETY

A question that still remains is whether or not a society at risk or a risk society is really as bad as many commentators might suggest. The notion of risk is active in other chapters, notably Chapter 13 where it helps to add meaning and understanding to the development of alternative or extreme sports. Whilst the spectre of risk increasingly hangs over us in terms of environmental disasters, Blackshaw and Crabbe (2004:54) remind us that it is the secure, monotonous, repetitive character of the contemporary condition that contributes to individuals engaging with risk. They draw upon: Midol and Broyer (1995), to note that it is partly a vision of risk society that influences the take up of a variety of extreme or whiz sports; Pilz (1996), to suggest that it is the sense of unselfconscious adventure that can help make sense of forms of German football hooliganism; and Rojek (1995), to illuminate that experiences at the edge of leisure are related to testing our limits in order to experience intense moments of pleasure and excitement. Most emphatically Blackshaw and Crabbe (2004:55) endorse an adapted working of Rojek's idea of abnormal leisure to suggest that such activities are always likely to occur in societies that set moral limits on what is and is not acceptable normal behaviour.

Debates about the emergence of a risk society also highlight a set of concerns pertinent to the individual at the beginning of the twenty-first century. Just as thinking socially about societies is a reflexive activity, the relationship between risk and identity also involves personal, individual reflexivity. These modern dynamics of identity have helped Cole (2002:445) make sense of what she refers to as embodied deviance and sport. The body plays a normative/non-normative role in forging identity through developing normal/ abnormal bodies that conjure up images of controversial sporting bodies – corrupt, criminal, cyborg, grotesque, hybrid, monstrous, subversive, queer and violent body images all of which represent forms of identity through sport and a perceived level of risk for the individual. In the contemporary world, argues Giddens (2001), individuals tread a tightrope between risk and opportunity. Individuals are obliged to choose between a vast array of lifestyle choices to the extent that everyday life amounts to an amalgamation of calculated risks. Risk opens up the individual to uncertainty whilst simultaneously serving the needs of increasingly individualistic cultures and identities. It forces him or her to live an uncertain life because there are so many choices.

Whilst individualisation may appear to be liberating on the surface it potentially undermines the ontological well-being of the individual. The individual is less and less certain about whether his or her actions are appropriate. He or she is more likely to feel that the world is quite literally spiralling out of control. The march towards global sports consumption may have liberated individuals from the constraints of sport and the local community but at the same time traditional forms of protection and support have also been lost as the shift towards global sport has created new political priorities. The violent litigation culture of contemporary professional sport may have contributed to the sense of risk in sport in society also being a paranoid society in which the perception of risk is either real or has grown out of all proportion. In December 2004 the Manchester United and England forward Wayne Rooney was served a three-match suspension after admitting a charge of violent conduct in a match against Bolton Wanderers. Commenting on the incident and changes in the game of professional football the Manchester United Captain Roy Keane added that

> a lot of players seem to be getting players booked or sent off . . . There are a lot of cases where players are reacting and trying to get fellow professionals into trouble. It's disgraceful – it needs to stop. Lots of stuff goes on in a game and if you went down every time a player touched you, every player would be down. They are trying to con the referee, con their fellow players and con the crowd
>
> (*Herald* 31 December 2004:36)

What Keane was actually alluding to was that the objective level of the risk of being sent off and being punished for violent conduct has changed and that the individual antics of players have meant that the perception of the risks associated with violent conduct has grown out of all proportion.

It is important not to forget that sociologists have portrayed children and/or young people as being at the forefront of both new and old forms of risk and violence. Young people are facing a greater diversity of risks and opportunities than ever before. Traditional family, work, school and sporting environments are more unpredictable and less secure and the journeys into adulthood are for some becoming increasingly precarious. Moreover because there is a much greater range of pathways to choose from, children may develop the impression that their own route is unique and that the risks they face have to be overcome as individuals rather than members of a collectivity. In concrete terms Hari (2002:24) reminds us that poverty is plainly a factor in the formation of what have become labelled 'feral children', the right-wing term referring to some of the most disadvantaged kids in Britain who have literally been raised without family support or without homes in urban inner-city housing estates. Kids Company is a responsive network set up in many of Britain's inner cities that aims at helping what the British right-wing press have dubbed feral children. Talking of these kids Hari (2002:25) reports 'It's not like these kids want much, they only ever have one pair of trainers, not five but it is not unreasonable for them to want one pair'. For poor kids in Britain's inner cities many areas are desolate, shrinking amounts of public space, no leisure centres and children who might once have played in parks, fields or even streets now have nowhere to go.

Ironically some of the most appealing avenues of escape in certain circumstances are risky forms of behaviour such as drug-taking, alcohol consumption, exercise addiction and sports consumption which simply serve to accentuate the risky and unpredictable nature

209

of youth lifestyles in a changing world. It is also important not to forget that children are in some respects equally threatened by the uncertainties of a risk society. Are children today more at risk of sexual abuse and violence in a sports context than in other settings, such as home or school? The author of one of the most comprehensive studies of sexual abuse in sport believes that we know too little to draw any conclusions (Brackenridge, 2001). So far only one study, in Norway, has compared the prevalence of sexual harassment in and outside the context of sport with the initial results revealing that twice as many athletes as non-athletes have experienced sexual harassment from authority figures (Council of Europe, 2000:6). Many experts believe that sexual harassment, abuse and violence in sports are widely under-reported due to the fact that many victims – mainly female, but also male – hesitate to report these abuses. They do not trust the system or society to respect their right to confidentiality and appear to become resigned to frequent acts of verbal and physical harassment in the strongly male-dominated world of sport. In 1998 studies in both Canada and Norway revealed that athletes experience a negative and uncomfortable environment ranging from mild sexual harassment to abuse (David, 2005:94).

Issues of sex discrimination, sexual harassment and sexual abuse in sport bring into question both the nature of sport within a risk society but also the very definition of violence that operates within sport, culture and society. Brackenridge (2002:257) questions any narrow definition of violence in sport from the point of view that one of the most important aspects of power in sport is the power to name or resist definitions made by those in power. With reference to sexual exploitation of children and women both within and beyond sport, Brackenridge (2002:257) notes that the power of men to define what counts as violence and what does not count often leads to narrow definitions of violence in sport which benefits men. Defining sexual violence purely in physical terms ignores the institutional forms of violence in sport against women, such as the violence of discrimination that is involved in pay, resources, career provision, safety, neglect, deprivation, insensitivity and oppression that, asserts Brackenridge (2002:257), face many women on a day-to-day, week-by-week basis. The solution is simply to define violence as that which violates and consequently allows the issue of violence in sport to be viewed in systemic terms rather than interpersonal terms. Brackenridge is right to question the notion of violence that has tended to operate in sport and her critique is a progressive and valuable step forward. Any evaluation of this and other research has also to note that paying exclusive attention to coaches and abused sports men and women tends to overlook other groups including 'experts' who are charged with identifying and protecting young people and/or children and others at risk in sport and society.

The social theory or notion of a risk society may not provide all the answers in helping students, teachers and researchers thinking about risk, violence and sport but what it does do is provide a useful framework or intervention within which you can come to your own conclusion about the nature of the problems and the solutions in the area of sport, violence and crime. It is particularly important that the notion of a risk society or a society at risk is not simply descriptive but adopts a critical approach to sport, violence and crime and perhaps the question is rather what can we learn about normal processes in different parts of the world that are either risky or seek to comprehend misfortune in the form of risk. If we were to try to prevent all undesirable consequences the danger might be inactivity due to the nature of the task, however in a society of risks the issues derive not so much from what each person does in isolation but from the very fact that because they often perceive a state of isolation the actions are often unco-ordinated and dispersed. If global sport is framed as a risk and if global sporting processes are taken to be a set of processes that no one controls then this should not be viewed as a reason for inaction simply because such forces are deemed to be overwhelming. Nor is the answer to the magnitude of the challenge of social change one of denial.

STATES OF DENIAL IN WORLD SPORT

Imagine for a moment a nice 30-something couple, interested in sport or fitness or exercise, having just finished a work-out or run and sitting with their coffee and newspaper in New York, London, Paris, Milan, Toronto, or some other epicentre of Western sport. They pick up the sports section of the newspaper and read about child jockeys being sold into slavery as camel racers, or of the hundreds of refugees who participated in the Twic Olympic Games in Southern Sudan, or of the street cleansing and removal of people from public spaces that accompanies certain visits of the International Olympic Committee to cities aspiring to host the Olympic Games, or of the World Cup Qualifying game of football which was interrupted because of claims of witchcraft, or of the illegal trafficking of young football, baseball and ice-hockey players across the frontiers of world sport, or of the sexual violence in sport mentioned in the previous section of this chapter, not to mention the opportunities for any sporting life or involvement denied the official number of 15 million Aids orphans world-wide or the 500 million children who have no access to sanitation facilities or those children who have accounted for 50 per cent of those killed in war between 1990 and 2003 (*Herald*, 10 December 2004).

To pick but one specific example – the case of Kailu, the Indian boy sold into labour at the age of 14. At his age other boys might dream of playing cricket or hockey for their country or of playing sport with friends at school and at home but these are areas of life, even dreams, that Kailu does not have access too. Kailu was among 200 boys from one village sold on to landlords to work in sugar, cane and rice fields. The transfer fee for Kailu was 1,200 rupees. He gets up at seven, carries out a 12-hour shift in the field, followed by housework before going to bed at midnight, before doing the same the next day (*Herald Magazine*, 11 December 2004:5). What does this news do to our 30-something sportsmen and women in New York, London, Paris, Milan or Toronto? What goes through their minds and does this register as part of the experience or lack of access to world sport today or is the response to the uncomfortable personal and political realities of world sport one of denial and evasion by individuals and states? Are these and other states of denial in world sport not also part of the reality of sport, violence and crime in the twenty-first century?

At least one common thread runs through these and many other stories of denial in world sport and that is that people, sports organisations, governments and even societies are often presented with information that is too disturbing, threatening or anomalous to be fully absorbed or acknowledged. The information is therefore somehow repressed, disavowed, pushed aside or reinterpreted. Blocking out, turning a blind eye, shutting off, not wanting to know, seeing what we want to see . . . these are all expressions of denial. At times denial may appear to be wholly an individual matter, but many forms of denial are public, collective and highly organised. The denial of certain matters of sport in society is often officially subtle – putting a gloss on the truth, setting the public sports agenda, spin-doctoring, leaks to the sports press and media, selecting victims for verbal abuse. Many classic sporting examples exist, none more typical than those fearful words that 'the board is behind the manager' or 'the player is not for sale' or 'no deal has been done behind closed doors'.

Cultural and social denials such as those in sport are neither wholly private nor officially organised by the state, since whole societies may slip into modes of denial independent of the authorities that are the official world of sport, the organisations, the clubs, the ministries and individuals. People, at times, tend to believe information that they know is false or fake in order to express their allegiance to sports slogans and ceremonies and rituals in the name of loyalty, identity, and other structures such as class, nation and religion. When sport denies something is it aware of what it is doing or is it an unconscious defence mechanism to protect sport from some unwelcome truths? Despite evidence to the contrary, many clubs for decades continued to deny that racism in sport was a problem in Britain – despite the physical and verbal abuse of players, and the lack of a non-white presence in positions of authority in British sport. Can there be cultures of denial in sport and how do organisations such as the United Nations, the Council of Europe, the World Health Organization or the International Olympic Committee try to overcome public indifference in certain countries towards violence in sport, to violations of children's rights and to criminality in the field of sport? The continued need for transparency and accountability in world sport, the greater scrutiny of public figures and the regular exposure of their private lives could no doubt lead to a corrosive cynicism about prospects for change in certain countries where athletes are bought and sold and where agents and middle-men stop monies going to where they are needed. At the very least it could create a reflex suspicion of official denials with regards to sports, violence and crime.

SUMMARY

The problem of violence in sport and how to lessen or prevent it is perhaps one of the most difficult questions to answer within the area of sport, culture and society. Clashes of viewpoints in sport, culture and society are often about how we should relate to basic dilemmas and problems. In this sense the study of sport, violence and crime is no different from many other areas covered within this book. The chapter has kept the notion of violence as wide open as possible in order to emphasise that the study of sport, violence and crime is not just limited to the phenomenon of crowd violence and player violence. It would be a mistake to regard this area of investigation in such narrow terms and as such this chapter has drawn upon the themes of deviance, crime and sport, risk and sexual violence in sport and states of denial in world sport. All of these themes and more raise all sorts of issues pertinent to sport and life at the beginning of the twenty-first century. Sport and related areas are no different from other areas of society in that statements of denial emerge rapidly when the personal and political ways in which many of the uncomfortable realities of sport in the twenty-first century in its broadest sense are avoided and evaded by both individuals and states. It has been suggested in this chapter that sport may be thought of at times as a form of cultural denial.

The literature on sport, violence and crime is often written as if it is irrelevant to the fact that the free market of sport in late capitalism accentuates violence and denial, in the sense that vast swathes of the world's populations are excluded from sport and are viewed as being marginal and superfluous to the real entertainment for the more affluent sectors, countries and regions. The exclusion and segregation of enclaves of losers and redundant sports populations separated from enclaves of winners, health enthusiasts and spectators in their guarded gyms, gated sports stadiums and modern sports villages is in itself a form of violence. The success stories are viewed as the real Olympics and not the Twic Olympics and yet these two very different worlds of sport are both part of the world of sport in the twenty-first century.

Furthermore, cultural denials are neither wholly private nor officially organised by global sporting organisations, states or powerful individuals. The social and cultural denials that accompany the façade of drugs in sport, sexual violence, racism and child labour are all areas of investigation that should not be excluded from the coverage of sport, violence and crime in the contemporary world. There is a very real danger of failing to recognise that that which violates is not simply limited to violence for private gain (crime), or violence between states and non-state actors (war, repression, terrorism), cultural and/or personal violence but all forms of violence. All of this can be acknowledged by the student of sport, culture and society without needing to deny or turn a blind eye to the very positive part played by sport in areas of the world suffering from atrocities of human violence, material greed and forms of conflict.

KEY CONCEPTS

Anti-slavery campaigns	Power
Compassion	Player violence
Crowd violence	Risk
Denial	Risk society
Deprivation	Racial abuse
Deviance	Racial violence
Identity	Sexual harassment
Labelling	Sexual violence
Media-sports violence	Violence
Normative values	Tolerance

KEY READING

Books

Blackshaw, T. and Crabbe, T. (2004). *New Perspectives on Sport and Deviance*: *Consumption, Performativity and Social Control*. London: Routledge.
Coakley, J. (2003). *Sport in Society*: *Issues and Controversies*. New York: McGraw Hill, 200–231.
David, P. (2005). *Human Rights in Youth Sport*: *A Critical Review of Children's Rights in Youth Sport*. London: Routledge.
Dunning, E. (1999). *Sport Matters*: *Sociological Studies of Sport, Violence and Civilization*. London: Routledge.
Young, K. (2002). 'Sport and Violence'. In Coakley, J. and Dunning, E. (eds) *Handbook of Sports Studies*. London: Sage, 382–408.

Journal articles

Benedict, J. (1997). 'Arrest and Conviction Rates of Athletes Accused of Sexual Assault'. *Sociology of Sport Journal*, 17(2): 171–197.
Hawkins, B. (1998). 'Evening Basketball Leagues: The Use of Sport to Reduce African American Youth Criminal Activity'. *International Sports Journal*, 2(2): 68–77.
James, M. and McArdle, D. (2004). 'Player Violence or Violent Players? Vicarious Liability for Sports Participants'. *Tort Law Review*, 131(12): 131–146.
O'Hear, M. (2001). 'Blue-collar Crimes/White-collar Criminals: Sentencing Elite Athletes who Commit Violent Crimes'. *Marquette Sports Law Review*, 12(1): 427–447.

Further reading

Beaumont, P. (2001). 'Kidnapped Children Sold into Slavery as Camel Racers'. *Observer*, 3 June: 27.
Brackenridge, C. (2002). 'Men Loving Men Hating Women: The Crisis of Masculinity and Violence to Women In Sport'. In Scraton, S. and Flintoff, A. (eds) *Gender and Sport*: *A Reader*. London: Routledge, 255–269.
Cole, C. (2002). 'Body Studies in the Sociology of Sport'. In Coakley, J. and Dunning, E. (eds) *Handbook of Sports Studies*. London: Sage, 439–461.
Jowell, T. (2002). 'Culture Can Cut Crime' at www.culture.gov.uk/global/pressw_notices/archive_2003/dcms06_2003.htm?mo...
Hari, J. (2002). 'Yah Boo to a Daily Mail Myth'. *New Statesman*, 23 September: 23–25.
Harris, P. (2002). 'Jumping the Gun'. *Observer*: *Sports Monthly*, March: 27–34.
Scottish Executive (2002). *Role of Sport in Re-Generating Deprived Urban Communities*. Edinburgh: Scottish Executive Publications at http://www.scotland.gov.uk/crukd01/blue/rsrdua-00.htm

REVISION QUESTIONS

1. Describe and critique the definition of violence provided by the World Health Organization as it might apply in the area of sport, culture and society.

2. Comment upon the role of sport in the area of crime prevention.

3. Explain what is meant by the notion of a risk society and the place of sport within it.

4. Outline and critically comment upon the correlates of gender violence and abuse based on cross-cultural studies, applied to sport as outlined in Brackenridge (2001:146).

5. How might the notion of denial be used to investigate aspects of world sport to day?

PRACTICAL PROJECTS

1. Outline five different policies in which sport is clearly used as an instrument of social control.

2. Compile a report of about 2,500 words on sport and violence in a country of your choice based upon investigating a national newspaper over a five-year period.

3. Use the Google search engine to find out information about the Twic Olympics and other sports competitions in different parts of the world that are aimed at helping countries affected by violence or even war.

4. Visit the websites of the World Health Organization, the United Nations and the Council of Europe and write a report on the official positions taken by these organisations on both violence in sport and children's rights as far as they apply to sport, exercise and physical activity.

5. Visit www.harassmentinsport.com, which is sponsored by Sport Canada and provides information and links to other sites on sexual harassment in sport. Develop a ten-point non-tolerance policy statement aimed at curbing sexual harassment in a sport of your choice.

WEBSITES

Australian Government: Australian Institute of Criminology Paper 165 Crime Prevention through Sport and Physical Activity
   www.aic.gov.au/publications/tandi/tandi1165.html

Department of Culture, Media and Sport (DCMS) on Sport and Crime
   www.culture.gov.uk/global/press_notices/archive_2003/dcms06_2003.htm?mo...

National Coalition Against Violent Athletes
   www.ncava.org

Rocks Twilight Basketball
    www.scottishrocks.co.uk

Sports, culture and the Scottish Executive
    http://www.scotland.gov.uk/crukd01/blue/rsrdua-00.htm

Twic Olympics play for the prize of peace
    http://www.christian-aid.org.uk/news/features/0202twic.htm

Chapter 10

Sport, body and society

Does the sporting body help to reproduce identity, sexuality and differences? © Nan Fang Sports (2005)

OBJECTIVES

This chapter will:

- introduce students, teachers and researchers to a vast body of research that takes as its focus in either a minor or major way sport, body and society;

- examine some of the key ways in which the sporting body is thought about in the twenty-first century;

- consider the argument that sport is a vehicle for disciplining, punishing, controlling and constraining the body;

- critically discuss sport and the body from the perspective of the 'other';

- explain and illustrate the way in which the body has become a marker for identity, recognition and difference in sport and related areas.

INTRODUCTION

Until relatively recently many have tended to view the body as a fixed, unchanging fact of nature, viewed in biological terms rather than as being social, cultural, historical or in terms of political economy. Today both naturalistic and social constructionist views have left their mark upon how academics and others have thought about human embodiment in relation to sport and related areas such as health, fitness and physical activity. Many new ways of thinking about the body have opened up sport, body and society as a rich and vibrant area of research, to such an extent that it is longer possible to think of the body solely in universal, fundamental or natural terms but rather in differentiated and plural terms. As Coakley (2003:140) testifies, changes in the ways that bodies have been socially defined or constructed over the years have contributed to different exchanges concerning how people think about the body in society and most notably in terms of sexuality, ideals of beauty, body image and identity, health, social differences, violence and power, the medical profession and high performance sport to name but a few robust areas of research and teaching.

Influential interventions such as Chris Shilling's *The Body and Social Theory* (1993); Sue Scott and David Morgan's *Body Matters* (1993); and Bryan Turner's *Body and Society* (1996) have all recognised at different periods of time sociology's neglect of the body and argued for divergent approaches to recognising the need to analyse humans as embodied persons. Much of this work has explored the varied cultural meanings attached to bodies and the way they are controlled, regulated and reproduced. The subsequent study of sport, body and society has proliferated into a healthy corpus of knowledge which has, for instance,

- challenged traditional Western ideas about the separation of mind and body;
- questioned the moral, cultural and sociological implications relating to how bodies are protected, probed, monitored, tested, trained, manipulated, re-habilitated and disciplined all in the name of sport;

218

■ questioned the simplistic way in which bodies are differentiated and represented as marks of gender, race, disability, age and other social divisions without really thinking about the recognition of difference or the dangers of thinking in differentiated terms;

■ questioned the way in which body culture figures as an alternative to conventional notions of sports policy.

It would be wrong not to relate the introduction to sport, body and society presented in this chapter to other chapters in Part 3 of this book. The body has figured prominently in accounts of *sports, violence and deviance*. Cole's (2002) review of sport and the body describes the role of science and technology in the production of a modern sporting body, which she describes in both normal and abnormal terms. Deviant/transgressive bodies are viewed as those which challenge or shock societies' orthodox attitudes to the sporting body. The language of deviance and violence is used to explain the appearance of non-normative bodies that do not conform to the conventional wisdom in a domain which often invests dedication to bodily perfection. Such views are often expressed in relation to female and male bodybuilders, male boxers and female bullfighters. Drawing upon the Eliasian analysis of European civilising processes, Shilling (1993) refers to the notion of civilised bodies. Elias's analysis of civilised bodies is both sociogenetic and psychogenetic in that it encompasses long-term processes underlying society's development and the personality structures of individuals. Changing rates of bodily violence, body manners and violence in sport have been drawn upon to substantiate and add weight to the theory of the civilising process. To simplify, the relatively civilised bodily characteristics and/or different rates of violence in sport of those involved in modern sport are compared with their medieval counterparts as a basis for explaining an ongoing process of change.

So, too, has the body figured in debates about *sport, nature and the environment*. Are our bodies to be thought of purely in biological terms or does nature or the environment in which bodies are located in time and space affect the relationship between body, self-identity and society? The naturalistic view holds that the capabilities and constraints of human bodies define individuals and generate subsequent social, political and economic relations. Women have challenged and buried the way in which natural bodies have historically been viewed as being a generic male form. Alternatively socio-biological or natural views of the female sporting body point out that feminists have often reproduced a distortion of the natural female body which because of social pressures requires women to pursue the tyranny of slenderness. The notion of feminine embodiment requires regimes of diet and exercise that are often far from healthy. The tyranny of slenderness is central to Lloyd's (1996) study of feminism, aerobics and the politics of the body. What determines the tyranny of slenderness, the body or the environment and to what extent can we change, manipulate one or the other or both? The relationship between natural bodies competing in natural activities in a natural landscape was, suggests Magdalinski (2004), a primary method of understanding the Sydney 2000 Olympic Games. When Sydney was awarded the 2000 Olympic Games in 1993, its success was in part due to its commitment to an environmentally friendly athletes' Games. The dynamics between spaces, sport and the body, argued Magdalinski (2004:102), revealed a plethora of social assumptions about the nature of nature.

Some of Bryan Turner's seminal contributions to both the sociology of religion and the sociology of body provide possibilities for thinking about *sport and religion*. The human body is typically central to shifting debates about whether modern sport is more or less secular. What we know about the body, sport and religion today exceeds what we knew in the late 1970s when Guttmann's (1978) pioneering history of modern sport from ritual to record informed us that organised games and physical bodily displays were often performed as forms of religious worship in which the outcomes were allegedly determined by religious necessity rather than physical ability. More recently, Hashemi (2000) has reminded us of the constraints that impinge upon the athletic body of Muslim women wishing to train for karate competitions in Afghanistan. In 1998 the second Islamic Women's Games took place – involving athletes from 24 Islamic countries. While much has been written about the place of sport and bodily practices in relation to the consuming body, the relationships between sport and divine bodies, secular bodies, Islamic bodies are potentially rich areas for any student, teacher or researcher wishing to explore sources of human mythology and religious dogma. Add to this Turner's (2000) challenge that the regulated body and the metaphors associated with right-handedness or left-footedness as being regarded as symbols and even sources of evil then the role of religious authority is not just about sport but all forms of body culture on display at festivals, gatherings and other collective rituals that may provide a rich vein of exploration in the past and the present.

SPORT AND THE BODY IN SOCIAL THOUGHT

Analytically speaking there has been a sociological debate about sport and the body in society for a quarter of a century, maybe longer. The range of social thought that has been brought to bear upon the study of sport, body and society is varied and while much progress has been made it would be misleading to suggest that while the importance of the body to fields such as sports studies is developing apace it remains less developed when compared to the centrality of the body to relatively contemporary concerns of social theory and thought. None the less various traditions of social thought have informed our understanding of sport and the body and in this section I should like to draw attention to some of the main contributions to sport and the body in social thought.

Civilised bodies and the quest for excitement

Although the human body is not the central focus of the work of Norbert Elias the analysis of bodily functions, bodily manners and bodily acts were substantive areas of concern that contributed to the theory of the civilising process. A key component of the civilising process was a concerted effort to understand how external restraints on behaviour could be replaced by internal, moral regulation. The civilised body, argued Elias (1978:140), has the ability to rationalise and exert a high degree of control over its emotions, to monitor its actions, and those of others, and to internalise a demarcated set of rules about what is and is not appropriate behaviour. Such a process provided the basis for making a contrast between the civilised and uncivilised body over a period of time (Shilling, 1993).

The notion of the civilising process has informed and sustained a rich vein of social thought that has been captured in collections of essays such as Dunning and Rojek's (1992) *Sport and Leisure in the Civilising Process* and more recently Dunning, Murphy and Malcolm's (2004) *Sports Histories*. One of the principle functions of sport and leisure activities talked about within this body of work was that those activities that took place within the spare-time spectrum were partly devoted to bodily maintenance, the control of emotional thresholds, and the enhancement of body appearance through utilising the outer body as a means of display. Thus the body contributed not only to the performing self but also to the promoting self. Both the quest for excitement and for identity were involved in physical and emotional bodily activities such as the controlled decontrolling of emotions, eliciting different rates of excitement, as well as pleasurable acts such as smiling or less pleasurable acts such as wincing with pain, which are both intentionally deployed symbols that can convey a range of messages as a result of involvement in sport and leisure activities. Sport and the civilising process provide a useful way of thinking about and exploring embodied emotions.

Both in society and the fields of sport the controlled and calculated management of the body becomes increasingly necessary and important for success. Such control is also a prerequisite, according to Shilling (1993:163), for the development of civilised bodies. The development of the civilising process and civilised bodies has involved a progressive social-isation, rationalisation and individualisation of the body. The rationalisation of bodies has been integral to the emergence of sport as form of physical contest of a relatively non-violent type. Despite de-civilising spurts of behaviour, such as witnessed in acts of football hooliganism in England throughout the 1980s and 1990s, by comparison with past eras in general sport as a form of physical contest of a relatively non-violent type was associated with the reduction of violence in society at large. Sport and physical activity provided an emotional release. The violence into which uninhibited drives were channelled in past eras, it is argued, has now been replaced by individuals witnessing mock contests in which behaviour is governed by rules. Sport provides the civilised body with release, with a re-charging, which helps it to return to highly controlled behavioural norms that help in the governing of society (Shilling, 1993:166).

Body, class and physical capital

The work of the French sociologist Pierre Bourdieu has also been central to an understanding of social reproduction. Key ideas such as the body as a symbol of distinction, body habitus, physical capital and social field are evoked by Bourdieu to provide a particular theory of social reproduction. Bourdieu describes his own work as constructivist structuralism. The production of different bodily forms is central to this theory of social reproduction as the symbolic values accorded to particular bodies vary. People's sporting tastes act as signifiers in the constant struggle for distinction. The instrumental body of the working class is differentiated from the bodies of the dominant class. The inter-relationship between social location, habitus and taste helps to produce distinct bodily forms and orientations. Social, cultural and economic processes affect the body for Bourdieu.

Habitus as a specific notion refers to the acquired patterns of thought, behaviour and taste which are said to constitute the link between social structures and social practices. It locates the middle ground between structures and actions. Bourdieu (1990a) likens habitus to the feel for the game but the game is the social game embodied and turned into a second nature of doing things without thinking. Being a competent social actor involves having a mastery over social practices that involves a feel for the game. Having a deeply embodied habitus develops this game. The knowledge of what it means to be a boxer, for example, involves the development of a particular body habitus. Conceived in this way the absorption of certain actions and specific feelings enables boxers to be at ease within a certain habitus, a boxing habitus. Yet it is not just membership of particular communities that such practices involve but also membership of humanity as a whole. Thus the boxer may be part of a particular boxing habitus which in turn is part of a broader habitus that is society. Habitus then is an embodied, internalised schema that structures but does not determine actions, thoughts and feelings (Jarvie and Maguire, 1994:191).

From Bourdieu's work it is clear that bodies are involved in the creation and reproduction of social difference. More specifically, bodies bear the imprint of social class because of three main factors, an individual's social location (material circumstances of daily life), the formation of their habitus and the development of their tastes. As a result of these factors people tend to develop bodies that are valued differently and serve to naturalise social differences through such features as accent, poise and movement. According to Bourdieu (1978), the working classes adopted an instrumental approach to the body in which the body is a means to end. The body tends to be characterised as a machine in relation to health, illness, exercise and lifestyle in that it is always important to put the body right. Working-class attitudes to bodies are marked by the demands of getting by in life and the temporary release from the demands of everyday living. By contrast, the dominant classes are characterised as viewing the body as a project and have available resources to choose whether to place an emphasis on the intrinsic or external functioning of the body. Again in comparison to working-class groups, middle-class groups are deemed to have more control over their health which can be exercised by choosing an appropriate lifestyle.

The relationship between physical activities, body habitus and lifestyles has been explored in a number of studies. Laberge and Sankoff (1988:285) concluded that the structure of relations between different physical practices, different types of attention to the body and various leisure activities provided information about the social meaning of participation in physical activities and the social logics that govern these activities. A summary of the results is presented in Figure 10.1. The variation or pattern of participation by women in physical activities according to social class depended not only upon the different capacities of women with regard to time and money but also the variations in perception and appreciation of the profits and/or immediate or long-term benefits that participation in various physical activities could bring them. That is to say, the relationship between physical activities, body habitus and lifestyle is essentially determined in part by class habitus.

Finally, social class according to Bourdieu, and as illustrated above, was not simply a function of belonging to a particular social category but also how one perceived one's self in relation to that category. Thus the relationship between the body, class and exercise could not be understood purely in terms of what a group or person did, but how they also perceived what they were doing in relation to class activity. The value of Bourdieu's contribution to this discussion is important because it places the body and sport as bearers of symbolic value. The general importance of the body's orientation through sport and leisure activities may be as an expression of elite status but there might also be a mismatch between a person's orientation to their body and a related taste for sport. Thus participation in certain sports might be seen as requiring social, cultural and economic capital before actual preferences or tastes are actualised in terms of participation.

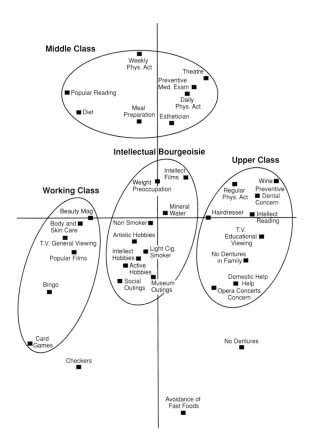

Figure 10.1 Physical activities, women, body habitus and lifestyles

Source: Laberge, S. and Sankoff, D. (1988) 'Physical Activities, Body Habitus and Lifestyles'. In Harvey, J. and Cantelon, H. (eds) *Not Just a Game: Essays in Canadian Sport Sociology*. Ottawa: University of Ottawa Press, 279.

Sexuality and the gendered body

The physical body has been the focus of much research concerning the construction of gender. Gender is experienced through the body and therefore experiences, feelings, representations and the body politic are fundamentally related not only to masculinity and femininity but heterosexuality, homosexuality and other cultures. Body-building for men and women is not only sport but also a body project that involves a practical recognition and changing understanding of the significance of the body both as a personal resource and a social symbol of self and a broader identity. The pervasive influence of new forms of twenty-first-century health consciousness re-confirms the way the body has become a project, the control of which is central, fundamental to gender politics. Plastic surgery has provided alternatives for radical bodily reconstruction in line with contemporary notions of femininity and masculinity of the time. These notions change over time, space and place, are not neutral and involve complex social processes and pressures that vary. They are not homogenous and in this sense bodies are constraining as well as facilitating.

It is impossible to provide an exhaustive list of the ground that has been covered by researchers in terms of gendered bodies, sport and physicality but it is crucial to realise that some of the orthodox questions, while still not being fully answered, have also been added to by a new wave of questions emanating from the study of sport and the gendered body. In a fairly comprehensive overview of this area Scraton and Flintoff (2002) remind us of different levels of analysis present and active at the beginning of the twenty-first century, which include

- theorising gender and acknowledging that shifts in thinking and theory are ongoing;
- the fact that the historical body has also changed as illustrated when one compares the Victorian cult of the family and the early years of female sport with the contemporary progress made by women's football;
- the representations of gendered bodies in sport through the media and, for example, how the body is used in displays of sexuality but also that such media representations contribute to the denial of women or the marginalisation of lesbian or homosexual sports coverage;
- the body diaspora and the ways in which notions of ethnicity, race and diaspora provide alternatives for reassessing the accepted gender hierarchy about sport and the body, for example, the role of the body in offering anti-national, anti-essentialist and non-European sophisticated accounts of the body and sport;
- accounts of different masculinities and men's talk in relation to women's sport, female body-culture, competition and homophobia;
- sexuality and how this manifests itself in sport, gym cultures, exercise clubs, sporting tastes and body movement;
- the body, physicality and power and how different permutations of these notions manifest themselves in terms of violence, sexual abuse, gender orders in sport, sports organisations and struggles/resistance to produce change.

The body, power and knowledge

One of the most fruitful and provocative lines of analysis that has touched upon all of the above and more has been the use of the work of Foucault in relation to the body, power and difference. This has not been limited to one particular form of social difference in that Foucault's ideas on control, discipline, punishment and the body have developed as a means of resistance to such control with possibilities for feminism, masculinity, sport and the emotions, and the body. Many have looked to the work of Foucault for insightful use of concepts such as power and resistance, bodily discipline, surveillance and self-surveillance to position the body in a social context. Foucault was particularly interested in the micro-politics of the regulation of the body and the effects of power on it. Self-surveillance was the means through which the individual, athlete, or women watched their own bodily behaviour to make sure it conformed to a prescribed norm. At the same time the body could be used to resist such control and this includes the implications for the use of the body in exercise, sport and leisure spaces.

Foucault's model of power and knowledge explained very clearly that knowledge is used by agencies wielding the power that they have at their disposal but also through the established language structures through which all forms of imposition on society are made. What is truth is decided by a powerful minority, it regiments and systematically regulates the subject to suit its own goals by operating through a discourse. Foucault believed that a group of people could have the power to influence or create a world-view if they had the knowledge. The exercise of power itself involved the creation and cause to form new objects of knowledge and accumulate new bodies of information. This notion has been applied to discussions about the body and health, the body and sexuality, the body and exercise, the political economy of the body, education and schooling, the body and masculinity to name but a few areas. These areas have been influenced by the idea that power constructs and dominates. The use of power and knowledge has helped to generate discourses about sport, the body, exercise and health that are viewed as natural and normal but are in fact legitimated through the use of power relation and knowledge. Simply put, for Foucault (1977:27) there could be no power relations without the correlative constitution of a field of knowledge, nor any knowledge that did not presuppose and constitute at the same time power relations.

Foucault argued that power was an inevitable part of the production of society, that its presence was dispersed through intellectual and bodily disciplines and that social relations were not to be understood as being dependent upon any single foundation. Gruneau (1999:121) points out that Foucault's influence forced an older generation of social critics writing about sport to broaden an understanding of the relationship between sport, power and the body not to mention radical politics. Various post-modern critics of sport, culture and society became more sensitive to a new line of critical analysis that focused attention on the problematic nature of any account or discussion of constraint or control that gave priority to any one axis of power, social division or one political subjectivity over another. This happened at the same time as new explanations of body, power and difference called into question the possibility of achieving any kind of universal freedoms in or through sport. Yet as will be expanded upon in the last chapter of this section, the work of Nancy Fraser (2000) points to the fact that such a broad Foucauldian approach to body/sport placing an emphasis on self-defined identity fails to connect with other struggles for recognition. Without any normative standards for evaluating if and when more forms of power are more anxious or self-indulgent the danger is always that yet another form of identity politics becomes reduced to just another form of lifestyle politics.

One more general point that needs to be made about the influence of Foucault is that perhaps his own source of power over knowledge, through the writings on the body and sport that his thinking has spawned, continues to be a contradiction. Over the last part of the twentieth century and beyond Foucault has lorded it over the fields of history, literary theory, queer theory, medicine, philosophy, sociology and sport, body and society. Some of his most powerful contributions are that the concept of truth is relative, that madness is a cultural creation and that history is little more than storytelling, which are all familiar. The pervading theme in Foucault's philosophy is that human relations are defined by a struggle for power. Right and wrong, truth and falsehood are but illusions and there can be such a thing as values and therefore such a thing as judgement. Yet many have subsequently suggested that Foucault was not just wrong but he erased any possibility of proving himself to be right since he asserted such things as that the author did not exist, since he or she was conditioned to write by the customs of literature, and the mores of the day. Therefore the body of work that is body, sport and society is nothing more than illusionary. By his own philosophy the logical conclusion leads to the question – how can we believe an author who tells us the author does not exist or the historian who tells us we can't write history or the sociologist of the body who tells us that body and society are illusionary? Foucault's contribution to sport, body and society is self-invalidating and perhaps it is time to listen to the French social historian Jean Baudrillard who asserted that it is perhaps time to forget Foucault (West, 2004).

THE BODY, IDENTITIES AND DIFFERENCES

As partially illustrated above, the study of the body offers endless possibilities and points of entry and exit from historical, geographical and contemporary examinations of sporting identities and differences. Even the most cursory glance at the critical academic literature on sport and related activities such as exercise, physical culture and health provides the reader with an array of bodies – the athletic body; the sporting body; the fascist body; the racialised body; the black body; the oriental body; the engendered body; the civilised body; the body-builder; the female body; the male body; the gay and lesbian bodies; the body habitus and the African body – all of which have been invested in as a basis of telling us about different identities, differences and representations. The rise of identity politics and the place of the body and sport within what Balakrishnan (2002) refers to as the age of identity may have increased our understanding of embodiment in some societies but such an approach also contains certain risks.

Given that the identity model and sport are brought into question and explored further in Chapter 14 of this book the discussion in this section limits itself to commenting upon three central ideas that any student or researcher needs to navigate or at the very least think about. The discussions that follow are necessarily succinct. The first of these is the notion of identities in relation to the body and sport. Although the term 'identity' has a long history, deriving from the Latin root *idem*, implying sameness and continuity, it was not until the twentieth century that the term came into popular usage. The usage of the term in relation to body, sport and society has taken many forms all of which have attempted to reinforce and challenge *essentialist* understandings of sport, body and society. Essentialism refers to that which is a core identity or identities after everything else has been peeled away and the extent to which sport and body cultures reproduce and reinforce essential identities. The historical contribution has highlighted the invented or constructed character of identity associated with many sporting traditions and body styles. The historical approach as with other approaches views identity as essentialist but also *contingent* in that the identities are associated with body change over time and are therefore contingent upon particular histories. The psychodynamic approach to identity, body and sport has attempted to answer the question who am I and to what extent are the sporting and bodily practices I am involved in a reflection of self in a psychodynamic sense? The sociological approach to identity also has links to a theory of self in that a sociological tradition of identity theory has been linked to the symbolic interactionism associated with George Herbert Mead, Erving Goffman and Peter Berger. In this sense body identities have been explained through the process of socialisation, communication and body language all of which have attempted to reconcile the inner subjective creative bodily 'I' with the more outer, partly determined and objective 'Me'. With particular reference to sport, discussions of national identity have drawn upon the notion of sport helping to construct an imagined community while developmental or process sociologists have asserted that sport and the body are but vehicles for an overall quest for identity.

The notion of *identity crisis* has been evoked on a number of occasions to imply that identity only really becomes an issue when a particular, culture, social group, or nation is facing a crisis of identity. The notion of the body or sport reflecting an identity crisis is problematic in that it reduces discussions of body identity to being simply reactionary rather than body or sporting identities being enabling. More importantly the framing of debates about the body and/or sport in this way is not sensitive to particular identity crises unique to sport or body culture at a particular point in time. Did the impact of football hooliganism in the 1980s, 1990s and beyond pose a particular crisis of identity for English football or was English football simply reacting to broader social and cultural forces? On the other hand if sport is viewed as a key component for the expression of national identity then the fragmentation of different parts of the world may pose a particular crisis of identity for particular body cultures at local, national and international levels. Although Chapter 14 will argue that identity politics on its own is relatively meaningless the notion of identity in crisis can contribute to an understanding of sport and body cultures in different parts of the world experiencing large-scale political upheaval or in places where new social forces attempt to dilute, replace or marginalise national identities. For example, to what extent have body cultures helped to reassert a new European identity that threatens national identities? To what extent has sport reflected or enabled forms of reconciliation or a hardened militancy amongst various ethnic identities who were part of the former Yugoslavia? Thus identities that are forged through sport, body and society may matter more if there is a real or perceived crisis of identity, globally, locally, personally and politically.

227

The second crucial concept is the notion of *difference* in relation to the body and sport. The marking of difference is crucial to the construction of identities in sport, body and society. In looking at how identities are constructed they tend to be formed in relation to other identities and thus essential differences are used to signify or represent identities. At its simplest this unsatisfactory trend tends to take the form of binary forms of classification such as us and them; insider and outsider; women and men; black and white; Arab and Jew; Protestant and Catholic; Serb and Croat. All the aforementioned depend upon differences marking particular forms of identity that in turn symbolise or represent forms of social exclusion and political difference. The notion of difference is integral to the understanding, construction and in some cases invention of identities all of which tend to be used to legitimate a particular social order or ways of being. More positively the recognition/acceptance of change and differences involving the body and sport may be seen as positively progressive in that it signifies an acceptance of a rich, diverse perhaps previously excluded set of body cultures such as gay and lesbian sporting culture; a sporting Olympiad rather than the able and disabled Olympics; and a secure place for Muslim Pakistani women in sociological accounts of sport and body cultures rather than a predominance of white/other feminist accounts of sport and the body. In this sense differences in and between sport and body cultures and identities may be viewed as a celebration of bodily diversity, heterogeneity and hybridity. Yet the notion of identity is not the same as difference in that one helps in the construction and legitimation of the other.

The final notion that needs commenting upon is the notion of *representations* in relation to the body and sport. Representation refers to the ways in which images and texts such as articles, books, radio or television programmes reconstruct an account of sport, body and society. Thus a painting, a photograph, a written text about sport and the body are never just an actual account of real sport or physical activity but how the painting, the photograph or the written text has represented sport and the body. Writers about gender and the body argue that representation is continually creating, challenging, re-creating and endorsing stereotypical images, stories, and ideas about identity, sport and the body. The areas of historiography and representation are crucial to developing post-colonial accounts of the sporting body. The work of Bale (2000) and other geographers of sport and Dimeo (2002) and other historians of sport offers alternative epistemological systems or ways of thinking about the sporting body that dislocate Eurocentric or colonial sporting histories and geographies.

Representing accounts of sport identities and the body can never be a neutral activity. Critical representations of sport and the body attempt to wrestle with and provide answers to who am I? What could I be? Who am I like and who do I want to be? Writers such as Bale and Dimeo could do a lot worse than take their lead from Edward Said who argues in *Culture and Imperialism* (1993:230) that studying the relationship between the West and its dominated cultural other is not just a way of understanding an unequal relationship between unequal stories but also a point of entry into studying the formation and meaning of Western cultural practices themselves. Thus Said implied that the discrepancy of power between Western and non-Western sport necessitates that any account of global, international or local sport must take such a disparity into account if we are to accurately understand sport, body and society in its totality and not simply as an illusion of totality. It is worthwhile exploring the issue of other sporting bodies in more detail if for no other reason than that they have made a profound contribution to the story of sport, body and society. The politics of representation are such that all accounts of sport and the body that are promoted as authentic, valid and true need to be closely questioned in order to ascertain just exactly where the authority and coherence for such claims may be located.

Other sporting bodies

In drawing attention to the fact that indigenous Australians grow up in historical contexts of racism both inside and outside sports, Gardiner (2003:43) concludes that indigenous players have to confront a sports culture in which traditionally white codes attempt to dictate, order and define black bodies. The texts that have emerged from indigenous people's lives in Australia have begun to produce an 'other' history of Australian football codes. In reality there is also a rich substantive terrain of women's sport in Africa, Asia and the Middle East but as Hargreaves (2004:197) points out there is a dearth of sport feminist literature from outside the West. She draws our attention to the need to develop multiple complex accounts of women in sport but also to the *vital* point that to many homogenous accounts of sporting identity for women tend to conceal many hidden forms of injustice, discrimination and activism in other worlds. This holds true for work on the body and identity as much as it does for sport. Anne Leseth (2003:243) talking of dance, sport and the body in Dar-es-Salaam contrasts the notion of a Western body image with 'other' points of view and in doing so draws upon the words of Betty, a 25-year-old woman living in a squatter area of Dar-es-Salaam, who explains 'it is not important whether you have a body shape like a body-builder, a beauty queen or a traditional figure, the crux of the matter is how this person moves when it comes to speed and style' (Leseth, 2003:242). This powerful piece of ethnography illustrates how the use of sport and dance in Tanzania can produce fundamentally different ways of thinking about bodily practice that takes us beyond the traditional way of thinking about colonial sport and the body. It vividly illustrates the power of sport and dance as a means of developing, changing and re-shaping lives in a post-colonial Tanzania.

As has been explored in Part 2 of this book it is important that both research and teaching about sport, body and society listen to the view from the 'other'. That is from the perspective of women and men who have been marginalised in some way as a result of colonial or other forms of Western sport. The work of post-colonial feminist studies on sport and the body would be critical of any forms of white, middle-class intellectual feminism which ignored the experiences of women who do not fit into this category. The notion of sport and the body occupying not only a personal but also a political space has the ability to address a research agenda and a teaching interest around other sporting bodies that would involve a revisionist approach to much if not all of the work on sport and the body related to the colonial experience, a project that in part has been kick started through Bale's work on the African sporting body, Dimeo's work on Indian sporting bodies and Hargreaves', Leseth's and Wearing's sensitive critical accounts of other sporting women. In terms of action the notion of body culture is perhaps utilised in policy terms within the Danish way of thinking more than other European countries and it is this that we turn to next.

229

Sport and body culture as cultural policy

Body culture is an important facet of Danish cultural policy in that it provides an alternative or third way of thinking about sport as part of national cultural policy (Danish Ministry of Culture, 1996). Danish cultural policy is informed by a number of underpinning principles. Cultural decentralisation entails that the state must ensure that all population groups and geographic areas have access to cultural products and cultural activities be they art, literature, film, sport, festivals, theatres or libraries. Thus culture is viewed not simply as art but as a dynamic social institution that acknowledges all cultural movements, including bodily movements found in play, festivals, dance and sport. The focus of Danish cultural policy since the 1960s has been on the dissemination of culture while sorting the principle of cultural decentralisation. The dissemination and production of culture in Denmark involves a division of labour between the state, country and the municipalities. Since the 1970s the Ministry of Culture has recognised the need for a pluralistic approach to culture rather than evoking the national mono-cultural approach that endorses one country, one culture. The Ministry of Culture thus recognises the differences with regard to cultural provision in the capital and the provinces, the city and the country and between various social groups and the population as a whole.

The second policy directive is the practice of cultural democracy. The connection between democracy and movement is explained by Eichberg (2004:129–130) who points out that democracy in the specific Danish sense is

- like movement meaning moving in rhythm with others and being aware of otherness;
- playing the game together and being implicit, mutual and communicative about the rules of play;
- to co-operate as a team in looking after the democratic character of sport;
- to elect a leader and although this implies the acceptance of authority for the duration of the contest the sovereignty remains with 'us';
- to respect human beings in contrast to carrying out acts of bodily and physical violence, manipulation, sexual abuse and forced doping;
- the right of bodily difference, to play the game together with 'the other' and always balancing equality and the acceptance of difference in sport and body culture;
- to divide power in that the existence of one central organisation for sport is a problem in itself.

As illustrated in Table 10.1 the notion of body culture is much broader than the simple notion of sport, sports cultures or sports policy. The added dimension of body culture moves the notion of sports and sports policy beyond the simple dualism of elite sport versus recreation or high performance sport versus mass sport or simply thinking of sport as sport without appreciating the nuances of sport, dance, games and sports festivals. Thus the third way or Danish way of sports implies a break from the unitary notion of sport. Sport *as body culture* includes not only competitive sport, with its problematic dualism of elite and mass sport, fitness and health-promoting initiatives, popular games, forms of play and festivals but all of these and more. Sport and body culture as cultural policy evokes a dialectic

Table 10.1 *The body, people and movement*

	Bodily movement	Emotional movement	Social movement
Basic experience:			
	"We play" motion	"I am moved" emotion, motive, motivation	"We are the people" people in motion
	Physical practice	Feelings of togetherness and difference	Self-organisation and conflict
How to discover:			
	Sports studies	Psychology/ sociology	Sociology/politics
What we discover:			
	People in sport, dance, festivals and games	People as social identities	People as civil society/other cultures
Differentiations and contradictions:			
	People in competition	Identity of achievement	People's will
	People in discipline	Identity of integration	Popular culture
	People in festivity	Identity of encounter	People's solidarity

Source: The information has been adapted from Henning Eichberg's insightful study of body culture in Denmark (Eichberg, 2004:129).

interplay between different forms of movement culture, performance and result-orientated sport; the lifestyle-promoting movement of exercise and fitness and popular activities of body culture such as play. In other countries, for example Scotland, there would be a natural place for sports festivals such as Scottish Highland Games within the democratic body politic of Scottish sports policy if such a broader approach to sports policy was considered.

SUMMARY

New ways of thinking about the body in social and cultural terms have led to a surge of interest in the study of the sport, body and society. The bodily practice of peoples in different parts of the world is a basis for their social life. The body remains central to struggles for recognition. A plethora of studies have been organised around the uses and abuses of the body in and beyond sport that have redressed the cultural and social blindness of biological paradigms that historically limited the body gaze to complex biological concerns. In reality the body in a physiological, medical, biological, religious and social sense is a key component to the practice of power, democracy, lifestyle, identities and to that end the fact that bodies of knowledge will interconnect and talk to one another is a refreshing breakthrough. This has helped to address some or all of the following concerns: (i) the process by which ideas about the body in sport and beyond are viewed as natural, deviant, different and/or biological; (ii) the ethical, social and legal implications of how bodies are protected, probed, monitored, rehabilitated, disciplined and/or evaluated; (iii) the extent to which the struggle by different professions for market control over different segments of the body continues to provide the rationale for developing accounts of the body that are driven by political economic concerns; (iv) the ways in which both old and new media represent bodies in sport; (v) the illusionary untouchable bodies associated with the marketing of celebrity sports bodies and (vi) anthropological studies which have made a real difference to the ways in which the sports academy of knowledge has opened up to other parts of the world.

It might be suggested that future thinking and action in relation to sport, body and society must attend to the dynamics and impact of new markets, social patterning, and state policies in different parts of the world in order to understand the new parameters of any post-twentieth-century body politic. On the question of social differences and identities the relation between the recognition of cultural differences and social equality and justice in different or all parts of the world remains a key tension and a fruitful study ground for teachers, students, activists and researchers interested in broadening or moving inter-ventions or policies beyond just sport. Studies of the body in sport provide for exciting opportunities to consider what is natural, what is ethical and what is social and for these reasons alone they must remain a valuable component of any future evaluation of the potential progressive contribution of sport to society.

KEY CONCEPTS

Body culture	Other bodies
Civilising process	Physical capital
Difference	Power
Disciplined body	Quest for excitement
Distinction	Regressive bodies
Habitus	Representation
Identity crisis	Secular bodies
Identity politics	Sexuality
Naturalistic	Social constructionist
Other	Transgressive bodies

KEY READING

Books

Brownell, S. (1995). *Training the Body for China: Sports in the Moral Order of the People's Republic*. Chicago: Chicago University Press.

Cole, C. (2002). 'Body Studies in the Sociology of Sport'. In Coakley, J. and Dunning, E. (eds) *Handbook of Sports Studies*. London: Sage, 439–461.

Dyck, N. and Archetti, E. (2003). *Sport, Dance and Embodied Identities*. Oxford: Berg.

Hargreaves, J. (2000). *Heroines of Sport*: *The Politics of Difference and Identity*. London: Routledge.

Scraton, S. and Flintoff, A. (eds) (2002). *Gender and Sports*: *A Reader*. London: Routledge.

Woodward, K. (2002). *Identity and Difference*. London: Sage Publications.

Journal articles

Dimeo, P. (2002). 'Colonial Bodies, Colonial Sport: "Martial" Punjabis, "Effeminate" Bengalis and the Development of Indian Football'. *International Journal of the History of Sport*, 19(1): 72–90.

Lloyd, M. (1996). 'Feminism, Aerobics and the Politics of the Body'. *Body and Society*, 2(2): 79–98.

Mewett, P. G. (2003). 'Conspiring to Run: Women, their Bodies and Athletics Training'. *International Review for the Sociology of Sport*, 38(3): 331–349.

Ozawa-De Silva, C. (2002). 'Beyond the Body/Mind? Japanese Contemporary Thinkers on Alternative Sociologies of the Body'. *Body and Society*, 8(2): 21–38.

Stone, E. (2001). 'Disability, Sport and the Body in China'. *Sociology of Sport Journal*, 18(1): 51–68.

Vertinsky, P. (1994). 'The Social Construction of the Gendered Body'. *The International Journal of the History of Sport*, 11(2): 147–171.

Further reading

Bale, John, and Philo, Chris (eds). (1998). *Body Cultures*: *Essays on Sport, Space and Identity*: *Henning Eichberg*. London: Routledge.

Cole, C. (2002). 'Body Studies in the Sociology of Sport'. In Coakley, J. and Dunning, E. (eds) *Handbook of Sports Studies*. London: Sage, 439–461.

Dimeo, P. (2004). '"A Parcel of Dummies?" Sport and the Body in Indian History'. In Mills J., and Sen, S. (eds) *Confronting the Body*: *The Politics of Physicality in Colonial and Post-Colonial India*. London: Anthem, 57–72.

Hansen, J. and Nielsen, N. (2000). *Sports, Body and Health*. Odense: Odense University Press.

Walseth, K. and Fasting, K. (2003). 'Islam's View on Physical Activity and Sport: Egyptian Women Interpreting Islam'. *International Review for the Sociology of Sport*, 38(1): 45–61.

REVISION QUESTIONS

1. Use examples from the literature on sport, body and health to explain the following terms: identity; difference and representation.

2. Choose two from the following list of body formations and compare and contrast the social theories behind them: the natural body; the civilised body; the engendered body; the body habitus; the socially constructed body; the fascist body; the African body; the oriental body.

233

3. Explain the difference between essential and contingent approaches to understanding sport, body and society.

4. Evaluate the contribution that post-colonial thinking has made to our understanding of the body in other cultures.

5. What are the advantages of the broader notion of body culture over sport in terms of policy formulation?

PRACTICAL PROJECTS

1. Select two popular health magazines and over a three-month period carry out a content analysis of the two magazines as a basis for writing a critical report on body representation and health.

2. Go to a local gym or exercise club in your area and carry out a series of interviews with three different populations in order to ascertain what their views are on the perfect body.

3. Identify five different articles in the journal *Body and Society* that have researched aspects of sport, exercise or physical activity and use these to compile a short case study on *representation* and sport, exercise and/or physical activity.

4. Identify three different local populations in terms of social class participation in exercise. Carry out a series of interviews with each population, enquiring about why exercise is important to the body and what sort of body people would like. Write a short report of about 2,000 words on the body, exercise and social class drawing on the findings from the three different populations.

5. List ten policy directives that would be derived from developing a policy based upon the broader notion of body culture as opposed to sport. Access the Danish website and compare your policy with that of Denmark.

WEBSITES

Australian Sports Commission website: Women and sport: Body image and Participation in sport
    http://www.activeaustralia.org/women/image.htm

Body and Society Journal
    http://tcs.ntu.ac.uk/body/

Denmark, Conditions of life, body culture and sport
    http://www.um.dk/english/danmark/danmarksbog/kap3/3-12.asp#3-12-3

Rethinking masculinity: Men and their bodies
    http://fathom.lse.ac.uk/Seminars/21701720/21701720_session1.html

Women, body and sport
    www.cddc.vt.edu/feminism/bod.html

Chapter 11

Sport and the environment

Ski events have caused a significant amount of environmental damage in some countries. How should you balance the environmental impact of such events with the economic impact that this activity has for local communities? JOHANNES SIMON/AFP/Getty Images

PREVIEW

Sport and the environment • Ski tourism • Sporting climate • Local and international perspectives • Sport and the weather • Cost of climate change • Sport and the weather forecast • Environmental determinism • Radical and reformist approaches to sport and the environment • Light green sport • Dark green sport • Agenda 21 • Sustainability • Environment and the International Olympic Movement • Naga Agreement on sport and the environment • Anti-golf movement.

OBJECTIVES

This chapter will:

■ introduce key themes in the discussion of sport and the environment;

■ critically discuss the relationship between sport and the weather;

■ consider radical, reformist, light and dark green approaches to sport and the environment;

■ answer the question what is environmental determinism?

■ evaluate ways in which sport and the environment are viewed as anti-global.

INTRODUCTION

Environmental issues are high on the international agenda for a whole generation of political leaders, activists, and to lesser extent sports leaders. Understanding the causes and impacts of environmental change may be more of an urgent task in the twenty-first century than it was in the nineteenth but so too is our knowledge of the impact of the environment upon sport. The environmental agenda for sport in the twenty-first century is a challenge in that certain sporting activities, such as Formula One racing on land, and powerboat racing on water, can create a threat to the local environment not to mention the loss of green space and the potential ecological damage caused by the international growth of sports. In Austria the impact of ski tourism meant that by 1991 there were 2,709 draglifts and 785 cable cars compared to 74 draglifts and 44 cable cars in 1952 (Weiss et al., 1998:369). The construction of new ski lifts to meet market demand for ski holidays in Austria meant the significant clearing of trees, soil and rocks above 1,500 metres bringing with it the increased risk of flooding to the habitats below 1,500 metres. The hosting of major sporting events creates numerous challenges and has forced major sporting organisations to at least think about the potential environmental impact and management of hosting such events. By the late twentieth century the IOC had raised the environment and environmental policy to being the *third dimension* of the Olympic Movement. In 1991 the IOC made amendments to its charter to promote the notion that future Olympic Games were to be held under conditions that were cognisant of the fragile nature of the environment. International environmental sporting issues have not yet emerged as a focus of international politics but they are part of any genuine understanding of sport, culture and society in the early twenty-first century.

Environmental sporting problems are not new. The wettest of cricket summers occurred in 1903 and 1924, with recorded rainfalls of 450 mm in four months, during which time 44 bowlers averaged fewer than 20 runs and only two batsmen achieved an average of more than 50 runs (Kay and Vamplew, 2002:27). The day Jack Dempsey beat Jess Willard for the heavyweight boxing championship in July 1919, 150,000 sweltered in the heat with hundreds of spectators fainting. In the 1924 Paris Olympic

Games 10,000 metres only 15 of the 39 runners completed the field in temperatures of over 40 degrees Celsius. In June 1952 when Sugar Ray Robinson fought Joey Maxim for the world light-heavyweight championship he was beaten as much by the heat as his opponent (Kay and Vamplew, 2002:185). 1947 was one of the coldest post-war British winters with more than 200 football matches being postponed by mid-March. 1976 was one of the driest and fast grass, worn courts and dehydrated players struggled in the above average heat accompanying the Wimbledon Tennis fortnight. Lightning fatalities occurred at the US golf open championships of 1988 and 1991. The environment then has long had an impact upon sport although different regions of the world have experienced different conditions unevenly and as a result climate in part has determined sporting choice. To take this to an extreme hot countries are to be renowned for their performance in Nordic sports.

Over much of human history the environmental impact on sport has tended to be local yet the contemporary environmental risks associated with global warming, large scale pollution, over-population, levels of security, changing seasons and nature mean that environmental sporting issues are no longer just local issues but potentially international and anti-global. Lack of ground or green spaces for sport and physical activity may be experienced in a particular way in a particular locality or nation but are also considered to be more than a local or national problem. Many environmental issues are intrinsically trans-national and many explanations for sporting performance draw upon the common environmental features such as high altitude or poverty. Indeed the nature versus nurture dualism to explain aspects of sport is itself not new.

The phrase 'environmental sporting issue' encompasses a wide range of types of problems and issues, posing different challenges to those who wish to develop effective responses. Although they share some common characteristics each environmental sporting issue needs to be analysed in its own right. Yet any committed eco sporting warrior or sporting conservationist must ultimately link sport and the environment to broader political and socio-economic changes that are impacting upon the environment. The eco sporting warrior may view golf course development as a social pollutant while sporting conservationists might defend the threatened village cricket green in rural England on more than just environmental green grounds but as a threat to the very nature of tradition and heritage. Thus students of sport, culture and society should recognise that many environmental sporting problems and concerns are not disconnected to the key causes of environmental problems related to the generation and distribution of wealth, knowledge, power, patterns of energy consumption, population growth, affluence and poverty. There is an inter-dependence and practical necessity to relate sport and the environment to other spheres of life.

SPORT, THE WEATHER AND ENVIRONMENTAL DETERMINISM

The changing nature of weather and climatic conditions not only poses an environmental threat to many winter sports but also results in an economic threat to certain communities that rely upon income from snow reliability and the resulting tourism. Mountain areas are sensitive to climatic change with the implications of less snow being, receding glaciers, landslides, and leading to the concentration of winter sports activities upon high mountain environments. In other words the ski industry will climb the mountain in order to obtain reliable snow at high altitude. While some regions may be able to maintain their winter tourism with suitable but expensive strategies, studies in Canada, the USA, Australia, Switzerland, New Zealand, France and the United Kingdom have all shown that the environmental threats to the winter sports industry brought about by climatic change are also real economic threats (Burki et al., 2003). The potential annual cost of climatic change in Switzerland is estimated to be $2.1 billion by the year 2050 which equates to about 0.8 per cent of the Swiss gross national product for 1995. In Canada it has been projected that based on the current patterns of climatic change, without snowmaking technology the ski industry would decline substantially by 37–57 per cent by 2050.

Kay and Vamplew (2002:157) remind us that everyone concerned with sport – players, administrators, promoters, spectators and many others – all pay attention to the weather forecaster who referees many a decision concerning whether sport is on, off, likely to be interrupted or likely to be safe from the elements. Information about the weather is a vital determinant which influences the decisions made by event organisers, ground staff, spectators and others. Some sports venues, they point out, such as Wimbledon and Old Trafford have their own weather centres while other sports rely on the local meteorological office. The All England cricket club has two radar systems while the Professional Golfers Association in the USA has two full-time meteorologists on site. Outdoor activities rely upon specialist weather services. Football grounds and racecourses require accurate assessments of the weather in advance of match or race day. The weather affects the preparation for Formula 1 races in terms of the tyres that the drivers will put on the car. Thus it might be argued that the weather is a vital environmental determinant influencing sports events and seasons.

The physical environment, to which Bale (2002a:152) alludes, has been a factor determining the athletic success of national groups and has been noted in studies of sport since at least 1910. In an article entitled the 'Geography of Games' published in 1919 it was claimed that the climate determines the games we play. In the 1920s and 1930s environmentally deterministic explanations of Finnish running success were not uncommon. In 1930 there were 12 Finns in the top twenty 5000-metre runners in the world. In the 1990s and early twenty-first century high altitude and other environmental factors have been highlighted as being almost a causal explanation in accounting for the phenomenal success of Kenyan and Ethiopian middle distance runners. The illustrations listed above are examples of ways in which forms of environmental determinism have been used as a kind of legitimating theory to explain sporting performance linked to different groups of people but they can also be read as racist.

RADICAL AND REFORMIST APPROACHES TO ENVIRONMENTALISM AND SPORT

Environmentalism broadly refers to a belief in and concern for the importance and influence of the environment within and between societies. The term environment is derived from the French verb 'environner' meaning to surround and therefore in one sense the term environment literally means our surroundings (McLean, 1996). The concept of the environment was evident by at least the mid-nineteenth century in that it was empowered through a range of ideas that suggested that human beings are to a degree formed by their surroundings. These included Darwin's discovery that the survival of the species was at least partly dependent upon their adaptation and suitability to their surroundings. German geographers through the notion of *Unwelt* placed an emphasis on the importance of the environment in determining economic and cultural differences between peoples. The history of the term environmentalist has referred primarily to a person who believes in the importance of the environment as a determinant of human life. Bale (2002a:147) observed that during the late nineteenth and twentieth centuries environmental determinism was a powerful social lens through which the world and its peoples and their sporting potential were read. In essence often colonialist and racist explanations of physical ability implied that physical activity and many of the qualities associated with sporting performance, vigour, health, energy, were *determined* by environmental factors.

Environmental determinism is but one of many environmental approaches from the standpoint of environmentalism. The concerns of environmentalism and sport can range from issues about architecture and stadium construction, to loss of green space, to explanations of human sporting performance and ability, to raising awareness of environmentalism, to political protest through movements such as the anti-golf movement, to questions about sustainability and a more green approach to world sport. Environmentalists can base arguments upon virtually any known philosophical assumption including those that are anthropocentric (concerned only with benefits to human beings) and those that are studiously opposed to anthropocentrism. Different approaches to sport and environmentalism are presented below.

Table 11.1 *Sport and environmentalism at the end of the twentieth century*

RADICAL SPORT AND THE ENVIRONMENT (*mainly anti-capitalism, tends to be proactive*)		REFORMIST SPORT AND THE ENVIRONMENT (*pro-capitalism, tends to be reactive*)	
Deep Ecology	Based on ecocentrism, intrinsic value in nature. Sport is not above nature.	*Conservatism*	Preservationism, NIMBYism, stewardship of nature. Sport as part of natural nurture management programmes would support the notion of sporting estates.
Social Ecology	Looks to both humanism and ecocentrism, based on anarchist and feminist principles.	*Free-market Liberalism*	Market mechanisms and privatisation of the commons. The relationship between sport and environment determined by the market.
Eco-socialism	Humanistic and socialist politics (libertarian, decentralist, utopian socialism). Sport as humanitarian values.	*Social Reformism*	Market intervention, e.g. environmental taxes, tradeable pollution rights plus voluntary agreements plus regulation.

Table 11.1 differentiates between *radical* and *reformist* approaches to environmentalism, many of which have grown out of Western or mainstream concerns over sport, capitalism and the environment/nature. While the discussion below broadly defines radical and reformist approaches to sport and the environment some have argued that the differences between the two collective camps of thought may be too profound to place them on the same continuum and that perhaps in the early part of the twenty-first century it might be more useful to think of paradigm shifts between each approach rather than a spectrum of thought which can be neatly compartmentalised as a continuum from reformist to radical environmental sporting politics.

Reformist approaches to sport and environmentalism at the end of the twentieth century would have embraced liberal and democratic socialist approaches to sport and the environment. As such the reformation of the relationship between sport and capitalism would be viewed as the key to reform and yet in practice would merely react to environmental problems in sport. The arguments would revolve around a greater or lesser degree of intervention within the sporting market or economy. Free-market liberals would look to increased privatisation to secure further environmental freedoms for sport while social reformists would increase environmental taxes and incentives while regulating firms and individuals. Elements of conservative thinking would also permeate reformist approaches to mainstream concerns about sport and the environment in that preservation, conservation, and a precautionary incipient approach to change would in the North be supported perhaps at the expense of those countries in the South.

Radical environmentalism on the other hand is inclined to be pro-active, seeking to eliminate environmental sporting problems at their root rather than simply reacting to the normal impulses of international or global capitalism operating through sport. The debate about sport and the environment is therefore shifted out of the cultural/economic mainstream sport debate to becoming counter-cultural and often drawing upon counter-cultural traditions of romanticism, anarchism and utopian socialism. At least three different strands of thinking might be mentioned in the first instance, namely social ecology, eco-socialism and deep ecology. Social ecology looks to both humanism and eco-centrism for inspiration and was often associated with anarchism and feminism. Eco-socialism looked to humanistic ideologies but drew heavily upon socialist politics. Deep ecology was based upon a strong eco-centrism that championed the intrinsic value of nature.

The reformist approach to sport and the environment has at times been referred to as the light green or technocratic approach to sport and the environment (Lenskyj, 2000:156–157). The latter embraces mainstream culture's ideologies of liberalism and democratic socialism and it would aim to reform capitalist sport to a greater or lesser degree by adopting a perspective that is technocratic. Technocentrist approaches to sport and the environment place faith in science, technology and the rational management of nature to solve environmental sporting problems. The arguments mainly relate to how much to intervene in solutions and choices provided through the market economy. The Atlanta 1996 Olympic Games were coined by environmentalists as the disposable Olympic Games because so many of the sporting structures including the velodrome, the water polo pool, the rowing venue, the archery facilities and much of the seating, fencing and tent space was dismantled and disposed of afterwards. Such practices clearly fail to qualify as ecological sustainable development but for reformists they offered a profitable, technical solution that was sensitive to some environmental issues but not others. The Atlanta 1996 Olympic Games adopted a light green approach to sport and the environment. By means of summary it might be suggested that the light green approach to sport and the environment involves putting a price on the environment in order to protect it unless degrading it is more profitable.

The discussion of reformist and radical approaches to the environment was often labelled as emphasising anthropo-centric versus eco-centric points of view on ecology (Grundmann, 1991). The anthropo-centric approach had the main advantage of providing a reference point from which to evaluate ecological phenomena. This can be defined in different ways (reference points might be currently living humans, society, future generations or gender) but no matter how we define it, it establishes clear criteria for how to judge existing environmental or ecological problems. Any eco-centric point of view is bound to be inconsistent unless it adopts a mystical standpoint. Eco-centrism is inconsistent because it tends to define ecological problems purely from the point of view of nature. It starts with the assumptions about nature and natural laws to which humans should adapt. The deep eco-centric approach tends to marginalise the social and therefore there would be a place for considering sport's relationship with the environment in social or human terms and yet it seems the very definition of nature's nature and ecological or environmental balance implies a human element. Sport and the environment may be thought of in terms of social needs, pleasures and desires and therefore it seems problematic to accept eco-centrism and see it as necessary to view sport and environmental problems as a result of the consequence of society's dealings with nature.

The radical approach to sport and the environment has, by way of an alternative, been referred to as the dark green or eco-centric approach to sport and the environment. Deep ecology's approach is eco- or bio-centric and is focused upon non-human nature. Eco-socialism is not so radical in that it sees humans as an ultimate source of value and is prepared to elevate human worth above that of plants and animals. Social ecology is said to transcend both anthropo-centrism and bio-centrism. Ecocentric or dark green approaches to sport and the environment would include the support of strategies aimed at energy conservation and use of renewable energy sources, water conservation, waste avoidance and minimisation, protecting human health with appropriate standards of air, water and soil quality and the protection of natural environments from the sports industry. The Sydney 2000 Olympic Games is perhaps the nearest example of a dark green approach to sport and the environment. The work of groups such as Greenpeace in relation to the planning of Olympic Games or the philosophy of the global anti-golf movement may be considered as being eco-friendly if not totally eco-centric in outlook. By way of summary it might be suggested that the dark green approach to sport and the environment views the natural environment as having an intrinsic worth and that existing political and economic systems are to be challenged when they pose a threat to the environment.

In answer to the question of what environmentalism is, it is important for students and researchers to start from the position that there are different environmentalisms. Environmentalism and sport is a wide-ranging, eclectic and diverse area of research that is influenced by and needs to move beyond orthodox social reformists and radical political traditions. To return to the weather, not surprisingly instances of cold, wet and snowy weather affect European sport more than issues of blistering heat but even this is changing as a result of environmental shift. Thus theoretically, spatially and temporally it is important to talk of *environmentalisms* and sport. It remains to be seen how global warming will impact upon sport in different parts of the world.

GREEN SPORT, AGENDA 21 AND SUSTAINABILITY

In 1972 the UN Conference on the Human Environment was organised in response to the dramatic increase in international environmental concerns. Held in Stockholm, the conference established a number of principles, institutions and programmes which helped to provide a framework for promoting the further development of international responses to trans-national environmental problems. Non-governmental groups such as Greenpeace, World Wildlife Fund and Friends of the Earth became as influential as many diplomats in shaping international environmental agreements. However the development agendas included in the Action Plan and Declaration of Principles agreed at Stockholm were never seriously followed up. Moreover the United Nations Environmental Programme (UNEP) lacked the institutional weight to co-ordinate other UN agencies and consequently largely failed to integrate the environmental agenda within the UN system. This caused an increasing international concern amongst many non-First World countries which suffered exploitation at the behest of trans-national, often Western based, multinational companies. NGOs became increasingly active in international environmental politics in the 1970s, 1980s and 1990s.

In 1987 the UN established a World Commission on the Environment and Development chaired by the then Prime Minister of Norway, Go Harlem Brundtland. The Commission promoted the notion of sustainable development. The Brundtland Commission's shorthand characterisation of development is development that meets the needs of the present without compromising the ability of future generations to meet their own needs. The prominence given to needs reflected a concern to eradicate poverty and meet human basic needs, broadly understood. The exact meaning of the concept of sustainable development remained unclear but it was important because it attracted support from a number of international constituencies. The UN General Assembly in 1989 decided to convene an Earth Summit in Rio de Janeiro in 1992, at which 27 general principles for guiding action on the environment and development were outlined.

Three new conventions were agreed at the Rio conference aimed at limiting climate change, preserving biodiversity and combating desertification. The institutions established in 1992 agreed to promote Agenda 21, aimed at providing a programme of action for sustainable development. The Global Environmental Facility provided alongside Agenda 21 is aimed at helping developing countries meet the costs of implementing aspects of Agenda 21. The institutions established to promote the implementation of Agenda 21, including the Olympic Movement, have stimulated the development of national plans for sustainable development and provided forums where plans can be reviewed and where networks of non-governmental groups, government representatives and international secretariats can develop and influence agendas and yet the influence on overall patterns of sustainable development has been small.

244

Global environmental issues exist in many different forms and although they share common characteristics each area needs specific examination in its own right. There has been a growth of green consciousness, policy and practice in the context of international sport (Maguire et al., 2002:89). The environmental dimension was critical to Sydney's bid to host the 2000 Olympic Games. The Sydney 2000 Olympic Games are viewed as being one of the most successful Green Games todate, with the environmental guidelines governing the Olympic Games focusing upon environmental protection and the *sustainable* development of Olympic sites. The Olympic approach to the environment was in part brought about by the resolution of the International Olympic Committee to adopt Agenda 21 in 1999 (see Box 11.2). The Sydney Olympic Games Committee followed the United Nations Agenda 21 resolution to implement a comprehensive plan of action to safeguard the environment from the impact of human interaction, including the hosting of major sports events, which committed the 2000 Olympics to demonstrating more sustainable site management practices; more sustainable event management measures and raising public awareness about environmental issues related to sport. The Executive Director of the United Nations Environment Programme argued in 2004 that

> the environment, like sports, knows no barriers or territorial borders and it tran-
> scends ideological cleavages. It does not recognise distinctions between North,
> South, East and West. . . . Athletes, as the main actors in the sports movement are
> role models and while only a few of us can aspire to join the Olympics we should
> all strive to achieve higher goals in order to help ourselves, our communities and
> our countries and most important of all the environment that we all depend upon.
> www.g-forse.com/enviro/e/index4.html

The 1999 agreement was re-emphasised in 2001 through the Nagano Declaration on Sport, Environment and Sustainable Development in which the participants of the IVth World Congress on Sport and the Environment resolved to uphold the principles of sustainability in their sports activities and to promote such principles on a global scale so as to ensure that the Earth is given a sporting chance. It is tempting to suggest that by 2004 the sports organisations such as the IOC are more green than they were prior to 1992 and it might be suggested that the IOC has acted uncharacteristically in a progressive manner with regard to perspectives on sports and the environment. On issues such as resource management and species conservation several other landmarks were achieved during the 2000 Olympic preparations. The Olympic village utilised solar power, construction work widely used recycled and plantation timber and an ecologically sustainable approach to design and building methods was pioneered. Major tree planting projects were planned throughout Australia so that the financial benefits of the Games could be experienced by the whole nation (Maguire et al., 2002:89).

There is no doubt that Sydney 2000 set an important new threshold for integrating environmental aspects into sports event planning and management. The concept of a Green Games with an integrated programme, which paid attention to transport methods, waste, energy, water, materials, pollution and biodiversity issues arguably set a benchmark for

BOX 11.1 THE OLYMPIC MOVEMENT AND AGENDA 21

In 1999 the International Olympic Committee (IOC) adopted the IOC Agenda 21 which proposed ways for individuals and groups in sports to develop sustainable societies.

■ *Improving socio-economic conditions*
Sustainable development implies satisfying the essential cultural and material needs of every individual to enable him or her to live with dignity and play a positive role in society. As a result, Agenda 21 pays particular attention to the lives of the most disadvantaged and to minorities. This includes helping to combat social exclusion, promoting a new approach to consumption, playing a more active role in health protection, promoting sports facilities which better meet social needs and better integrating development and environmental concepts into sports policies.

   Promoting the socio-economic dimension of Agenda 21 matches the goal of Olympism, as set out in the Fundamental Principles of the Olympic Charter, which is 'everywhere to place sport at the service of the harmonious development of man, with a view to encouraging the establishment of a peaceful society concerned with the preservation of human dignity'.

■ *Conservation and management of resources for sustainable development*
The Olympic Movement's environmental protection policy should come within the wider framework of sustainable development. Thus the environmental work of the Olympic Movement is now focused on the conservation and management of resources and the natural environment necessary to improve socio-economic conditions. These should encourage education about the environment and specific action to help preserve it. This is the most visible aspect of the IOC's environmental work, especially at the Olympic Games.

■ *Strengthening the role of the main groups*
To ensure the success of sustainable development, it is helpful if all of the groups that make up society are active and respected players in the process set in motion. To this end, the Olympic Movement can make a meaningful contribution to strengthening the roles of two groups in particular, women and young people.

future international sporting events. The Sydney 2000 Environment Programme managed to extract pledges from multinational corporations that have added credibility to notions of sustainable environmental development through sport. Corporations such as Coca-Cola pledged to introduce Green Freeze technology through its global operations by the time of the Athens 2004 Olympic Games. The relationship between trade and environmental issues has also served as a reminder that virtually all environmental issues are intimately linked to the dynamics of international if not global political and economic processes. Such concerns have given rise to movements such as the anti-golf movement.

THE ENVIRONMENT AND THE ANTI-GOLF MOVEMENT

The spread of golf courses on an international basis has not only spawned the global anti-golf movement but has also been a catalyst for a movement that calls for a moratorium on the development of golf courses. Huge amounts of water, 2.4 million litres a day world-wide it is argued, are needed to keep golf courses bright green and much of this activity takes place in countries where water is scarce. The global anti-golf movement was launched on World Golf Day in April 1993. The three initial sponsoring organisations were the Global Network for Anti-Golf Course Action (GNAGA) based in Japan, the Asian Tourism Network (ANTENNA) based in Thailand and the Asia-Pacific People and Environmental Network (AEN) based in Malaysia. The anti-golf movement is active in Europe, Australia, Asia, Latin America and the USA. Various environmental groups are opposed to the construction of golf courses. The anti-golf course manifesto revolves around the following observations that include: (i) golf courses and golf tourism are part of a global package that is capitalist-orientated with most of the money arising from the activity being exported out of the locality; (ii) the speculative nature of the industry makes it a high-risk investment for small countries and localities with many golf courses, resorts and companies becoming bankrupt; (iii) the environmental impact of golf course development is negative in that it facilitates water depletion and toxic contamination to such an extent that the golf green is fraught with ecological problems; (iv) it promotes an elitist and exclusive leisure class with the globalisation of this lifestyle encouraging wealthy urban elites to absorb a particular way of life regardless of the environment and other members of society; and (v) in the face of growing criticism the golf industry is falsely promoting the notion of pesticide-free, environmentally friendly golf courses in the knowledge that such a golf course does not exist. A survey by the UK Sports Turf Research Institute found massive overdosing of British greens with phosphate fertilisers.

Between August 1995 and April 1996 the town of Tepozitan in Mexico was involved in a conflict with a real estate development corporation, the Kladt-Sobri Group (KS), over the construction of a golf course and country club. The project represented a $500 million investment in the town and promised to augment the tourism industry but local activists became concerned about the negative environmental impact of the development. The arguments against the development included excessive water usage, toxic runoff, and the negative social and cultural impacts caused by creating an enclave community of extremely wealthy individuals within a relatively poor community. The opposition group, which called itself the Committee for Tepozteco Unity (CUT), managed to convince the majority of the population that the golf course was a bad idea and they pressurised the town council into promising not to issue the zoning waivers that would facilitate planning permission. The council subsequently issued permits, resulting in their physical expulsion from the town. The state government organised a fraudulent assembly (they bussed people in from other municipalities) to ratify the decision; CUT threw the state government out of town, erected barricades and a month later held their own elections to name legitimate authorities. The confrontation between the state, the townspeople and KS continued until April when an elderly activist was then killed in a police ambush. The scandal forced the KS to drop out of the project and the state to suspend its aggressive polices towards the town.

247

Yet with specific reference to golf what is required is an increased awareness of the environmental threats posed by the ideas and practices of people involved in the development of golf at local and international levels. Should golf as a sport become a resource intensive and environmentally harmful activity then it may be defined as an unsustainable sport. The paradox of sustainable development often means that environmental issues are sidelined in favour of economic development when the latter is more convenient, more commercially attractive and supported by more powerful interest groups (Maguire et al., 2002:96). However, as the case in Tepozitan serves to illustrate, organised, committed and locally driven anti-golf protests can succeed in bringing about social and political change at the local level.

SUMMARY

Environmental issues emerged as late as the last quarter of the twentieth century as a major focus of international concern and activity. Sport is not immune from the environmental gaze and intervention. Many environmental problems are intrinsically international and consequently stimulate international political activities in response to the degradation of the planet. Sport and the environment problems have been shown to connect with international movements such as Agenda 21 but also at the local level as in the case of Tepozitan. International environmental issues in the field of sports pose significant challenges for students and researchers of sport. They raise questions about the significance and the role of states and trans-national corporations in the field of environmental politics, about the relationship between power and knowledge and about the distinction between international and domestic or local spheres of activity. The issues of sport and climatic change, sport and international sporting agendas, sport and environmental thinking and the notions of dark green and light green sport have figured in this chapter. Yet sport and the environment has also figured in broader social and political protests concerning the control of communities over their own local environs as is illustrated in the anti-golf course movement.

The activities of the anti-golf course movement have been highlighted as illustrative of the fact that sport has linked with broader environmental impacts which in many cases have reflected the way in which different parts of the world connect on an economic, social and political level. The core concerns of the anti-golf movement have been economical, environmental in this sense that it is a protest against a reliance on toxic chemicals and in some cases water wastage, but also social in the sense that the protests have also been against the closed door policies of many golf clubs which often leave locals out in the cold in terms of club membership. The profits also bypass local communities. The average cost of developing a golf course in Thailand has been estimated as being as much as $47 million, not including the cost of hiring consultants. In Indonesia, the construction of a golf course in Cimacan, West Java, displaced 287 peasants in 1991. The Badung Asri Mulia Construction Company paid villagers who lost their lands 1.5 cents per square metre.

The issue of sport and the environment or the question of how sport can be greener may not be one of the prime directives of the sports industry in the Western world but the environment and survival of human life itself is one of the foremost early twenty-first-century concerns. According to Edward O. Wilson the earth is entering a new evolutionary era in that we are on the brink of extinction the likes of which have not been seen since the end of the Mesozoic era, 65 million years ago. Species are vanishing and as Wilson puts it, our children will be practically alone in the world (Gray, 2002a:27).

Given the magnitude of such concerns you would expect the environment to be at the centre of public debate, as would be discussion of the alleged causes of concerns about mass destruction. According to most mainstream political parties and environmental organisations the destruction of the environment is mainly the result of flaws in human institutions. The predominant view of the northern countries has tended to be that potentially we are entering a desolate world with the reason being that humans have overpopulated and injustice prevents proper use of the earth's resources. Such a view is not accepted in many of the world's poorer countries, China, Egypt, India and Iran. Ideas about population control tend to be concentrated in or emanate from within rich parts of the world. Such an issue is raised here to illustrate the complexity of implementing a course of action even if it were to be accepted that Wilson's era of solitude is about to fall upon the world. A policy of zero population growth requires universal acceptance of contraception and abortion and limits on freedoms to breed but the authority to impose such conditions does not exist. On the one hand if population growth is about to collapse is it more likely to come about as a result of wars, genocide or generalised social entropy rather than environmental degradation, or will new technology provide the answers to the scarcity of water, oil, natural gas and food aggravated by environmental destruction? A world of 8 billion people competing for vital necessities is highly unlikely to be at peace. Thus the loss of biodiversity is very real and often irreversible but has perhaps not yet led to an age of solitude. Sport may not be able to halt major environmental catastrophes but its undoubted popularity in many parts of the world means that it provides a popular target for organisations such as Greenpeace, the anti-golf movement and the IOC to spread or carry environmental messages. Perhaps the real question for environmentalists is can we have sport at all without nature?

KEY CONCEPTS

Agenda 21	Global anti-golf movement
Conservation	Greenpeace
Dark green sport	Light green sport
Deep ecology	Olympic Movement
Eco-centrism	Radical environmentalism
Eco-socialism	Reformist-environmentalism
Environment	Social-ecology
Environmental determinism	Weather
Friends of the Earth	

KEY READING

Books

Baylis, J. and Smith, S. (2001). *The Globalization of World Politics*: *An Introduction to International Relations*. Oxford: Oxford University Press.
Brennan, T. (2003). *Globalization and its Terrors*: *Daily Life in the West*. London: Routledge.
Lenskyj, H. (2000). *Inside the Olympic Industry*: *Power, Politics and Activism*. New York. New York University Press.
Maguire, J., Jarvie, G., Mansfield, L. and Bradley, J. (2002). *Sport Worlds*: *A Sociological Perspective*. Illinois: Human Kinetics, 83–97.

Journal articles

Bale, J. (2002a). 'Lassitude and Latitude: Observations on Sport and Environmental Determinism'. *International Review of the Sociology of Sport*, 37(2): 147–159.
Cantelon, H. and Letters, M. (2000). 'The Making of the IOC Environmental Policy as the Third Dimension of the Olympic Movement'. *International Review of the Sociology of Sport*, 35(3): 249–308.
Grundmann, R. (1991). 'The Ecological Challenge to Marxism'. *New Left Review*, 187 (May/June): 1–15.

Further reading

Burki, R., Elsasser, H. and Abegg, B. (2003). 'Climate Change and Winter Sports: Environmental and Economic Threats' at www.google.co.uk/search?q=cache:cyMNECTWTnm8J:www.unep.org/sport_en/Documents/toribuerki.doc+SPORTS%2ENVIRONMENT&hl+en
Chatterjee, P. (1993). 'Clubbing South East Asia: The Impacts of Golf Sports Development' at http://multinationalmonitor.org/hyper/issues/1993/11/mm1193_13html
Gray, J. (2002a). 'When the Forests Go, Shall we be Alone?' *New Statesman*, 22 July: 27–30.
Kay, J. and Vamplew, W. (2002). *Weather Beaten*: *Sport in the British Climate*. Edinburgh: Mainstream Publishing.
Stubbs, S. and Chernushenko, D. (2004). 'Guidelines for Greening Sports Events' at www.committedtogreen.com/guidelines/greening.htm

REVISION QUESTIONS

1. Discuss four different approaches to sport and the environment taking care to differentiate between light green and dark green strategies.

2. Comment upon the potential impact of Agenda 21 in sport in relation to sustainable development in different parts of the world.

3. What are the arguments against the development of golf courses and are the arguments essentially eco-centric?

4. What considerations would you have to take into account when designing an environmentally friendly sports event?

5. Evaluate the development and philosophy behind the anti-golf movement and consider whether such policies might be viewed as dark green or light green.

PRACTICAL PROJECTS

1. Carry out a Google search on sport+environment. Look for studies by Rolf Burki, Hans Elsasser and Bru Abegg and write a short synopsis of 500 words explaining how environmental and economic threats to winter sports are brought about by climatic change.

2. Explore the guidelines for the greening of sports events outlined by the Committed to Green Foundation and compare this with the values of the anti-golf movement. Write 1,000 words describing and comparing this specific foundation and movement.

3. Assess the impact of environmental pollution caused by a local sports event. Interview five local residents and five visitors to the event with a view to exploring issues relating to sport and the environment.

4. Keep a diary of the weather in your country or region over the period of (i) a month and (ii) a year and write a report on how the weather has affected sport.

5. Design two different policy statements in relation to sport and the environment, one which is radical in orientation and one which is reformist in orientation. Each strategy should contain ten items or directives.

WEBSITES

Golf Ecology website
www.glofecology.co.uk

Green Games Watch
www.nccnsw.org.au/events/greengames/index.html

Greening Sports Events
www.committedtogreen.com/guidelines/greening.htm

Olympic Games report
www.greenpeace.org.au/archives/olympics

The global anti-golf movement
 www.utenti.lycos.it/dossiersarenas/manifest.htm

Tunza Sport
 www.ourplanet.com/tunza/issue0201en/pages/contents/html

Chapter 12

Sport and religion

The Maccabi Games remain one of the few exclusively Jewish International Sports Festivals. The Maccabi Games are associated with the Maccabi Movement which dates back to 1895. What is the relationship between sport and religion today? Getty Images

PREVIEW

Sport and sabbatarianism • *Chariots of Fire* • Amateurism and muscular christianity • The tyranny of materialism • Nation of Islam movement • Muhammad Ali • Sport and religion • Faith invaders, religion and liberal humanism • The Maccabi Games • The Promise Keepers • Fundamentalism • Celtic Football Club, Irishness and identity • Faith and football • Liberal humanism • Muslim fundamentalism, the war against feminism and physical activity • Sport as civil religion, worship and capitalism • The cathedral of sports business • Better faith, better ethics, better sport?

OBJECTIVES

This chapter will:

- highlight the historical and contemporary relationship between sport, religion and business;
- provide empirical case study examples of single faith orientated sports organisations;
- critically evaluate the dangers of fundamentalist approaches to religion and sport;
- examine the relationship between Islam, gender and physical activity;
- question the notion of better faith, better ethics and better sport.

INTRODUCTION

In August 2004 on the beaches around the north-western tip of a small Scottish island, could be found Nicola Breciani and Francesco Palatella, professional surfers from Italy, who have dedicated their lives to finding the perfect wave; a quest that had taken them from California, to Costa Rica, Australia, Bali, South Africa, Burma and Scotland. This is one of 'the top places in Europe' raves Palatella but he is unaware of the controversy that surrounded them about surfing on a Sunday (Martin, 2004:13). 'Lewis hands surfers never on Sunday warning' was how Martin (2004:13) introduced her feature story in a leading national newspaper, the *Observer*. The article explained the tension between the quest to increase tourism and income generation and the long-standing tradition of Sunday being a day of worship, rest and reflection. The Rev. Iver Martin of the Stornoway Free Church of Scotland commenting upon the issue of surfing on Sunday pointed out 'that the Sabbath is very special here and we have to fight to keep it sacred' (Martin, 2004:13). The Rev. Martin was referring to plans by a local businessman to host an international surfing competition and festival on the Island of Lewis from 2004 onwards. The local Western Isles Council had earlier voted unanimously against opening a multi-million pound sports hall on the Sabbath while a paintball company twice had its application for a Sunday licence refused.

The issue of sport on Sunday has had a long history. By July 1982 David Putnam's film classic *Chariots of Fire* had amassed £49.4 million making it, at the time, the biggest money-making foreign film in US box office history. The narrative in the film was built around Eric Liddell the Scottish athlete, later to become a missionary in China, who was picked to run in the 100 yards at the 1924 Paris Olympic Games but refused to run because the final was scheduled for a Sunday. Liddell is introduced in the film as an establishment Scottish rugby international who turns to running as a form of secular preaching. The conflicts in the film between amateurism, idealism, realism, god and nation, sport and social class are crucial to the narrative. Liddell's metaphysical evangelical running qualities are a core theme throughout the film. Liddell's faith was deep-rooted within a Scottish evangelical fundamentalist tradition. The core of this faith was a burning conviction in personal salvation through the merits of Jesus. To bring men and women to this spiritual climax was one of the ultimate aims of the Scottish evangelicals. The evangelical fundamentalists shared many similarities with the Scottish covenanters; both were ferverent, both were puritanical and both in their heyday were anxious to see their ideals adopted by the rest of society. The story presented in *Chariots of Fire* transforms Liddell's evangelical ideology into a metaphorical statement about the ultimate possibilities that could be achieved through sport. The framing of this story about the athlete tended to depoliticise the role of the evangelicals within Scottish society but also framed the notion of freedom within a religious frame of reference.

The clashes between sport and sabbatarianism are not merely early twentieth- or nineteenth-century phenomena. The orthodox history of the relationship between sport and religion has been reproduced in numerous accounts of the connection between amateurism, class, colonialism and religion through the advent of the muscular Christian. Perhaps too much has been made of the moral power of this ideology, exercised through the connections and power of a networked society and closely associated with the British public school system. Too many have uncritically accepted the orthodox story of the development of muscular Christianity emanating from the athletic missionaries of the British, not simply English, public schools. What is often overlooked in these accounts of muscular Christianity is not only its *contemporaneous* meaning for some athletes, such as Jonathan Edwards, the former 2000 Olympic Triple Jump champion, but also that like all forms of religion, amateurism itself was/is a social system. A social system that reproduced power relations, colonialism and sexism. Like all -isms, amateurism as a social practice consisted of sets beliefs and rituals that were supported by social institutions. For the muscular Christian who adhered to amateurism the attitude towards money and economic reward was viewed as being secondary to other more important aspects of human life (Allison, 2001). The poor across a range of colonised countries were invariably left to live on forms of metaphysical income rather than materially sustainable livelihoods.

The tyranny of materialism was a value not simply present within the practice of amateur muscular Christianity but other forms of religion, notably Islam. According to Smith (2002:189) it was the clash between profit and faith that led to the rift between Muhammad Ali, the former world heavy-weight boxing champion, and Elijah Muhammad, leader of Nation of Islam movement. After Muhammed Ali indicated in the late 1960s that he wished to return to the boxing ring because he needed to make money, Elijah Muhammad suspended him from the Nation of Islam. He removed his holy name on the grounds that he had rejected the spiritual platform and replaced it with the search for money. Elijah Muhammad went on to to assert that Ali had become too dependent upon white America and his return to the world of sport had revealed a lack of faith in Allah (Smith, 2002:188). Just as the boxer's sporting popularity had been used to the full advantage of the Nation of Islam movement in the beginning, so too at the end of this association was Muhammad Ali's return to sport used by the

Nation of Islam to promote key values. Ironically one of the movement's most popular messengers was removed from office for returning to the very activity that had provided a popular platform for the Nation of Islam movement. The relationship between sport and religion in this instance was not only contradictory but paradoxically financially rewarding, providing the movement with an international audience through the fame and athleticism of a boxer. Muhammad Ali continued to follow the Muslim faith after the death of Elijah Muhammad in 1975.

Religion has had a significant historical presence in sport. Some or all of the following themes are common to many sport, culture and society studies:

- rates of change in various historical periods with a view to commenting upon whether sport has become more or less secular or religious;
- the relationship between early Puritanism and folk games;
- the religious symbolism of sporting festivals and events, most notably the Olympic Games;
- the specific religious identity and stereotypes associated with particular sports teams;
- muscular Christianity, amateur sport and social class;
- the relationship between body, spirit and mind in the practice of sumu;
- the relationship between particular sport, particular countries and particular faiths such as rugby in Afrikaner South Africa and the Dutch Reformed Church or gymnastics, Catholicism and France;
- the relationship between sport, religion and capitalism;
- the relationship between gender, physical activity and Islam.

The research literature grounding the substantive presence and forms of sport and religion may be used to suggest that religion and sport have rarely been indifferent to one another. Certain fundamental beliefs have come to form part of the juridical religious dogma that sustains several institutional structures in the West. Sport is not immune from the effects of these. The problem here is not particularly new but it is posed today with particular urgency. Sport is far from secular but the issue is in part whether doctrinal systems are impenetrable and therefore reduced to either condemning each other or in the case of fundamentalism, potentially doing battle with one another. The catalogue of atrocities committed in the name of religion shows how dangerous all forms of dogma may be, and not just those that have emanated from the West. The relationship between sport and religion is far from innocent.

FAITH INVADERS, RELIGION AND LIBERAL HUMANISM

The following is an illustration concerning the relationship between religion and politics. Puritanical yet wealthy, convinced of their God-given mission to the rest of the world,

Saudi Arabia and the United States are surprisingly similar in terms of religion, politics and interference in other countries' affairs. Saudi Arabia in part is wedded to Wahhabi Islam while a large section of Middle America is devoted to evangelical Christianity. Historically they are at odds with one another; both see themselves as exponents of the purest version of their faith, are suspicious of modernity and see no distinction between politics and religion. Both of these spiritual empires have been invading Britain since the last part of the twentieth century onwards. Increasingly foreign-financed and foreign-inspired religious conservatives have been recruiting volunteers, establishing schools, setting up publishing houses, think tanks, places of worship and cultural outlets.

A single faith, Saudi-funded Wahhabi influenced curriculum has been at the heart of the King Fahd Academy set up in London for 600 primary and secondary school children. Christian evangelical training is at the heart of new theologies such as the Alpha Course, a ten-point plan to salvation which has been heavily supported by middle-class fundamentalist groups. Far from being secular it is perhaps time that the secular establishment noted that religion now identifies many people in the way that other forms of social division have done in the past. It may be suggested that single faith organisations have used sport in a number of ways, notably (i) to promote spiritual growth; (ii) to recruit new members and (iii) promote religious beliefs and organisations. Yet at the heart of these doctrines are certain problematic concerns. Often a strict adherence to absolute interpretations of sacred texts promotes certain forms of behaviour, for example, no drugs, no sex outside of marriage, male superiority over women and a profound conviction that the wider society is living in sin.

The Maccabi Games remains the only exclusively Jewish international sports festival. The games are the largest Jewish teen event in the world, with 6,000 Jewish teenagers between the ages of 13 and 16 participating each summer. The games are sponsored by the Jewish Community Centre Association of North America, the Maccabi World Union, Maccabi Canada and Maccabi USA. The Maccabi Movement began in 1895 with the first games proposed in 1929 and held in 1932. Sport has been one of the many institutions that have sought to conserve religious traditions and ethnic culture as well as communicate important lessons about Judaism and society. The first American Maccabi Games were held in 1982. Sporting activities held a considerable place within the lives of numerous Jewish women and girls at local, national and international levels. Borish (2002:90) in particular points out that Jewish women's participation in American sport was contoured by their gender and ethnic roles in American society and therefore sport helped in the construction of what it meant to be a Jewish American woman. Sport therefore helped in the construction of ethnic, gender, religious and national identities.

Fundamentalism

The Promise Keepers, according to Randels and Beal (2002), are a Protestant Christian evangelical group which acts as a social movement through religion. In this sense it is similar to a range of other groups such as the Freemasons, the Knights of St Columba, the Young Women's Hebrew Association and the Young Men's Christian Association. In other senses it is different. The Promise Keepers do not simply invoke sport in the name of Christianity but as a partial solution to what Randels and Beal (2002) refer to as the crisis of masculinity. By this it is implied that success in sport might help to define certain aspects of masculinity and religion. They acknowledge that patriarchy is reproduced not just through athletics but other fields including politics, business and religion. The Promise Keepers as a movement seeks recognition through a blend of sport, masculinity and religiosity. The Promise Keepers, it is argued, endeavour to enable men to become more Christ-like and masculine (Randels and Beal, 2002:163). The Promise Keepers reject secularism, use sporting symbols to reach a broader audience and promote an overt relationship between religion and sport. The boundary maintenance offered in promoting such forms of religious and gender exclusivity through sport requires forms of surveillance and soft policing.

The extent to which the Promise Keepers also promote Conservative fundamentalist beliefs through sport may be brought into question when tested against a number of political beliefs held by other fundamentalist groups such as pro-life, pro-family and pro-American expansion. Many fundamentalist Christian groups have embraced sport as mechanism for reducing their separation and exclusion from society while increasing their legitimacy and power within it. Fundamentalists in all religions tend to emphasise a need to return to basic, moral religious roots and develop a personal relationship with God, Allah, Christ, Mohammad, or the Other whoever that maybe. The Fundamentalist view is the absolute view that allegedly offers clear cut answers to personal and social problems. The key point however is to recognise that in the quest for seeking legitimacy and exclusivity all forms of fundamentalism promote forms of reification and separatism. By shielding internal tensions, a fundamentalist approach to sport would repress forms of communitarianism, and promote conformism, intolerance and patriarchalism.

The dangers of an uncritical acceptance of fundamentalism are also evident in certain forms of research into sport, religion, politics and identity. Bradley's (2004) vibrant collection of essays on Celtic Football Club, Irishness and identity in Scotland tends to rest upon a reified dogmatic approach to football, culture and society in Scotland. This is evident in the opening the essay which sets the context for the rest of the book. In the introduction, Scotland is considered a secular country in a positive sense (Bradley, 2004:34) and yet in the conclusion in a more negative, almost lamenting sense, football clubs such as Celtic have apparently succumbed to the forces of secularisation and have been forced to conform to the dominant acceptable ways of Scottish life in the twenty-first century – whatever these may be (Coll and Davis in Bradley 2004:232). It seems strange to emphasis the relationship between faith, football and Celtic supporters in the conclusion (p.230) and in the introduction argue 'that religious *identity*, as opposed to religious *faith* and lifestyles, still have a significant role to play in Scottish life', (Bradley, 2004:34). The issues of identity and faith in this collection seem to be confused, but more of a concern is the fact that the initial concepts upon which the research is based are perhaps not robust enough to deliver what the authors want them to deliver.

Bradley asks us, as many authors tend to do, to accept his organising assumptions and principles as a matter of faith and yet the assumptions based upon notions of identity, diaspora, and selective notions of community cast a shadow over the analysis of Celtic Football Club, Catholicism, Irishness and identity. Such notions or ideas are presented throughout in a reified form that unfortunately reduces the social possibilities within sport and in this case Scotland. It could be suggested that just as the struggle to ban fox-hunting was viewed as one of last bastions of naked class warfare in Scotland and Britain, the effort to reify the significance of football clubs such as Celtic and Rangers, in terms of identity and religion, is perhaps one of the few spaces where core ideologues fight out a sectarian war without weapons and sadly either unconsciously or consciously contribute to the reproduction of forms of sectarianism in Scotland. This rich collection of essays may have been better premised upon notions of recognition, redistribution and respect rather than identity. It is not without reason that the *Record of the Summit on Sectarianism*, held by the Scottish Executive in February 2005, highlighted football as one of four areas of required action in Scotland (Scottish Executive, 2005).

One final comment needs to be made in relation to the liberal humanist claim that religion can be eradicated from human life. This remains an article of faith for many secular humanist groups and yet it should not be forgotten that at best (i) liberal humanism itself may have been rooted in nineteenth-century Christian denominations such as the Quakers or the Unitarians and (ii) at worst in its extreme form liberal humanism itself is often viewed as religion-like in terms of its adherence to particular views about humanity, politics and religion. According to Gray (2002b: 69) liberal humanism is an absolute form of religious doctrine. Gray argues that the secular view that we live in a post-religious era is a Christian if not Western invention. Liberal humanism in other words is framed as a form of religious humanity forged in a period before the work of John Stuart Mill (1806–1873) and whose intervention, lest we forget, upheld the abolition of slavery. Today's liberal humanism could be viewed as a contemporary version of an eccentric nineteenth-century cult that is clearly modelled on Christianity despite the secular claims that are made. Yet the Christian principle of individual liberty contrasts with and is often at conflict with other faiths.

MUSLIM FUNDAMENTALISM, THE WAR AGAINST FEMINISM AND PHYSICAL ACTIVITY

Many of the traditional early sociological thinkers believed that a process of secularisation was bound to occur as societies modernised and became more reliant upon technology and science. In this sense secularisation was utilised as a comparative concept that described the processes whereby religion lost its influence over various aspects of the social world. By contrast the notion of fundamentalism is used to describe a strict adherence to a set of principles or beliefs and within this context religious fundamentalism describes the approach taken by different religious groups who adhere to a strict interpretation of various religious doctrines, texts, and/or scriptures. The strength of religious fundamentalism is often viewed as an indication that secularisation has not triumphed in the modern world. Religious fundamentalists believe that only one view of the world is possible and that their view of the world is the correct one.

A number of feminist thinkers have attempted to explain the appeal of fundamentalism in the predominantly Muslim societies of the Middle East, North Africa and Southeast Asia (Afary, 1997). Such studies have generally been divided into at least three groups: those that have (i) stressed the economic and political issues that have given rise to the emergence of fundamentalist movements; (ii) explored the disruptive impact of modernisation on the

259

family and (iii) argued that militant Islamist movements and organisations have actually empowered students and professional women in certain ways by restricting their lives. Gender relations are not a marginal aspect of such movements because an important facet of the work of many Islamic fundamentalist groups has been the creation of the illusion that a return to traditional patriarchal relations is the answer to the social and economic problems of both Western and non-Western societies (Afary, 1997:1). The notions of fundamentalism, secularism, traditionalism and modernism are all contested ideas in terms of their continued and precise value to explaining late twentieth- and early twenty-first-century capitalism.

It is clear from the above that the emergence of Muslim beliefs and fundamentalism is a complicated phenomenon. It is only recently that feminist researchers have begun to fuel, question and intensify the stance taken by forms of Muslim fundamentalism in relation to women's physical activity. Walseth and Fasting's (2003) study of Islam's view of physical activity and sport is based upon the interpretations offered by Egyptian women over a four-month period. Studies that have looked at the relationship between Islam and participation in physical activity and sport, they argue, have generally been divided into at least two groups: (i) those that draw upon Islam's positive attitudes towards sport and (ii) those that have focused on women's sports participation in Muslim countries (Walseth and Fasting, 2003:48). What is interesting about the conclusions drawn from this fieldwork is the common opinion, that contained within Islam was a positive attitude towards participation in sport and physical activity that could be interpreted as a way of pleasing God – a finding that challenges the secular interpretation of the nature of sports participation in certain parts of the world and warns against too much of a Western interpretation being placed on the relationship between sport and religion. The second conclusion from this study was less positive in that it noted that some of the barriers to women's participation in certain physical activities resulted from a different interpretation of Islam in relation to the body, dress, religion, sexuality and the locus of power in society (Walseth and Fasting, 2003:57).

It has been suggested that certain religious beliefs have curtailed the freedom of expression that women in parts of the world have in comparison to, for example, women in many non-Islamic countries. It has also been recorded that feminist politics is viewed by some religious fundamentalists as a form of fundamentalism which is in part why some traditionalist Islamic fundamentalist groups have waged war on feminism. Afary (1997:15) contends that for feminist politics to be more effective in this area it must work in conjunction with other grassroots movements in order to mainstream an emancipatory rather than a reactionary feminist agenda as a basis for undermining traditional Islamic fundamentalism. Certainly progressive alliances might help to produce a more reality-congruent view of the relationship between sport and religion in the twenty-first century. Research into Islam and physical activity needs to become more mainstream to the debate about sport and religion today. The stories of the struggle for Muslim woman attempting to find God through sport and physical activity are much more religious than the moderate view that sport is a form of civil religion or worship contoured by the developments of contemporary capitalism. Yet other challenges exist within some forms of Islamic belief in relation to the redistribution of wealth within areas of the world that might not be Muslim, that is, in relation to humanity as a whole.

SPORT AS CIVIL RELIGION, WORSHIP AND CAPITALISM

Today many major league baseball clubs and more than 100 minor league teams arrange non-denominational religious services each Sunday morning before the Sunday afternoon game (Levinson and Christensen, 1996:317). Approximately 50 per cent of all major league players attend these sessions of prayer and bible reading. The Fellowship of Christian Athletes and other evangelical sports groups are thriving in certain parts of America. Ministers have become part of the army of support services attached to major sport franchises. The Fellowship of Christian Athletes was founded in 1954; it has doubled in size over recent years, according to Nixon and Frey (1996:69), has a multi-million dollar budget, a staff of more than 100 and a membership in excess of 100,000. Signs with biblical references, note Levinson and Christensen (1996:317), sprout like mushrooms with fans, coaches and athletes during the post-game prayer sessions. Sport is often uncritically described as a form of civil religion, worship and capitalism without necessarily forging the links between these three social forces.

The relationship between religion and sport has relatively recently been explored in a collection of essays entitled *With God on Their Side*: *Sport in the Service of Religion* (Magdalinski and Chandler, 2002). The assumptions informing this collection are that sport and religion are both cultural institutions with a global reach, a claim that may be more realistic in relation to Catholicism than sport. The authors go on to suggest that each of these institutions is characterised by the ecstatic devotion of followers and ritualistic performances. The premise upon which the historical and geographical case studies of sport and religion, presented in this book, are based is one of international pluralism. Thus Magdalinski and Chandler (2002:1–2) write

> we have conceived this volume to investigate the role of sport and religion in the social formation of collective groups and we are specifically concerned with the way in which sport might operate in the service of a religious community and assist in the promulgation of its theology.

Magdalinski and Chandler (2002) avoid the somewhat common assertion in the age of late modernity that sport has taken on the character of modern religion. In many cases such assertions are critically advanced as a statement about the alleged increasing secularism associated with modern life (Gruneau, 1999:10). Consequently sport is viewed as form of civil religion, controlled through hierarchical structures of authority, a celebration that seeks to reproduce certain sets of power relations, a sacred form of activity that lifts the human spirit and like religion is dependent upon rituals before, during and after major sports events. The extent to which sport is viewed as a modern substitute for religion, a new popular opiate, is often questionable but the idea that sport acts as a form of religion is often a question of emphasis. The most extreme position is to suggest that sport is like a new form of religion while others stop short of this position by suggesting that sport is *religious-like* thus sharing certain characteristics with religion but not being a religion or a religious movement.

At its most extreme the relationship between sport, religion and capitalism is ever present in Smith and Westerbeek's (2004) account of the new sporting cathedrals of the

Western world. The writers point out that sport is a kind of religion that satisfies religious needs for participants and spectators and that at the heart of the optimal sporting and religious experience is spiritual enlightenment (Smith and Westerbeek, 2004:90). The sports business, they warn, could destroy everything that makes sport suitable as a religious substitute (Smith and Westerbeek, 2004:91). In other words they believe the specialness of sport can be destroyed by business if it fails to comprehend the spiritual components of the product by diminishing the power of the rituals, the stories, the gods and the temples that can be promoted through sport as religion. The authors uncritically buy into the idea that sport like religion mobilises communities, forges identity, provides meaning, infuses passion and enlivens the soul. Many of the problems that limit this sort of analysis are closely tied to a frame of reference that is presented as universal but in reality rarely unpacks or delineates within or between matters of faith. Perhaps more importantly development is based upon spiritual rather than social possibilities. The political implications of this lack of social thinking can often be disturbing. By framing development purely in spiritual and capitalistic terms Smith and Westerbeek (2004), while acknowledging the potential of the cultural sports business, tend to reproduce certain social arrangements that are idealist and far from liberating for some people.

BETTER FAITH, BETTER ETHICS, BETTER SPORT?

In the contemporary world is it necessary to have a strong relationship between sport, religion and faith or does an adherence to religious faith make things worse in terms of tolerance, recognition and reconciliation? Faith carries a premium with it in the contemporary world and yet from faith schools, faith-based welfare through to religious justifications for debt relief and even warfare it is hard to escape from it. Faith-based sports movements continue to have a presence despite the increasing secularisation of certain societies. Those who support the notion of better faith, better ethics, better sport tend to view forms of faith as an ethical underpinning for debates about not just religion and politics but also sport. Those who do not support the notion of better faith, better ethics and better sport tend to argue from a humanist perspective that being in the possession of a divinely-prescribed rulebook does not put you on the moral high ground in which there is a hierarchy of moral ideologies. It is worthwhile briefly considering the arguments for and against such propositions.

The arguments for better faith, better ethics and better sport tend to rely on a number of assumptions. The assumed demise of old political ideologies has left all areas of public life including sport with a sense of uncertainty about what is right and wrong. Developments in genetic science continue to present ethical dilemmas for sport, not least the possible cloning of athletes. Broader bio-ethical issues such as abortion and euthanasia are rarely out of the headlines. For those who support faith-based answers to difficult problems it is argued that faith can make an important contribution in the prioritising of policies. Faith groups are frequently sought out by government and related agencies because they contain highly motivated and committed volunteers. A major English study into sport volunteering confirmed the need for more informal patterns of sports volunteering given the chaotic lifestyles of young people in general (Sport England, 2003). Faith-informed volunteers often run local schemes and while the faith element may be strong it often remains in the background. The problematic assumption is that better faith, better ethics, better volunteering in sport is part of an answer to the broader crisis of volunteering. Faith-based welfare provision has become so popular in the United States and to a lesser extent Britain that governments want to remain neutral on matters of faith but all parties whether it be in politics, religion or sport seem to want dedicated adherents.

The arguments against better faith, better ethics, and better sport also tend to rely upon a number of assumptions primarily associated with humanists or atheists. Humanists tend to deny the possibility of moral rulebooks but believe that certain actions are right and wrong in areas such as freedom, tolerance, equality and justice. Emotive arguments about sport need to be informed by relevant comparative evidence as the possible antidote to making uninformed choices. Humanists view too strong an adherence to religion and sport as divisive and serving self-interests. Humanists would seek to provide forms of intervention that promoted tolerance in areas such as ethnicity and racism in sport and be naturally suspicious of sporting organisations that promoted single-faith sport as a model for better faith, better ethics and better sport. Humanist sport would promote pluralist sport based upon the assumption that cultural and religious based sporting groups will only come to tolerate each other if they are educated together through sport and other areas. To humanists, seeking to promote or privilege forms of sporting experience at the expense of others is immoral but also dangerous because it promotes a sort of tribalism that capitalism, globalisation and the contemporary world needs to outgrow. Yet the problem, for anyone seeking faith-based forms of sporting involvement as the antidote to the contradictions of the modern sporting world, or even a faith-based model of global sport, of realism and hierarchies remains with sport as in other facets of life – namely, which faiths and why?

SUMMARY

The sense of allegiance that many hard-core sports fans have for a particular team is almost religious-like in the sense that fans share a common history and stand in a particular relationship to other sports fans and groups that are integral to a sense of who one is. Hard-core sports fans and strong believers of faiths share a common distinguishing aspect of ascriptive identity, namely that those who belong to such groups identify deeply with them and typically experience membership of such groups as morally significant. The sectarian hate that attaches itself to Celtic versus Rangers football matches is often characterised as groups of hard-core football fans partaking in a common history and standing in a particular relationship to another group of fans who are integral to one's sense of self. In the same sense to be a Muslim or a Jew or a Christian is also to suggest that one's identity is intimately bound up with membership of a group or at least the value that such a belief has is fundamentally important to the believer in a similar but also different way that a hard-core old firm sports fan values the allegiance to a team.

Religion exists in all known societies; religious beliefs and practices vary from culture to culture and to the extent that sport involves a set of symbols and rituals, some of which may be religious, it is not difficult to see why academics are quick to point out that sport continues to invoke religion in the early twenty-first century. Today we find religious organisations using sport and sports participants turning to religion in different ways. Despite the onward march of secularism in some Western communities it is far from clear whether sport inhibits or promotes religious beliefs, and whether in certain instances such religious beliefs help to develop social cohesion, networking, or even psychological advantage in sport today.

History has also taught us that proclaiming the principle of tolerance and justice in a multi-faith society is not sufficient to make a reality of it. There is some truth in the observation that the cultural wars between the religious and the secular is an important social division locally, nationally and internationally and yet it is not an openly acknowledged problem in the sense that other social divisions involving race, gender and forms of social inequality are. The influence of religion on sport may have declined but it certainly has not disappeared and we have seen in this chapter that the potential influence of faith of different varieties does not necessarily mean better sport or a more acceptable world to live in today. While other areas of conflict in the world today have observed the power of fundamental religious groups, conflict in and through sport has not yet been characterised by a class of fundamental religious beliefs or dogma and in this sense sport might thankfully be viewed as being more secular than, for example, some aspects of American politics, culture and society. Just as the identity model of sport may be viewed as being problematic so too is the ascriptive identity model of religion in its most fundamentalist forms – a point we shall return to in the last chapter of this section.

KEY CONCEPTS

Capitalism	Islam
Catholicism	Jewishness
Christianity	Liberal humanism
Civil religion	Masculinity
Ethics	Muslim
Faith	Power
Feminism	Religious dogma
Fundamentalism	Sabbatarianism
Identity	Secular
Ideology	Sectarianism

KEY READING

Books

Coakley, J. (2003). *Sport in Society*: *Issues and Controversies*. New York: McGraw Hill, 526–561.
Magdalinski, T. and Chandler, T. (eds) (2002). *With God on Their Side*: *Sport in the Service of Religion*. London: Routledge.

Nixon, H. and Frey, J. (1996). *A Sociology of Sport*. Albany: Wadsworth, 60–77.

Ruthven, M. (2000). *Islam: A Very Short Introduction*. Oxford: Oxford University Press.

Sugden, J. and Bairner, A. (1993) *Sport, Sectarianism and Society in a Divided Ireland*. London: Leicester University Press.

Journal articles

Afary, J. (1997). 'The War against Feminism in the Name of the Almighty: Making Sense of Gender and Muslim Fundamentalism'. *New Left Review*, 24 (July/August): 1–21.

Lacombe, P. (2001). 'The Breton Body in Culture and Religion'. *Culture, Sport and Society*, 14(3): 27–40.

Supiot, A. (2003). 'Dogmas and Rights'. *New Left Review*, 21 (May/June): 118–137.

Walseth, K. and Fasting, K. (2003). 'Islam's View on Physical Activity and Sport: Egyptian Women Interpreting Islam'. *International Review for the Sociology of Sport*, 38(1): 45–61.

Further reading

Beer, S. (2002). 'Better Faith, Better Ethics?' *Fabian Review*. Spring: 8–12.

Gardiner, G. (2003). 'Black Bodies–White Codes: Indigenous Footballers, Racism and the Australian Football League's Racial and Religious Vilification Code'. In Bale, J. and Cronin, M. *Sport and Post-colonialism*. Oxford: Berg, 29–45.

Gunnell, R. (2004). 'Religion: Why Do We Still Give a Damn?' *New Statesman*, 3 May: 18–22.

Scottish Executive (2005). *Record of the Summit on Sectarianism*. Edinburgh. Scottish Executive Publications.

Smith, A. and Westerbeek, H. (2004). *The SportsBusiness Future*. Basingstoke: Palgrave Macmillan, 90–117.

REVISION QUESTIONS

1. Explain the usage of the following terms to illuminate the relationship between sport and religion today: fundamentalism, secularism, traditionalism and faith.

2. Evaluate the key themes that have dominated the research literature on sport, religion and society.

3. Explain the assertion that Islam has been both a barrier and a source of empowerment for Muslim women's involvement in sport and physical activity.

4. Argue for and against the idea that the relationship between religion and sport is based upon profit rather than faith. Illustrate your answer using three examples from sport.

5. How would humanists view the adherence to religion from sporting outlets and vice versa?

PRACTICAL PROJECTS

1. Identify a single faith organisation of your choice and explain the way in which faith informs the organisation's understanding of its sporting practices.

2. Develop a ten-point strategy aimed at increasing participation in sport and physical activity amongst Muslim women. (http://www.islam.org.au/articles/19/women.htm).

3. Develop a series of four short historical case studies of any sports clubs that have religious affiliations and use the material you have collected to write a report arguing for or against the notion that sport has become more or less secular over time.

4. Carry out a content analysis of the newspaper coverage of Celtic versus Rangers football matches, or any other two teams associated with forms of religious identity, between 2000 and 2005. List and evaluate references to religious themes associated with this match. Write a research report of about 3,000 words analysing your findings and providing a set of recommendations aimed at changing fan culture at these matches.

5. Make a list of five actions/behaviours from observing sport which have religious connotations. Explain the action, the meaning of the action, the religion the action is associated with and give a critical comment.

WEBSITES

Christian sports groups
    www.crosssearch.com/Recreation/Sports/

Fellowship of Christian Athletes
    www.fca.org/

Jews in sports history
    http://jewishsports.com/jewsin/history/

Islamic women's sports
    www.salamiran.org/Women/Olympic/history.html

The Maccabi Games
    www.jccmaccabi.org/index_home.php

The Maccabi World Union
    www.maccabiworld.org/

Chapter 13

Sport, lifestyles and alternative cultures

How do core extreme sport fans resist the absorption into mainstream sport – indeed should they? Getty Images

PREVIEW

Introduction • Alternative, extreme and free-sports • The growth of alternative sports in the USA • Alternative versus mainstream sports trends • Alternative sports and the IOC • Rationales and arguments about extreme sports • Sports, sub-cultures and lifestyle sports • Sport as popular resistance and hegemony • Freedom, constraint and alienation – an old sporting paradox • Negative freedom • Positive freedom • Liberation and sport • Sport and alienation • Alternative or lifestyle sports as social movements • Utopian alternatives • Sport as a social movement or social forum.

OBJECTIVES

This chapter will:

■ examine the emergence of extreme sports and the differences between extreme and alternative sports;

■ introduce concepts for thinking about sport, lifestyles and alternative cultures;

■ discuss the processes by which some alternative sports threaten to evolve into mainstream sports;

■ evaluate the use of the term freedom in relation to alternative sports cultures;

■ suggest ways in which sports, lifestyles and alternative cultures might be thought of as social movements.

INTRODUCTION

Alternative sports like alternative cultures have often been linked ideologically and in practice as an expression of resistance to both mainstream sport and mainstream culture. Alternative sports have at times been linked to extreme, action and/or free-sports. *One* approach to activities coming under the banner of free-sports has been to firmly locate or associate such activities with counter-cultures or 'other' alternatives to mainstream sport. Data from the USA illustrates that the demand for alternatives to mainstream sport choices has emerged at such a rate that the large traditional commercial powerbrokers in American sport may struggle to win back a generational cross-section of traditional devotees to sports such as baseball, basketball and American football. The values associated with alternative sports have often been linked with notions of individualism, lifestyle, risk, freedom, alienation, excitement, volun-tarism and invoking a high degree of agency when compared with mainstream sport and mainstream lifestyles. The spectre of generation X or Y rebelling or protesting against the way things are is not new since counter-cultural movements have been active throughout the twentieth century and before. BMX biking and skateboarding have more than a 30-year history but it is only relatively recently that they have been brought to the attention of mainstream advertising. It is not so long ago that the popular trend of jogging struggled to become a mainstream form of activity for certain groups of people and yet at the beginning of the twenty-first century the attraction of organised fun runs, marathons and half-runs continues to be a pull for people of all ages. The same cannot be said for pursuits such as surfboarding, skateboarding, snow-boarding, BMX biking or undertaking the eco-challenge, all of which mean different things to different groups of people and oscillate between conformity and fighting to remain as an alternative. There are those who see the difference between alternative sport as a cult or a religion being purely a question of numbers. If this is the case then when does an alternative lifestyle become a mainstream activity? Or given the demographic ageing profile in countries such as the UK are there likely to be as many alternatives in the future as there have been in the past?

Research carried out by the Sporting Goods Manufacturers Association in the USA (see Table 13.1) indicates that the growth rates of skateboarding and snowboarding remain around the 50 per cent a year mark and that five of the top ten fastest growing sports in the USA can be bracketed as extreme or free sports. Yet the issue is complicated not just by the emergence of a diverse range of sports but by genre and geographical location. The evolution of non-mainstream sport is not simply youthful rebellion against the sporting choices of parents or elders. Surfing between 1987 and 2000, for example, remained the second most popular sport to soccer in Brazil and yet in America skateboarding, windsurfing and snowboarding are all associated with rebellion against the sports participation of one's parents including those who were part of the free sports associated with the Californian surfing communities of the 1950s. Many traditional sports in America are in decline in terms of participation growth, a fact that is supported by the table in Box 13.1 which shows that sports such as baseball, basketball and tennis have all been in decline. Mainstream sports lag behind alternative sports in terms of US participation trends but not number of participants. The story can be repeated in different parts of the world, particularly in Australia and Europe, where the lifestyle choices inherent in extreme sports make them an attractive alternative to those that were available to their parents (Gillis, 2001:15).

In the USA the term generation Y, also known as the new millennials, is specifically used to refer to the 75 million children between the ages of 6 and 24 who allegedly show a higher degree of individualism than their predecessors. There is no longer a youth culture, but youth cultures plural, that are turned off the old school of sport and yet what you do is still seen to be an important part of the type of person you are. As Gillis (2001:15) reminds us there is no contest when you ask a contemporary 18-year-old whether they like snowboarding, skateboarding, bands, girls and boys or rugby, baseball, or cricket. Further defining the nature of generation Y is a disdain for authority and the desire for sport is in part characterised not by the traditional values of team sport but by the desire for risk-taking with the common denominators being the thrill-seeking experience culminating in an adrenalin rush. The choice of sports of future rulers of twenty-first-century America may in fact be organised on a continuum not according to health, safety and co-operation but the likelihood of danger, recklessness, and potential injury. Between now and 2010 it is estimated that generation Y will grow at twice the rate of the general population and that the future leaders of American society will be those weaned not on baseball, basketball and American football but also extreme sports.

The emergence of alternative sports has also had an impact upon an International Olympic Committee eager to develop youth appeal and take a hard line on traditional minority specialist sports. In 2004, alarmed that the Olympics were increasingly viewed

Table 13.1 *Alternative versus mainstream sport in the USA*
US participation trends (1000s)

Alternative sports	1987	1990	1993	1999	2000	% change (1999–2000)	% change (1987–2000)
BMX	n/a	n/a	n/a	3,730	3,977	6.6	6.6
Inline skating	n/a	4,695	13,689	27,865	29,024	4.2	518.2
Kayaking	n/a	n/a	n/a	4,012	4,137	3.1	18.2
Mountain biking	1,512	4,146	7,408	7,849	7,854	0.0	419.4
Rock climbing (indoor)	n/a	n/a	n/a	4,817	6,117	27.0	30.3
Skateboarding	10,888	9,267	5,388	7,807	11,649	49.2	7.0
Skiing (downhill)	17,676	18,209	17,567	13,865	14,749	6.4	−16.6
Snowboarding	n/a	2,116	2,567	4,729	7,151	51.2	237.9
Snowmobiling	n/a	n/a	n/a	5,490	7,032	28.1	8.3
Surfing	1,459	1,224	n/a	1,736	2,180	25.6	49.4
Wakeboarding	n/a	n/a	n/a	2,707	3,581	32.3	58.9
						21.3% (average growth)	244.7% (average growth)
Maonstream sports	1987	1990	1993	1999	2000	% change (1999–2000)	% change (1987–2000)
Baseball	15,098	15,454	15,586	12,069	10,881	−9.8	−27.9
Basketball	35,737	39,808	42,138	39,368	37,552	−4.6	5.1
Golf	26,261	28,945	28,610	28,216	30,365	7.6	15.6
Ice hockey	2,393	2,762	3,204	2,385	2,761	15.8	15.6
Soccer	15,338	15,945	16,365	17,582	17,734	0.9	15.2
Tennis	21,147	21,742	19,346	16,817	16,598	−1.3	−21.5
						8.6% (average growth)	1.9% (average growth)

1. These statistics are based on the 'Superstudy' of sports participation commissioned by the Sporting Goods Manufacturers Association, and conducted by American Sports Data, Inc in January 2001, monitoring 103 sports and fitness activities.
2. All percentage figures represent positive growth unless preceded by a minus symbol.

Source: 'Extreme Sports', *SportsBusiness*, 14 August 2001: 17.

as being too staid and out of touch, IOC president Jacques Rogge suggested to senior IOC officials that younger people were into newer more demanding pursuits, such as dirt-biking and extreme sports. In 2002 Rogge tried to axe modern pentathlon, baseball and softball and pointed out how sports such as equestrian and tae kwan do often draw very small crowds. In 2004 the IOC wrote to five governing bodies of sport concerning potential inclusion in the programme for the 2012 Olympic Games, namely squash, karate, golf, roller sport and rugby. At the Beijing Olympic Games of 2008 it has already been agreed to substitute two track cycling events with two BMX cycling events. Keen to make the games a more truly global or international event it has been argued that people in every country in the world play golf but that only a few do modern pentathlon (Campbell: 2004). The inclusion of Rugby Sevens would open up opportunities for many 'other' countries to participate and not simply the traditional nations such as Britain and Australia. Yet if extreme or alternative sports were to become part of a mainstream attraction such as the Olympic Games does this mean that they would lose something of the essence of being extreme or alternative in the first place? Would the threat of being absorbed into the arena of international capitalist sport mean that extreme or alternative sports would lose their appeal through becoming associated with other values and pressures?

In one of the most recent attempts to account for the growth of extreme sports Rinehart and Sydnor (2003) choose to highlight several observations as a basis for grounding a critical discussion of the area. This provides an insightful summary of some of the main themes that have shaped the debate about alternative and or extreme sports to date, these are:

- Sports labelled alternative, extreme, gravity, lifestyle and adventure have proliferated trans-nationally.
- Contributions from cultural studies, anthropology, sociology, history, literary criticism and other areas of knowledge have impacted upon the study and interpretation of extreme sports.
- While the individual, as opposed to team approach, fundamental nature of present day alternative sports remains, the march of corporate capital and the promise of lucrative sponsorship has encroached upon many of these activities.
- The image of class-related freedom that is often attached to certain activities when they are presented as cultural commodities in film and photography is frequently an illusion if not a misleading image, if not an illusion.
- While grassroots communities of surfers, snowboarders, skateboarders and windsurfers remain the participants are conscious of their insider/outsider status brought about by the different reasons and values attached to the consumption of alternative sports.
- The history of many extreme sports illustrates the potential to explode and threaten the monopoly of mainstream sport and yet at the same time struggle to

avoid being absorbed into the mainstream and consequently lose the essence of the attraction to the sport in the first place.

■ Speed, time, risk, uncertainty, temporal issues and adrenalin rushes are all central to the ontology of being in alternative sports.

■ Notions of identity, consumption and difference remain prominent analytical angles for grasping the phenomenon that is alternative sport today.

Let us consider some of these central issues in more detail.

SPORTS, SUB-CULTURES AND LIFESTYLE SPORTS

Throughout at least the last quarter of the twentieth century the notion of sub-cultural theory was formative in discussions of sport, culture and society. The formation of sub-cultures as a collective solution or resolution to problems of blocked aspirations of certain sections of society was widely used in discussion of youth sport, violence and sport and the much wider usage of the way in which hegemony operated through sport. In this sense sport was framed as a site of popular resistance and cultural struggle. While the politics of state involvement in sport continued to dominate much of the politics of sport literature at the time the question of sport's capacity to provide resistance to what was then a debate about sport and capitalism rested very much upon the role of sport in civil society and its capacity to define itself as a credible social alternative.

A significant impact was made by those researchers who set out to illustrate the oppositional promise of sport, the meaning of style, the significance of sporting rituals and alienation from mainstream sport in the sense that many dropped out of sport. As mainstream society becomes increasingly subject to potential processes of globalisation there are those who through their actions seek to dissociate themselves from what is perceived to be the homogenising nature of global culture. Many feel that they do not wish to consume the products of a global culture and seek to find alternative sources of pleasure while others simply reject the process of globalisation. Yet the uneven development of alternative sports and lifestyles amongst the peoples of the world increasingly points to the uneven distribution of those sports mentioned in the introduction to this chapter. Is alternative sport a metaphor for Western or affluent sporting cultures and places?

One of the significant dangers in this sort of work was that many critical studies of sport that set out to analyse the wide variety of apparent popular forms of resistance to hegemony were drawn into theoretical and practical positions that lost sight of the importance of political economy and what was then discussed as capitalism's powerful forces of containment. One of the greatest weaknesses of contemporary discussions about sport today is the continued failure to realise that the new parameters of political ideas and action in sport result not so much from the demands of global markets and states and various social patternings in sport but the tension between all three of these planes (see Chapter 3). It is within this triangle of states, markets and social patternings that political ideas about sport gain ascendancy and political action occurs. Almost a quarter of a century ago the Canadian writer Richard Gruneau (1988:126) wrote that the moment of resistance always needs to be understood both in the way it opposes hegemony and is often contained by it.

It is a common mistake to associate all alternative sports with extreme sports. Many extreme sports fall under the umbrella of alternative sport but not all alternative sports are extreme. Any sport that may threaten a particularly powerful ideology may be deemed to be an alternative sport and yet not all alternative sports are associated with lifestyle, opposition or have the potential to be a social movement. Many sports that have positioned themselves as being alternative to mainstream sports tastes and choices may share some of the same characteristics as the mainstream – perhaps male dominated, suburban and exclusive to certain groups. Traditionally alternative sports have been enjoyed by smaller groups of people, and cherished a lack of competition, organisation and commercial intervention. Yet sports such as surfing have their own Grand Prix world circuit with surfing in 1999 being Coca-Cola's third largest sporting sponsorship deal behind international football and the Olympic Games. Beal's (1995) exploration of forms of social resistance presented through the sub-culture of skateboarding tried to tease out a contemporary statement about the differences between skateboarding as an alternative to mainstream sport. Three factors highlighted as important were:

- participant control of the sport;
- a desire to individualise the sport as standing apart from corporate sponsorship and thus being a symbol of self-determination and definition;
- the devaluing of competition in that what tended to define high status was not competitiveness which was viewed as negative but skilfulness and a willing co-operation in sharing experiences and expertise with group members.

FREEDOM, CONSTRAINT AND ALIENATION: AN OLD SPORTING PARADOX

The notion of freedom has often been associated with alternative sports and sub-cultures and yet the popularity of the term freedom is often matched by confusion about what it actually means. Does freedom mean being left alone to act as one chooses or does it imply some kind of fulfilment, self-realisation, personal and social development or simply escape? One of the most popular ideologies associated with the consumption of lifestyle or alternative sports is the close association with fun, hedonism, involvement, self-actualisation and expression. If we are to avoid simplistic views that alternative or lifestyle sports are simply expressions of freedom, voluntarism or even spontaneity then we have to be more sensitive to the complexity of meanings and possibilities attached to the term freedom.

Freedom is a difficult term to discuss because it is employed by sociologists, philosophers and others as commonly as political theorists. In each case the concern with the notion of freedom is rather different. In philosophy, freedom is usually examined as a property of the will. Do individuals possess free will? Do individuals possess free will to enjoy sport or are their actions entirely determined? Clearly the answer to this question depends upon one's conception of human nature, opportunity and perhaps more importantly the human mind. In economics and sociology freedom is invariably thought of as a human social relationship. To what extent are individuals or groups free agents in sport, able to exercise choice and enjoy privileges in relation to others or other places? By contrast political theorists often treat freedom as an ethical ideal or normative principle, perhaps as one of the most vital principles. Moreover throughout the twentieth century the language of freedom became closely associated with other notions such as liberation. This took many forms such as national liberation, women's liberation, sexual liberation, racial liberation and consequently the question must be asked to what extent has sport contributed to the notion of liberation? The idea of liberation seems to promise a more complete inner fulfilment than that implied by emancipation or liberty. This notion is addressed in some depth in Part 4 of this book.

Perhaps sport continues to be haunted by the same fundamental paradox alluded to by Gruneau (1999) more than a decade ago, namely that forms of sport can at times give the impression of being at once an independent and spontaneous aspect of human activity and action while at the same time being a dependent and regulated aspect of it. Certain sports at times allow us to be totally frivolous and escapist from the stresses, strains and realities of hardship in everyday life and yet the very same sports remain inherently rule-bound, structured through not just rules and rituals but space and time and therefore the paradox is simply this. How can something that is essentially structured, rule-bound, ritualised and culturally specific be free? Forms of sport might be seen to entail a high degree of freedom, choice and voluntarism but at the same time be constrained by the rules, tensions and pressures that are themselves constitutive of the same social reality. How free are we in sport? To what extent are the runners at the beginning of a race standing on the same starting line all equal, are some more equal than others, more free than others? Has sport contributed to the politics of liberation or has sport won freedoms for different groups of people in different parts of the world?

At its worst sport goes beyond the notion of constraint in that for many it is deemed to be alienating. The notion of alienation has historically been central to discussions about young women and sport and more generally youth and sport. The notion of a certain type of freedom was clearly reflected in Marx's concept of alienation. By virtue of not being able to control the product of their labour Marx asserted that workers would suffer from alienation in that they would become de-personalised by market forces and separated from their own genuine or essential natures. Such ideas have been used to provide insights into the world of contemporary sport particularly where athletes drop out of sport or where they have little control over their own labour as athletes. Thus dropping out from sport may be explained by suggesting that such athletes or that sports labour have experienced the process of being alienated from labour itself, alienated from their fellow athletes and finally alienated from their true selves. This use of the term, alienation from sport is presented in such a way that freedom is linked to personal fulfilment that only unalienated labour could bring about. At the same time the popularity of sport was also linked to alienation in the sense that sport was viewed as historically helping people cope with alienation at work.

Thus the fairly simple question: Are people free to participate in sport or do alternative sports provide a sense of freedom that is no longer encapsulated in mainstream sport? — turns out to be not that simple at all. In its simplest sense freedom means the absence of constraints or restrictions. There is a distinction drawn between the liberty to do anything or participate in anything and a licence to do anything and participate in anything. It is often unclear whether liberty becomes licence when rights are abused, when harm is done to others or when freedom is unequally shared out. Thus the most common qualified answer to the question of whether people are free to participate in sport is often yes but only within certain limits and possibilities. Although a formal neutral definition of freedom is possible, negative and positive conceptions of freedom have commonly been advanced. Negative freedom means non-interference, the absence of external constraints, while positive freedom is conceived variously as autonomy, self-mastery, personal self-development and/or some form of moral or inner freedom.

ALTERNATIVE SPORTS, LIFESTYLE OR SOCIAL MOVEMENTS?

Social movements play a significant role in radical politics not so much because of what they try to achieve but because they dramatise alternatives that might otherwise go unnoticed. It is clear that social movements favour different politics and while the aspirations of some social movements may be close to forms of socialism or a progressive way of life their objectives are disparate and sometimes actively opposed to one another. Social movements are not totalising nor do they all promise social reform or a clear strategy of social development aimed at social change or moving beyond the existing order. Grassroots organising remains crucial for building up relationships of mutual support and coalitions of resistance and yet organising from below while remaining the life-blood of many social movements remains a fragile process.

Writers such as Kusz (2004) have attempted to make sense of the emergence of extreme sports in America during the 1990s and beyond by praising the identities, values and desires that the American press have articulated and associated with the growth of extreme sports in America. The story that is told is that extreme sports are a symbol of a revival of so-called traditional American values such as individualism, self-reliance, risk taking and progress. What Kurtz means by this is that extreme sports have enabled and celebrated the return of white masculinity, white privilege, and a close articulation between American images and whiteness brought by the mainstream space colonised by white, male participation in extreme sports. To quote directly from Kusz (2004:209) 'extreme sports are celebrated . . . because they enable the apparent return of the strong, confident white male no longer paralysed by feelings of anxiety, uncertainty, resentment and paranoia'. Thus the rise of extreme sports in America is caught up in the cultural logics of white male backlash politics of the 1990s.

The story told by Wheaton (2004:149) and Beal (1996), while acknowledging that gender relations and competing notions of masculinity remain core entry points for thinking about and participating in windsurfing cultures, is slightly different from that presented by Kusz (2004). The accounts presented here are not of any single monolithic sporting masculinity but of perceived strains in the sport/masculinity relationship in windsurfing and other lifestyle sports. Add to this the rejection of formal competitiveness and the overt emphasis on winning then the ethos, action and representation of sports such as windsurfing and skateboarding culture in the USA and the UK is slightly different from that referred to by Kusz. However the examples do serve to illustrate that alternative or extreme sports are capable or at least have the potential of mobilising meanings, networks, resources and ideologies which may contribute to social conflict or at least have the potential to realign aspects of alternative or lifestyle sports with aspects of larger social movements such as the women's movement or the ecological or green movement or other socially driven movements which have been seeking social change in society.

World-wide, 60 per cent of learner surfers are women. Women and girls, while not forming themselves as a social movement, have made and won space for themselves in the world of surfing. The first Australian surfer was a woman, Isabel Letham, who started surfing in 1914 and is now in the Australian Surfing Hall of Fame. In California, women started surfing in the 1920s. During the 1960s the skill and number of female surfers increased. Margo Godfrey, in particular, represented a new breed of female surfer – athletic and aggressive – and later became the first female professional. Layne Beachley is the most successful female surfer of all time to date and her success has helped to attract more girls to take up the sport. She acknowledges the importance of powerful women such as Pam Burridge, Freida Zamba and Lisa Anderson who broke down barriers, adding 'Now there is an industry that supports women's surfing with all-girls magazines, movies and professional circuits all of which have contributed to social change within the sport of surfing. At one National Surf Centre in Britain in 2003, 40 per cent of new surfers coming through are women' (Pearson, 2003:14).

The extent to which it can be claimed that alternative or extreme sports may be considered as a social movement or making a contribution to a new social movement remains open to question. The term 'new social movements' is often applied to a set of social movements that have arisen primarily in Western cultures since the 1960s in direct response to the changing risks facing human societies. While the ways in which sports contribute to risk, uncertainty, agency, values and certain notions of freedom can be illustrated, the extent to which alternative and/or extreme sports consciously form new social movements remains uncertain. Wheaton (2004) notes that any understanding of such sports necessitates challenging the characteristic hegemonic masculinity associated with traditional and/or mainstream sport; not all alternative sub-cultures or lifestyles have to be linked to the promise, utopian or otherwise of an alternative future. Utopian alternatives to mainstream sport would remain inoperative without the visions of alternative futures and utopian transformations presented in certain alternative lifestyle sports, and in that sense they remain both an important component of and a threat to any social movement in sport. It is clear however in the research by Wheaton (2004:4) and others that part of the particular experience of, for example, windsurfing was the lifestyle that participants sought. A lifestyle that was distinctive, often alternative and closely associated with social identity although not necessarily in the progressive sense of the word. Whether it be in the promise of the surfing sub-cultures of the 1960s or twenty-first century or adventure racing and epic expeditions as 'another kind of life' (Bell, 2003:219) or the uncertainty or risk experienced in what Watters (2003:257) in his accounts of kayaking refers to as 'the wrong side of the thin edge' or style, prestige and tension encountered in Booth's (2003:315) research into surfing in Hawaii, California and Australia, something has to be said about the pleasures and compulsions of the potential utopias presented through these and other lifestyle or alternative sports.

Wheaton insightfully suggests that like other alternative lifestyle groupings that have emerged out of counter-culture movements, sporting cultures may at times invoke certain identity politics and lifestyle practices. While the emergence of lifestyle politics and lifestyle sports in the late twentieth and early twenty-first century may have deflected from the ideal of social class as a driver of social change it remains clear that the politics of sport, lifestyles and alternative cultures remains one of the key terrains of any post-twentieth-century politics of sport. Yet without firmly associating at least some of the terrain of sports, lifestyles and alternative cultures with notions of social movement or social forums the promise of these alternative sporting lifestyles and alternative cultures may remain utopian.

Social movements are amongst the most powerful forms of collective action. Social movements come in all shapes and sizes and often arise with the aim of bringing about change on a public issue. Many claim that the term 'new social movements' seeks to differentiate contemporary social movements from that which preceded them in earlier decades and is in part a reflection of changing risks facing human societies. The cumulative effect of new challenges and risks is often expressed in a sense that people are losing control of their own lives in the midst of rapid change. The notion of sport as an old or new social movement in itself or contributing to broader social movements may help to acknowledge the collective efforts to promote or resist political and/or cultural change in and through these sports. A change that acknowledges that alternative, extreme or free-sports may be viewed as a collective or individual attempt to conquer risk, take control of part of one's sporting life separate from global sport or that the sort of grassroots organising remains a crucial aspect, perhaps a primary or core reason why people participate in old or new alternative/extreme sports. These characteristics are not unlike some of the key reasons that give rise to the development of social movements. The notion of sport as a social movement remains a fruitful area of exploration for students, teachers or researchers interested in sport, culture and society.

The idea of skateboarding as a social movement aligning itself with feminist, environmental, anti-global or civil or human rights movements is a key silence within the contemporary story of lifestyle sports. While Wheaton (2004) acknowledges the potential power of skateboarding and the transforming nature of twenty-first-century sport in the USA the analysis stops short of asking what is the transformative or even liberating capacity of these sports to link themselves to progressive or even social forms of change. If the notion of social movements can add anything to the story of sport, lifestyles and alternative cultures it is simply that the very essence of social movements through and in sports involves a collective attempt to further common interests by collaborative action outside the sphere of mainstream sport and/or society. This would appear to echo many of the stated values, spirit and forgotten promises within contemporary discussions of sports, lifestyles and alternative cultures.

In Chapter 3 we have already indicated the ways in which political space has changed under the impact of new social patterns. It should be noted that newly emerging forms of sporting politics exist as well as traditional ones, rather than replacing them. New politics of sport have come onto the agenda, such as lifestyle politics, human rights in sport, environmental politics as well as old ones such as inequality, violence, nationalism and internationalism. The characteristics often associated with lifestyle sports cultures such as those of choice, self-expression or freedom of expression, differentiation, individuality, creativity, health, fitness and the body may be seen not simply as some of the variables that attract different groups of people to lifestyle sports but also as a set of values that have the possibility to unite a sea of people looking for something different from that provided by global or mainstream sporting forms. Alternative sports and lifestyle sport have been referred to as being an expression of people's cultural beliefs and values but potentially they are much more since the various sports may be viewed not simply as a widely differentiated set of sports but also as containing a mutual link to an expanding network of anti-global pleasures, pastimes and protest.

SUMMARY

Sports, lifestyles and alternative cultures have attracted a considerable degree of attention not least because they have offered a popular alternative to mainstream sport. So popular have alternative sports become that multinational corporations have seized upon the opportunity to capitalise upon the commercialisation of them. The media endorsement of athletes such as Tony Hawk meant that at age 14 the skateboarder could command a market value estimated at $250 million. The arrival of new alternative sports in the broadest sense of the word continues to pose new questions, new issues and demand new notions of explanation while at the same time necessitating evaluation of the real social choices that are offered by such new developments, characterised as they are by colonial powers, world markets and trans-national companies. The thirst for risk, uncertainty adrenalin rushes, chance and the quest for excitement are not new but the limits and possibilities presented by sport, lifestyles and alternative cultures in the twenty-first century are also matched by unpredictability, uncertainty, and a new set of parameters from those that were faced in the mid-twentieth century.

It would be unfortunate if the spirit of lifestyle or alternative sports were left solely to either theories of collective behaviour or the politics of utopia. At least two practical issues are at play in the struggle over alternative and/or extreme sports. On the one hand the notion of grassroots involvement and an antithesis to the essence of sports such as surfing, skateboarding and others being defined primarily by the need for alternative forms of competition would seem to indicate that the notion of alternative sports is more closely aligned to social-democratic reform than mainstream sport. On the other hand the inherent potential within alternative sports to become mainstream due in part to their free-market potential would seem to indicate that the notion of alternative extreme sports is also closely aligned to free-market fundamentalism due to its potential of being absorbed by free-market forces and transformed into being a mainstream popular alternative to traditional sports. A genuine confrontation with such utopias remains possible within a broader social forum or movement involving alternative sport forms and the lifestyle politics of sport, because without visions of alternative futures in and through sport utopian transformation remains politically and existentially inoperative, mere thought experiments and mental games without visceral commitment.

Thus it has been suggested here that the possibilities of real freedoms in and through alternative sporting choices may be achieved if alternative and/or extreme sports actively engage with the spirit and ethos of new social movements and social forums of the time rather than identifying with the ethos of free-market individualism or being lost to identity politics. Alternative and/or extreme sports must also become more than just the choices of a Western play-world; the options of real lifestyle sports choices must remain open to all parts of the world and not simply be a North/South divide in lifestyle and or sport as a facet of lifestyle politics. The co-operation so evident within Wheaton's (2004) accounts of lifestyle sports must move beyond being a symbol of experience and identity to making room for a more international alternative sports forum that can accommodate innumberable lifestyles and sport for life projects. Such an orientation maybe discernable in embryonic form amongst those, primarily young people, who commit themselves to the new politics of sport in the twenty-first century.

KEY CONCEPTS

Alienation	Lifestyle sports
Alternative sports	Masculinity
Constraint	Negative freedom
Counter-culture	Positive freedom
Environmental politics	Risk
Extreme sports	Social forum
Generation X	Social movement
Generation Y	Sub-cultures
Liberation	Uncertainty
Lifestyle politics	Utopia

KEY READING

Books

Donnelly, P. (1993). 'Sub-cultures in Sport: Resilience and Transformation'. In Ingham, A. and Loy, J. (eds) *Sport in Social Development*: *Traditions, Transitions and Transformations*. Illinois: Human Kinetics, 119–147.

Heywood, A. (2004). *Political Theory*: *An Introduction*. Basingstoke: Palgrave, 252–283.

Rinehart, R. (2002). 'Arriving Sport: Alternatives to Formal Sports'. In Coakley, J. and Dunning, E. (eds) *Handbook of Sports Studies*. London: Sage, 504–519.

Rinehart, R. and Sydnor, S. (eds) (2003). *To the Extreme*: *Alternative Sports Inside and Out*. Albany: Suny Press.

Wheaton, B. (ed.) (2004). *Understanding Lifestyle Sports*: *Consumption, Identity and Difference*. London: Routledge.

JOURNAL ARTICLES

Beal, B. (1995). 'Disqualifying the Official: An Exploration of Social Resistance through the Sub-culture of Skateboarding'. *Sociology of Sport Journal*, 12(4): 252–267.

Jameson, F. (2004). 'The Politics of Utopia'. *New Left Review*, 25 (Jan/Feb): 35–54.

Rinehart, R. and Grenfell, C. (2002). 'BMX Spaces: Children's Grass Roots, Courses and Corporate Sponsored Tracks'. *Sociology of Sport Journal*, 19(3): 302–314.

Stranger, M. (1999). 'The Aesthetics of Risk: A Study of Surfing'. *International Review for the Sociology of Sport*, 34(3): 265–276.

Wheaton, B. and Beal, B. (2003). 'Keeping it Real: Sub-cultural Media and the Discourses of Authenticity in Alternative Sports'. *International Review for the Sociology of Sport*, 38(2): 155–176.

Further reading

Booth, D. (2001). *Australian Beach Cultures*: *The History of Sun, Sand and Surf*. London: Frank Cass.

Booth, D. (2004). 'Surf Lifesavers and Surfers: Cultural and Spatial Conflict on the Australian Beach'. In Vertinsky, P. and Bale, J. (eds) *Sites of Sport*: *Space, Place Experience*. London: Routledge, 115–131.

Campbell, D. (2004). 'Game Over for Minor Olympic Events'. *Observer* 3 October: 5–6.

Gillis, R. (2001). 'Ready to Board?. *SportsBusiness*, August: 14–17.

Pearson, B. (2003). 'Say Aloha to Sisters of Surf'. *Herald*, 12 April: 14.

REVISION QUESTIONS

1. To what extent do participants experience a sense of freedom in lifestyle sports?

2. List and critically and evaluate six of the main themes that have been used to frame discussions about alternative or extreme sports.

3. What does the term alienation mean and how might it be used to explain the emergence of alternative sports and cultures?

4. Define both negative and positive freedom and explain how these notions differ in relation to alternative sporting cultures.

5. In relation to lifestyle politics and sport in what sense might we consider these activities as forming a social movement or social forum?

PRACTICAL PROJECTS

1. Identify five extreme sports websites and write a short report (1,000 words) on how these differ from mainstream sport choices today.

2. Choose any alternative sport, interview five individuals who regularly participate and form a discussion group from this sport. List the reasons they give for participating in the sport.

3. Use either newspaper or television coverage of alternative or extreme sport events to critically examine how these events to are reported by the media. How would you make sense of what you have found?

4. What arguments would you use to forge a policy aimed at increasing provision for alternative sports in your area? What objections would you envisage coming from the authorities and how would you address these objections or concerns? Draft a letter to your local authority making the case for the increased provision of alternative sports in your area.

5. Choose two different lifestyle sports and using ethnographic methods of enquiry write a comparative report explaining how the different sub-cultures within these two sports experience the sport.

WEBSITES

American sports data
   www.americansportsdata.com/pr_01-15-02.asp

Extreme-sports
   www.itzalist.com/spo/extreme-sports/

Insane-Riders
   www.insane-riders.com/females.html

Ripping-boardletters
   www.riing.com/boardletters.htm

Chapter 14

Sport, identities and recognition

Many authorities argue that sport is important because it helps with identity formation but if taken too far is this not dangerous? Ian Stewart

---

PREVIEW

Identity and sport • Recognition through sport • South African sport • Sport and political identities • The rise of identity politics in sport • Sport and national identity • Key questions about identity • Fragmentation in sport • Common ground in sport • Sporting heroines • The construction of identity • Sport as positive recognition • Reification of group identity • Irish sporting culture • Identity in sport as separatism • Rethinking recognition in sport • Status model of identity • Redistribution • Sport and social justice.

OBJECTIVES

This chapter will:

■ examine the rise of identity politics in sport;

■ provide an overview of the key ways in which identity in sport has been thought about;

■ provide examples of ways in which identity has been used in relation to sport such as South African sport, Irish sport and sporting heroines;

■ critically evaluate the way in which the notion of identity is used in discussions about sport, culture and society;

■ suggest reasons and ways in which the identity model needs to be replaced by a politics of recognition and status in sport.

INTRODUCTION

More than five years ago I wrote in the introduction to an edited collection of essays on sport in the making of Celtic cultures that identity history and politics in sport was no longer enough as a justification for writing about sport, culture and society (Jarvie, 1999:11). Formulaic constructions of identity in sport have become a symptomatic feature of much of the present body of knowledge that is sport, culture and society. Yet it is perhaps time to move on or at least think differently about a concept that has grown out of all proportion, is vaguely misrepresented and at times appears to be a signature phrase or rationale in itself for talking or writing about a wide range of topics such as sport and nationalism, sport and religion, and sport and ethnicity to name but three areas where the word is loosely used. Part 3 of this book has explored various notions of identity in some detail and yet the term identity itself while tending to assert a common essence to which special meanings are attached is weaker than terms such as recognition. Is it not recognition in and through sport that so-called collective identities are seeking to establish, challenge and consolidate?

One such example of how the notion of identity is presented in research about sport, culture and society is the analysis of sport presented in John Nauright's (1997) *Sport, Cultures and Identities in South Africa* which claims to explore the meanings attached to sport in South African societies, past and present. It argues that in the past, meaning the apartheid era 1948–1992, only white South Africans could represent South Africa in international sport whereas in the new post-apartheid, post-1992 South Africa, the formerly white-dominated sports have been promoted as unifying forces for a nation in the process of forging a new national identity. Apart from the title, the notion of identity is central to at least 50 per cent of the main headings that structure this cultural history of South African sport. In specific parts of this story about the development of South African sport the notion of identity is active in relation to discussions about sport, memory and performing white South African culture and identity; the

Springboks and white South African identity; coloured rugby, masculinity and community identity in Cape Town; rugby, politics and white identities in South Africa between 1948–1990; the development of soccer and urban black culture and identity; nostalgia, place and identity in the new South Africa and sport, unity identities in the Rainbow Nation.

Identity within the above mentioned book, as in many others, has a prominence as an answer to many questions. Here it features not as an explicit theory but as a magical incantation as a password into the story of South African sport that is expected to illuminate explanations of such areas as identity behaviour and the ways in which sporting ceremonies in South Africa have helped to generate identities among white South Africans (Nauright, 1997:21); the generation of national feeling in that sport played a role in shaping national identity for the white communities of the Cape and Natal colonies and the former Boer Republics prior to the 1920s (1997:45); the role of rugby in galvanising and symbolising white identity in apartheid South Africa (1997:95); the role of soccer as an emancipatory sport and as a signifier for respectability, African identity, political struggle and individual freedom (1997:123); the implementation of sporting sanctions against South Africa in the 1960s, 1970s and 1980s and bringing about a crisis of white South African identity (1997;144); the role of sport in nation building and forging a new national identity (1997:161); or more specifically the prospects of sport helping to promote a new non-racial pan-South African identity and presenting this within the new global sports order (1997:183).

There are numerous of shades of the same basic argument about sport, namely that sport can provide the technical means for creating political identities and these are thereby reflected or embedded within national cultural identities and often accompanied by an invention of tradition. This is often reinforced by suggesting that such political identities in sport challenge a certain world order and allegedly prepare the way for democratisation: table tennis in China; rugby and soccer in South Africa, cricket in the Caribbean and athletics in Kenya are all illustrative of this line of thought. The term identity often obscures a wide range of questions, scientific, political and sometimes religious and in this sense it is tempting to suggest that the concept of identity as it is used in writings about sport seems particularly well suited to function as an ostensive screen, camouflaging vagueness of content in a blaze of expression. If identity is a signifier that carries with it histories of sport or people or nation then it is important not to conflate or camouflage the complexity of sport through the use of stereotypes or plastic words such as identity and it certainly must not be confused with the struggle for recognition that is ongoing through sport.

THE RISE OF IDENTITY POLITICS IN SPORT

The rise of identity politics and identity history in sport forms a certain kind of logic of its own that has been attractive to writers who have sought to comment upon changes in sport, culture and society after about 1990 and yet few writers have offered an analysis of sport during what Balakrishnan (2002) critically refers to as the age of identity, or what Woodward (2002) refers to as the crisis of identity. The march towards global sport has meant that the processes associated with globalisation have placed questions of identity centre stage in terms of explaining the importance of sport to those countries, for example, that have emerged out of the break up of the former USSR or other former European countries such as the former Yugoslavia. Many nationalist movements during the later part of the twentieth century have fought to develop and sustain forms of identity and sport has become one of the very visible forums for the expression of such imagined communities whether they be nationalist in orientation or not.

The rise of identity politics in sport is a mode of logic, a badge of belonging and a claim to insurgency. It operates across states but also through the personal in the sense that the calls for identity have come from a myriad of traditionally marginalised groups. Identity politics presents itself as a quest from anonymity in an individualised impersonal world in that groups, countries, individuals are searching for answers to a cluster of questions such as who am I? Who is like me? Whom can I trust and where do I belong? Identity politics in sport in practice slides toward an uncritical acceptance of the premise that social groups have essential identities which if enforced run the tendency to forge divisions, separation and fragmentation. Yet in essence all identity politics involve a search for community, a quest for belonging and recognition. The problem with this and the point I wish to assert is that the thickening of identity politics through sport is inseparable from the fragmentation of sport as different groups assert their identity. In large measure the hypothetical challenge to sport is that while being the focus for a myriad of identities, personal politics as well as national identities, something at the centre needs to hold sport together. The idea of commonality or social sport or the quest for community runs the danger of being replaced by separate assertions of fundamental identities that can only lead to fragmentation.

Very rarely do you find carefully crafted accounts of identity politics in sport that empirically substantiate different accounts of identity while at the same time confirming what Naomi Klein (2001) has called reclaiming the commons. What this means is the formulation of a political framework that can take on corporate power and control and empower local organisation in sport while at the same time valuing human diversity and recognition. There are concerns about all kinds of prosaic issues in sport in the twenty-first century to the extent that sport at times is taken out of its own hands and into the law courts or the board rooms of the major global companies. There is little room here for local decisions or concerns about human diversity. The 2004 Olympic Women's marathon in Athens was run at a time to suit American television, not the athletes and not the local organisers of the games. The goal for sport should not be better far-away rules or forms of governance by faceless rulers but close up democracy on the ground.

Sporting heroines

One of the few carefully crafted studies of human diversity and identities in sport that respects the common ground is Jennifer Hargreaves' (2000) account of the politics of difference and identity amongst sporting heroines. The story of these sporting heroines does not lose sight of the common ground of social relations, different social divisions and women's sporting experiences across the globe. At the same time the stories of sport that are told illuminate exclusion, difference and identity in sport as experienced by black women in South Africa, Muslim women in the Middle East, Aboriginal women in Australia and Canada, lesbian and disabled women. All of these accounts of heroines in sport have contributed to knowing more about the lives of ordinary women, many of whom are on the margins of mainstream sport and how their own personal and group identities tell you something about who they are and who they belong to and trust. This courageous account of sporting heroines is all the more politically powerful because it avoids the danger of presenting a fragmented list of identity politics in sport that are unconnected from the common ground of social relations, power and human diversity in sport. It is very much a social account of sport that champions the cause of the public intellectual in sport making a difference, struggling for a new world order and recognising that identities in sport are not fixed but subject to continuous interpretation and re-interpretation. This account of the identities of sporting heroines avoids the temptation of so many 1970s and 1980s feminist accounts of sport which tended to champion the ego of white middle-class women in sport.

THE CONSTRUCTION OF IDENTITY

The usual contemporary approach to identity politics in sport tends to start from the idea that identity is constructed dialogically (Fraser, 2000). The proposition is that identity is forged by virtue of the fact that one becomes an individual subject only by virtue of recognising and being recognised by another subject or group. Recognition is seen as being essential to developing a sense of self and being mis-recognised involves suffering a sense of distortion of one's relation to one's self and consequently feeling an injured sense of identity. This logic is transferred onto the cultural and political terrain. As a result of repeated encounters with the stigmatising gaze and the resultant internalising of negative self- or group-images, the development of a healthy cultural identity is affected. Within this perspective the politics of recognition through sport is mobilised as a potential strategy in the repair of self or group dislocation by affirmative action that challenges derogatory or demeaning pictures of the group. The argument is that members of mis-recognised groups or groups suffering from a lack of identity can jettison such images in favour of self-representations of their own making and collectively produce a self-affirming culture of recognition. Add to this public assertion the gaining of respect and esteem from society at large and a culture of distorted mis-recognition changes to being one of positive recognition.

This model of how identity politics in sport may operate contains some genuine insights into the effects and practice of racism, sexism, colonisation, nationalism, imperialism and other forms of identity politics that operate through sport and yet the model is both theoretically and politically problematic in that such an approach leads to both the reification of group identity and the displacement of resource distribution. The problems of displacement and the reification of social and political identities in sport are serious insofar as the politics of recognition displaces the politics of redistribution and may actually promote inequality. In the 1970s and 1980s identity politics of sport was imbued with emancipatory promise and potential and yet at the turn of the century the identity politics of sport has transformed itself into a reified school of thought that recognises identity as an end in itself rather than recognition accompanied by resource redistribution. Those who promote identity politics in sport as opposed to the politics of recognition run the danger of encouraging separatism, intolerance, chauvinism, authoritarianism and forms of fundamentalism. This then is the problem of reification and identity politics in sport which will be discussed further in this chapter. What is being argued here is the need to develop accounts of recognition in sport that can accommodate the full complexity of social identities instead of promoting reification and separatism. This means developing accounts of recognition in sport that allow for issues of redistribution rather than displacing or undermining such concerns in relation to sport, culture and society.

By means of summary it might be suggested that some or all of the following arguments listed in Box 14.1 have been utilised in an examination of identity politics in sport.

It has been suggested here that students, teachers and researchers exploring identity politics in sport need to avoid decoupling the politics of identity in sport from social issues relating to the redistribution of wealth and power in sport. Identity in sport should not be viewed as an end in itself and by the same token it is not being suggested that recognition in sport can be remedied by redistribution of resources. Properly conceived struggles for recognition in sport can assist in the redistribution of power and wealth and should be aimed not at a promotion of essential fundamentalism but interaction and co-operation across gulfs of difference in sport.

BOX 14.1 THE RELATIONSHIP BETWEEN SPORT AND IDENTITY

- Essentialist arguments view identity in sport as fixed and unchanging.
- Sporting identity is linked to essential claims about nature, self and/or culture.
- Sporting identity is relational and differences are established by symbolic marking in and around sport. Sport contributes to both the social and symbolic processes involved with the forging of identities.
- Sport simply reflects the changes that have accompanied the age of identity and in this sense identity in sport refers to a period or phase in history.
- Identity politics in sport is reproduced and maintained through changing social and material conditions.
- Identity in sport involves classifying people into different permutations of us and them.
- Identity in sport involves both the promotion and obscuring of certain differences.
- Identities in sport are not unified and contradictions within them involve negotiation.
- Identity politics in sport when reified leads to forms of fundamentalism.
- The quest for identity through sport involves the quest for recognition.

Source: These arguments have been modified using Woodward's (2002:12) classifications of identity and difference.

THE REIFICATION OF SPORTING IDENTITIES

The identity politics model of recognition tends to reify identity in sport as an end in itself. In the first instance the construction of identity involves the construction of opposites and others whose actuality is always subject to continuous interpretation and re-interpretation of differences. It is crucial that all such representations that are promulgated as authentic or true accounts of identity in sport are questioned and their authority and coherence closely examined (Walia, 2001). Alternative accounts are usually decried by fundamentalists within the group as inauthentic and branded as outsider accounts not to be taken seriously. Yet this need not be the case since rarely do accounts of identity in sport elaborate upon the struggles within reified enclaves.

For example, Irish culture in Bradley's (2004) collection of essays on religion, politics, society, identity and football is presented as a cosy culture. The group, the authority and power to represent a particular version of identity in Irish sporting culture is presented as being almost immune to self-criticism. Bradley is hesitant to dissect the authority and the conflict within what he refers to as the Irish-Catholic Diaspora. Irish identity is presented as a relatively homogenous happy family, despite little mention of women's experiences within what Bradley (2004:83) asserts as 'one of the most significant institutions in world football, Celtic Football Club, a definition of Irishness itself'. By shielding certain internal struggles from view this approach masks the power of different groups to reinforce intra-group domination within and between forms of Irishness. Such an approach to identity politics in sport lends itself too easily to repressive forms of communitarianism, conformity, intolerance and fundamentalism. Many accounts of identity in sport tend to deny the possibility of recognition because of the premises or silences within the narrow discussions of sport, culture and society. They seek to laud all forms of collective self-representation as exempt from challenges as if cultural identity through sport is the end game. Such approaches to identity in sport fail to foster social interaction, social capital or *trust across differences*. The identity model thus conceived can encourage separatism, group enclaves and insider authority. In Bradley's case the tight juxtaposition of Irishness versus Scottishness versus Britishness in the end tends to reproduce some of the very forms of sectarianism that the author seeks to address. The reification and almost exalted notion of Irish identity through football is exempt from any rigorous self-criticism as if it is beyond reproach. It reifies group identity and replaces the politics of redistribution and recognition in sport with the politics of identity in sport.

A further problem with the approach to identity politics as represented within much of the research into sport, culture and society is to confuse or to misunderstand the issue of mis-recognition and maldistribution. This is akin to the way that much of the cultural Marxist literature on sport addressed the problem in the later part of the twentieth century. Marxism allowed the politics of redistribution to displace the politics of recognition in sport whereas the identity model allows the politics of recognition to replace the politics of redistribution. The idea of a purely cultural society with identity being perceived without reference to any economic relations is far removed from the current reality in sport and yet so many accounts of identity in sport, culture and society are written without due reference to political economy as if it is no longer relevant. The vagaries of

289

academia in sport have at times become too detached from the world in which sport operates.

Displacement, however, is not the main problem that the identity politics model of sport suffers from. As mentioned above this model of recognition tends to reify identity in sport thus stressing the need to confirm and display an authentic, self-affirming and self-generated collective identity. It puts pressure on individual members to conform to given group culture, cultural dissidence is accordingly discouraged and intra-group division is suppressed. The overall effect is to impose a single drastically simplified group identity that denies the complexity of people's lives and the multiplicity of their identities in sport. Ironically, adds Fraser (2000:112), the identity model runs the danger of serving as a vehicle for mis-recognition; in reifying group identity it obscures the politics of identity in sport and the struggles within the group for the authority and power to represent it. The identity model then, as certain writers in discussions of the body and sport use it, is deeply flawed both theoretically and politically.

RETHINKING RECOGNITION IN SPORT

There is no neat theoretical model that can be used to neatly resolve the dilemma of identity and recognition in sport. However the dilemma can be softened in various ways by acknowledging in part that the status model at least continues to recognise that social justice and a redistribution of wealth provides a social framework for thinking about sport, culture and society The status model recognises that not all distributive injustices in sport can be overcome by recognition alone but it at least leaves the door open for a politics of redistribution. Unlike the identity model in sport the status model continues to strive to understand recognition in sport alongside distribution. The status model of identity politics in sport works against tendencies to displace struggles for redistribution. It recognises that status subordination is often linked to distributive injustice and therefore any notions of identity in sport would be closely aligned with notions of injustice and social change in sport (see Part 4). The status model also avoids the problem of reification of group identities because the status of individuals and sub-groups within groups is part of the total pattern of recognition and social interaction. Thus identity in sport can invoke notions of social and political solidarity without masking forms of authority and power within such a collective form of identity.

It is not unrealistic to see such issues being played out in the world of sport. Following the collapse of apartheid in South Africa in 1992 the chief executive of the newly formed Department of Sport and Recreation in South Africa argued in 1997 that sport and recreation in the new South Africa had to meet the needs of the people and the nation. Identity through sport in the new South Africa was not enough but rather one of the questions facing the Department of Sport and Recreation and the government of South Africa was how to compensate the black athlete in South Africa for the decades of injustice inflicted as a result of apartheid polices. Speaking in Edinburgh in 1997 the chief executive asserted 'From that premise of recognition of past injustices, we should be able to move forward to say: how then can we address and redress this legacy of denial and deprivation in sport for the majority of athletes in South Africa?' (Department of Sport and Recreation, 1997:4). At the same time it was suggested that sport in South Africa should not be just the concern of the South African Department of Sport and Recreation but also the Supreme Council for Sport in Africa and the South Africa Truth and Reconciliation Commission, and in this way sport in South Africa may be able to contribute to the renaissance of sport in Africa. It was this notion of sport in Africa that was behind Cape Town's bid to host the 2004 Olympic Games and the 2010 Football World Cup. Thus as argued above such an example can be viewed as being illustrative of the fact that identity in sport can invoke notions of social and political solidarity without masking forms of authority and power within such a collective form of identity. Clearly the initial phase of policy development in post-apartheid sport in South Africa practically illustrates that recognition in sport in the new South Africa was a collective effort but also that the international community should compensate South Africa for past injustices in some way.

Today's struggles for recognition in sport often assume the disguise of identity politics in sport. This is usually aimed at countering demeaning cultural representations of social, cultural, national or local groups in sport. The result of mis-recognition in sport is that the struggle for identity by emphasising differences has enforced forms of separatism, conformism and intolerance but more importantly has displaced struggles for economic justice with the formation of reified identities. What is required is not the rejection of the politics of recognition in sport but rather an alternative politics of recognition that can remedy mis-recognition without fostering displacement and separatism or reification. The forgotten notion of status can provide a possible basis for examining recognition and struggles for redistribution in sport and with the help of sport. The status model of sport tends to reject the view that mis-recognition is free standing and it accepts that status subordination is often linked to distributive justice. Identity in sport cannot be understood in isolation nor can recognition be abstracted from distribution.

Cultural recognition then should not displace socio-economic redistribution as the remedy for injustice in sport even in a post-socialist age. It is possible to think of one world of sport with many worlds in that world. The goal for sport should not be identity as the end game but a framework that is not scared of close up local democracy in sport and on the ground. Even the academic left in sport, the traditional guardians of social inequality, have lost interest in the commonalities that underpin differences and identities as if the logic of global sport has arrived in every corner of the globe. Global sports has not but capitalism has and to talk of identity in sport as if nothing else matters is to accept a zero-sum game that only serves to recognise and consolidate separatism and injustice in global sport.

SUMMARY

The concept of identity has had a long history in relation to sport. It has been suggested in this chapter that the concept is not sufficient or weighty enough to encompass all the differences or representations presented through sport. Consequently there is an urgent need to rethink recognition in sport. Contemporary struggles for recognition in and through sport often take on the guise of identity politics. This is often aimed at championing the cause for a particular social difference or form of representation from disenfranchised or less powerful sections of sport. It has been suggested in this chapter that such approaches are misconceived on at least three accounts (i) the failure to foster authentic collective identities across differences has tended to enforce separatism, conformism and intolerance; (ii) the struggle for identity politics in and through sport has tended to replace struggles for economic justice and wealth redistribution which condemns different sporting groups to suffer grave injustices; and (iii) the failure to realise that while levels of social inequality between and within certain groups may be decreasing levels of poverty remain on the increase. Identity politics in sport is not enough and alternative forms of thinking about recognition in sport that make a real difference need to be urgently addressed. Only by looking at alternative conceptions of redistribution and recognition can we meet the requirements of justice for all.

KEY CONCEPTS

Collective identities	Local
Commons	Maldistribution
Difference	Mis-recognition
Displacement	Recognition
Distribution	Reification
Diversity	Resources
Fundamentalism	Social interaction
Globalisation	Social justice
Identity	Status
Intolerance	Trust

KEY READING

Books

Dyck, N. and Archetti, E. (2003). *Sport, Dance and Embodied Identities*. Oxford: Berg.
Hargreaves, J. (2000). *Heroines of Sport: The Politics of Difference and Identity*. London: Routledge.
Kenny, M. (2004). *The Politics of Identity*. Cambridge: Polity Press.
Nauright, J. (1997). *Sport, Cultures and Identities in South Africa*. London: Leicester University Press.
Woodward, K. (2002). *Identity and Difference*. London: Sage Publications.

Journal articles

Fraser, N. (2000). 'Re-thinking Recognition?' *New Left Review*, 3 (May/June): 107–120.
Fraser, N. (1995). 'From Redistribution to Recognition? Dilemmas of Justice in a Post-Socialist Age'. *New Left Review*, 12 (July/August): 1–24.
Gitlin, T. (1993). 'The Rise of Identity Politics an Examination and Critique'. *Dissent*, Spring: 172–179.

Further reading

Department of Sport and Recreation (1997). 'Pulling it Together: Developing a Sport and Recreation Policy That Meets the Needs of the Nation'. South African Department of Sport and Recreation. Cape Town: unpublished paper.

Jarvie, G. (ed.) (1999). *Sport in the Making of Celtic Cultures*. London: Leicester University Press.

Maynard, M. (2002). 'Race, Gender and the Concept of Difference in Feminist Thought'. In Scraton, S. and Flintoff, A. (eds) *Gender and Sport: A Reader*. London: Routledge, 111–126.

Niethammer, L. (2003). 'The Infancy of Tarzan'. *New Left Review*. 19 (Jan/February): 79–91.

REVISION QUESTIONS

1. Compare and contrast the way in which the notion of identity is used in discussion about sport, culture and society.

2. Develop a critique of the identity model and provide an alternative approach to thinking about recognition in sport.

3. In relation to two of the following texts mentioned in this chapter Nauright (1997); Hargreaves (2000); or Bradley (2004), explain how the concept of identity is used to describe aspects of sport, culture and society.

4. Compare and contrast the way in which identity is used to define symbolism and rituals in two different sporting settings.

5. This chapter has talked about the reification of sporting identities – what does this mean and what are the dangers of a reified sporting identity?

PRACTICAL PROJECTS

1. Carry out a Google computer search using the words Sport+Identity+Recognition and write a short report (1,000 words) on your findings.

2. Interview five different groups of people as defined by such variables as age, gender, sexuality and/or nationality with a view to ascertaining different attitudes towards exercise, eating and body image. Write a short report comparing and contrasting the views of the different groups.

3. Over the period of a month visit a popular local sports team and talk to the regular core fans about what the team means to the locality, the group, the nation.

4. Develop a ten-point sports plan or policy designed to produce a fairer redistribution of the wealth generated through sport from the rich countries of the world to the poorer countries of the world.

293

5. Carry out a content analysis of the opening ceremony of a major sporting spectacle. Use the evidence from your content analysis to substantiate and critically evaluate the existence or otherwise of a world order in sport in terms of recognition, wealth and coverage of the opening ceremony.

WEBSITES

Boxing bodies and identities
  http://ww.boxinginsider.com/gallery/index.php

Cultural and national identity in New Zealand
  http://www.stats.govt.nz/looking-past-20th-century/culture-national-identity/default.htm

Sport and identity
  http://irs.sagepub.com/cgi/search?qbe=spirs;36/4/393&journalcode=spirs&minscore=5000

Lesbian identity formation and sport
  http://www.findarticles.com/p/articles/mi_hb3589/is_199709/ai_n8538108

Part 4

Sport, social division and change

INTRODUCTION

The chapters that form the final part of this book emphasise issues of social division and social intervention. They look at well-documented forms of social division such as sport and social class, sport and gender and sport and racism. They acknowledge that particular forms of social division have tended to be singled out for particular attention in the study of sport, culture and society. They take a broader view of looking at sport and social division. They are also sensitive to other notions such as community, social cohesion and human rights, which are highlighted as having an important influence in the real world of sport at the beginning of the twenty-first century. They champion the power of sport to produce change and make a small difference to people's lives. Part 4 of this book necessarily focuses upon the extent to which sport has figured in various campaigns and policies aimed at producing change in and through sport. The final chapter of this book explains some of the excitement, commitment and challenges facing the student, researcher or teacher who is captivated by and committed to the power of education and education through sport today.

Sport and social divisions

It is impossible to begin to think about people, including sportspeople without immediately encountering social divisions. Human beings are almost automatically perceived as being male or female, black or white, old or young, rich or poor. How people come to think of their own identity is often influenced by social divisions such as age, gender, ethnicity and class to name but four primary social divisions. Chapter 15 in highlighting certain social divisions and the nature of the evidence in relation to sports participation, aims to clear a lot of the substantive groundwork relating to sport and social division while emphasising the importance of taking a broad view.

It acknowledges that different social divisions are not just statements about identities and difference but also about hierarchies. It is also necessary to consider the way in which class, gender, age, ethnicity and other factors interact in sporting contexts. The analysis of sport and social divisions must involve coming to terms with complexity in sport. The celebration of sporting differences implies differentiation, which as Part 3 showed, can be problematic if reified.

Sport, community and social capital

The relationship between sport and the community has become central to various policies of social inclusion and on a broader international scale community regeneration. Community building is a live agenda and yet it is set within a context or a world that champions the triumph of the individual within a consumer-orientated culture. Within this type of thinking all sporting choices are allegedly valid and open to everybody. Chapter 16 examines the relationship between sport and a cluster of concepts and policy ideals that have collectively asserted the positive influence of sport and communitarianism. Sport's contribution to communitarianism is examined drawing upon the notion of social capital. We often hear of the contribution that sport can make in terms of producing economic capital but what social capital can be built or sustained through sport? It is argued that it is unrealistic to expect sport to sustain a notion of social capital or civic engagement without addressing certain issues such as community ownership of sports clubs, obligations to the community or stakeholding in international sport. Should sport be viewed as a form of entertainment or a social right?

Sport and social change

In the introduction to this book one of the core questions that was raised was: What is the transformative capacity of sport? It has subsequently been stressed throughout this book that it is important to go beyond explaining or analysing sport by asking the question: What difference can sport make? Chapter 17 answers this question by looking at where sport has been part of campaigns and policies aimed at bringing about social change through sport. The chapter draws upon illustrative examples of where sport has been part of broader campaigns to bring about change in society at large and internal campaigns where the focus of change has been sport itself. While many of the examples relate to sport and social class, sport and gender and sport and racism the chapter is conscious of the fact that the underlying factors linked to social division and inequality are also geographical and that all students interested in thinking about and addressing social change in sport must acknowledge that the root causes of many of the social injustices in sport today may also involve differences, for example, between the North and the South. The chapter explains that in practical terms the formulation of sports policy is but one of the most effective methods of bringing about social change in sport. The link between analysis and action for change can take many forms but ultimately the student, teacher and researcher of sport must move beyond the issues of what is going on in sport and how we make sense of it to decide what is to be done about what is going on. Chapter 17 argues for informed social intervention in and through sport.

Sport, human rights and poverty

Chapter 18, Part 4 finishes by asking whether sport should be seen in terms of it being a form of entertainment or more of a social right. In this penultimate chapter the relationship between sport, poverty and human rights is examined. The aspirations of many groups to bring about social change should not lose sight of the fact that whatever the advances made by forms of progressive globalisation many areas of the world continue to experience human rights violations and both absolute and relative forms of poverty on a massive scale. The power of sport to influence poverty is negligible but sport itself should not hide from the fact that it has been a vehicle for help in many parts of the world. Talking of the political responsibility of the athlete, the former Olympic 1500 metre gold medallist Haile Gebreselassie commented that 'eradicating poverty, this is all that matters in my country. When I am training I think about this a lot; when I am running it is going over in my mind – as a country we cannot move forward until we eradicate poverty and whereas sport can help – the real problems will not be overcome just by helping Ethiopians to run fast' (White, 2004). This final chapter examines the ways in which sport has been used to help with issues and campaigns that have made a difference in terms of human rights and poverty in parts of the world today. Those who are committed to advancing opportunities not just for a more humane sporting world but also a more humane world overall should not lose sight of the role of sport in helping to produce social change in a world that is left wanting and in need on so many fronts. It seems that for many governments change, policies change but the need remains the same.

Chapter 15

Sport and social divisions

Are the key social divisions of today the same as those that moulded twentieth century struggles for sport? DIMITRIMESSINIS/AFP/Getty Images

PREVIEW

Social differences • Sport and social differentiation in Flanders • What are social divisions? • Sport and social class • Sports participation and social class • Lacrosse and social class • Privilege • Sport, social class and social differentiation • Sport and gender • Sports participation and gender • Sex and gender • Gender and American sports stadiums • Gender power relations and sport • Female body use and body image • Female bull-fighting in Spain • Muslim women and physical activity • Sports participation and ethnicity • Arab-African sportswomen • Sport, ethnicity and ethnic identity • Scottish Highland Games in America • Sport, race and black power in America • Sport, ethnicity and racism • Sport and social divisions.

OBJECTIVES

This chapter will:

■ consider social divisions as a way of thinking about sport in society;

■ answer the question what are social divisions?

■ outline substantive material about sport, gender, social class, racism and ethnicity;

■ re-visit the notion of limits and possibilities in contemporary sport;

■ argue for an approach to social divisions that recognises tensions between fragmentation and cohesion of social order.

INTRODUCTION

It is impossible to think about sport, culture and society without immediately recognising the social differences that exist. Gruneau (1999:99) and others have reminded us that it is useful to think of sport in terms of limits and possibilities in the sense that people are free to participate in sport but only within certain limits. Such limits are not necessarily of people's own choosing with some of the most regularly commented upon limits being social divisions such as class, gender, ethnicity but also age, health and location. Different people have different degrees of freedom and the fact that they differ in their freedom of choice and the range of actions they decide to take is, according to Bauman (2001:113), the essence of social inequality. The difference in the degree of freedom is often considered as a difference in power in the sense that power is an enabling capacity and the more power that people have at their disposal the wider is the range of sports choices available to them. Nobody is powerless but being less powerful often, sometimes wrongly, equates to moderating one's choices and dreams of what is, should be or could be possible.

Throughout the last quarter of the twentieth century and the early part of the twenty-first century substantive empirical research has shown that sporting practices tend to reflect patterns of social differentiation within sport, culture and society (Back et al., 2001; Bourdieu(a), 1978, 1990; Hargreaves, 1994, 2000; Gruneau, 1976, 1999; Scheerder et al., 2002). A relatively recent study of sport and social differentiation in Flanders (Scheerder et al., 2002: 219–245) concluded that during the period between 1969 and 1999

■ socio-educational status and socio-professional status had increased in Flanders but socio-geographical status had diminished;

■ people from all social positions, men and women, had higher rates of participation in sport towards the end of the century;

■ people from the lower social positions in society experienced the most marked increase in sports participation;

 300

- sports diversity remained socially stratified with socio-professional status having a significant impact upon the number of sports practised;
- the number of sports participated in by low status groups remains small;
- many sports retain their class-related status with golf, sailing, tennis, skiing and gliding remaining high status sports while boxing, wrestling, angling, cycle-cross and archery are more frequently participated in by people from low socio-professional status groups;
- at the end of the twentieth century active involvement in sports was still related to social position and social class and consequently the democratisation and promise of sport has still to be realised.

One further introductory comment is to recognise that one of the significant shifts in thinking about sport and social differentiation has been that while sports research in the 1970s and 1980s was sensitive to issues of power and wealth the available empirical evidence in the 1990s and beyond has tended to replace issues of wealth, power and poverty with debates about sporting identities. The rich substantive material available is illustrative of the fact that sport has contributed to the struggles for differential recognition and emancipatory promise. Sports researchers and enthusiasts remind us that, whether it is in terms of sexuality, gender, ethnicity, social class or race, sport has been a key factor in forging and sustaining forms of social and cultural identity. Sport, moreover, has been viewed as a legitimate even necessary terrain of struggle, a site of injustice in its own right, and yet as Chapter 14 reminded us one of the fundamental flaws within the debate about sports identities and recognition for different groups through sport is that discussions of identity have become uncoupled from debates about the redistribution of power and wealth in and through sport. Consequently it might be suggested that accounts of social division and identity in sport need to take account of the full complexity of social identity instead of promoting separatist and reified enclaves of sporting practice and identity.

It is impossible then to think about sport without encountering certain social divisions. Traditionally people have perceived other human beings as being male or female, black or white, older or younger, richer or poorer and yet much of the vocabulary and language of these social differences in and between sports is deeply problematic because of the priorities that tend to be given to one single category at any given time and place. Such categories fail to acknowledge the way in which multiple forms of identity or social differentiation actually require a mid-range set of concepts that are capable of explaining the complexity of social divisions and social identities. The idea of identity through sport is important but it must remain secondary to that of social division and recognition because the multiple forms of identity that people draw upon are in fact socially constructed and change from time to time and place to place. That is to say that patterns of participation in sport are not fixed purely in terms of class, gender and ethnicity but also other forms of social division and inequality.

WHAT ARE SOCIAL DIVISIONS?

It might be useful in the first instance to distinguish between several terms that are commonly used in discussions relating to social divisions in sport. *Social inequalities* may refer to the differences in people's share of and access to resources and opportunities. The term 'social inequality' in relation to sport and other areas can be thought of in at least two senses (i) inequality of condition which may refer to variations in factors such as income, education, occupation or the amount of time to spend on sport, exercise and recreation and (ii) inequality of opportunity which focuses more on the individual and is concerned with the degree of freedoms that people have in moving within and between the restrictions set by a reward structure. People are free to participate in sport at different levels but only within certain limits that are in many ways relatively set by social divisions and conditions. Social inequalities in and through sport are often related to *social stratification* which is a term used specifically in relation to discussions of class, status and power in sport. Social division however is a much wider term than just social class since it has the potential to place an emphasis on many forms of social division. On the other hand social division is a more restricted and focused idea than social differentiation, a general term used to describe the increasing complexity of specialised roles and relationships that are evident as societies grow in size, develop more elaborate social institutions, and utilise new technologies in production. In the past non-sports researchers tended to be interested in social class aspects of sport at the expense of other social divisions or even the complexity of social class itself.

Sport and social class

Table 15.1 Sport and social class

** Participation in most popular 2 months %		Social class				Base number
		AB %	C1 %	C2 %	DE %	
% of adult population		19	26	22	33	
Walking (2+ miles)	31	24	30	20	26	5269
Swimming	23	26	31	21	22	3773
Cycling	11	27	32	20	21	1486
Football	10	19	32	25	24	1727
Golf	10	33	32	20	15	1342
Keep fit/aerobics	9	25	34	20	21	1452
Dancing	9	21	32	20	27	1365
Snooker/billiards/pool	8	17	30	23	31	1293
Tenpin bowling	7	21	34	24	22	1009
Multigym/weight training	7	28	36	20	17	1139
Running/jogging	6	30	34	18	17	946

Hill-walking/climbing/mountaineering	5	36	34	16	13	846
Bowls	4	22	32	21	25	654
Fishing/angling	4	16	27	29	28	452
Badminton	3	29	40	19	12	470
Tennis	2	40	31	16	12	191
Basketball/netball/volleyball	2	25	35	22	18	240
Ice skating/Ice hockey	1	18	31	22	29	202
Sailing & other water sports	1	41	37	14	9	160
Squash	1	39	41	15	5	139
Yoga	1	36	32	13	19	210
Athletics	1	24	30	24	16	126
Horse riding	1	23	42	16	18	153
Rugby	1	30	31	21	18	130
Table tennis	1	34	29	15	23	145
Martial arts	1	22	29	26	23	184
Skiing	1	43	25	21	10	73
Hockey	1	31	38	18	13	67
Gymnastics	1	29	33	24	14	79
Curling	*	49	43	5	3	37
Cricket	*	44	39	5	12	41
Judo	*	0	60	20	20	10
Other	1	24	33	22	22	188
All sports	65	23	30	21	26	11,388
Selected sports (excluding walking, dancing and snooker/billiards/pool)	52	24	31	21	23	8,858
None	35	13	22	21	44	7,587

Notes:
* less than 0.5%
** The first column shows the percentage of adults participating in each sport in the four weeks prior to interview during the two months in which the survey participation rates are highest. Sport profiles relate to sports participation and social class in one country between 1998–2000.

Source: Sport Scotland (2001). 'Sports Participation in Scotland 2000'. *Research Digest 84*. Edinburgh: Sportscotland.

The figures presented in Table 15.1 relate to sports participation and social class in one country towards the end of the twentieth century. The survey results provide for a detailed discussion of sports participation in one country for those people aged 16 and over. Social class differences are represented by four distinct categories. Social class AB refers to higher and intermediate managerial, administrative and professional people who at the time of the survey made up 19 per cent of the population. Social class C1 refers to supervisory, clerical and junior managerial, administrative and professional people who at the time of the survey accounted for 26 per cent of the population. Social class C2 refers to skilled manual workers who at the time of the survey made up 22 per cent of the population. Finally Social class DE who accounted for 33 per cent of the population and were made up of semi-skilled or unskilled manual workers, apprentices in skilled trades; casual or lowest grade workers; state pensioners or widowers/widows and those entirely dependent upon the state long-term through sickness, unemployment, old age or other reasons. Even at this level it is clear that social class is influenced by other social divisions such as age and therefore cannot be viewed as a single homogenous social division.

Students, readers and researchers should be able to draw certain empirically informed statements from various readings of the figures presented in Table 15.1. The following statements are but some examples that may be inferred from the figures:

1. the most popular participatory sports amongst the AB category are curling, cricket ski-ing, sailing and tennis;
2. the most popular sports amongst the DE category are snooker/billiards/pool, ice-skating/ice-hockey, fishing/angling, dancing and walking;
3. sports participation in all sports is most popular amongst social class C1 (30%); followed by DE (26%), AB (23%) and C2 (21%);
4. with reference to particular sports; golf participation by social class is made up of AB (33%), C1 (32%), C2 (20%) and DE (15%); football participation by social class is made up of AB (19%), C1 (32%), C2 (25%) and DE (24%); bowls participation by social class is made up of AB (22%), C1 (32%), C2 (21%) and DE (25%); and athletics participation by social class is made up of AB (24%), C1 (30%), C2 (24%) and DE (16%);
5. sports such as squash would appear to be extremely elitist in terms of participation, AB (39%) and DE (5%);
6. sports such as walking, AB (24%), C1 (30%), C2 (20%) and DE (26%), swimming AB (26%), C1 (31%), C2 (21%) and DE (22%) and cycling, AB (27%), C1 (32%), C2 (20%) and DE (21%) are fairly democratic in terms of participation.

Sport has long been viewed as a graphic symbol of meritocracy despite the fact that sociologists and others have been questioning the substantive basis for such a claim for more than a quarter of a century. Thus the popular image of sport as an unquestioned democracy of ability and practice is somewhat over-exaggerated if not mythical. Generally speaking, the term 'democratisation' tends to imply a widening degree of opportunity or a diminishing degree of separatism in varying forms of sports involvement. The term has also been

304

used to describe the process whereby employees or clients have more control over sporting decisions and sporting bodies. The expansion of opportunities in sport over the last quarter of the twentieth century might be used at one level to argue that sport, at least in the West, has become more open. But, as Moffat (2000:33) suggests, the reality in Britain is that the extremes of privilege and poverty remain sharply drawn. An emphasis on social class cannot explain all aspects of the development of British sport – it tends, for example, to occlude the place of women in British sport – but there is good reason for believing that sport and social class have been mutually reinforcing categories in British society for a long time. Indeed, the claim that the secular decline of British sport in the international arena during the twentieth century is to be understood in part as a result of the exclusionary nature of sport in Britain is one that cannot lightly be dismissed (Hill, 2002).

'What's in a game but Class and History?' was the title that recently captioned an article explaining the extent to which the game of lacrosse had striven to become a more meritocratic sport in America (Stephen, 2000:20). The earliest documented reference to lacrosse dates from the mid-1600s but given its folk origins in the cultural practices of the Huron, Chippewa and Iroquois such a date might seem to be conservative. At one point, lacrosse was made illegal in order to prevent Native Americans using it for war-like purposes. Geographically, Montreal is considered to be the cradle of modern lacrosse, although the French, according to Jackson (1996: 219), are likely to have engaged in informal competition long before the Montreal Lacrosse Club was formed in 1856. By the nineteenth century lacrosse had grown into one of America's most exclusive sports, fashionable among the elite schools and colleges and a mainstay of the white anglo-saxon protestant Ivy League universities. In 2000 lacrosse remains one of America's chic fashionable status sports and a mainstream sport of the north-eastern private schools and colleges, while slowly filtering into state schools. It is still practised by marginalised sectors of North American culture that conveniently overlook the origins of the game.

Such cases allow for the assertion that sport has been transformed by the changing social conditions of modern life but it would seem premature in either case to assert that sport in all its different forms is democratic. A significant amount of substantive evidence exists which challenges the notion of meritocratic sporting practices permeating sporting cultures. The contemporary scene has changed dramatically when one compares twenty-first-century sport with nineteenth-century sport. The case can be made that extreme class and status-linked barriers to sports participation have been greatly challenged by the changing nature of democracy in Britain, America and other places. Such an argument can be made without necessarily accepting that sport is widely available to all.

Two initial points are important to note. The first is that that while terms such as class, democracy and privilege are always on the move the gap between privilege and poverty remains. This is the case whether one is referring to Britain or America. Unlike the British, Americans do not tend to conceive of their society hierarchically. By comparison with British society, Americans are not interested in the language of class, or in the models of society which in Britain that language has in the past described. The result, as Lord Beaverbrook once remarked, is that in the New World, unlike the old, the only difference between rich and poor is that the rich have more money. This remains a shrewd insight. Britain or at least parts of Britain remain besotted with issues of class, privilege and how the rest of

305

the world perceives Britain to be. A nation that debated whether the late Princess of Wales, following her divorce, should be allowed to retain the prefix, Her Royal Highness, is clearly concerned with its class image. A nation that was gripped by a courtroom battle between two cricketers, Imran Khan and Ian Botham, a large part of which was devoted to considering their social origins, was as obsessed with class in the late twentieth century as it was with gentlemen versus players in the nineteenth century. None of these examples illustrate an overwhelming desire to be rid of divisive social distinctions such as class, poverty and privilege.

The second point is that while there have been inequalities in wealth and power in most societies throughout history, it seems unreasonable to define a classless society as one in which inequalities have been abolished. It might in the first instance be useful to adopt an approach that Bourdieu (1990) has described as a 'reasoned Utopia'. These examples serve to remind us that we need to think more carefully about how we think about ourselves as social individuals or as social groups, how previous social groups thought about themselves and what future patterns of involvement in sport will say about particular societies. Only then will we better understand the complexities of sport, privilege and democracy that have operated within sport, culture and society.

Like all areas of social life, sport has been and continues to be influenced by multiple social divisions and social inequalities that differentiate groups of people. Sociologists have traditionally used the term 'social class' to explain some of key relational and distributive characteristics of culture and society. In the first instance many of the traditional core social differences experienced by sport might be summarised under these same two headings: (i) differences in distributive characteristics which may refer to the way in which sport reflects such symbolic factors such as wealth, occupation, prestige, social esteem, education, status, distinction and (ii) relational characteristics which refers to the way in which different groups of people relate to one another within and between sports as a result of the above characteristics.

By means of summary it might be suggested that arguments about sport, social class and social differentiation have tended to follow some or all of the following lines of departure:

- that it is possible to identify a leisure class that is involved in the conspicuous consumption of sport;
- that sport helps to sustain and reproduce status, prestige and power;
- that the struggle for sport has been influenced by social class;
- that the practice of sport is socially stratified and differentiated by social class;
- that sport within and between social classes acts as a hallmark of distinction;
- that sport is intimately associated with classes that exist on the basis of the differential distribution of wealth, power and other characteristics;
- that sport contributes to a distinct way of life associated with certain class categories;
- that social class has contributed to the discourse of colonial sport within and between certain former colonies and nations.

Everybody does not have to believe in the existence of class, nor constantly perceive of themselves in class terms or class identity for class to be a social division. Contrary to the position adopted by Bourdieu, class situations are not dependent upon economic and cultural capital alone. Social divisions do not always systematically lead to a sense of distinctive group identities or the same action based upon shared personal identities. However in an empirical sense as the earlier studies indicate social class may not be the single determinant of sports participation or life chances and increasingly it has been recognised that other forms of social division may act alongside, with or against class as a single independent variable. Age, gender and ethnicity are all social divisions that impinge upon sport, social inequality and social division in a distributive and relational manner. It is misplaced to talk of Western cultures such as Britain as classless societies but its members may no longer spontaneously use the language of class as the sole way for describing social inequality. As Scott (2000) indicates class is not dead but perhaps the monolithic social imagery of class is not as forceful in the early part of the twenty-first century as it was in the twentieth century.

Sport and gender

Table 15.2 *Sport and gender*

** Participation in most popular 2 months %		Sex		Base number
		Male %	Female %	
% of Adult Population		48	52	
Walking (2+ miles)	31	45	55	5269
Swimming	23	40	60	3773
Cycling	11	62	38	1486
Football	10	93	7	1727
Golf	10	88	12	1342
Keep fit/aerobics	9	25	75	1452
Dancing	9	26	74	1365
Snooker/billiards/pool	8	84	16	1293
Tenpin bowling	7	53	47	1009
Multigym/weight training	7	62	38	1139
Running/jogging	6	72	28	946
Hill-walking/climbing/ mountaineering	5	61	39	846
Bowls	4	68	32	654
Fishing/angling	4	92	8	452
Badminton	3	52	48	470
Tennis	2	59	41	191
Basketball/netball/ volleyball	2	63	37	240
Ice skating/ice hockey	1	31	69	202

continued

Sailing & other water sports	1	65	35	160
Squash	1	84	15	139
Yoga	1	13	87	210
Athletics	1	71	29	126
Horse riding	1	25	75	153
Rugby	1	92	8	130
Table tennis	1	72	28	145
Martial arts	1	65	35	184
Skiing	1	62	38	73
Hockey	1	53	47	67
Gymnastics	1	29	71	79
Curling	*	51	48	37
Cricket	*	78	22	41
Judo	*	70	30	10
Other	1	62	38	188
All sports	65	52	48	11,388
Selected sports (excluding walking, dancing and snooker/billiards/pool)	52	55	45	8,858
None	35	42	58	7,587

Notes:
*   less than 0.5%
**   The first column shows the percentage of adults participating in each sport in the four weeks prior to interview during the two months in which the survey participation rates are highest. Sport profiles relating to sports participation and gender in one country between 1998–2000.

Source: Sportscotland (2001). 'Sports Participation in Scotland 2000'. *Research Digest 84*. Edinburgh: Sportscotland.

The figures presented in Table 15.2 relate to sports participation and gender in one country towards the end of the twentieth century. The survey results provide for a detailed discussion of sports involvement in one country for those people aged 16 and over. Gender differences in terms of sports participation specifically refer to male and female participation in the majority of sports participated in by those aged 16 to 55+. Such figures as presented in Table 15.2 need to be treated with caution in that they represent patterns of sports participation within a snapshot in time in one country. It is easy for students, researchers and teachers to be critical of all figures since they can be read in a number of different ways. With particular reference to this discussion about gender and social divisions. They illustrate a basis for thinking about two aspects of social division, in that they illustrate that a gender gap in sports participation exists but also that it is difficult, if not impossible, to consider single aspects of social division without thinking about issues such as age and how this may impact upon these figures or how in fact social class and gender in this case cross-tabulate to provide a more complex picture of sports participation in this one cultural setting, namely Scotland.

Students, readers and researchers should be able to draw certain empirically informed statements from various readings of the figures presented in Table 15.2. The following statements are but five examples that may be inferred from the figures:

- that the most popular participatory sports amongst women are aerobics (75%), dancing (74%), swimming (60%), yoga (87%) and horse-riding (75%) whilst the least popular sports in terms of participation are football (7%), fishing/angling (8%), rugby (8%), golf (12%) and squash (15%);
- that the most popular participatory sports amongst men are football (93%), rugby (92%), golf (88%), fishing/angling (92%) and squash (84%) whilst the least popular sports in terms of participation are yoga (13%), aerobics (25%), dancing (26%), horse-riding (25%), and gymnastics (29%);
- that women's participation in sports in this country is dominated by four activities while men participate in a much wider range, with 12 sports having participation rates of above 5% compared with six such sports for women;
- that sports that have the smallest gender gap in terms of participation include curling (51% M and 48% F = 3% difference), badminton (52% M and 48% F = 4% difference), tenpin bowling (53% M and 47% F = 6% difference), and hockey (53% M and 47% F = 6% difference);
- that in terms of total sports participation a gender gap of 4% exists between men (52%) and women (48%).

Like many areas of social life, sport carries with it assumptions about gender and gender differentiation. Gender refers to the female and male differences created by social, cultural, historical and political expectations about behaviour, interests, abilities and attitudes to men and women in sport. Gender is not a fixed concept and gender and sport relations while transcending boundaries of culture and region are also differentiated by many cross-cultural differences. In identifying gender as an important social division it is important to go beyond the argument that men and women experience sport differently. It might be tentatively suggested that we are concerned with providing accounts of sport and gender that are based on the idea that differences are structural, perhaps social in origin and that historically men in sport as a category have more power than women as category. Drawing from American experiences Eitzen (2003:23) suggests that male dominance is maintained when communities build expensive stadiums and arenas to keep professional teams or to entice professional teams to move there. Stadiums costing millions of dollars in tax revenue to be primarily filled by men as owners, athletes, coaches, trainers, male media controlled corporations and mainly male fans. The symbolic sports message is clear, that men count for much more than women. However, although men are often in a position of advantage they are also structurally constrained in different countries and places by different ideas of masculinity.

From consciousness raising, to political campaigns, to theoretical analysis, to empirical concerns about the place of women and the very nature of sport, women have increasingly placed their own experiences of sport, labour, education and other social spheres centre stage. Although there was Olympic competition for women in golf and tennis as early as 1900 it was not until 1928 that the Olympic Games admitted female track and field athletics. In 1921 at the first International women's athletic meeting staged in Monte Carlo, Britain along with France, what was then Czechoslovakia, Italy, Spain and the United States of America formed the Fédération Sportive Féminine Internationale. This body staged a women's Olympic Games in Paris in 1922, as an act of defiance of the International Olympic Committee's decision not to allow women's athletes to compete in the Paris Olympic Games of 1924. More recently the introduction of Title IX in 1972 has legally enforced the right that no person in the United States, can be excluded on the basis of sex, from participation in, can be denied the benefits of, or can be subject to discrimination in any educational programme or activity receiving federal financial assistance. Money for women's sports programmes went from virtually nothing before Title IX to about 33 per cent of athletic budgets in 2002. Before Title IX about 23 per cent of women received athletic scholarships compared to 41 per cent of all athletic scholarships in 2002 (*USA Today* 21 January 2002:10a).

The gendered sports story is not an exception and yet it is important to continue to ask a number of questions in order to explore and reveal particular aspects of sex and gender in sport in different countries. Asking fundamental questions such as where are the women in sport can lead to different kinds of answers. It may lead students and researchers to highlight sporting heroines – to name but a few examples: Martina Navratilova, Evonne Goolagong or Billy Jean King (all women's tennis); Paula Radcliffe, Marion Jones; Lorna Kiplagat or Hassiba Boulmerka (all women's athletics) or Annika Sorenstam or Catriona Matthews (all women's golf), for example. Others may use the question where are the women to identify places in sport where women are not, because they are women? For example, golf clubs in different parts of the world where women are not elected to the key committees or allowed to join the club. Where women's participation in sport is influenced by religious beliefs, as in many Islamic countries it is often the case that few statistics on women's sports participation exist. During the late 1990s Nabilah Abdelrahman was the only woman represented in Egypt's Supreme Council of Youth and Sport. She established the Arab Women and Sports Association and is mentioned here as an illustrative example of the fact that different stories of women's sport are not just structured by gender but other factors such as religion.

When we find women and/or men, we find gender relations but careful distinctions and similarities need to be made between different stories about gender relations in sport. At one level the gendered sports story is not different from other areas of social life. The public/private split coincides with other splits in explaining gender relations such as reason/emotion, mind/body and male/female. These splits often associate different kinds of character or sporting temperament with particular genders. Feminism would assert that the male side of the dichotomy is usually given more value, and privileged while the female side is devalued. During this process gender becomes both relational and a power relationship. Furthermore certain feminisms fundamentally assert that women's experiences of sport are systematically different from men's. Both masculinity and femininity are powerful sets of values that can control and regulate female sporting behaviour. It is important to recognise that there are layers of power within sport that are influenced by gender relations. Gendered power relations are embedded in sport in the following ways:

- the language, ideas, beliefs, norms and values in sport that; for instance, promote the belief that women's sport is not as valuable as men's sport or that men are better;
- the space for sport is structured by other factors such as women's freedom to go running in open spaces or at night for fear of attack;
- hierarchical and institutionalised practices in sport;
- embodied sporting practices that result in physical activity and sport being performed in certain ways also reproduce power relationships;
- historically specific forms and notions of sport that change over time.

An important early intervention by feminists was to distinguish between sex and gender in that sex was seen primarily to refer to biology in that we are born male or female where as gender is viewed more as a social construct. The role of the body has often been prioritised within this social division given the ideological weight that is often viewed in the weak or strong female athletic body or the masculine or feminine sporting body. Women have asserted that rather than being a vehicle of disempowerment in terms of physicality women's bodies themselves can be agents of empowerment in terms of physicality and sexuality.

Sarah Pink (1996) argues that the female bullfight represents a statement about female body use and body image. The development of female bullfighting and their actions is not unrelated to the issue of women's status in Spain. Pink (1996:47) argues that female bullfighting represents a significant and contrasting model of physicality and the body and those who can't accept breasts as being compatible with the bullring are traditionalists who are resistant to boundary crossing into male domains (refer to Chapter 11 for a more extensive discussion of sport and the body). The advent of female bullfighting maybe indicative of shifting gender relations in Spain. It could be argued that female bullfighters are only accepted as a novelty value and could be marginalised as curious oddities, exceptions to be marvelled at rather than revolutionary agents of social change in Spain. The female bullfighter is a passive actor, she performs her art as a person, as herself, someone who has succeeded in the public sphere through becoming a bullfighter. The advent of female bullfighting in Spain indicates that the ritual structure of the bullfight no longer simply represents the drama of masculine experience. Perhaps more importantly this example illustrates that the body, as well as gender, is socially, culturally, politically and historically constructed.

Gender relations will always be differently combined in different sport settings. An examination of gender ideologies within several fundamentalist movements and how these impact upon sport has recently been explored by writers such as Jennifer Hargreaves (2000) and Walseth and Fasting (2003). In the latter study of Islam's view of women and physical activity in Egypt it is pointed out that the view that Egyptian women have on the relationship between physical activity and Islam has consequences for their level of involvement in physical activity and sport. The results supported the notion that Islam was not against involvement in physical activity and sport and that the women who most shared this view were supporters of a fundamentalist interpretation of Islam. Some Muslim women have a non-secular relationship between sport and religion. Walseth and Fasting (2003:45) argued that different interpretations of Islam impacted upon their experiences of sport and physical activity. These experiences were related to such factors as use of the veil, gender segregation, the concept of excitement and the power relationship between women and men. Most of the barriers, it was argued, tended to be products of Muslim society's view of women and their sexuality.

It is impossible to cover all the areas impacted upon in sport by gender relations yet the studies such as those relating to sport, gender and Islam are important because post-modern feminists in particular have warned about the perils of generalisations in feminist theory that transcend the boundaries of culture and religion. On the other hand feminist critics of post-modernism have tended to abandon cross-cultural and comparative theoretical perspectives. Indeed the work by feminist sports writers in this field might be amongst the most ground-breaking and original in terms of research that attempts to make sense of gender and Muslim fundamentalism. At the same time Western readers and students of sport, culture and society need to become more attentive to the ways in which progressive Islamic discourses impact upon sport, the body and physical activity. It might be further suggested that the study of sport and gender relations in Islamic countries and regions may provide empirical evidence of internationality, tolerance, diversity and comparative gender relations in and through sport.

The coverage of gender and sport in this chapter is by means exhaustive but by way of summary it might be suggested that the arguments about sport and gender have tended to follow some or all of the following:

- that different structures of masculinity and femininity have historically influenced the development of sport;
- that it is necessary to ask where are the women in sport in order to highlight issues of oppression, marginality and empowerment of women in sport;
- that gender is a fundamental category through which all aspects of life are organised and experienced including sport;
- that experiences of gender in sport need to be sensitive and aware of 'other' experiences of sporting struggle outwith mainstream and/or colonial gender relations;
- that body culture and physicality are important facets of gender relations that also need to be explored and explained in terms of social division and social differences;
- that sport and gender relations have contributed to both reformist, emancipatory and evolutionary aspects of social change and continuity;
- that sport and gender remains an important and insightful element of social division in its own right.

Gender and sport remains an important and fascinating element of social division and sport in its own right but so does ethnicity and racism.

Sport, ethnicity and racism

The figures presented in Figures 15.1 and 15.2 relate to sports participation and ethnicity in one country towards the end of the twentieth century. The survey results provide for a detailed discussion of sports participation in one country for those people aged 16 and over. The results relate to sports participation and ethnicity in a specific part of the United Kingdom, namely England, for the year 1999/2000. Defining ethnicity is fraught with methodological problems and any label given to a group in society simplifies the nature of diversity in sport. This applies particularly to ethnicity but the approach adopted within the survey asked respondents to consider which of the following groups they belonged to, white, black Caribbean, black African, black other, Indian, Pakistani, Bangladeshi, Chinese or none of these. Given that most if not all in the survey may also think of themselves as English or British such social divisions merely reinforce many of the issues about identity and sport raised in Chapter 14. A large minority of respondents (17 per cent) chose none of these when asked to select the ethnic group to which they belong (Rowe and Champion, 2000:9).

The figures presented in Figures 15.1 and 15.2 enable four broad generalisations to be made about sports participation and ethnicity in England towards the end of the twentieth century.

- Black African (60%) and Black Other (80%) men have higher participation rates than the national average for England (54%).
- Indian (47%), Black Caribbean (45%), Bangladeshi (46%) and Pakistani (42%) men are less likely to participate in sport than men in the population as a whole.
- National participation rates for women (39%) are matched or exceeded by women from Black Other (45%), Other (41%) and Chinese (39%) ethnic groups.
- Women who classify themselves as Black Caribbean (34%), Black African (34%), Indian (31%), Pakistani (21%) and Bangladeshi (19%) have participation rates below the national average for all women.

As with issues of social class and gender the popularity and social significance of sport has meant that it has often been influenced by a multitude of ethnic and racial contexts and tensions at different points of time in different parts of the world. Sport itself has had to address and think about challenging specific problems emanating from at least three forms of racism. Structural racism refers to the racism embedded within the history of societies and the extent to which it impacts upon sport. Factors commonly associated with structural racism include gaps between different racial and ethnic groups in terms of income, education, health and employment. Institutional racism refers to the practices and procedures within sport that discriminate against people of colour and ethnic groups. Areas commonly associated with institutional racism in sport include the gap between different groups which have experienced discrimination in terms of people in positions of influence and power in sport or the extent to which tensions between different ethnic groups become visibly crystallised at sports events. Individual racism refers to the actions and attitudes of individuals to members of ethnic or racial groups.

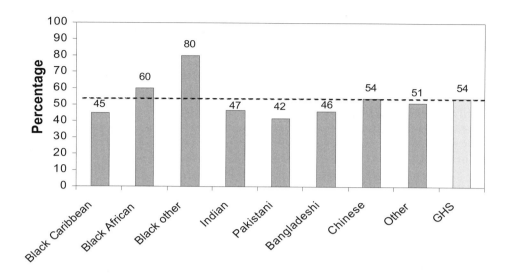

Figure 15.1 *Sports participation figures relating sport and ethnicity among men over 16 for 1999/2000.*

Note: GHS = General Household Survey.

Source: Rowe, N. and Champion, R. (2000) Sports Participation and Ethnicity in England. *National Survey 1999/2000.* London: Sport England.

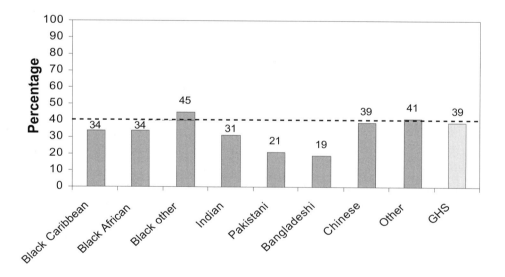

Figure 15.2 *Sports participation figures relating sport and ethnicity among women over 16 for 1999/2000.*

Note: GHS = General Household Survey.

Source: Rowe, N. and Champion, R. (2000) Sports Participation and Ethnicity in England. *National Survey 1999/2000.* London: Sport England.

There is no simple answer to what constitutes ethnicity or racism and yet it is important not to confuse the two terms since they are often used interchangeably. Both ethnicity and racism as terms have been used in a multitude of different ways. Even those who argue that ethnic minorities are united by a common experience of racism often fail to be sufficiently alert to the fact of the diverse ways in which racism impacts upon different social divisions in sport. For example, the case of Hassiba Boulmerka, a much loved Arab-African sportswoman forced at a particular point in her career to leave Algeria for France in order to escape the backlash from Muslim zealots of the time (*Independent*, 12 August 1991). Winner of the women's 1500 metres final at the 1991 World Athletic Championships, Boulmerka became the first Algerian, first Arab and first African woman to win a gold medal at any World athletic championships. On her return to Algeria, the then President Chadli Benjedid greeted her as a national heroine. But Muslim zealots denounced her from the pulpit for baring her most intimate parts (her legs) before millions of television viewers. Furthermore President Benjedid was himself publicly denounced for embracing a woman in public. The row at the time underscored the clash between modernity and Islamic fundamentalism. It was a clash which at the time was all the more surprising given Algeria's position in the Arab world as the torchbearer of modernism, socialism and successful struggle for independence from colonial rule. Hassiba Boulmerka moved to France and the Islamicists at the time lost an opportunity to promote national unity in Algeria during the early 1990s. As a student or researcher of sport, culture and society how would you have approached this case study – from the standpoint of ethnicity or gender or colonialism or racism? – all of which would only provide a partial explanation.

The most popular point of origin of the term ethnicity is taken from the Greek word *ethnos*, translated as people or nation and its meaning being somewhere between the two. Ethnicity does not mean race but ethnic conflict between groups may be caused by racism. The concept of ethnicity has been popular within sociological and political accounts of sport partly because of a reaction to the perceived inadequacies of terms such as race which has tended to legitimate forms of biological reasoning. In sport such subtle determinism associated with biological, genetically mapped differences between peoples is viewed by many as being potentially racist. The term ethnicity then is broader than the term race but is incorrectly often used interchangeably with the term race and racial identity. Multi-ethnic societies are not new or rare – the first state level societies of the Middle East were multi-ethnic yet ethnic differences within societies have taken on a different importance in post-Enlightenment times. Anthropologists define ethnic groups as having shared customs, religious practices, linguistic traditions, geographical origins and sometimes common descent. Anthropologists studying ethnicity have tended to look for markers of social boundaries between groups often described as ethnic boundary markers and referring to things such as language, music, style of dress, religious expression and loyalties to particular sports teams.

Ethnic identities, like other identities, evolve over time and far from being primordial are often quite voluntary. When an ethnic identity is claimed those who assert it often form an ethnic group. When an ethnic group is imposed from the outside (generally on a minority group) it is an ethnic category. Occasionally an ethnic category goes through an ethnogenesis and becomes an ethnic group – as with labels such as Hispanic or Latino. In eighteenth-century America Scottish was an ethnic category, the ethnonym Scottish-Irish was first employed to distinguish Patriot Ulster Scots from Highland Scots and later to distinguish Protestant Scots from Ulster from the Catholic 'Famine-Irish'. In the late eighteenth and early nineteenth centuries Scottish-Irish was an emergent ethnicity whereas the Scottish-American ethnic group of today may be called resurgent. Perhaps symbolic ethnicity is often a nostalgic reclamation of an ethnic identity already lost.

The discussion that follows considers the relationship between the emergence of the Scottish Highland Games in Canada and America (Jarvie, 2005). It is illustrative of the complex relationship between sport, ethnicity and racism involving one sport in several cultural contexts. The American-Scottish Foundation was founded in 1956 by Lord and Lady Malcolm Douglas Hamilton (www.asgf.org/). The Foundation's broad purpose was to build bonds of interests and co-operation, both social and commercial, between the people of Scotland and the United States of America. An increasing number of Americans of Scottish descent have joined regional Scottish and clan societies, attended Highland Games and subscribe to Scottish-orientated publications. The US Senate conceived of Tartan Day in 1998 in recognition of the contribution made by Scots to the foundation, character and prosperity of America. The date selected was 6 April, the same day in 1320 when the declaration of Arbroath, initiating an independent Scotland, was signed and presented to the Pope. The same declaration of 1320 allegedly informed the American declaration of Independence (Jarvie, 2005). Enter the American-Scottish Foundation website (http://www.asgf.org/) and you will be informed that there are at least 13 million Americans claiming Scottish ancestry according to the latest census figures, and that further research indicates that the figure might be nearer 35 million. The American-Scottish Foundation is one of seven organisations which form a Scottish Coalition of American-Scottish Organisations, the others being, the Caledonian Foundation, USA; Scottish Heritage, USA; the Council of Scottish Clans and Associations; the Association of St Andrew's Societies; the International Association of Tartan Studies; and the Association of Scottish Games and Festivals.

The Association of Scottish Games and Festivals was itself founded in 1981 as a modern clearinghouse for information about American-Scottish Highland Games and Gatherings that are held in locations from Alabama to Arkansas, California to Connecticut, Idaho to Iowa, Maine to Montana, Nebraska to north Dakota, Ohio to Oregon and Washington to Wyoming (http://www.asgf.org/). These Highland Gatherings and Games can be found in every month from January with the Central Florida Highland Games until November with the Foothills Highland Games in North Carolina. The Calendar of Highland Games and Gatherings in America is longer than that in Scotland. The Foothills Highland Games are presented by the Scottish Clans of the South who in part aim to educate and promote an interest in traditional Scottish arts of piping, dancing, athletic achievement and culture (http://www.asgf.org/1html). The specific Highland Games schedule involves traditional events such as highland dancing, piping, and strength events such as the tug of war but also more bizarre *inventions* of tradition such as the bonny knees contest, the border collie contest, the clan challenge, the kirking of the tartans and the golf classic. The Association of Scottish Games and Festivals adopted as its logo the Scottish thistle and the St Andrew's flag.

On the one hand the descendents of early émigrés from the Highlands of Scotland would appear to have much to celebrate within this modern international North America (Ray, 2001). The contribution made by Scots is acknowledged within the Scottish American Hall of Fame (Jarvie, 2005). Stornoway-born Alexander Mackenzie and Simon Fraser from Strathglass left their names on two of Canada's greatest rivers. Glasgow-born Sir John A. MacDonald, whose father was from Strath Oykel and his mother from Strathspey, was to become Canada's first Prime Minister. It was MacDonald along with two other Scots, George Stephen and Donald Smith (later to become Lord Strathcona), who was to be instrumental in building the Canadian Pacific Railway. The only minister to sign the Declaration of Independence was of Scots descent as was the founder of universities such as Princeton. On the other hand a more critical acknowledgement of the totality of the Scots émigrés' investment in north America would also acknowledge the darker side of this émigré culture. The nineteenth-century white South was by no means wholly Scottish, let alone Highland in origin. The 'bonnie blue flag' of the breakaway and slave-holding Confederate states was modelled on the Scottish national flag or Saltire (Jarvie, 2005). The organisation, which tried to rebuild white supremacy among the wreckage of the Confederate defeat, became known in an unwanted tribute to the Highlands – as the Klan. Scotland's influence on north America manifests itself in ways other than the continent's long-standing fondness of Highland Games, pipe bands and tartan.

The discussion above raises important questions for students of sport, culture and society in relation to what exactly is being celebrated at these American-Scottish Highland Games. At one level it might be insightful to think about the extent to which terms such as ethnicity, race, racism help to explain the development and popularity of the Scottish-American Highland Games in America, Canada or elsewhere. To what extent: (i) do these Scottish Highland Games reflect an ethnic identity? (ii) does this form of sport or athleticism help to create or break down boundaries between ethnic groups? (iii) might it be argued that the Scottish Highland Games in America may be viewed historically as contributing to particular forms of racism? (iv) do the Scottish Highland Games in America remind us that the relationship between sport and ethnicity is situational and that people might have different ethnic identities in different sporting situations? or finally (v) do we hear of sport being associated with an ethnic majority in that the term is almost exclusively used in relation to ethnic minorities while at the same time ethnic minorities are frequently seen to have certain experiences which are more in common with one another than with the majority? Many of these questions can be asked as a basis for examining sports associated with ethnicity, ethnic identity and racism.

Mention here must be made of what came to be termed in the early 1990s the new politics of race and racism. A number of commentators suggested that while the physical prowess of the black body has in the 1990s been acknowledged and exploited as a fertile zone of profit within American society, the symbolic dangers of black sporting excellence need to be highlighted (Cashmore, 1997; Dyson, 1994; Markovits, 2003). Because of the marginalised status within the overall sphere of American sports, black athletic activity, argues Dyson (1994), has often acquired a social significance that transcends the internal dimensions of the game, sport and skill. Black sport becomes an arena for testing the limits of physical endurance and forms of athletic excellence while at the same time repudiating or symbolising the American ideals (often mythical) of justice, goodness, truth and beauty. It also becomes a way of ritualising racial achievement against socially or economically imposed barriers to sporting performance. That is to say that many ethnic sports celebrities or athletes of colour may all be equal when they line up at the start of an Olympic final but the social, economic, political and emotional struggles that any given athlete has to overcome to get to that final are far from equal.

There is a danger too in celebrating uncritically any black or other sports industry. More specifically, the question that is posed in both Hoberman (1997) and Cashmore (1997) is whether there can be such a thing as an authentic black sports culture when the sports industry that produces it is controlled by so many white dominated corporations. In developing a history of black culture in the West from the 1960s to the present Cashmore (1997: 172–181) argues that inflating the value of a commodified black sports culture may actually work against the interests of racial justice. Black entrepreneurs, when they have reached the top, have tended to act in much the same way as their white counterparts in similar circumstances. They failed to destabilise the racial hierarchy and yet remained part of an African-American elite. Add to this the fact that Arthur Ashe, the first American winner of the All England Wimbledon Tennis Championship back in 1979, used to be critical of any policy which specifically channelled ethnic minorities into particular sports because it often closed off other channels of social mobility. In that same year Ashe pointed out that of the 3 million black kids in America who committed themselves to the athletic dream only 900 managed to make a professional living from sport. Thus the sport as a field of dreams thesis has to be qualified because for many it can lead to dangerous fantasies.

There is also empirically the danger of overstating the athletic, physical dominance of black athletes in American sport. Statements such as those made by John Hoberman (1997) in *Darwin's Athletes: How Sport has Damaged Black America and Preserved the Myth of Race*, 'that there is not a white star left in the National Basketball Association' (1997:64), or that 'the idea of a white quarterback playing in today's National Football League' (1997:85) have to be treated as historically specific to a particular year or phase. Both statements, several years later, are untrue with Jason Sehorn, the white quarterback of the New York Giants up until March 2003 being known for his natural athleticism while a white player Brent Barry won the 2002 National Basketball Association's annual slam dunk competition, the league's purest test of exuberant physical creativity. The influx of white European stars into the American game has also offered renewed evidence that athletes are produced by complex cultural, social and physical interactions and not simply racial differentiation. Thoughtful black and white players have taken the occasion to dispel racial/ethnic myths. At the end of the 2001 season, Chris Webber said of Turkish guard Hidayet Turkoglu 'This summer I am taking Hedo the hood with me to play. By the end he will be the god of my hood' (Markovits, 2003:153). Of course to such an extent such claims perpetuate the stereotype – the white player's brilliance can only be viewed in the context of black athleticism. The point guard Jason Williams was dubbed 'white chocolate' to reflect what was seen as an element of African-American improvisation in his style. Yet the point to be made is that such examples may belong to transitional stages of hybrid sports that may eventually dissolve rather than reinforce notions of racial differentiation.

Many popular arguments about sport, ethnicity and racism have contributed to a number of racist beliefs about different people's sporting abilities. A number of popular arguments have contributed to particular explanations of race relations within discussions of sport, culture and society. The coverage of sport, ethnicity and racism in this chapter is by no means exhaustive but in summary it might be suggested that core arguments have tended to rely upon some of or all of the following arguments.

- That sport is inherently conservative and helps to consolidate patriotism, nationalism and racism.
- That sport has some inherent property that makes it a possible instrument of integration and harmonious ethnic and race relations.
- That sport as a form of cultural politics has been central to processes of colonialism, imperialism and post-colonialism in different parts of the world.
- That sport has contributed to unique political struggles which have involved black and ethnic political mobilisation and the struggle for equality of and for black peoples and ethnic minority groups.
- That sport is an important facet of ethnic and racial identities.
- That sport has produced stereotypes, prejudices and myths about ethnic minority groups which have contributed both to discrimination against and an under-representation of ethnic minority peoples within certain sports.
- That race and ethnicity are factors influencing choices that people make when they chose to join or not join certain sports clubs.
- That sport needs to develop a more complex set of tools for understanding the limits and possibilities that influence sport, racism and ethnicity and in particular the way such categories historically articulate with other categories and social divisions.

SPORT AND SOCIAL DIVISIONS

It has been suggested here that the complexity of sport is such that to talk of sport and social divisions emphasises the multiplicity of social division or divisions rather than the limited focus on sport and one form of social inequality or social injustice. Whichever division(s) is (are) prioritised or used to explain sport the question remains as to how the multiplicity of divisions in sport intersect, at times form alliances of social cohesion. To talk of social divisions in and through sport is not an intellectual exercise designed for neat scholarly purposes; they are about the sporting worlds in which we live in. Thus despite issues of social inequality, social differentiation and unequal distributive and relational aspects of sport it is vital to be sensitive to the fact that social division in sport may refer to two, three or more categories of social differences that may at times provide and express connection and cohesion between forms of social inequality. Even the figures presented in this chapter in relation to sports participation suggest that other factors such as age and perhaps even geographical location have an impact upon social divisions in sport. Thus it may be suggested that when students, teachers and researchers are considering the relationship between sport and social divisions it would be useful to keep in mind that which is summarised in Box 15.1.

BOX 15.1 SPORT AND SOCIAL DIVISION

- A social division is a principle of social organisation resulting in a distinction in sport between two or more logically interrelated categories of people, which are socially sanctioned as substantially different from one another in material, cultural and other ways.

- Although not permanently established in a given form, a social division in sport tends to be long-lasting and is sustained by dominant cultural beliefs, the organisation of social institutions and the situational interaction of individuals.

- A social division in sport is socially constructed, in the sense that it is not a simple manifestation of 'natural' or 'inevitable' laws of existence. This does not mean that it can be ignored or revised by the moment-to-moment social interactions, interpretations, decisions or social acts of individuals in or out of sport.

- Membership of a social division in sport confers unequal opportunities of access to desirable 'resources' of all kinds – and therefore different life chances and lifestyles – from membership of other categories.

- The extent of differentiation between categories in sport varies from social division to social division, but movement across a divide is either rare, or relatively slow to be achieved.

- Being socially divided tends to produce shared social identities through sport for people in the same category, often expressed by reference to their perceived difference from those in an alternative category of the same division.

- Each social division encompasses all members of society in one or other of its categories, but individuals seldom have matching profiles of category membership across the range of social divisions.

- An examination of sporting life chances and sporting lifestyles is an empirical method of identifying social divisions and categories in sport.

- Many *specific* social divisions in sport are challenged by those disadvantaged by them, the *principle* of social divisions is a universal systematic feature of sport.

SUMMARY

The value of social divisions as a way of thinking about sport and society has been highlighted in this chapter for a number of reasons. The coherence of studying these social divisions lies in the notions of hierarchy, social inequality and social injustice that permeate the worlds of sport. These complex social divisions are not just about the reality of everyday sport nor are they simply about intellectual problems of sociology and history but rather they reinforce the fact that whatever categories are used unequal access to sport tends to continually impinge upon the same categories of people. In a simple sense the gap between rich and poor remains a significant gap. To reduce the discussion of sport and social inequality to that of class, ethnicity gender, or any singular category fails to raise issues of poverty, human rights, and the precise nature of the limits and possibilities that are open to people. It is worth reiterating the point made by the Canadian sociologist Richard Gruneau (1999), when he suggested that one single story cannot address every form of oppression, identity or political aspiration but that sport in the world today has to be much more sensitive to the sheer diversity of the axes of power and inequality. The broadest possible range of voices in sport needs to be heard but individual students, teachers and researchers of sport need to choose their own entry points to the debate about sport, social division and change.

The changing nature of class imagery and utility does not deny the existence of very real social divisions within contemporary sport, culture and society. Social divisions refer to the substantial differences that exist between people that run throughout society. Social divisions may not be natural but come out of various events, struggles, decisions and interactions. The advantage of a more inclusive term such as social divisions is that it marginalises the one-dimensionality of much of the literature on sport whether this is a question of social class, gender, ethnicity, race or increasingly age in Western societies. It is increasingly important for students, activists and scholars of sport, culture and society to acknowledge the way in which a large number of social divisions influence sporting choices and outcomes. It is increasingly important to recognise that these voices are international and not just Western or the voices of the core economic social formations. The absent voices of Nike's sub-contracted Asian workers can add a lot to our under- standing of world sporting experiences. The study of sport and social division is therefore not simply a means of examining different sections of sport in society. Its approach and coherence lies in the notions of hierarchy, social inequality and social injustice which have perhaps been marginalised too much in discussions about sport in society. While this chapter has attempted to outline some of the areas of concern when looking at sport and social division the next chapter considers the role that sport has played in producing social capital and communitarianism.

KEY CONCEPTS

Distributive characteristics	Power
Distinction	Relational characteristics
Ethnicity	Sexuality
Ethnic identity	Social class
Freedom	Social differentiation
Gender	Social divisions
Individual racism	Social inequality
Inequality	Social injustice
Institutional racism	Status
Meritocracy	Structural racism

KEY READING

Books

Archetti, E. (1999). *Masculinities: Football, Polo and the Tango in Argentina*. Oxford: Berg.
Eitzen, D. (2003). *Fair and Foul*: *Beyond the Myths and Paradoxes of Sport*. New York: Rowan & Littlefield Publishers.
Markovits, B. (2003). 'The Colours of Sport'. *New Left Review*, 22 (July/August): 151–160.
Payne, G. (2000). *Social Divisions*. Basingstoke: Palgrave.
Scraton, S. and Flintoff, A. (eds) (2003). *Gender and Sports*: *A Reader*. London: Routledge.

Journal articles

Afary, J. (1997). 'The War Against Feminism in the Name of the Almighty: Making Sense of Gender and Muslim Fundamentalism'. *New Left Review*, 24 (July/August): 1–21.
Eilling, A., De Knop, P. and Knoppers, A. (2003). 'Gay/Lesbian Sport Clubs and Events: Places of Homo-Social Bonding and Cultural Resistance'. *International Review for the Sociology of Sport*, 38(4): 441–456.
Fraser, N. (1995). 'From Redistribution to Recognition? Dilemmas of Justice in a Post-Socialist Age'. *New Left Review*, 12 (July/August): 1–24.
Pink, S. (2003). 'She Wasn't Tall Enough and Breasts Get in the Way: Why Would a Woman Bullfighter Retire?' *Identities*: *Studies in Global Culture and Power*, 10(4): 427–450.
Van Ingen, C. (2003). 'Geographies of Gender, Sexuality and Race: Reframing the Focus on Space in Sport Sociology'. *International Review for the Sociology of Sport*, 38(2): 201–216.

Further reading

Bradley, H. (2000). 'Social Inequalities: Coming to terms with Complexity'. In Browning, G., Halcli, A. and Webster, F. (eds) *Understanding Contemporary Society*: *Theories of the Present*. London: Sage, 476–489.
Jarvie, G. (2002). 'Sport, Racism and Ethnicity'. In Coakley, J. and Dunning, E. (eds) *Handbook of Sports Studies*. London: Sage, 334–343.
Gems, G. (1995). 'Blocked Shot: The Development of Baseball in the African-American Community of Chicago'. *Journal of Sports History*, 22(2): 135–148.
Pink, S. (1996). 'Breasts in the Bullring: Female Psychology, Female Bullfighters and Competing Femininities'. *Body and Society*, 2(1): 34–51.
Rowe, N. and Champion, R. (2000). *Sports Participation and Ethnicity in England*: *National Survey 1999/2000*. London: Sport England at www.english.sports.gov.uk.
Walseth, K. and Fasting K. (2003). 'Islam's View on Physical Activity and Sport: Egyptian Women Interpreting Islam'. In *International Review for the Sociology of Sport*, 38(1): 45–61.

REVISION QUESTIONS

1. Explain the advantages and disadvantages of using terms such as social divisions and social inequality to explain difference in sport in terms of class, gender and ethnicity.

2. How does sport influence class, democracy and privilege in today's world?

3. Discuss the assertion that power relationships are central to understanding sport and gender relations today.

4. Critically evaluate core assumptions that have influenced popular arguments about sport, ethnicity and racism.

5. Evaluate the idea that different degrees of freedom of choice are the essence of understanding sport and social divisions and social divisions in sport.

PRACTICAL PROJECTS

1. Use the empirical data presented in Tables 15.1 and 15.2 and Figures 15.1 and 15.2 to critically discuss social divisions in terms of social class, ethnicity and gender participation rates in sport.

2. Select ten sporting organisations of your choice, identify the members of the executive or top committee and if possible interview some of these people to ask how they got onto the committee. Write a short report entitled 'An Investigation into Sporting Democracy' drawing upon your findings.

3. Identify between eight and ten points that would form the basis of any anti-racist or gender equity sport policy in your local sports organisation, school, college or university.

4. Where are the top 50 wealthiest sports clubs located in your country? Identify where they are located on a map and try to find out how the clubs are supported financially (access annual accounts if possible) and who provides the money. Use your findings to explain how wealth creates social divisions between local and regional areas or urban and rural areas in terms of sporting provision and location.

5. Examine the committee structure of a major international sporting organisation and the processes by which individuals get elected. Comment on the extent to which organisations such as the International Olympic Committee or major international sports organisations are representative or divisive.

WEBSITES

Black Athlete sports network
    www.blackathlete.com

European Women and Sport group
    www.ews-online.com/

Let's Kick Racism Out of Football
www.kickitout.org

Women's Sport Foundation
www.womenssportsfoundation.org

WWWomen
www.wwwomen.com

Chapter 16

Sport, community and social capital

The social value of sport is often underestimated – does sport help to build a level of trust between communities? TORSTENBLACKWOOD/AFP/Getty Images

PREVIEW

Introduction • Sport and community • Associational nature of sSport in Denmark • What is communitarianism? • Critique of communitarianism • Sport, civil society and ownership • Sport as a site of civic engagement • Sport and human rights • Sport and civil society • Ownership of sports clubs • Community stakeholder model • What is social capital? • The importance of social capital • Sport and voluntary associations • The dark side of social capital • Sport and social capital • Bowling alone • The decline of the public sphere • Sport as entertainment or social right? • Local sports worlds • Sport in a safe and secure world.

OBJECTIVES

This chapter will:

- examine the argument that sport is good for the community;
- consider different theoretical approaches to the term communitarianism;
- define and discuss the relationship between sport and social capital;
- provide examples of projects where sport has been part of the community philosophy;
- evaluate whether sport is a form of entertainment or a social right.

INTRODUCTION

The contribution that sport can make to community has been a common theme within historical, sociological and political thinking about sport. As a term the word community is often invoked to imply democratic legitimacy, citizenship, part of civil society or a feel-good factor. For some the term has simply been used as a synonym for the people or society or the state and an antonym for the private sector and competition. Sport in different parts of the world is often associated with community building, social welfare, social capital and stereotypical notions of making a contribution to working-class communities. The latter often refers to a lost network of trade unions, craft associations, friendly societies, co-operatives, women's organisations, religious organisations, sport and social clubs, causes and campaigns and unitary organisations. Community in this sense of the word may be characterised by close-knit bonds or social relationships but more often than not the term refers loosely to a collection of people in a given location, a particular town, city or nation described as community. Community as place is often viewed as warm and friendly.

People rarely have bad words to say about the community or sports policies or initiatives that are premised upon rationales of contributing to the community. The associational nature of sport in Denmark may be viewed as a particular example of sport in the community that involves a high degree of local democracy but is more than just the local community. Sport in Denmark belongs to the non-governmental sector and is dependent upon an active degree of voluntarism. Despite substantial public support the freedom and independence of sports organisations, federations, associations and clubs, are respected by the public authorities. The voluntary contribution is regarded as a valued aspect of democracy within Danish civil society. Sport remains at arm's length from government. Sports associations, like all cultural associations in Denmark, are approached from an ideal perspective characterised by notions of solidarity, reciprocity, community and personal initiative. Solidarity in a sports association can be manifested as responsibility for the whole, which each individual is a part of. The whole which the association is part of, will often be a local community and association and solidarity through sport necessitates a broader sense of awareness of the needs of the broader local community. Sport occupies a central position in the consciousness of young Danish people and therefore it is deemed as having the opportunity to inspire the form of solidarity and responsibility inherent within Danish democracy.

A wide range of thinkers, socialists, conservatives, nationalists and more emphatically fascists have at different times styled themselves as anti-individualists. In most cases, anti-individualism is based upon a commitment to community and the belief that self-help and individual responsibility are a threat to social solidarity. In social and political thought the term community usually has deeper implications, suggesting a social group or neighbourhood, town, region, group of workers or whatever, within which there are strong ties and a collective identity. A genuine community is therefore often distinguished by the bonds of comradeship, loyalty and duty. Some of these terms are often readily used to describe the notion of particular sporting communities be they local fans, places, national supporters or groups of people who wear a badge of allegiance to a particular sport such as marathon running or wushu in China or baseball in Cuba, Japan or America. One final point by means of introduction is that the notion of identity is often a surrogate term for community where community refers to the social roots of individual identity. Both the notions of identity and community although hotly desired often remain imagined rather than real. Neither of the two is readily available in a rapidly privatised, individualised and globalised world and to some extent the challenges facing sport in the early twenty-first century are different from the challenges facing others spheres of activity that are dominated by market-mediated consumer choice and the power of individualism.

WHAT IS COMMUNITARIANISM?

The notion of community means different things to different groups and by means of summary Box 16.1 illustrates some of the most common characteristics of the term community as it is used today.

Approaches that place an importance upon the notion of community are usually referred to as forms of communitarianism. Communitarianism is a very good example of a phenomenon that reveals common ground in the relationship between political and social theory and practical politics. Traditions of social and political thought such as socialism, Marxism and conservatism, have all emphasised the ideal of community. Communitarians have tended to view community not simply as an object of analysis but as the true source of values, particularly of self-reliance and self-help. Recurring themes are those of social justice, mutuality, a rejection of individualism, social networks, power devolved to local communities and an emphasis on family, neighbourhood and kin. Furthermore, it is suggested that community rather than the individual or the state should be the main focus of analysis.

Communitarianism might be thought of as being divided into at least three categories, namely the social, the political and the vernacular (Frazer, 2000:180). Social communitarianism consists of a core group of texts or abstract canons that have developed a sustained

> ### BOX 16.1 SOME OF THE MOST COMMON CHARACTERISTICS ASCRIBED TO THE NOTION OF COMMUNITY
>
> - There is no such thing as 'the community' as a homogenous entity. There are many and overlapping communities, with new forms developing all the time. Some are chosen by their members, some are the product of ascribed characteristics
> - Communities exist beyond geography; they encompass a wide range of social ties and common interests which go beyond proximity or common residence
> - Communities benefit and enhance the lives of individuals, through fellowship, development and learning, and engendering a strong sense of mutual rights and responsibilities
> - Communities can give the individual a sense of identity and culture
> - Communities must be democratic, giving people a collective say over their destinies
> - Communities must be tolerant towards, and respect other communities, and where disputes arise, there must be mediation by law
> - Communities, in their diverse forms, create a civic society where the forces of decency can act to countervail anti-social behaviour
> - Community is usually expressed through association with others in voluntary institutions

attack on the philosophy of liberal individualism. The arguments are very much centred upon a number of abstract notions that question our knowledge of social processes and values (epistemology); the nature of the individual and the social world (ontology and metaphysics); and the nature or issue of what we do value and what we should value (ethics). Political communitarianism relates to a core set of policy ideals or positions and arguments adopted by politicians who have attempted to propel the notion of communitarianism onto the twenty-first-century political agenda. The alleged strength of such a policy is that it lies beyond left and right politics. Vernacular communitarianism is more concerned with the ideas, ideals and values of a range of social actors and movements who think of their central *raison d'être* as being that of community activists and that community building is the most important political project.

Liberal individualism is a natural target for forms of communitarianism that seek to establish solidarity and mutuality. From the communitarian point of view the central defect of liberalism is its view of the individual as an asocial atomised self. The critique of liberal individualism arises out of its rightly or wrongly assumed dominant position not simply within academic thought but also key political institutions such as the free market, individualism and the rule of law. The individual, according to liberal thought, must be protected from the state. Communitarian engagement with liberal individualism tends to include some or all of the following arguments. First, that liberal theories of rights are overtly individualistic and fail to recognise that bonds of obligation are not necessarily freely chosen and that mutuality, reciprocity and co-operation are pre-conditions of human life.

Second, that while an individual rights culture is historically admirable it has gone too far, in that it produces a society that has encouraged people to think of themselves as disconnected from others. This, it is argued, leads to a distortion or misunderstanding of the real meaning of rights *per se*. Finally, communitarians point to a wholly undesirable and unintended upshot of a society that emphasises too many rights and too little duty or mutuality. It is therefore within the gap between the state or governmental provision and free-market ideals, and the perception of their twin failure, that communitarianism as social theory and political practice has become popular.

The emphasis on community rather than the individual or the state has raised questions about the lack of definition over the term community. Are we talking about community as place or community as a set of interests? Some feminists, while supporting the notion of communitarianism, have implied that terms such as community are hierarchical and that communitarian arguments are non-egalitarian. The claims of individual liberty and rights versus the claims of community raise difficult issues of the common good, public interest, and notions of justice and exclusion. The communitarian stance has particular implications for any understanding of justice. Liberal theories of justice tend to be based upon assumptions about personal choice and individual behaviour that, communitarians argue, make sense because they apply to the individual without society, community or others. Thus for communitarians, universalist theories of justice must give way to ones that are strictly local.

Are sporting communities more likely to be formed through friendship or friendship-like relations arising through work and associational ties? If so, then one might expect notions of community to be closely tied to issues of social capital and civil society. Borrowing Anderson's concept of imagined communities, writers such as Bricknell (2000) suggest that the very ideal of local imagined communities remains highly emotive and a potent political and social symbol to those it includes and those it excludes. Others, such as Krieger (2000), tend simply to refer to two categories of community – actual and imagined.

It must be acknowledge that all concepts are continually contested on an ongoing basis. The notion that there is a proven link between communitarianism and social capital or that friendship is a prerequisite for continual development are all valid critiques that might be questioned by robust empiricists or non-athletes. In response to many of these criticisms communitarians stress the importance of community, social capital and a strong civil society and the practical goal of an inclusive community with layered loyalties. The notions of communitarianism and community are likely to remain active but often illusionary or slippery principles and/or notions of not just contemporary social thought and political practice but also the normative or real potential of sport to form bonds or bridges between groups of people.

SPORT, CIVIL SOCIETY AND OWNERSHIP

The view that it was good to have sources of power in society that were independent of the state was both popular and controversial as early as the eighteenth century (Keene, 1988). Hegel used the term civil society to denote the sphere of contact, or of free association amongst individuals. For Antonio Gramsci civil society was the bastion of class hegemony and ultimately viewed as being supportive of the state (Jarvie and Maguire, 1994:113). It is enough to say that civil society is an arena between the spheres of the state, on the one hand, and domestic or interpersonal relations, on the other. Sports policy in various Western democracies has attempted to operationalise this aspect of civil society through the notion of sport being at arm's length from direct government intervention. In other words civil society is an arena in which the struggle for the hearts and minds of what is important to sport takes place, is negotiated and is won or lost.

By the twenty-first century civil society has come to be defined in not just social but political and economic terms. Thus civil societies today have been described as a constellation of forces that provide a series of checks and balances upon the power of the nation-state or the local state. At a micro-level civil society is also the terrain of civil associations that are potential forces of civic engagement and mutuality (Marquand, 2000). These forces might include the market in all its forms or professional associations or mutual societies or voluntary public bodies or sports associations to name but a few of the bodies which actively hold the middle-ground between the government, the state and the individual.

The idea that sport and other forms of cultural activity may be viewed as sites of civic engagement has often led to the suggestion that such activities might be viewed as important arenas of community revitalisation. Community fun runs and sponsored marathons are often used as a means of subsidising sporting provision in areas where state provision for sport is inadequate. Such perspectives reflect a change of emphasis from viewing urban regeneration or community development in purely economic terms to one that places a greater emphasis on people and the development of social capital. The role of professionals in the development of civil society or the development of social capital may be paradoxical. As Harris (1998:144) suggests the horizontal, equitable nature of civil society makes professional efforts to strengthen civil society somewhat problematic because professionals usually have more power than the people they often serve and the conventional top-down approach to the development of community and civil society is not likely to bring about the desired outcomes.

Sporting activity historically has been associated with political protests that have championed human rights, progressive socialism and social inequality. Kidd and Donnelly (2000) have recently explored the contribution which sport has made to the struggle for human rights. They argue that the aspirations for democracy and liberation evoked under the banner of human rights cannot be achieved without human rights in sport. They conclude by drawing attention to the Sports Act in Finland which came into force in 1998 and stated that the purpose of the Act was to promote: (i) equality and tolerance and to support cultural diversity and sustainable development of the environment through sport and (ii) recreational, competitive and top level sports and associated civic activity, to promote the population's welfare and health and to support the growth and development of children and young people through sport (Kidd and Donnelly, 2000:145).

Sport and physical activity, as Harris (1998:145) has recently asserted has played its part in 'fostering self-esteem, human agency and social equity . . . an important step toward strengthening and expanding civil society'. Daniel Tarschys, then Secretary General to the Council of Europe suggested in 1995 'that the hidden face of sport is also the tens of thousands of enthusiasts who find, in their football, rowing, athletics and rock climbing clubs, a place for meeting and exchange, but above all, the training ground for community life' – she goes on to assert that within this microcosm, people learn to take responsibility, to follow rules, to accept one another, to look for consensus and to take on democracy 'seen in this light sport, is par excellence, the ideal school for democracy' (Sportsengland, 1998:12). If this is the case then community itself must mean more than just a common bond between individuals or a sense of belonging and obligation to others. The term community must therefore mean in part democratic community in which members of the community or the club have a real say over decisions affecting them.

Sport as a site of civic engagement

The issue of ownership of community-based sports clubs needs more careful consideration. The importance of the sports club to the city or the community has been widely recognised and yet in the increasingly commercial global sport market-place there remains the danger of certain sports clubs becoming increasingly divorced from the local or grass-roots fan base. Increasingly demutualised societies and communities have failed in most cases to give sports fans any form of stakeholding in the community sports club. The conventional wisdom in relationship to the ownership of sports clubs remains that of the profit-maximising, investor-owned plc with the public sector remaining the natural and unchallengeable giants of the modern economy (Morrow, 2000a). In the twenty-first-century global economy a number of third sector, non-profit-making organisations continue to flourish. When it comes to building sustainable forms of social capital, generated by a sense of local self-responsibility, neither the private sector nor the public sector seem to offer the ideal solution. The private sector has a history of crowding out the third sector from capital markets and the public sector of bludgeoning mutual or co-operative ventures out of existence. There will continue to be many areas of economic activity where investor-owned, profit-maximising companies will remain dominant but there are many other instances where there remains a need for stronger state/civil regulation or a different form of ownership, or possibly a combination of both. When consumers or employees become owners, their sense of self-esteem, responsibility and participation can be transformed.

It is not unnecessary to dismiss a debate about mutuality as irrelevant to sport. Sport in many ways is ideally suited to mutuality because of the way in which groups attach themselves to a sporting ideal or common objective. The idea of football trusts which developed in England is simple; if supporters want an increased say in the way that football clubs are run they can achieve it only by ownership. Supporters Direct, as a unit of the Football Trust in England, supplies legal and financial advice in addition to model constitutions while the Co-op bank helps with funding. The first Scottish attempt to form a mutual trust, operating upon co-operative principles, was made by a small group of shareholders in Celtic Football Club back in January 2000 (*Scotland on Sunday*, 23 January:6). The Scottish Executive at the time refused to inject money into the setting up of football supporters' trusts in Scotland and yet, mutual self-help, historically has been an important aspect of the development of Celtic Football Club. As Morrow (2000b:23) points out, one distinctive aspect of the 1995 share issue is that the available shares were nearly all bought by football supporters as opposed to city institutions. The willingness of supporters to take up the share offer in the club demonstrates a sustained level of community pride in the football club. Morrow (2000b:24) goes on to assert that one of the most important things that Celtic supporters have to thank the former club Director Fergus McCann for is the opportunity to buy and own part of Celtic Football Club. He commented that 'I believe it is important the ordinary supporter has a say in the running of their football club . . . Celtic Football Club is an institution which should not be in the hands of one individual or the City' (quoted in Morrow 2000b:24).

The community stakeholder model provides but one model of possible conduct for sports clubs who first, aim to demonstrate that they are a vital part of the community and second, aim to promote and sustain social and economic capital through facilitating the community role in the decision-making structures of the sports club (Morrow, 2003). The organisational thinking behind increasing community ownership of sports clubs owes much to the principles of mutuality. The co-operative is but one organisational form that is based upon the notion of mutuality. The above case is but an illustrative example that questions the inaccurate assumption that the profit-maximising investor plc is the natural form of sports organisation for the professional sports club. Co-operative, mutual philosophies work best when there is a clear opportunity and incentive for people to work closely together for practical mutual interest in increasingly demutualised societies. In truth few democratic governments have got to grips with the important issue of community ownership of sports clubs and organisations. Its natural pragmatism whispers that which works is right, but there is a danger that in rejecting the sterility of the polarised argument about state versus private ownership, the case for diversity in forms of ownership goes unexamined. Ownership matters. The socially excluded need a sense of ownership. One of the most intransigent aspects of twenty-first-century welfare reforms in Britain is that the poorest 15 per cent cannot afford to put cash aside to save for retirement – because they lack capital either in terms of savings or real estate (Hargreaves, 1999). In all the meanings of that word, the issue of ownership and community lies at the very heart of a larger debate concerning sport's contribution to civil society.

WHAT IS SOCIAL CAPITAL?

While it was the sociologists James Coleman and Pierre Bourdieu who developed the term, it was the political scientist Robert Putnam who packaged and developed a theory as a basis for analysing American society. Social capital, according to Putnam meant those features of social life – networks, norms and trusts – that enabled participants to act together more effectively to achieve shared objectives. It has been viewed as the elixir that thickens civil society with the potential to create strong reciprocal relationships and energetic communities. For Putnam the best indicators and generators of social capital included involvement in voluntary associations, a choir, a political party, a football or a bowling league. James Coleman's (1988) concept of social capital has also become popular within contemporary policy-orientated discourses about sport and leisure (Coalter, 2000; Harris, 1998). Coleman introduced his now well-known concept in a discussion of a society's capacity for educational achievement but implicit within the notion of social capital was a potential meaning that extended well beyond education in that social capital can be involved in any sphere that involved trust. Since the late 1980s, developing social capital has been viewed as a way of renewing democracy. It refers to the network of social groups and relationships that fosters co-operative working and community well-being. It involves communities and other social groups exercising a certain degree of trust through taking on mutual obligations.

There are at least two reasons why social capital has attracted so much attention. On the one hand civil society and communities depend upon it. Social capital has been seen as a way of contributing to social inclusion. Social groups and individuals learn more when they can draw upon the cultural resources of people around them. They learn from each other directly but they also learn to trust that the social arrangements are in place to ensure that learning, through a multitude of mediums including sport, will benefit them both culturally and for employment opportunities. They also trust that their own family or friends will grow up in a community that is intellectually stimulating. Social capital can have these effects most readily where it is embodied in the social structure – most notably, formal educational institutions and cultural organisations that have a commitment to other outcomes such as learning.

On the other hand democracy depends upon social capital. This is true in one very obvious sense, that democracy depends upon everyone trusting that everyone else will operate the system constructively. When that trust breaks down – for example, as a reaction to certain screening practices aimed at the control of drugs in athletes or the failure to deliver sustainable sporting and economic benefits for deprived inner-city urban ghettos, or the adequate funding arrangements for sport in universities or local authorities – the result is cynicism about democracy in general. But the potential role of social capital is more profound than this because citizenship requires knowledge and that people know how to work with others towards common goals.

The political scientist Robert Putnam has recently (1995) documented the decline of social capital in America which he defined as those features of social life – networks, runs and trusts – that enable participants to work together more effectively to pursue shared objectives. Putnam used this notion to analyse the phenomenon of what he called civic disengagement. By this he referred to the decline in participation not just in formal political activity but also in all kinds of social activities, including sport and physical activity. The decline of social capital allegedly included the decreasing membership in voluntary organisations, decreased participation in organised activities and the decrease in time spent in informal socialising and visiting. Americans were viewed as becoming less trusting of one another with a close correlation existing between social trust and membership of civic associations. Television emerged as the prime suspect in the decline of social capital with viewing per television in 1995 accounting for more than a 50 per cent increase in viewing time in comparison to the 1950s. Television privatised time for sport and other activities and in doing so destroyed the networks and values that supported social capital and the pursuit of shared objectives.

The concept of social capital carries with it a heavy burden of claims that only recently have been subjected to critical review (Johnston and Percy-Smith, 2003). At its heaviest, as typified by writers such as Putnam, the presence or absence of social capital is used as an explanatory factor for economic and political performance. More modest claims are also made for social capital in that it allegedly contributes to the formation of strong formal and informal networks, shared norms and trusting social relationships. In relation to communities it is asserted that high-trust communities typically experience less crime, anti-social behaviour and social fragmentation. For individuals social capital it is suggested contributes to better health, higher levels of educational attainment and access to employment. Social capital it is maintained is a factor that contributes to higher levels of civic and voluntary activity and in turn such activity enhances democracy by offering citizens greater choices and opportunities.

The dark side of social capital

On the other hand Portes (1998) has identified at least four negative consequences associated with social capital. First, the exclusion of outsiders as a result of strong ties that exist within a particular group or community. Second, group or community closure which inhibits the economic success of its members as a result of free-riding on the part of some group members. Third, conformity within the group or community resulting in restrictions of personal freedom and autonomy. Finally social capital is partly responsible for a downward levelling as a result of group solidarity that arises out of opposition to mainstream society and inter-generational experiences of exclusion and discrimination. In all of these ways social capital is viewed as excluding outside influences and enforcing damaging group norms if you do not belong to a community or group. Thus it is important to be aware that the notion of social capital has a dark side as well as a positive side and that discussion of sport and social capital must be sensitive to both the positive and negative aspects of social capital in action.

SPORT AND SOCIAL CAPITAL

While credit for the notion of social capital remains with sociologists such as James Coleman and Pierre Bourdieu it was Robert Putnam who packaged and developed the theory subsequently presented in *Bowling Alone: The Collapse and Revival of American Community* (2000) and earlier works. Putnam's firm belief that investment in bowling leagues and other voluntary associations could save democracy and community in the West has been encouraged by both American and British political administrations. Rarely has a work revolving around aspects of sport, culture and society had such a political impact. *Bowling Alone* articulated the unease many, initially Americans, felt about the state of their communities and Putnam provided the numerical evidence that fuelled those initial fears. Putnam saw deep parallels between the turn of the twentieth century and the turn of the twenty-first century in which major technological, economic and social change was destroying the nation's stock of social capital and yet no action was taken to fix the problem. Between 1890 and 1910 all the major American civic institutions of the twentieth century – from the Urban League to the Knights of Columba – were invented. At Harvard, Putnam engaged in a range of seminars to encourage a new wave of voluntary associations aimed at rebuilding bonds of civic trust among Americans.

 334

Much of what was happening in America also related to the British experience at the turn of the twenty-first century and perhaps expressed most forcibly in the work of David Marquand (2004) in *The Decline of the Public* in which the writer charts the decline of citizenship, equity and service that had been crucial to both individual fulfilment and social well-being. From the Women's Institutes and the Women's League of Health and Beauty to the working men's club and local sports clubs Britain has always had a strong record of voluntary association and social capital in sport and other areas of public life. With specific reference to sports clubs in Scotland a 1999 survey identified the following concerns; 50 per cent identified a general shortage of volunteers; 33 per cent identified a shortage of volunteer staff with technical skills and 29 per cent identified a shortage of volunteer staff with management skills (Jarvie, 2004).

On the other hand Hunt (2001) points out that we still manage to maintain levels of sociability and community investment commensurate with the 1950s. Yet at the same time we are trusting people less, our faith in politics is declining and the kinds of associations we are joining tend to have more to do with private needs than civic engagement. The results of the shift away from ways that were concerned about the public domain and social capital to individualism and market fundamentalism are there for everyone to see, according to Marquand (2004); resource-starved public services, the marketisation of the public sector, the soul-destroying targets and audits that go with it and the erosion of public trust. One further observation upon this general malaise is made and that is the observation that citizenship rights are by definition equal. Market rewards are by definition unequal. If the public domain of sport is annexed to, or invaded by, the market domain of buying and selling the primordial democratic promise of equal citizenship and sporting equity will be negated.

The promise in the notion of social capital is that sport and other associational activity can make a contribution to building up levels of trust in sport, culture and society and consequently contributing to democracy, community spirit and a weakening public domain. Yet the explanatory power of the relationship between sport and the promise of renewed forms of social capital needs to carry with it a cautionary note. The work on sport and social capital has been predominantly based upon evidence drawn from British and American sport and recreational activity and if broader international comparisons with other places were brought into play the picture may be different. There is little evidence of the decline in associational activity in certain parts of Europe and in Scandinavia and in other parts of the world such as South America it may still be constant if not increasing (Da Costa et al. 2002). Stolle's (1998) work in Germany and Sweden suggests that sport and the arts facilitate few bridging links with ethnic groups. Whereas sport and the arts may encourage bonding at the expense of bridging little contribution is made to linking disadvantaged groups to other levels of the decision-making hierarchy. Insofar as many people are excluded from sport how can the notion that sport is said to increase social capital be accepted as a general or universal truth? Are there not differences between regions, within nations and more importantly between rich and poor parts of the world?

While not wanting to imply that an uncritical devotion to certain observations and facts does not mean that sport cannot make a contribution to social capital or healthy democratic communities it is important to heed Putnam's (2000:77) own words in *Bowling Alone* where he challenges readers to understand the complexities involved in creating civic engagement and just precisely what types of organisations and networks most effectively embody or generate social capital in the sense of mutual reciprocity, social obligations and community action. Many on the left have viewed the politics of social capital and civic renewal as a diversion from the politics of social democracy and as such students, teachers and researchers may want to consider or emphasise that in sport, culture and society social capital is a complement and not an alternative to the more egalitarian fundamentals of social democracy and a more just and equal world beyond Britain and America.

Current debates about social capital and social cohesion may, at one level, raise questions concerning the direction of sport within urban policies. Sports have been at the heart of city life in many parts of the world for some time and yet urban policy needs to address the issue of whether the role of sport remains that of entertainment or whether sport is a social right or both. If sport were to facilitate social capital then cities, rather than using sport as a basis for attracting the national and international destination of major events or sports festivals, might wish to resurrect the notion of sport as a social right rather than a spectacle or form of entertainment. Cities in all parts of the world are first and foremost places to live for millions of people and yet access to sport remains problematic for many vulnerable groups of people. The citizens who seem the most ignored are those with the fewest resources (Harvey, 2003). The Canadian Council on Social Development points out that more than 60 per cent of children in the poorest households almost never participate in organised sports, whereas the figure is 27 per cent for children from affluent homes. The Council also confirmed the theory that cities that give young people a voice in policy development are more inclusive than others. Thus it might be argued that if sport does help to facilitate notions of social capital and/or community then a prerequisite of any such approach necessitates viewing sport as a social right rather than a form of entertainment. Harvey (2003) is insightful when he suggests that the sociability networks that may develop in and around community sport and recreation initiatives may help to strengthen social bonds and consequently a potential source of social capital. If this is the case then sport as a social right for children and all vulnerable groups cannot be left to chance.

SUMMARY

The themes of community and the place of sport in the community have been commented upon for more than half a century. From at least the 1950s the sociological analysis of community has existed in the work of writers such as Tönnies (1963) and others who distinguished between relations of *gemeinschaft* and *gesellschaft* through to the twenty-first century where writers such as Frazer seek to push a modern communitarian agenda that draws upon concepts such as cohesion and mutuality. There remains a substantive, moral and political disagreement between those who value community in itself and those who value it instrumentally. The notions of social capital and citizenship have been associated contemporaneously with the above agenda. Sport's role in the regeneration of twenty-first-century communities also remains well documented but problematic. This chapter has argued that it is unrealistic to expect sport to be totally responsible for sustaining a sense of community or citizenship or even for reinforcing notions of social capital. However, sports projects and the place of sport within both imagined and active senses of communities can make a valuable contribution. More importantly it is the potential contribution that sport makes to civil society, the space between the state and the individual, that provides sport with the opportunity to promote a communitarian philosophy based upon mutuality and obligations rather than individualism and some ideological notion of sport for all.

The assertion that local sports clubs provide communities with a sense of place and identity is one of the popular contributions that sport can make to communitarian thinking. Other arguments include:

- that the associational nature of sport helps in the production and reproduction of social capital;
- that sport contributes to a sense of civic pride and civic boosterism;
- that sport has a vital role to play in the regeneration of deprived urban communities;
- that sports facilities can provide an important contribution to the physical infrastructure of communities, provide a social focus for community and consequently influence people's perceptions of neighbourhood;
- that the power of sport has been diminished along with the decline of civil society and social capital;
- that a strong sense of collective identification with some teams rather than being communitarian has been divisive;
- that sport alone cannot sustain vibrant living communities;
- that global sporting markets and patterns of consumption have marginalised and replaced local sporting identity and taste;
- that the mutual ownership of sports clubs can contribute to social capital within the community.

In answer to the question is sport good for the community it might be useful to qualify any notion of universality by suggesting that (i) sport can play a positive role in a number of wide-ranging community initiatives that can help to sustain a sense of community; (ii) sport on its own is not the solution to community social and economic problems but it can be part of the solution; (iii) policy advisers and social theorists need to test empirically a number of statements concerning the role of sport and its associated outcomes in specific settings before concluding on the issue of sports relationship to communities and (iv) communities themselves change over time and whether one is talking about a community of Internet sport enthusiasts or the place and space associated with sport in the geography of communities recognition must be given to the fact that the relationship between sport and the community is never static but always changing.

One final comment is that at the beginning of the twenty-first century community is missing in the worlds we inhabit and yet it is potentially a crucial quality to a happier life. The worlds of sport and beyond would be safer, more secure and less vulnerable if community was more of a reality (Bauman, 2001). Given the insecurity and concerns about safety in a rapidly globalising interdependent world we need to gain control over the conditions under which we struggle with the challenges of life and for most people such control can only be gained by working collectively. If there is to be any notion of active community in a world of many individuals it needs to be a community woven together from sharing and mutual care. If sport can help to provide moments of safety, security and hope for vulnerable groups of people then it has a part to play in creating a community of concern and responsibility for the equal right to be human and the equal ability to act on that right. At present those excluded from sport in many parts of the world do not have access to that right.

KEY CONCEPTS

Civic engagement	Social bonds
Civil society	Social capital
Community	Social rights
Communitarianism	Solidarity
Democracy	Sports clubs
Local sport	Supporters trusts
Mutuality	Trust
Networks	Vernacular communitarianism
Ownership	Voluntarism
Political communitarians	Voluntary sport

KEY READING

Books

Bauman, Z. (2001). *Community: Seeking Safety in an Insecure World*. Cambridge: Polity Press.
Eichberg, H. (2004). *The People of Democracy: Understanding Self-determination on the Basis of Body and Movement*. Arhus: Klim.
Field, J. (2003). *Social Capital*. London: Routledge.
Maguire, J., Jarvie, G., Mansfield, L. and Bradley, J. (2002). *Sport Worlds: A Sociological Perspective*. Illinois: Human Kinetics.
Marquand, D. (2004). *Decline of the Public*. Oxford: Polity Press.

Journal articles

Dyreson, M. (2001). 'Maybe It's Better to Bowl Alone: Sport, Community and Democracy in American Thought'. *Culture, Sport, Society*, 4(1): 19–30.
Harris, J. (1998). 'Civil Society, Physical Activity and the Involvement of Sport Sociologists in the Preparation of Physical Activity Professionals'. *Sociology of Sport*, 15: 138–153.
Jarvie, G. (2003b). 'Sport, Communitarianism and Social Capital: A Neighbourly Insight Into Scottish Sport'. *International Review for the Sociology of Sport*, 38(2): 139–153.
Johnston, G. and Percy-Smith, J. (2003). 'In Search of Social Capital'. *Policy and Politics*, 31(3): 321–334.
Putnam, R. (1995). 'Bowling Alone: America's Declining Social Capital'. *Journal of Democracy*, 6: 65–78.

Further reading

Bliers, H. (2003). *Communities in Control: Public Services and Local Socialism*. London: Fabian Society.

Da Costa, L., Lamartine and P. and Miragaya, A. (2002). *Worldwide Experience and Trends in Sport for All*. Aachen, Germany: Meyer and Meyer Sports Books.

Heywood, A. (2004). *Political Theory and Introduction*. Basingstoke: Palgrave Macmillan, 15–50.

Palm, J. (2003). *Global Perspectives on Sport, Community and Inclusion: Sport for All in Policy and Practice*. London: Routledge.

Portes, A. (1998). 'Social Capital: Its Origins and Applications in Modern Sociology'. *Annual Review of Sociology*, 24: 1–24.

REVISION QUESTIONS

1. Compare and contrast at least four different ways in which sport is said to contribute to the notion of community.

2. What do the terms communitarianism, community stakeholder and social capital mean?

3. Provide a summary of Putnam's thesis in relation to sport and social capital and describe ways in which sport might contribute or not contribute to the notions of social bridging and social bonding.

4. Use the work of Marquand to argue against any policy that suggests that sport should be annexed to the private domain.

5. What is social capital and does sport help to develop it? Illustrate your answer with at least five examples from sporting contexts.

PRACTICAL PROJECTS

1. Identify one socially excluded group of your choice. Develop a policy document designed to promote social inclusion in sport.

2. Look at the constitution of three different sports clubs and compare and contrast the different ways in which the constitution promotes or discourages communitarianism or mutual obligations to the community in which the clubs are located.

3. Interview ten different local people, taking into account different generations of people, and ask them how sport has helped to develop or fragment social cohesion within the neighbourhood. Based upon your findings write a report on sport and community within your neighbourhood.

4. Identify the board members of three major professional sports organisations and explore their social backgrounds prior to writing a critical report on how representative the board is and how it protects the interests of its members.

5. Interview ten volunteers and explore with them the way in which they see their role in sport in terms of obligations and active citizenship.

WEBSITES

Scottish Executive Publications
   www.scotland.gov.uk/crukd01/blue/rsrdua-00.htm

Scottish Parliament proceedings
   www.scottish.parliament.uk/business/chamber/mop-00/mop-06-15.htm_42095

Social capital statistics
   http://www.statistics.gov.uk/socialcapital/

Sports Policy Research Initiative Canada
   http://policyresearch.gc.ca/page.asp?pagenm=horsunset_06_01

Chapter 17

Sport and social change

Can street football or basketball initiatives help with social change? © cocopics (2005)

PREVIEW

Capitalism • Global sport and capitalism • Neo-liberalism • Tiger Woods and Augusta • Sport and social change in Brazil • Law of moralisation for football • The transformative capacity of sport • Women's sport and social change • The Women's International Sports Movement • Sport, social class, irreverence and deference • Workers' Sports Movement • Social class, the lottery and gambling • Sport, racism and black activism • Campaigns against racism in sport • Historic sporting moments in the fight against racism in sport • Sport, power and the South • The Games of the Newly Emerging Forces • Women, sport and Islam • Cricket and Zimbabwe • Sport and the North–South divide • Sport, social change and social forums • Non-governmental organisations, social movements and sport.

OBJECTIVES

This chapter will:

■ examine ways in which sport has contributed to bringing about social change;

■ consider examples of campaigns for social and political change through sport;

■ illustrate that sport is not immune from campaigns for change not only between groups but also within and between countries and regions;

■ examine sport's contribution to the politics of social forums and movements;

■ draw upon empirical material as a basis for critiquing neo-liberal sport.

INTRODUCTION

In 1919, Canadian sport was divided between amateur and professional, east and west, male and female, bourgeois and workers' sports organisations, so wrote the Canadian historian of sport Bruce Kidd. Writing almost a decade ago about the struggle for Canadian sport in a text that still remains an exemplar for students, teachers and researchers thinking about the capacity of sport to produce social change, Kidd (1996:270) concluded that capitalist sport had triumphed and that the effort to create alternatives to commercial sports culture continued to be an uphill fight. Any progressive strategy aimed at bringing about social change in sport, suggested Kidd (1996:270), while fighting for scarce resources and political support must at some point confront consumer loyalties, conventional wisdom, economic power and the political force generated by sports corporations. But such alternatives do exist and they have an active and long history in the real world of sport.

An important priority in any contemporary discussion of capitalism is to first acknowledge that it still exists but perhaps more importantly to acknowledge that it exists in new forms. Capital today is much more fluid, it flows much more readily looking for the optimum conditions with which to reproduce itself and in turn accumulate greater capital. Sports businesses look around the world, not just around the locale, the region or the nation for greater profit. Contemporary capitalism is marked by the rise to pre-eminence of the trans-national corporations that in terms of their size and power are able to take advantage of whatever opportunities exist to lower the costs of production, typically by shifting aspects of sports production from wealthier to relatively poorer countries, or through consolidation, merger or takeovers. Contemporary capitalism also takes place within an alleged regime of international governance that seeks to accommodate the interests of nation-states and the needs of trans-national capital.

At the same time there is the almost unquestionable challenge that global sport in many ways is part of the hallmark of the triumph of capitalism coupled with the growing ascendancy of economics over politics, of the corporate demands for sport over public policy and of private sporting interest over public sporting interests. Neo-liberal thinking about sport in many ways implies the end of politics because of the centrality of the market as the resource allocator and the submission of public life and the commons to commodification. It is tempting to suggest that globalisation represents but a further acceleration towards the capitalisation of the sporting world but to accept such an analogy would be to acknowledge *uncritically* the rhetorical promotion of globalisation as capitalism and the submission of public life and the commons to com- modification. That is to say that at one level the services that remain in the public sector according to neo-liberalism have to be compelled to run themselves as private enterprises and the role of different sporting worlds is simply to compete for customers. At another level global neo-liberalism also advocates a clear path towards economic convergence between the richest and poorest parts of the world if the governments of poor countries strictly adhere to liberal policies. While global neo-liberalism is an intellectually complex body of knowledge involving diverse strands of argument its politics are pristinely simple in that politics ceases to have any meaning beyond terms prescribed by the market.

To accept such logic would be to deny or reduce to a matter of insignificance the many opportunities for social change and social reform that are presented by and through contemporary sport. To deny that such opportunities for social change exist would be just as utopian as thinking that older variants of capitalism remain the way of the twenty-first century – this is not the case. New parameters of global politics exist just as capitalism continues to forge an increasing inter-dependence with global sport. Yet, as outlined in Chapter 3, politics are thought and fought, policies are forged and implemented, political ideas wax and wane within an increasingly global space that at one level is geo-political and at another level is socio-economic. Opportunities for social change in and through sport exist at both these levels and arise in both intended and unintended ways.

In 1997, when Tiger Woods won the Masters and donned the green jacket that accompanied the winning of the coveted title, golf became thrilling to watch for an entirely new audience. On the hallowed putting greens of Augusta, where Woods would not have been allowed membership a few years earlier, history had been made. Social change through sport occurred and at the time America did not have the language to deal with the change. Not since Lee Elder squared off against Jack Nicklaus in a sudden death playoff at the American Golf Classic in 1968 had a black golfer gained so much televised attention (Bass, 2002). The sports press cast the feat of Woods as breaking a modern colour line, yet no one including Woods himself could fully describe exactly what colour line had been broken. The press conveyed his parental heritage as variously African–American, Asian and Native American, overwhelmingly others portrayed Woods as a black athlete, a golfer who had brought about change in the same way attributed to the likes of Jesse Owens, Tommie Smith, John Carlos, Muhammad Ali, Tydie Pickett, Louise Stokes, Vonetta Flowers and Alice Cochrane. Woods himself did not consider himself in such terms but embraced a more nuanced racial heritage more representative of the melting pot imagery associated with American history and a determining demographic factor of so-called Generation X (Bass, 2002:xvi).

In 2002, Luiz Inacio Lula da Silva was elected President of Brazil. The former shoeshine boy, economic migrant, lathe worker and militant brought a change of style to political life in Brazil. Lula's administration tried to bring about social change in a number of key areas of Brazilian life. It is alleged that the administration aimed at succeeding in at least two areas – the promotion of economic growth after 22 years of economic stagnation and an attempt to develop a sense of increasing justice so that the poor were not so poor at the end of his administration as they were at the beginning. In August 2003 when Lula wanted his ministers to commemorate a victory in the battle for pension reform, he invited them for a kick-about game of football. A game in which Lula's team beat the side captained by the fisheries minister 5–3. Lula while trying to reform the tax and pension system and deliver economic policy that helped drive social change, had already proved himself a sound tactician in the democratisation of Brazilian football.

The content of the administration's policies were also influenced by football in that the first two laws that the President signed in May 2002 concerned football. Football in Brazil is one of the key battlegrounds upon which the struggle to make the country a fairer place is being fought. The sport had been run by a network of unaccountable largely corrupt figures known as *carrolas* or 'top hats' who had become obscenely wealthy while the domestic football scene remained broke and demoralised (Bellos, 2003:32). The public plundering of football was viewed by the President as a continual reminder of the previous administration's failure to stamp out corruption in areas of public life. Lula in an attempt to force the football authorities to become transparent ratified a *Law of Moralisation* in sport that enforced transparency in club administration (Bellos, 2003:32). On the same day he sanctioned a more ambitious and wide ranging law, the 'Fans Statute', a bill of rights for the football fan.

At the beginning of this book we asserted that one of the key sporting questions of our time needed to be what is the transformative capacity of sport to produce social change? There are a number of fault lines running through the different worlds of sport that have sustained progressive agendas for change. Any number of entry and exit points may be chosen as a basis for substantiating the transformative capacity of sport. Forms of action may be classified along the continuum from reformism to radicalism or from ideological to non-ideological or from issue-orientated to more collective forms of action. Forms of change may also have both intended and unintended outcomes but whatever the basis for thinking about sport and social change in the early twenty-first century it is imperative to acknowledge that the parameters of sport and social change are both geo-political and socio-economic. The analytical distinction and separation of these two elements does not of course imply that they are literally distinct. In the different worlds of sport these two fault lines may become conjoined but as a method of thinking about sport and social change they help to highlight not just the particular social patterning of movements for change in sport but also that the impetus and pressure for change may result from a more geo-political faultline of North and South or East and West.

The categories that follow are not exhaustive but they help to illustrate the capacity of sport to produce change in a way that is not limited simply by ideology. Effective reform whether it be radical or evolutionary can only be based upon an understanding of current global or international pressures, sporting tensions or fault lines and these are continually shifting. While much attention in recent years has focused upon the emerging real or mythical notion of a global civil society with the power to engage with and challenge institutions of global governance the place of sport has not figured greatly within such developments. Where sport has figured has mainly been, for example, where it has provided a means to an end rather than focusing upon being a progressive end in itself with its own house in order. The relationship between sport and social change must encapsulate and acknowledge both forms of activity in that sport and social change may refer to social change within sport itself but also the way in which sport has been instrumental in contributing to broader campaigns for social and political change in different parts of the world. The following themes encapsulate some of that promise.

SPORTING HEROINES AND COLLECTIVISM

In 1792, commenting upon the vindication of the rights of women, Mary Wollstonecraft noted that it was justice and not charity that was wanting in the world at that time. Throughout the late twentieth-century, women and feminist movements have continually questioned male radicals' leadership of movements for liberation and equality in which traditional gender roles have remained unchanged. Overall feminism has been a movement of the left, in the broadest sense, although more so in Western Europe and, in its own way, in the Third World – questioning the masculinist rule of capital as well as patriarchy – than in the USA. Whether or not the contemporary women's movement or other forms of activism involving women's issues provides the prototypical alternative social movement is open to question but certainly struggles for women's sport have benefited from international support, collectivism and forms of solidarity. Struggles for women's sport and other forms of justice for women have been sensitive to other traditions of emancipatory internationalism and in this sense a similarity exists between labour and women's movements. One of the major reasons for the advances, policies and interventions won by women in sport has not only been the heightened sense of forms of common orientation but also the linkage of the women's movement to struggles for women in different parts of the world.

The normative potential of sport to produce social change is self-evident in the following example from the Sydney 2000 Olympic Games. Maria Isabel Urrutia was a gold medal winner having lifted 75 kg in the clean and jerk weightlifting category. The Olympic gold medal winner represents a country where young athletes have had to pass through guerrilla and paramilitary roadblocks while travelling between cities to national competitions. Columbia holds the unfortunate distinction of being the world's leading country in terms of kidnapping with some 3,000 reported cases per year. Commenting on her gold medal victory Urrutia said that 'she hoped that her victory would reach others like her – poor, black and female' (*Sunday Herald*, 1 October 2000:18). She went on, 'as a poor person, I hope others see that you can make a living, see the world and get an education through sports or even music and other arts. As a woman I hope that girls who are now 13, like I was when I started, now realise that they don't have to become teenage mothers and as a black person I hope the country sees that there's another Urrutia besides the white man who signs our pesos' (*Sunday Herald*, 1 October 2000:18).

On the other hand writers such as Bruce Kidd (1996:144) commenting upon the struggles for women in sport in Canada point out that women's sport run by women is such a utopian ideal that it cannot be imagined. As a result girls and women in Canada struggle to develop identities and healthy womanhood in a cultural practice largely controlled by males and steeped in the discourses of masculinity. Despite the acceptance of gender equity in many sports organisations women remain under-represented in positions of leadership although perhaps not as woefully as their early twentieth- or late nineteenth-century counterparts. The following list is not exhaustive but illustrative of some of the key areas of social change fought for by women in and through sport:

1. a more representative coverage for women within the Women's International Sports Movement;
2. concerns over the existence and strategies aimed at the amelioration of sexual harassment in sport;
3. raising awareness of women in sport across the world;
4. improved conditions for women in sport;
5. increased representation for women in sport both through the existing structures and new structures;
6. women's health and well-being in all parts of the world;
7. ensuring that the women executives in positions of power listen to and do not distance themselves from ordinary women who are the majority;
8. acknowledgement that the culture of movement is different for ordinary women in different parts of the world.

The Women's International Sports Movement has been an effective advocate for change in sport but also a successful conduit between sport and other organisations such as the United Nations. The reality of speaking as one voice may be utopian but co-operative work between women in sport has meant that there is a greater potential or hope for the international voice of women in sport being heard within the mainstream of other international movements supporting and advocating for women in different parts of the world. The Women's International Sports Movement continues to struggle with the question of representation, but as Hargreaves (2000:233) concludes the future of a global sports feminism and the Women's International Sports Movement lies in the potential to unite women across social divisions and differences and as such the future remains international in focus and dependent upon effective coalitions both within sport and between sport and other forms of difference including generations of feminisms.

SPORT, SOCIAL CLASS AND IRREVERENCE

The great epoch of the industrial working-class movement has come to an end. The relationship between sport and the labour movement was probably at its strongest during the 1930s, 1940s and 1950s in that sport was always viewed as popular and therefore worthy of serious political attention. This varied between countries. Yet the relationship between sport and social class has certainly changed as a consequence of the values associated with modernity. Crucial developments such as the erosion of traditional forms of deference have resulted in the breaking down of certain traditional barriers of social control. What we might call social modernisation in sport resulting from sports migration, education, mass communication and the forging of further democratic rights in sport. These and other changes have resulted in the erosion of many different kinds of deference such as the forms of social class deference that operated through the reproduction of amateur and professional codes of sporting practice and a more party political notion of deference that operated through the formal workings of various workers sports movements of the twentieth century in which progress in part was determined by due deference not only to elder statesmen, they usually were men, but also to the political ideology of the party.

The work of Jones (1986, 1988) remains a classic account of the relationship between sport and the labour movement in Britain during the inter-war years. Both the British Workers Sports Federation and the British Workers Sports Association campaigned for the state to provide facilities and services for sport, to regulate and even suppress certain sports and to secure the right of access to the countryside for all. The former of these organisations was aligned to the International Union of Red Sport and Gymnastic Associations that later became the International Union of Workers and Peasants Sports Associations. Fabians from at least the nineteenth century had challenged the need for an increased sport and recreation provision in Britain at a municipal level while Labour throughout the 1920s and 1930s raised concerns over the fact that urbanisation would reduce the number of sports grounds. Labour MP Jack Jones was fairly typical of the time when he asserted that it was essential to preserve recreation and sports grounds and release more space for parks so that youth could indulge in weekly sports. The *Clarion* newspaper of the 1930s also regularly commented upon the glaring injustices brought about by the lack of proper sporting amenities. Clarion Cycling and Rambling Clubs had been formed in Britain since at least 1894 in order to help with the distribution of the *Clarion* and other socialist newspapers.

Such activities were not limited to Britain or indeed Europe. The work of Kruger and Riordan (1996) tells the story of workers' sports movements in Germany, France, Finland, Austria, Sweden, Norway, Israel, the former Soviet Union and Canada. In 1931 the Socialist Workers Sports International (SWSI) included membership from the those countries listed in Table 17.1.

Table 17.1 *Socialist Worker Sports International members in 1931*

Country		Clubs	Members
Alsace-Lorraine		249	13,560
Austria		2,500	293,700
Belgium		421	12,900
Denmark		?	20,000
Czechoslovakia			
	Czech	1,220	136,977
	German	585	70,730
England		?	5,000
Estonia		29	1,600
Finland		419	30,257
France		138	10,895
Germany		15,730	1,211,468
Hungary		?	1,750
Latvia		94	5,171
Netherlands		76	16,759
Palestine		?	4,250
Poland			
	Polish	?	7,000
	German	?	938
	Jewish	110	4,369
	Ukrainian	68	1,925
Romania		?	2,500
Switzerland		289	21,624
United States		12	697
Yugoslavia		?	1,800

Source: Kruger, A. and Riordan, J. (1996). *The Story of Worker Sport*. Champaign, IL: Human Kinetics, p.171.

The detailed work of social historians such as Mark Clapson (1986) and Ross McKibben (1994) illustrates the enduring relationship between social class, betting and the lottery in Britain that pre-dates the emergence and growth of football pools in the 1920s. The growth of illegal commercialised betting from the 1880s, a time of relative working-class prosperity, reflected its importance as a means of intellectual and rational expression amongst working-class punters. Wagering was an opportunity for those who possessed little money and a limited formal education to study the form of a horse or a greyhound in past races, to predict its likeliness of winning and to back up their considered opinion with a small investment which carried a measure of hope. Even in America during the great depression of the 1930s queues of unemployed and the debt-ridden shuffled to buy lottery tickets and betting slips, praying for what the American depression playwright Clifford Odets called the rocket to the moon that would whisk people into a world of instant wealth, security and respect (McMillan, 1995:16).

Perhaps there are times in human history when liberalisation in the direction of harmless fun can be absorbed in an upward movement of an optimistic and expansive society. For many in the Britain of much of the second half of the twentieth century the answer lay in labour with a small and large L, in work itself, in the organisation of people who did the work so that their rewards began to match the value of their efforts and in the progress of the political party that historically represented the working class, the unrepresented and those in poverty. However, for many the relationship between sport, class and the lottery in the twenty-first century is just another symptom of decline, a change of focus, a feeling of uncertainty and insecurity in a world in which collectivism and solidarity in many instances has been replaced by irreverence and individualism. A nation of subjects who historically felt that they had some control over their fate through elections, security of pensions, representation and the communities where they lived has been replaced by a loose collection of individuals living in a global world of uncertainty where even the winnings from the sports lottery are distributed elsewhere. A nation of ricocheting pinballs in some vast global bagatelle machine in which the anonymous financial masters of the universe pulled the levers.

The national lottery has for some become an icon of uncertainty, individualism, false hope which even in sporting terms has failed to supply the financial security and provision that was promised with its introduction. The number of good causes funded through lottery provision has meant reduced funding for sport in many if not all parts of Britain. A Britain in which some people are doing rather well for themselves while others remain marginalised, disadvantaged within sport and in terms of the opportunities for physical activity (Jarvie, 1997). A 30/30/40 society, in which the privileged 40 per cent remain comfortable, can access private sporting clubs and have increased their power in the market-place. A further 30 per cent who due to their changing relationship to the market-place, insecurity of pension provision and an ageing society have become marginalised but also increasingly politically active as a result of the changes and a further 30 per cent who remain disadvantaged. Twenty-five per cent of children living in Scotland under the age of 16 continue to live in poverty according to figures published in 2005 (*Herald*, 31 March 2005:2). It has been suggested in the Britain of the twenty-first century that while the lottery draws more of a working-class support in terms of distribution of ticket sales, the distribution of prize-money is disproportionately biased towards middle- and upper-class sporting tastes. The poor have always had to live with insecurity and uncertainty, sport used to be a traditional avenue of social mobility but even this has been increasingly left to chance. Yet the relationship between sport, social class and campaigns for social change is not irrelevant.

It would be misleading to suggest that as a major driver of social change social class is no longer relevant to bringing about transformation in sport despite the fact that the extent to which political education was fostered through sport in say the Britain of the 1930s,

1940s and 1950s may have reduced. It is evident even in sport that social class cannot be viewed as a static entity. It has a life form that changes as result of social and historical processes and consequently finds different forms of expression in political movements that endorse forms of social change in and through sport.

Many forms of class conflict have in certain parts of the world been deflected into anti-immigrant and anti-Muslim campaigns. Many forms of traditional urban and rural social class activism have re-emerged and confronted each other over the fight to ban fox-hunting in Scotland and England. The International Labour Organisation in conjunction with FIFA and UNICEF launched the Red Card to Child Labour campaign in conjunction with the 2002 African Nations Cup while Fabians in the twenty-first century have campaigned not only against corruption in world sport but also for the need to develop a more progressive politics of sport that promotes co-operation, mutuality and a fostering of trust between different groups who share such concerns (Katwala, 2004). Even the traditional working-class game of football struggles through partially state sponsored movements such as supporters' trusts to gain or acquire an increased say in the running of clubs. The very cost of viewing contemporary, elite football is in itself a barrier to many people. The very poor of course are not in the main seats and as John Underwood writing in the New York Times has explained:

> The great damage done by this new elitism is that even the cheapest seats in almost every big-league facility are now priced out of reach of a large segment of the population. Those who are most critically in need of affordable entertainment, the underclass (and even the lower middle class), have been effectively shut out. And this is especially hateful because spectator sport by its very nature has been the great escape for men and women who have worked all day for little pay and traditionally have provided the biggest number of a sports core support. As it now stands, they are as good as disenfranchised – a vast number of the taxpaying public who will never set foot inside these stadiums and arenas.
>
> (Cited in Eitzen, 2003:18)

Social class continues to impact upon campaigns for social change in sport and yet this particular expression of social class activism has combined diverse social and political protests with different forms of ideological awareness. While one of the elements of the erosion of deference has been the creation of new forms of rebellious collectivism, the motor of sport and social class as an engine of social change is not dead. It may have shifted geographically and as we shall examine in the next chapter many of the progressive successes and challenges in and for world sport continue to be linked to traditional areas of concern such as poverty and labour. Classical irreverent collectivism linked to sport and working-class movements may have passed its historical high point and may be progressively weakening and yet it would be foolish and unscientific not to acknowledge the continuing significance of social class politics in bringing about social change in sport. There may be less class but there is certainly more irreverence which may also express itself in repulsive forms in xenophobic violence or crime.

SPORT, RACISM AND BLACK ACTIVISM

Sport has explicitly been involved with campaigns, activism, policies and protests aimed at discrediting explicit racism and the power of colonialism. The struggle for sport has involved drawing attention to the fact that up until the 1960s many black and other peoples of colour in the United States were still denied human and civil rights. The de-colonisation of Africa, the attempt to defeat institutional racism in the United States, the overthrow of apartheid in South Africa and the defeat of US imperialism in Cuba and Vietnam have all implicated sport as an area of activism if not policy intervention.

The following introductory list includes some but not all of the most prominent areas of print, discussion, legislation and injustice:

- The period of *apartheid* sport in South Africa from 1948 to 1992 when specific racial legislation which separated the practice of sport by racial groupings gave rise to the international slogan 'You cannot have normal sport in an abnormal society'.
- The practice of *colonialism* in many parts of the world which formed the backcloth to sporting relations between many countries. During the 1960s and 1970s the cricket rivalry between England and the West Indies reflected racial tensions and racism rooted in years of colonial struggle. Terms such as White Wash and Black Wash were used to refer to English or West Indian victories while at the same time sport took on the mantle of symbolic colonial/anti-colonial struggle both between the two teams but also in the selection of the West Indian team as is explained in C. L. R. James's (1983) classic period account of West Indian cricket.
- The popularity and world-wide coverage of sport has meant that *sport as vehicle for protest* has been a successful medium for drawing attention to the treatment of Black Americans as second-class citizens in the United States of America and in American sport as evidenced by the Black Power protests at the Mexico 1968 Olympic Games. The extent to which Aborigines or Inuit peoples have also been marginalised in mainstream Australian or Canadian sport has been another target for sporting activists. For example much of the coverage of the Sydney 2000 Olympic Games revolved around the performances of the 400 metre Olympic Gold Medallist Cathy Freeman and the plight of Aborigines living in contemporary Australia.
- *Legislation* such as the Race Relations Acts of 1976 and 2004 in Britain which provides the legal machinery of the law to investigate and act against racism in all walks of life in Britain, including sport.

Equally there are important historical moments that can symbolise a prejudice, a protest, an ideology or a breaking down of barriers. Historically sport has both been racist but also provided some of the most poignant anti-racist moments. In 1881 Andrew Watson became the first black player to play for Scotland at football/soccer. In August 1936 Jesse Owens won an unprecedented four gold medals at the Nazi Olympic Games in Berlin. Two years later Joe Louis crushed Max Smelling to signal the end of a period of white supremacy in boxing. In 1967 Muhammed Ali, the world heavyweight boxing champion condemned the war in Vietnam arguing that he did not have any quarrel with the Vietcong. One year later in October 1968 American black athletes protested from the Olympic medal rostrum against the treatment of black people in America and elsewhere, notably South Africa. Evonne Cawley (Goolagong) became the first aboriginal Australian to play in a Wimbledon Tennis final in 1971, two years before Arthur Ashe became the first black American to win the Wimbledon Men's Tennis Championship in 1973. In 1995 Nelson Mandela, following South Africa's victory in the Rugby World Cup, talked of sport as force that could mobilise the sentiments of a people in a way that nothing else could. Three years later when Zinedine Zidane lifted the Football World Cup for France the French President talked of the French football team as being symbolic of the new multi-racial integrated France. In 2001 arguably the world's greatest footballer, Pele, endorsed a world wide anti-racist campaign in football with the words that racism is cowardice that comes from fear, a fear of difference. In February 2002 Vonetta Flowers became the first African-American to win a gold medal at the Winter Olympic Games.

SPORT, POWER AND THE SOUTH

The struggles for social change commented on above have clearly been linked to issues of social inequality and the distribution of resources between different groups. Inequality is a complex issue and varies both within and *between* countries and communities. An important although not causal determinant would be the inequality of opportunity or lack of access to good education, healthcare, clean water; poor economic and social services, markets, information and the lack of democratic right to participate in the key decision-making processes. Often the root cause of poverty, marginalisation and injustice is the unequal power distribution that impacts upon many regions and areas of the South. There are historical causes linked to colonial impositions, extraction of resources (human and natural) and the reality of globalisation and international affairs only seems to perpetuate certain benefits of power. Within the South there are cultural, social political and historical reasons today for poor governance and power in certain groups and places. Most noticeable are the fault lines between the North and South. This is to say that there exists a very definite tension, sometimes ideologically based and sometimes intuitively based between the demands of those from the wealthy countries and those from the poorer countries.

The Games of the Newly Emerging Forces or GANEFO Games were founded in Indonesia in 1962 in response to sanctions imposed upon Indonesia by the International Olympic Committee in 1963 when it suspended Indonesia indefinitely from the IOC. Indonesia responded by going ahead with plans for the GANEFO Games, an idea that had originally been proposed by the Indonesian President Sukarno in a speech in November 1962 in Tokyo. In November 1963, 3,000 athletes from 48 nations participated in the first GANEFO Games. The hope had been to establish a quadrennial competition with the 1967 games to be held in Cairo or Peking. Shifting political alliances meant that following a coup in Indonesia the government established business relationships with Taiwan while relationships with mainland China cooled. In September of 1965 a smaller group called the Asian GANEFO was formed with the first and last Asian GANEFO Games being held in December of 1966 in Phnom Penh, Cambodia with 15 nations participating.

The female badminton player Susi Susanti became the first Olympic athlete to wear a gold medal for Indonesia, the world's most populous Muslim nation. In 1992 the Islamic Countries Women's Sports Solidarity Congress gathered to decide on the manner of organising sports competitions for women from Islamic states, primarily from the countries of the South such as those Islamic Countries in Asia, Africa and the Arabic region. Faezeh Hashemi opened the First Islamic countries Women's Sports Solidarity Games in Iran in 1993 (http://www.salamiran.org/Women/Olympic/history.html). For many Muslim sportswomen, Islamic traditions can have a direct influence upon participation in international sports events such as the Olympics. Faezeh Hashemi is the daughter of the former Iranian President Rafsanjani and was director of a women's organisation tied to the Foreign Ministry in Tehran. She brought female athletes together from the Third World in 1993 for the first Islamic Women's Olympic Games. At the time 33 Islamic countries did not send women to the Olympics in fear of compromising Islamic dress codes. The group called Atlanta–Sydney–Athens Plus started to campaign after the 1992 Olympics, when 35 countries – half of them Muslim – sent no Muslim athletes to the Olympic Games. Only nine countries failed to send women to the Sydney 2000 Olympic Games with most of these male-only delegations coming from Middle Eastern countries. In Athens in 2004 Robina Muqimar and Friba Rezihi were the first ever women to represent the primarily Muslim country of Afghanistan. In March 2005 Laleh Seddigh became the first female champion, in the otherwise all male field, to win the national motor speed race championship in Tehran (*Sunday Herald*, 27 March 2005:21). For Faezeh Hashemi women's sports are an important step to evoking social change because they promote an awareness of women's physical strength and thus foster a spirit of self-awareness.

The flow and distribution of resources between Europe and Asia resulting from television broadcasting has become increasingly subject to criticism by Asian broadcasters (Roberts, 2005:27). The way forward, according to Total Sports Asia is first to recognise the unique characteristics of the Asian broadcasting market and facilitate local operators controlling the international sports opportunities that are arising out of Asia. Put more critically each territory in Asia is different and independent and international broadcasting companies located in the West, argues the Chief Executive of Total Sports Asia, need to recognise that Asia is not a golden goose designed to service European television demands for sport. European companies 'if they wish to help develop the local in Asia need to show a commitment and the days are gone when you can sit in Europe and expect it all happen for you' (Roberts, 2005:27). The Asian sports market is still expanding and more and more initiatives are coming up with new channels, broadband and video on demand services. There has been a massive investment in infrastructure with the result that Asia is arguably ahead of other parts of the world. Asia is an increasingly sophisticated television sports market and gone are the days, points out Mike Mackay of Octagon CSI, when Asia 'was a dumping ground for content from the rest of the world' (Roberts, 2005:27). The example of Asian broadcasting is utilised here to illustrate and emphasise the dynamics of sporting capital and the potential of the local in the South to challenge and produce change within broader international sporting opportunities which have traditionally been controlled out-with the South.

The international campaign against apartheid sport in South Africa helped to topple a system of legalised racism in South Africa. The notion of no normal sport in an abnormal society was not the causal factor that brought about change in South Africa but it was an important facet of the strategy for reform adopted by the African National Congress (ANC) prior to coming to power in 1992 under the leadership of Nelson Mandela. Given the history of struggle for social and political change in South Africa and the place of sport within that campaign it is ironic that both South Africa and countries such as Great Britain have been less than progressive in relation to democracy in Zimbabwe under the leadership of Robert Mugabe. Thabo Mbeki, South Africa's Premier in 2005, has refused to decry the regime of Robert Mugabe, a stance that has hurt the international reputation of the new South Africa. Both the *Mail* and *Guardian* newspapers, valiant supporters of the ANC during the era of apartheid, have reported that South Africa has lost the moral high ground and that democracy has been sacrificed by both the South African and Zimbabwean governments and in its place there is the slavish adherence to democratic form without substance (*Sunday Herald*, 27 March 2005:19).

Unlike the actions taken by President Luiz Inacio Lula da Silva of Brazil in passing legislation in relation to the morality of Brazilian football, when faced with the option of intervening to prevent England cricketers touring Zimbabwe both the chairman of the England and Wales Cricket Board and Jack Straw the then British Foreign Secretary accepted by their actions that morality had no part to play in English cricket (Wilson, 2004:27). In contrast Stuart MacGill, the Australian cricketer who refused to make himself available for the Australian cricket tour of Zimbabwe on the grounds that he could not maintain a conscience in the light of the human rights violations being perpetrated in Zimbabwe, was commended by both the Australian Prime Minister and Foreign Secretary. One year earlier two members of the Zimbabwean cricket team, Henry Olonga and Andy Flower, made a powerful political statement by wearing black armbands as they took the field in a World Cup match in Harare – a protest in their words against the death of democracy in Zimbabwe. A group of church leaders in Bulawayo hailed the gesture as hitting a six for freedom and democracy and which cost both players their position in the side. While the International Cricket Council (ICC) did not allow tours to be cancelled on political or moral grounds they did allow for *force majeure* and it was this failure by Jack Straw to issue a clear statement by the government cancelling the tour on these grounds that was a missed opportunity. Despite the preparation of a framework paper that could have lead to the abandonment of the 2003 tour in the end the Foreign Secretary stated that he did not have the power to order sportsmen around even when they begged to be ordered, and this was from a government that had no problem with finding powers to invade Iraq on the basis of little substantive evidence of weapons of mass destruction.

In passing it is necessary to draw clear parallels between the position in which the ICC finds itself today and the position of the major sporting bodies under apartheid-ruled South Africa more than a decade ago. The South Africans' experience taught them that they could have no normal sport in an abnormal society. The ICC and other sporting bodies and governments who support the approach taken by the ICC to cricket in Zimbabwe have to learn that lesson all over again. The most enthusiastic sporting authorities in South Africa eventually had to face the truth that there were occasions when overriding social if not moral considerations need to transcend the interests of sport. In the end the power of capital and loss of cricketing funds influenced the decision to tour Zimbabwe rather than influence both social change and cricket in Zimbabwe. Both have been let down by a weak foreign secretary, and betrayed by an international cricket community dominated by the financial vested interests of the first-class countries. How wise were the words of C. L. R. James: 'What do they know of cricket who only cricket know?' (James, 1983:ix).

These examples are far from exhaustive but they help to illustrate factors that impact upon sporting worlds that are only partially governed and influenced by unbalanced power structures that operate along or between different fault lines between northern–southern geopolitical sporting worlds. That is to emphasise the fact that sporting worlds are differentiated not only as a result of social patterning but also geo-political power structures and markets. How capital is allocated or misallocated is important for the success or failure of sporting development in different parts of the world. Sport can also help in the development of different parts of the world by virtue of its visibility and capacity to publicise the need for social change in different places. The differential relationship of sport and power is evident between, for example, northern and southern hemispheres' influences; the migration of sporting talent; the support for local or indigenous sport; the flows of sporting capital in and out of certain places; rates of child labour violations and human rights violations. The worry is that continuing injustices in sport and the failings of global sport will contribute to the undermining of trust not only in sport but also between local, regional and international communities.

It is not necessary to view sport as irrelevant to the geo-political concerns that might figure in the reform of sporting structures and power balances that cause fissures within the North–South fault line or divide. Some or all of the following actions might figure in the reform of neo-liberal or global sport:

- to reform global sporting institutions to permit greater representation of currently under-represented groups and regions of the South;
- to develop sporting treaties and legislation to draw attention to secure better working conditions on a universal basis and the end of child labour in sport;
- to recognise that the primary causes of child labour lie in poverty and traditionally sport has been an avenue for escape from poverty in many parts of the world;
- to support and publicise attempts by women from Islamic countries to participate in international sporting forums and competitions;
- to draw upon existing charters, declarations, covenants and laws that point the way to a more humane forms of international sport not only within but also between countries and communities;
- to monitor and evaluate the percentage of profit made from migrant sports labour and sporting exiles and ensure that it returns South and does not simply remain circulating within the North;
- to legislate to ensure that sport addresses and chases corruption with the same zeal that it chases the ideal of drug-free sport;
- to make sporting exchange and trade work for the poor.

355

SPORT, SOCIAL CHANGE AND SOCIAL FORUMS

We should not over-emphasise the capacity of sport to collapse social barriers. At the same time it is crucial to acknowledge the capacity of sport to facilitate social change within sport. The ways in which sport may contribute to other alternatives should not be over-emphasised either but neither should they be ignored. The strength of sport's capacity to produce change perhaps lies in its popularity in different parts of the world, its capacity to symbolise graphically and poignantly social and political success and failure. The old and new politics of sport have been commented upon in Chapter 3 while this chapter has illustrated further some of the ways in which sport has attempted to produce and struggle for alternative ways of change, of reform and intervention. Such alternatives both influence and are influenced by different visions of a world that continues to struggle with inequality, turmoil and lack of clarity about the nature of both capitalism and democracy. It is a mistake to think that contemporary researchers, teachers and thinkers about sport in the world today have not been concerned about the type of world we do or could live in.

In a general sense sport has contributed to at least three different visions of what the world is and should be. These might be referred to as (i) the global neo-liberal view of sport in society in which the convergence of the opportunity gap between sport in the richest and poorest parts of the world might be possible (dependent upon a strict adherence to liberal policies); (ii) the hard third way view of sport in society that requires a more limited adherence to democracy but an enthusiasm for sporting partnerships funded between private/public sources, decentralisation, arm's length sports policy, an acceptance of global sporting values and less of a concern with sporting inequality while still embracing certain egalitarian goals through provision for targeted or vulnerable sports groups; and (iii) a softer but less likely third way in which sporting relief is used as part of an overall policy of managing capitalism's social contradictions with the typical role for sport being that of being a means to an end or a bridge-builder of reconciliation in areas of conflict. Within this model, Third World democracy and sport as a facet of social welfare come first, not last.

Much attention has focused in recent years on the possibility of an emerging global civil society with the power to engage with and challenge institutions of governance. The protests of Seattle, Washington, Chiapas, Prague, Barcelona, Genoa, Porto Alegre and elsewhere have all highlighted the presence and work of civil society. Non-governmental organisations (NGOs) and various social movements have found themselves in the limelight, becoming front-page news and the subject of international debate and action. The development of, at a European level, civil society over the past ten years has been impressive. NGOs from local to the international level have increasingly realised the importance of organising themselves into coherent alliances in order to gain influence within the European Union. Both European and World Social Forums have been set up in the early part of the twenty-first century as focal points for various activists, students, intellectuals, environmentalists, economists and researchers amongst others to meet and link together in an expanding network of opposition to the neo-liberal cause.

The geography of the current climate of social and political protest and change in many ways signals a new political landscape. One which is arguing for diverse forms of social change and points towards an entirely new ideological, political and geographical design than that which characterised the Cold War or other ideologically driven left versus right sporting battlegrounds of the twentieth century. The social and geographical diversity of calls for social and political change can be found in places such as Chiapas, an impoverished region of southern Mexico, Seattle, the symbol of the microchip and American post-modernity and Porto Alegre, a European city in Brazil's deep south, not to mention the many smaller specialist campaigns that have revolved around single issues such as the environment, poverty, hunger, child labour, religion, democracy and war to name but a few. What has happened is that new groupings, new emblems of protest and new possibilities have given rise to a host of hopes, fears, illusions, questions and actions for change. In a way that differs somewhat from liberalism, the ideas of civil society, social forums, NGOs and social movements have been used to voice and proclaim opposition to irresponsible states, governments, parliaments and political parties while at the same time searching for effective partnerships with socially responsible and responsive multinational corporations.

Thus a new form of internationalism is emerging in a way that is entirely different from the old historical internationalism in which solidarity was premised upon the universalised exploitation of labour. In 2005, UN Secretary-General Kofi Annan, pointed out that sport was a universal language that could bring people together, no matter what their origin, background, and religious beliefs or economic status (www.un.org/sport2005/index.html). The use of child labour in sport is still very much part of the use of a debate about labour in sport and it is vital that such areas of concern are not isolated as single areas unconnected to other local, and/or international forms of resistance. The use of child labour in sport is related to labour rights and the rights of the child. The movements that emerged so effectively in Seattle in November of 1999 resulted from ecological, feminist, ethnic, human rights and other movements combining with anti-world trade groups that created new space. The notion of the social forum as a meeting place for anti-systemic forces to gather at a world level is attractive both in terms of its diversity but also because it creates a space in which anti-neo-liberal struggles can escape from the narrow limitations of the global sport versus national or local sport binary. The common framework provides not so much an alternative to globalisation and global sport but a different kind of globalisation and global sport. The advent of social forums represents a milestone and marks the possibility of a shift from sterile debates about global sport or identity sport to that of asserting yet again the idea that sport can contribute to social change but also articulate international political, social and cultural concerns about neo-liberal sport and overcome them.

SUMMARY

In this chapter we have examined different ways in which sport has contributed to bringing about social change. It is crucial that workers in the field of sport, culture and society do not lose sight of the many forms of intervention that have helped to contribute to what sport in the world is today. Forms of legislation, declarations of policy, political party manifestos and single and multi-lateral issue campaigns about sport have all had an impact and are continually in a state of flux. At the time of writing the Supreme Court in America was expanding the protections given to sport under the provision of the 1972 Title IX on sex discrimination to include protections for those people who were fired from school educational boards for drawing attention to the inequalities between the provision for girls and boys within the school system (Greenburg, 2004:1). This chapter has also questioned the comprehensive nature of capitalist triumph in sport by drawing attention to the campaigns that effectively have been against globalisation and consequently global sport. Furthermore it has built upon the old and new political successes and failures of sport outlined in Chapter 3.

The chapter has highlighted the effectiveness of the Women's International Sports Movement for the way in which it has not only forged forms of internationalism but actively campaigned for women's sport in a way that has effectively militated against women's sport been sidelined as a single issue movement or cause. The demise of the relationship between class and sport has been brought into question and while social deference in and through sport may have declined the need for more irreverence through sport is ever-present.

KEY CONCEPTS

Black activism	Racism
Capitalism	Radicalism
Collectivism	Reform
Deference	Revolution
Global Sport	Social change
Irreverence	Social forum
Neo-liberalism	Social movements
Non-governmental organisations	Transformative capacity
North/South divide	Women's International Sport Movement
Power	Workers sport

KEY READING

Books

Bass, A. (2002). *Not the Triumph but the Struggle*: *The 1968 Olympics and the Making of the Black Athlete*. Minneapolis: University of Minnesota Press.
Eichberg, H. (2004). *The People of Democracy*: *Understanding Self-determination on the Basis of Body and Movement*. Arhus: Klim.
Hargreaves, J. A. (2000). *Heroines of Sports*: *The Politics of Difference and Identity*. London: Routledge.
Kidd, B. (1996). *The Struggle for Canadian Sport*. Toronto: University of Toronto Press.
Tormey, S. (2004). *Anti-Capitalism*. Oxford: Oneworld Publications.

Journal articles

Fraser, N. (1995). 'From Redistribution to Recognition? Dilemmas of Justice in a Post-Socialist Age'. *New Left Review*, 12 (July/August): 1–24.

Katwala, S. (2004). 'Political Footballs'. *Fabian Review: The Age of Terror?* 116(2): 14–16.

Mertes, T. (2002). 'Grass-Roots Globalism'. *New Left Review.* 17 (September/October): 101–113.

Sader, E. (2002). 'Beyond Civil Society'. *New Left Review.* 17 (September/October): 87–101.

Therborn, G. (2001). 'Into the 21st Century'. *New Left Review,* 10 (May): 87–111.

Further reading

Alexander, T. (2003). 'Uniting Humanity – Strategies for Global Democracy and Progressive Globalisation'. *Fabian Global Forum.* London: http://www.fabianglobalforum.net/forum/article026.html

Allison, L. (2005). *The Global Politics of Sport: The Role of Global Institutions in Sport.* London. Routledge.

Arrighi, G. (2002). 'The African Crisis'. *New Left Review,* 15 (May/June): 5–39.

Bellos, A. (2003) 'The President wins the Midfield Battle'. *New Statesman,* 3 November: 32–34.

Deacon, B. (2003). 'Global Social Governance Reform'. *Fabian Global Forum.* London: http://fabianglobalforum.net/forum/article033.html

Eitzen, D. (2003). *Fair and Foul: Beyond the Myths and Paradoxes of Sport.* New York: Rowan & Littlefield Publishers.

Jarvie, G. (1997). 'Sport and Social Problems in Unprincipled Societies'. In Nardis, P., Mussino, A. and Porro, N. (eds). *Sport, Social Problems, Social Movement.* Milan: Edizioni Seam, 16–28.

Mertes, T. (2004). *A Movement of Movements: Is Another World Really Possible?* London: Verso.

Wallerstein, I. (2002). 'New Revolts Against the System'. *New Left Review,* 18 (November/December): 29–41.

Wilson, D. (2004). 'Cricket's Shame: The Inside Story'. *New Statesman,* 6 December: 27–31.

REVISION QUESTIONS

1. List the different forms of activism that may be utilised to bring about social change in sport.

2. Evaluate the notion that women's sports movements have been successful in terms of collective action.

3. Explain what alternative forms of globalisation and/or global sport mean and discuss the ways in which social movements and social forums may impact upon or use sport to bring about social change.

4. Use the notions of irreverence and deference to discuss the way in which the relationship between sport and social class has changed.

5. How might the gap between sport in the North and South be changed?

PRACTICAL PROJECTS

1. Carry out a Google search using the terms Sport+Social Change, Sport+Social Movements, Sport+Reform and write a short 1,000 word report explaining how sport contributes to campaigns aimed at bringing about social change in the world today.

2. Collect a series of about 10–20 charters, declarations and/or laws that have been specific to sport and develop a ten-point charter of your own aimed at bringing about social change in some aspect of sport in your locality.

3. Use the Internet and newspaper sources to research the way in which major sports organisations such as FIFA, the IOC or any other major sports organisation of your choice have associated themselves with movements or examples of solidarity in the world today.

4. Imagine you are leader of an international political party and an important part of your party manifesto is going to address the question of how sport can make the world a better place today. What would your key party pledges be in relation to your sports policy for international sport? (List and explain 20 points of intervention aimed at bringing about social change in and through the world of sport.)

5. Monitor and evaluate five contemporary and/or historical initiatives that have used sport as a means of addressing poverty. Write a short report of 1,000 words thinking about the relationship between sport and poverty. Finish your report with a list of ten recommendations.

WEBSITES

FARE, Football Against Racism in Europe
www.farenet.org/

International Year of Sport and Physical Education
www.un.org/sport2005

Sokwanele Civic Action Support Group
www.sokwanele.com/articles/sokwanele/cricketnonormalsportinanabnormal_12...

Stamping out racism in football
www.scottish.parliament.uk

Street football for peace
www.dados.org/frieden_int/grundkurs_5/fussball/htm

Twic Olympics
    www.christian-aid.org.uk/news/features/0202twic.htm

Women's International Sports Movement
    www.iwg-gti.org/e/about/index.htm

Chapter 18

Sport, human rights and poverty

Sports are often implicated with fighting forms of inequality and poverty. Can sport make a difference? © Telegraph Group Limited (2000)

PREVIEW

Millennium development goals • Human rights and sport • Sport and conflict resolution • The Beijing 2008 Olympic Games • The Human Rights Act and sport • Civil and political rights • Mexico 1968 Olympic Games • Cathy Freeman and the Sydney 2000 Olympic Games • Social, economic and labour rights • Child labour and sport • Cultural and solidarity rights • Inuit sport and culture • SOS Children's Villages and football • Civil society and obligations • Poverty • Sport as humanitarian aid • Maria Mutola and Mozambique • Kenyan women athletes • Mathare Youth Sports Association • Homeless World Cup • Poverty recognition and redistribution.

OBJECTIVES

This chapter will:

- explore the notion of human rights as it applies to sport;
- answer the question, what are human rights?
- evaluate the relationship between sport and poverty;
- identify a number of sports campaigns that might be viewed as humanitarian;
- argue for a solution that prioritises recognition and redistribution in sport and through sport, culture and society.

INTRODUCTION

In 2000, at a Millennium Summit in New York, 189 world leaders agreed to implement a series of Millennium Development Goals (MDGs) by the year 2015. These goals included (i) reducing world poverty and hunger by 50 per cent; (ii) achieving universal primary education; (iii) empowering women and promoting gender equality; (iv) reducing child mortality; (v) improving maternal health; (vi) combating HIV/Aids and other diseases such as malaria; (vii) ensuring environmental sustainability and (viii) developing a global partnership for development (Ogi, 2004). Talking of the role of sport in international development, in 2005 Kofi Annan, United Nations Secretary General, noted the potential of sport to effectively convey humanitarian messages, help to improve the quality of people's lives while helping to promote peace and reconciliation (www.un.org/sport2005/index.html).

The Statute of Rome, established in April 2000, provides for a permanent International Criminal Court for the prosecution of crimes against humanity. It has been suggested that ideas of human rights and international norms have become increasingly diffuse around the world (Gorman, 2003). Yet the question remains as to whether the labyrinth of human rights and other concerns refer to a common resource or credo determined by a few global powers. The collection of human rights specified in international human rights law draws upon long-standing traditions of rights, from philosophy, history and political theory, all of which may provide initial benchmarks for critically engaging with the world of sport. At least three categories or sets of rights might be mentioned by means of introduction (i) civil and political rights; (ii) economic, social and cultural rights, and (iii) solidarity rights. The issue here is two-fold in the sense that it is about human rights in sport, but it is also about the role that sport can play, because of its popularity, to draw attention to human rights violations in different parts of the world. In a simple sense, should international sports competitions be used to bring publicity to human rights issues?

The end of World War II has been but one of the many periods when international concerns about human rights and social justice emerged as an appealing idea with potential universal applicability. Such concerns found their expression in the 1945

United Nations Charter and the 1948 Universal Declaration of Human Rights. These two documents were soon followed in 1976 with the International Covenant on Civil and Political Rights (ICCPR) and the International Covenant on Economic, Social and Cultural Rights (IESCR). By the year 2000 some 190 states had demonstrated support for the idea of human rights, illustrating that the issue had gained considerable international recognition. At the beginning of the twenty-first century it would seem to many that we live in an 'age of rights' and yet despite progress in many areas poverty remains one of the enduring characteristics and experiences for many in a global world that is left wanting on many fronts.

HUMAN RIGHTS AND SPORT BEYOND THE WEST

It is not necessary to view the issue of human rights as divorced or separate from the world of sport. The struggle for and diffusion of human rights in the post-twentieth-century world has become an international concern and yet only recently has the re-emergence of a human rights agenda in sport become part of the contemporary debate within the area of sport, culture and society (David, 2005; Kidd and Donnelly, 2000; Donnelly, 1988; Kidd, 1996, 1982). More importantly, despite the potential possibilities inherent within the idea of sport supporting the notion of human rights and a growing sense of equality and social justice in sport, culture and society such a reality has not emerged from the many, often unconnected, campaigns for social change. The persistence of economic inequality, poverty and labour violations means that the world in particular and sport in general has a long way to go before the potential of sport, culture and society being free from such practices becomes much more than utopian thinking.

The recent work of Giulianotti and McArdle (2005) has sought to suggest the ways in which sport may be used as a development tool in areas of conflict resolution and thus might be viewed as a vehicle for internationalism. They go on to argue that sport may (i) help to resocialise people who have been traumatised by conflict and (ii) be useful as a means of promoting programmes of conflict resolution and reconciliation between sharply divided communities. Thus sport can be used to develop humanitarian goals. Kidd and Donnelly (2000) consider whether a strategy for establishing, and publicising and then demanding rights, modelled on the Universal Declaration of Human Rights could in fact help with some of the most difficult social changes faced in contemporary sport, culture and society. These might include the shrinking of the public sphere, the widening inequality of condition, the rights of the child in sport, the trafficking and sale of young athletes, the right of refugees to sport, reflecting the millennium development goals as well pursuing sports-based approaches to internationalism, peace and an engagement with the politics of sport for the twenty-first century outlined in Chapter 3. Human rights have been a central international issue over the last quarter of a century and longer and yet only relatively recently have sports-based initiatives become prominent within certain select United Nations initiatives.

At the heart of the decision to award the Beijing 2008 Olympic Games to China was the issue of human rights. On 13 July 2001, the International Olympic Committee chose Beijing over four other candidate cities, Toronto, Paris, Istanbul and Osaka, as the venue for the 2008 Olympic Games. Beijing had previously lost out to Sydney in the bid to stage the 2000 Olympic Games. At the heart of the debate about whether China should host the 2000 and 2008 Olympic Games was a simple struggle essentially between two points of view. Supporters of the Beijing 2008 Olympic bid argued that staging the Olympics would help to narrow the gap between China and the rest of the world. The media coverage of the event would illustrate that China had come of age as a member of the international community. A sport-obsessed younger generation in a country that contains about a quarter of the world's population would benefit from the legacy of Olympic investment. State media in China estimated that as much as $30 billion could be invested in the reconstruction of Beijing – in creating not just a new Olympic district, but in basic public services such as sewers, subway lines and new roads. The Olympic factor saw the value of Beijing-based construction and real estate companies rise significantly on the stock market.

Critics of the Beijing 2008 bid contended that China's history of human rights violations should have meant that one of the other contenders for the 2008 Olympics should have been victorious. The critics argue that many Beijing citizens will be forced to move out of their homes to make way for Olympic construction, that China's rural peasantry will gain little from Olympic mega-events and that China cannot afford massive investment when it still has more than 20 million people below its own very low poverty line. Conservatively estimated at 13–16 per cent of China's GDP, corruption is said to be one of the major political and economic challenges facing twenty-first century China, so who will benefit from the massive infrastructure spending that will need to accompany any Olympic buildings programme? The desire for new markets for IOC sponsors and the need to complete a large number of infrastructure projects in Beijing has proved to be a major challenge to an IOC that claims that it no longer wishes to be associated with corruption. Critics of the 2008 Olympic bid point to the fact that China should have lost the right to host the 2008 Olympic Games because of the massacre that took place in Tiananmen Square, and they highlight the continuing attitude of the authorities to Falun Gong, Tibetan religious institutions and the blocking of BBC television coverage of events in China during the early part of the twenty-first century. Human rights activists argue that just as environmental factors are taken into account in evaluating Olympic bids, so too should human rights. Are human rights taken into account when bidding for the Olympics and if so how should they be measured and thought about? Such a question is not for answering in this book but it remains an important question for anyone interested in researching the contradictions within Olympic movements.

The Human Rights Act in Europe came into being in 1998 and came into force in the United Kingdom in October 2000. There are a number of clauses within the Act that have an immediate impact on European sport but are also relevant in terms of substance if not legislation to other areas of global sport. Article 2 states that no one shall be deprived of his or her life intentionally and has labour and practice implications for the sports labour industry in general and high level contact or dangerous sports in particular (Blackshaw, 2002:42). Although the rules of sport are designed to reduce the risk of death such risks do occur. In such cases should there be a legal action against the governing body or other players by the victim's family for breach of their human rights? Article 3 states that no one shall be subjected to torture or to inhuman or degrading treatment or punishment and has implications for children in sport and training regimes that necessitate extreme weight control such as those potentially involved in the control of weight by jockeys and gymnasts. What about what Americans call hazing and other ceremonies and rituals that are parts of some sports cultures? Can someone harmed by such practices claim a breach of their human rights (Blackshaw, 2002b:42)?

Article 4 states that no one shall be required to perform forced or compulsory labour and this applies as much to sport as it does to any other area of work. What about the restrictions that still exist in the transfer system of some professional sports? Article 6 states that in the determination of civil rights and obligations or of any criminal charge, everyone is entitled to a fair hearing within a reasonable time by an independent and impartial tribunal established by law. Article 6 raises questions about the governance of sport and the practice of sports law within and external to sport itself. Did the UK athlete Diane Modahl get a fair hearing over her alleged, subsequently dropped doping offence? The abolition of the right of the referee to rescind the issue of a red card may be considered unfair treatment of the offending player? Article 8 states that everyone has the right to respect for his/her private and family life. Is there a right of privacy in the UK that will protect sports personalities' images from unlawful exploitation for commercial gain? Article 10 states that everyone has the right to freedom of expression and that this may be applied both on and off the field of play in relation to crowd behaviour at sports matches. Freedom of speech includes commercial speech and so is the ban on sports advertising by tobacco and alcohol a stand against this benchmark? What about outbursts by one athlete against another – do these fall within the domain of freedom of speech or are they punishable on the grounds of bringing the sport into disrepute (Blackshaw, 2002b:42)?

Political debate is littered with references to rights – right to work, right to education, right to abortion, right to play, right to sport, right to own property and so forth. The idea of human rights developed out of natural rights theories of the early modern period that sought to establish some limits upon how individuals may be treated by others, especially by those who wield political power. Although it would be wrong to suggest that the doctrine of rights is universally accepted, most modern social and political thinkers have been prepared to express their ideas in terms of rights and entitlements. Although such ideas are now commonplace, it is less clear what the term rights refers to and how it should be used (Heywood, 2004:185). Who for instance is to be regarded as human? Does this extend to children and embryos as well as adults? Are particular groups of people entitled to special rights by virtue of their biological or social position and should the conventional definition of rights be challenged given the arguments about nature and animals championed by environmental and animal liberation movements?

A further issue is that whereas the idea of human rights might be viewed as universal, human beings are not identical. This can clearly be seen in the way that women in some sense enjoy rights that are different from men and vice versa. To advance the cause of women's rights historically it might have been useful to activate the notion of human rights as being available to all and highlight specific areas where sexist ideologies have been blind to instances where rights have specifically been framed by men with men in mind. However, the idea that certain groups of people have special rights might also be based upon specific needs and capacities that might have been historically denied. Much of the work of the Justice, Truth and Reconciliation Committee in the new South Africa was to establish levels of compensation for past injustices perpetrated during the period of apartheid rule. Insofar as rights are based upon a commitment to equal treatment it can be said that they draw upon the notion of human rights. However it is difficult, for example, to regard women's or men's rights as fundamental human rights because they are not allocated to all human beings. Rights that arise out of unequal or unjust treatment will be meaningful only so long as the inequality or injustice that reproduces or justifies their existence persists.

Even when such controversies are set aside there are very deep divisions over what rights human beings should enjoy. Writers such as T. H. Marshall (1963) have argued that the rights of citizenship entail the development of civil rights, political rights and social rights. The provision of social rights required the development of a welfare state and the extension of state responsibilities for economic and social life but the model failed to acknowledge the differential capacity of different states either to have the capability or indeed to want to develop such a level of provision. The following overview of human rights is far from exhaustive but it is illustrative of the ways in which rights provide a plethora of avenues for legislation, charters, and antisystemic possibilities for social change.

Civil and political rights

Civil rights include such rights as the right to life, liberty and personal security; the right to equality before the law; the right to protection from arbitrary arrest; the right to the due process of law; the right of a fair trial and the right to religious freedom and worship. When protected, civil rights guarantee one's personhood and freedom from state-sanctioned interference or violence. Political rights include such rights as the right to speech and expression; the rights to assembly and association and the right to vote and political participation. Political rights in a very orthodox sense of the term guarantee individual rights to involvement in public affairs and affairs of state.

In 1968, at the Olympic Games in Mexico City, African-Americans Tommie Smith and John Carlos finished first and third in the 200 metres final. Tommie Smith and John Carlos also used the 1968 Mexico City Olympic Games as a forum for protesting against the racial inequalities in America. Harris (1999:169) writes that when Tommie Smith and John Carlos raised their black-gloved fists in a Black Power salute on the medal rostrum they engendered feelings of pride in African-Americans. The then proposed boycott of future Olympic Games and the resultant protests by black athletes has been described by authors such as Spivey (1985) as the cornerstone in the wakening of black America, although athletes such as Muhammad Ali undoubtedly paved the way. Ali influenced generations not just of black athletes but of all those who were prepared to challenge the racial injustices of sport in America and South Africa at the time. The actions of Tommie Smith and John Carlos to bring attention to civil rights injustices were not dissimilar to the methods used by political leaders such as Mahatma Gandhi and Martin Luther King who used forms of non-violent civil disobedience as a powerful weapon in political campaigns for Indian independence and black civil rights in America respectively.

Against all the odds, Catherine Astrid Salome Freeman became the first Aboriginal woman to represent her country at the Olympics, at Barcelona in 1992, its First World champion, and first Olympic champion. In doing so she became a symbol for reconciliation between a black and white Australia in which she had much to forgive (Gillon, 2003:15). Her grandmother, Alice Sibley, was one of the so-called stolen generation, taken from her parents at the age of 8 by a reviled Australian government policy that was designed to help integration. As a consequence of the 1950s programme which saw Aboriginal children removed from their parents and settled with white families, Freeman remained unaware of her ancestry on her mother's side (Gillon, 2003:15). Her father, an outstanding footballer, left home when she was 5 and died of an alcohol-induced stroke aged 53, she was sexually molested at 11 and later abused by whites (Gillon, 2003:15). Her Olympic success has perhaps helped to change the face of prejudice, almost a taboo subject in a modern Australia. Her Olympic reception following victory in the final of the 400 metres may be viewed in stark contrast to the day she travelled to an athletics meeting aged 13. Waiting outside Melbourne's Flinders Street Station, she was ordered to move on by a group of middle-aged white housewives, when the whole adjacent seating area lay vacant (Gillon, 2003:15). As Cathy Freeman held the Olympic torch aloft during the opening ceremony of the 2000 Sydney Olympic Games she did so in a different Australia from the one experienced by her parents. She herself had become perhaps one of Australia's greatest ever sporting icons but also a symbol of the struggle that Aboriginal Australians had to endure in order to win many civil and political rights.

Social, economic and labour rights

Social and economic rights include the right to a family; the right to education; the right to health and well-being; the right to work and fair remuneration; the right to sport and leisure time and the right to social security. When protected these rights are meant to support and promote individual flourishing, social and economic development and self-esteem. The inclusion in the UN Universal Declaration of Human Rights of a battery of social rights invested the idea of social citizenship with the authority of international law. The notion of social rights has been closely associated with the notion of social or active citizenship and historically has been inextricably bound up with the idea of welfare provision. The idea of social rights has been ferociously attacked by neo-liberals who are committed to rigorous individualism and self-reliance.

Throughout the 1990s the Nike brand continued to be closely associated not only with sporting goods manufacturing but unjust, inhumane and dangerous labour practices, not only but primarily in Asian countries. Between 1992 and 1995 the Nike Trans-National Advocacy Network campaigned to bring about change in the working practices in Nike factories. Between 1991 and 1998 Nike factories in Asia were visited by a number of organisations including human rights organisations. More than three-quarters of Nike workers were women, mostly under the age of 24, routinely working more than 10 hours a day, 6 days a week and earning on average between $1.60 and $2.20 per day. Perhaps unwittingly Nike indirectly helped to pioneer a new brand of activist strategy (Klein, 2001:85). Students facing a corporate takeover of American university campuses by Nike linked up with workers and other groups including youth groups and church groups who were all united in resistance by their different relationship to a common enemy. Nike is a gateway drug, in the words of one Oregon student activist (Klein, 2001:85). Exposing the social and labour violations perpetrated by such sports consumer brands has provided an alternative under-standing of the stories that companies such as Nike tell through advertising and public relations. The Trans-National Advocacy Network demonstrates how an advocacy network can delineate basic human labour rights, organise against trans-national corporations but also connect with other movements that start off as single-issue campaigns but are united by certain common denominators.

Cultural and solidarity rights

Cultural rights include the right to the benefits of culture; the right to indigenous land; rituals and shared cultural practices and the right to speak one's own language and bilingual education. Cultural rights are mean to maintain and promote sub-national cultural affiliations and collective identities while protecting minority communities against the incursions of national assimilation and nation-building projects. Solidarity rights include the rights to public goods such as development and the environment. This collection of rights seeks to guarantee that all individuals and groups have the right to share in the benefits of the earth's natural resources as well as those goods and products that are made through the process of economic growth, expansion and innovation.

Aboriginal cultural groups including those living in small parts of Greenland, Canada, Alaska and north-eastern Siberia refer to themselves as Inuit – meaning the people. Inuit cultures have their own range of traditional games and pastimes that are invariably under threat from global mainstream sport. The Saskatchewan Games were created in 1974 to address the issue of exclusion of First Nation children from mainstream sport. Classical, ancient and traditional sporting heritages are never dead, only dormant and their value in part is that they have much to say about not just the contemporary sporting world but perhaps more importantly about the way we live, who we are, where we have come from and where we want to go. Indigenous sports in different parts of the world, particularly those associated with minority cultures, often ask the question whether the sports of minority, indigenous cultures should be protected if not prioritised as a cultural right. Many European countries have developed cultural strategies to develop and protect the arts and cultural heritage. Yet indigenous cultural sports such as shinty in Scotland often get over-looked or marginalised and discriminated against because they don't neatly fit with a global or Olympic strategy designed to win medals. Some of these sports are as old as the Olympic Games themselves. In essence the local, traditional and at times international cultural heritage that is part of a living cultural sport or tradition may at times be the natural defence against global, American or other cultural forces of the day. Perhaps cultural legislation, campaigns and charters should protect traditional minority sports under threat.

The official FIFA Solidarity web-pages (www.fifa.com) regularly draw attention to campaigns and issues that FIFA wish to attach themselves to by virtue of the popular power of football to raise awareness over solidarity issues in different parts of the world. In 2003, 44 children between the age of 7 and 12 from SOS Children's villages accompanied the players onto the field during the FIFA Confederations Cup in France 2003. The media information accompanying the campaign stated that in an effort to respond to the needs of countless underprivileged children around the world to play football in good conditions, FIFA supports the activities of SOS Children's Villages, an international humanitarian organisation (www.fifa.com/en/display/mrel,70019.html). Since 1995 FIFA has supported SOS Children's Villages in Liberia through co-operating with the efforts of the International football star from Liberia George Weah. FIFA's commitment to SOS Children's Villages came about initially through the work of former president Joao Havelange who singled out SOS and its work in 131 countries, helping some 300,000 deprived children in different pars of the world. Football's social responsibility to these children has to be kept in context given the football industry's dependency upon child labour to stitch footballs in places such as India, Pakistan, Indonesia, China and Africa (www.globalmarch.org). In 1998 some 80 per cent of the world's footballs provided to international companies such as Nike, Reebok and Adidas allegedly were produced in Sialkot, an army town near the Kashmir border in which between 5,000 and 7,000 children worked in the football stitching industry.

Thus human rights have emerged in different forms but as an appealing ideal with potential universal applicability, a development fortified by the growth of the international law of human rights and the diffusion of human rights norms through the emergence of trans-national advocacy networks. The struggle for human rights has become synonymous with globalisation, a proliferation of systems, mechanisms and groups trying to transform very uneven state behaviour across the world. That is to say that the relationship between groups who struggle for human rights and the change in state behaviour is often fragmented, uneven and contradictory such that some states make initial concessions to opposition groups prior to reverting back to repressive tactics.

Much more could be said about the evolution, history and impact of human rights movements and campaigns in and out of sport but in this brief overview I shall limit myself at this point to three concerns prior to moving on to consider some substantive research that indicates whether sport can contribute to a specific and enduring humanitarian cause such as poverty – but only within certain limits and possibilities. First, human rights movements have often been associated with the push to create new spaces within and beyond civil society (Sader, 2002). In the context of providing resistance to both capitalism and neo-liberalism, human rights movements have at times combined with other local and sectoral forms of resistance but many such forces have also implicitly renounced any attempt to construct an alternative society. As such the implication and perhaps the problem within such an approach to human rights in and through sport is that it is confined within the limits of capitalism and liberal democracy since they are accepted as fact.

Second, the notion of rights is often connected with a qualifying concern about obligations. The notion of citizenship often entails a blend of rights and obligations. While sports organisations and personnel may be involved in claims over rights in sport they also carry with them responsibilities or mutual obligations. Any hope of sport contributing to a more just world of sport or broader aspirations of any global civil society depends not only upon an accepted minimal level or benchmark standards of provision. It also means taking on obligations to others on the basis of enabling full participation in the life of the community whether this be local, regional, or global. Critics of the notion of obligations of the individual to the broader community often question the universal quest for obligations as utopian given the level of not only cultural but other forms of diversity in the world today.

Finally it might be suggested that there is a need to re-claim or at least acknowledge the *common ground* between many different struggles for change in sport and life itself. What is referred to as the anti-globalisation movement must turn into thousands of local movements fighting the same way as neo-liberal politics of sport are played out on the ground. Single-issue rights or other campaigns about space for sport, provision for sport, a say in taking decisions about sport that affect local communities can often be marginalised if they remain as single-issue campaigns. The common ground is very often concerns over privatisation and deregulation or a neo-liberal economic and social agenda for sport that values central-isation, consolidation and homogenisation. This in itself is a war waged on diversity but if global sport is going to stand for much more than neo-liberalism and privatisation then it must convey resources of hope, empower local organising and be committed to a single sports world but with many sports worlds within it.

It is perhaps alarming that despite the relative progress and success of various sanctions and campaigns aimed at the rights and reasons of various rights in and out of sport poverty remains one of the enduring facets of the early twenty-first century in many parts of the world. The relationship between sport and poverty is not a new one since one of the traditional defences of sport in different parts of the world was that sport provided an avenue of social mobility for many talented athletes in different parts of the world.

POVERTY, SPORT AND PROGRESS

Nelson Mandela has described it as the modern slavery; thousands have demonstrated against it; New Labour on coming to power in Britain in 1999 vowed to eradicate child poverty within a generation; eradicating it has been viewed as been one of the most successful strate-gies to halt terrorism and it has been the object of fundraising campaigns by some of the world's top musicians and sportsmen and women. In July 2004, James Wolfensohn, head of the World Bank, noted that in terms of expenditure the priorities in world spending were roughly $900 billion on defence, $350 billion on agriculture, and $60 billion on aid of which about half gets there in cash (Settle, 2004:16). Oxfam recently noted that it would cost £3.2 billion to send all the world's children to school. Poverty may be one of the few truly global phenomena in that in relative and absolute terms it exists world-wide and while governments change and policies change the needs of the world's poor invariably remain the same.

The notion of poverty is not new but it is often suppressed in the academic literature about sport, culture and society as other debates take centre stage. Discussions of poverty have tended to draw upon some or all of the following ways of thinking about poverty: (i) poverty is a matter of behaviour; (ii) poverty does not exist but some people are too unequal; (iii) poverty must be viewed in both relative and absolute terms; (iv) a symptom of poverty is social exclusion; (v) poverty is about how society distributes its resources through its structures and processes; (vi) poverty is what economists say it is but also much more in terms of social poverty; (vii) poverty is about having an income below some statistical percentage of the national income distribution and (viii) poverty is not just relational in socio-economic terms but also geo-political terms (Alcock, 1997; Lister, 2004; Pacione, 2001).

Many NGOs have been at the forefront of initiatives involving sport as a facet of humanitarian aid in attacking the social and economic consequences of poverty. The Tiger Club Project in Kampala, Uganda is one of many initiatives that use sport as a basis for reaching street children and young people in need. The objectives of the Tiger Club include: (i) helping street children and young people in need; (ii) providing children with food, clothing and other physical needs; (iii) helping with education and development; (iv) enabling children to realise their potential so that they can gain employment; (v) providing assistance to the natural families or foster carers of children and young adults and (vi) providing medical and welfare assistance (Tiger Club Project, 2003). The 2003 Annual Report reported the fact that in 2002, 263 children had been offered a permanent alternative to the street; a further 116 street children and young people were in the START programme which meant full-time schooling; and 161 young people were resettled in their village of origin and provided with means for income generation. Of those resettled children, 76 per cent have remained in their villages (Tiger Club Project, 2003:2).

Every year about 200 million people move in search of employment – about 3 per cent of the world's population (Seabrook, 2003:32). Legal migrants who leave their homes in poor countries to provide labour or entertainment in other parts of the world are generally regarded as privileged. Sociologists such as Maguire (1999, 2005) have helped to pave the way for an extensive body of research into the causes of sports labour migration across different parts of the world and yet very little has been written about the part played by some athletes in earning money to support whole families even villages in their country of origin. When the career of a leading world athlete from a developing country is brought to a premature end the consequences often extend far beyond the track. The Mozambican Maria Mutola, the Olympic and five-time world indoor 800 metres world record holder routinely sends track winnings back to her country of origin. Chamanchulo, the suburb of Maputo in which Mutola grew up, is ravaged by HIV, passed on in childbirth or breast milk to 40 per cent of the children (Gillon, 2004:30). In 2003 when Mutola became the first athlete to collect $1 million for outright victory on the Golden League Athletic Grand Prix Circuit, part of the cash went to the foundation she endowed to help provide scholarships, kit, education and coaching for young athletes (Gillon, 2004:30). Farms and small businesses have often been sustained by her winnings on the circuit. They have provided for the purchasing of tractors, fertilisers and the facilities to drill small wells.

A recent survey of more than 250 Kenyan women athletes prioritised the following motivations for women athletes wanting to run: (i) money (48 per cent); (ii) role models (22 per cent); (iii) to run in the Olympics (12 per cent); (iv) scholarships (6 per cent); (v) significant others (6 per cent); (vi) fitness (4 per cent) and (vii) fun (2 per cent) (Jarvie and McIntosh, 2006). The most prominent barrier facing Kenyan women was a lack of money, with a staggering 98.5 per cent finding this prohibitive. Closely related to this was a lack of equipment (97.5 per cent). These barriers were also faced by young boys starting out on an athletic career but boys were much more likely to receive support from their families, the government and the Kenyan Amateur Athletic Association. The findings from the survey are supported by other sources of information that support the priority of money as the main motivation for women athletes in Kenya.

> An audit of property in the Eldoret Central Business District owned by athletes reveals a remarkable departure from the past where athletes only had their medals to show for the years of jet-setting and scaling heights of sporting success.
>
> (*East African Standard*, 17 November 2003)

Nowadays money is arguably the most important motivation for athletes. While Kenya is better off than many other African countries, many areas are still poor and unemployment high. To a European athlete, an Olympic gold medal is the pinnacle of their career; however for many Kenyan athletes it is simply a gateway to earn money that will transform the lives of themselves and their communities. In a country where the average wage is less than a dollar a day, the lucrative European and American road race circuits are attractive career options for even second-rate Kenyan athletes. The majority of Kenyan athletes, prior to the change of visa regulations introduced in 2005, lived outside of Kenya as they travelled the world to earn a living (Bale and Sang, 1996). When Catherine Ndereba broke the world record in the Chicago marathon in October 2001, she received a $75,000 prize purse, $100,000 for breaking the world record and a Volkswagen Jetta worth $26,125. This was in addition to a not insignificant appearance fee merely for turning up (Schontz, 2002). A world championship gold medal has been estimated to be worth $60,000, as well as opening other lucrative avenues in terms of qualification for appearance fees in big races (*East African Standard*, 17 November 2003).

Money is perhaps more of a motivation to women due to the independence it buys them, 'Once a woman begins to earn her own money, she is valued immediately by her family and her community' (Schontz, 2002). Under customary law, women cannot *inherit* land in Kenya. They must live on land as a guest of their male relatives. Women can however buy land in Kenya. Therefore as Kenyan women win road races and track meets, they are not only gaining control of substantial amounts of money which allows them to invest in their own land – a once unlikely prospect for women not born into wealthy families – but also gives them more control over their own lives. The importance given to money by female athletes may explain the fact that while they routinely collect the top prizes at the big city marathons, they have yet to triumph over the distance at the Olympics.

Founded in 1987, the Mathare Youth Sports Association (MYSA) in Kenya lies in one of the country's poorest slum areas (Hogenstad and Tollisen, 2004). An area with a population of nearly one million people and with an average household income, for a family of eight, of about 63 pence a day. Here, sport is placed at the centre of a humanitarian aid programme precisely because it is a point of contact with young kids that can entice them to learn. It is a vehicle for facilitating mutual self-help and education on a massive scale. Organised sports leagues involving participation figures far in excess of 14,000 children run on a 'pay it back' approach in which in return for help with facilities and organisation, players help keep the neighbourhood clean, plant trees, attend Aids, pregnancy and drug awareness classes. Scholarships exist for photography, music and drama classes. Teams get points for their work as well as their sport.

374

Reflecting back on the impact of MYSA one former goalkeeper said: 'Older kids who have been involved since its beginning have become leaders and role models in the community and football has been the catalyst for their social, physical and intellectual development'. The ethos here was pretty straightforward, ask kids what they want, use sport and physical activity as a basis for developing economic and social capital, local solutions to local problems, education and a track record of success all of which has been recognised internationally through a number of awards. MYSA was short-listed, indeed got down to the last five, for a Nobel Peace Prize in 2003 for its contribution to attacking poverty. Other nominees included Tony Blair, George Bush and Jacques Chirac.

The examples above are illustrative of the way in which sport is often used as strategy within an overall approach to humanitarian aid and yet relative and absolute forms of poverty are not simply limited to the places discussed above. In Scotland Scottish Executive figures published in 2005 reported that 25 per cent of children are living in poverty, a factor that the National Sports Strategy for Scotland fails to acknowledge. Since 2003 teams from 18 nations have competed in the Homeless World Cup, an international project that seeks to exploit the popularity of football for men and women to help combat homelessness and poverty. The organisers state that they want to view football as not simply a once or twice a week event but a vehicle for social change (*The Times*, 10 August 2003:42). The event is organised by the International Network of Street Papers (INSP). In 2003, 18 teams from Europe, Brazil, the United States and South Africa took part in this event (www. streetsoccer.org). The equivalent of Sports 21 in Canada actually uses words such as citizen and draws the links between things like education, sport and poverty. In Canada, the Progress of Canada's Children 2001 Report draws upon the analyses of several national surveys to show, for example, the link between poverty and children's access to organised sports and physical activity. In particular, the council points out that more than 60 per cent of children in the poorest Canadian households almost never participate in organised sports, whereas the figure is 27 per cent for children from more affluent homes.

Sport is clearly not an answer to the eradication of absolute or relative poverty in that in certain circumstances it can only make a small contribution. In certain parts of the world it may contribute to escaping from certain local contexts but this in itself does not change the context. Certain celebrity role models may draw attention to the plight of many of the world's poor and underprivileged but the number of socially committed sporting role models is more than often outweighed by the overall impact of global sport that in itself is part of the problem. Athletes on the world stage can keep the issue of human rights and poverty in the media headlines for a small period of time. There are also humanitarian support initiatives, such as Sport Relief held in the UK in July 2002 which helped to raise £10 million for projects aimed at improving the lives of children and young people suffering from the effects of poverty and deprivation. Numerous initiatives involving education through sport, in which sport is viewed as a means to an end, have been cited in this chapter. It is evident according to the Chairman of Olympic Aid, J. O. Koss, that participating in sport may provide a number of psychosocial benefits (Roberts, 2002:24). Yet the important thing to remember about poverty and the exploitation of human rights is that they continue to exist whether the spotlight is turned on or off in that governments change, policies change, initiatives change but the need often remains the same.

375

In the final chapter of Part 3 of this book, the work of Nancy Fraser (2000) was viewed as providing an insight into the weakness of accounts of sport and identity that were uncoupled from questions of recognition and redistribution and in drawing this discussion on poverty, sport and redistribution to a close it is again to Fraser (2003) that this book turns. Although she does not write about poverty, Fraser's recognition is helpful here. The mode of thinking that is encouraged through Fraser's work is to view recognition and redistribution as key social, cultural and economic dimensions to understanding social justice and injustice. Fraser contends that the politics of recognition and redistribution are central to thinking about social justice and the same might be said for thinking about sport and poverty. People in poverty are denied participatory parity for a multitude of reasons, material deprivation, processes of otherness, the infringement of human and citizen rights, lack of voice and relative powerlessness. The continuing struggle for social justice in sport at both a socio-economic and geo-political level necessitates not simply discussion and analysis involving redistribution, recognition and the development of mutual trust (social capital) but also intervention. The debate and problem of global sport is notoriously silent on all of these issues as if the public intellectual, amongst others, has no place in this world – a point we shall return to in the last chapter.

SUMMARY

A final related issue might be the right of all people to have access to education through sport, participate in sport and be represented through sport. With the twentieth-century campaign against international debt proving to be less than effective – even the G8 Summit of July 2005 failed to agree over the terms relating to Africa – new ideas and progressive values are needed to cure the problems in part caused by international finance institutions attempting to solve the debt problem of the global South. Sport is popular in places such as Brazil where it is estimated that some 250 million children work and a further 250 million who are not working are not in school. The need to raise money for the family unit through working the informal economy means that many children do not have access to education and the failure to study only serves to maintain a cycle of poverty (Landman, 2003).

Yet projects such as the Mathare Youth Sports Association are illustrative of the fact that sport and education through sport can assist in breaking the cycle. Sport cannot do this on its own but swapping international debt for education, including education through sport may be one of the possible strategies open to a progressive, humanitarian, international approach to sport which could challenge the very values at the heart of global sport. It may assist in creating the conditions that allow education through sport to thrive. In short swapping debt for education and including education through sport may assist millions of children to gain substantive education and transferable skills, and enable them ultimately to become active participants in the national economy and escape a cycle of poverty.

However, there is often perceived to be a messianic fundamentalism that tends to propagate a particular Western interpretation of human rights and aid across the developed world, one that promotes and sustains the full use of the arsenal of the modern missionary, from grants in the social sciences to structural adjustment plans and schemes for paying off world debt. To open the doors to other interpretations of human rights necessitates viewing human rights as a resource open to all humanity (Supiot, 2003). There is no need for a Western monopoly of their interpretation. Opening up Western conceptions of human rights to African or Chinese values might help to resolve certain ethical problems that Western societies face themselves. The problems stated here are not particularly new, but should be posed today as a question or problem and as a matter of particular urgency given the current state of world relations. Are there beliefs common to all humanity, are certain values universally recognised and should such concerns be reflected in the process of bidding for major sporting events in all parts of the world? Perhaps such an approach might manage to move beyond viewing human rights as dogma to being one of a common resource? However, the condition for such a move might involve the countries of the West and the North ceasing to impose their own ideas on the rest of the world and starting to learn from or at least listen to other cultures in a common enterprise of self-examination.

Perhaps one of the last words in this book prior to concluding should be left to the Ethiopian athlete and politician, once Olympic champion and world record holder Haile Gebreselassie who has left us in no doubt about both the social and political responsibility of the athlete but also the limits and possibilities of sport in relation to poverty in his country. In an interview with the athlete reported in *The Times* of March 2002 in an article entitled 'Gebreselassies's rise provides hope in the long run', the Ethiopian drew attention to the context and circumstances that were the early life of Haile Gebreselassie. Talking of his life aged 15: 'This was all at a time when my father was cross with me because I was doing athletics and my country was going through famine in which millions died and all I had was running – I just ran and ran all the time and I got better and better'. Talking of the necessity to run: 'I only started running because I had to – we were six miles from school and there was so much to be done on the farm that I ran to school and back again to have enough time to do farming as well as school work'. Finally talking of the political responsibility of the athlete we were left in no doubt about the priorities: 'eradicating poverty this is all that matters in my country. When I am training I think about this a lot; when I am running it is going over in mind – as a country we cannot move forward until we eradicate poverty and whereas sport can help – the real problems will not be overcome just by helping Ethiopians to run fast'. In reality sport can only make a small contribution but small contributions can sometimes make a difference. How sport can help in the fight against poverty should not be shelved as a historical question until much more has been done to fight both relative and absolute experiences of poverty world-wide.

The truth about global sport as a universal creed is that it is also a ruthless engine of injustice. The social dimension and possibilities of global sport remain as empty slogans amid constant historical reminders that proclaiming the principles of equality, justice and the eradication of poverty does not suffice to make a reality of it. There is just one thing that many corporate lobbyists and social movements both understand and that is that the real issue is not trade but power. A fundamental gap continues to exist both within sport and capitalism between the outcome of universal, often Western prescriptions and local realities.

KEY CONCEPTS

Absolute poverty
Child labour
Citizenship
Civil rights
Common resource
Cultural rights
Economic rights
Human rights
Obligations
Political rights

Recognition
Redistribution
Relative poverty
Rights of citizenship
Social rights
Solidarity rights
Sport as aid
Sport and human rights
Sport and poverty
Western dogma

KEY READING

Books

David, P. (2005). *Human Rights in Youth Sport*: *A Critical Review of Children's Rights in Competitive Sports*. London: Routledge.

Giulianotti, R. and McArdle, D. (eds) (2005). *Sport, Civil Liberties and Human Rights*. London: Routledge.

Heywood, A. (2004). *Political Theory*: *An Introduction*. Basingstoke: Palgrave Macmillan, 184–220.

Hogenstad, H. and Tollisen, A. (2004). 'Playing Against Deprivation: Football and Development in Nairobi, Kenya'. In Armstrong, G. and Giulianotti, R. (eds) *Football in Africa*: *Conflict, Conciliation and Community*. Basingstoke: Palgrave, 210–229.

Pacione, M. (2001). *Urban Geography*: *A World Perspective*. London: Routledge, 562–576.

Journal articles

Cunningham, J. and Beneforti, M. (2005). 'Investigating Indicators for Measuring the Health and Social Impact of Sport and Recreation Programs in Australian Indigenous Communities'. In *International Review for the Sociology of Sport*, 40(1): 89–98.

Grenfell, C. and Rinehart, R. (2003). 'Skating on Thin Ice: Human Rights in Youth Figure Skating'. *International Review for the Sociology of Sport*, 38(1): 79–98.

Kidd, B. and Donnelly P. (2000). 'Human Rights in Sport'. *International Review for the Sociology of Sport*. 35(2): 131–148.

Supiot, A. (2003). 'Dogmas and Rights'. *New Left Review*, 21 (May/June): 118–137.

Further reading

Baylis, J. and Smith, S. (2001). *The Globalization of World Politics*: *An Introduction to International Relations*. Oxford: Oxford University Press, 470–491; 559–581; 599–614.

Cammack, P. (2002). 'Attacking the Global Poor'. *New Left Review*, 13 (January/February): 125–136.

Fabian Society (2003). 'Human Rights'. *Fabian Global Forum*. London: Fabian Society, http://www.fabianglobalforum.net/knowledge/article002.html

Lister, R. (2004). *Poverty: Key Concepts*. Cambridge: Polity Press.

REVISION QUESTIONS

1. What are human rights and how has sport figured within United Nations initiatives?

2. Explain how the Human Rights Act of 1998 might impact upon European Sport.

3. Explain why a universal approach to sport and human rights might be problematic in different parts of the world.

4. Consider both historical and contemporary ways in which sport is associated with the fight against poverty.

5. To what extent might the existence of human rights violations in sport and pockets of world poverty be used as a critique of global or neo-liberal sporting policies?

PRACTICAL PROJECTS

1. Carry out two separate Google searches using the search words sport+human rights and sport+poverty and write a 1,000 word report on your findings from each of the searches. (Two reports in total.)

2. Examine the clauses within the European Human Rights Act and provide a list of ten ways in which the Act may impact upon sport.

3. Research the different ways in which four sporting celebrities of your choice have used their public profile to bring attention to poverty in the world today.

4. Develop a case study of a sports association or club such as the Mathare Youth Sports Association explaining how sport has helped contribute to humanitarian causes.

5. Historians have long been aware of the differences between British, European and or International socialist movements. Examine the place of sport within the politics of any two socialist movements of your choice and compare and contrast the way in which sport has been has figured within the politics of the labour movement in two different countries.

WEBSITES

Human Rights Watch
   www.hrw.org

The Homeless World Cup
   www.streetsoccer.org/en/home

The Right to Play
   www.righttoplay.com

United Nations
   www.un.org/sport2005

Conclusions

![book icon] **PREVIEW**

India, Pakistan and cricket • Sport, culture and society • Evidence, analysis and intervention • Alternative worlds of sport • The role of the public intellectual in sport • The dangers of identity-orientated accounts of sport • The limits of global sport • Sport and social change.

OBJECTIVES

This chapter will:

- Comment upon the inter-related nature of evidence, analysis and intervention;
- Review some of the key building blocks that have informed the thinking behind this book;
- Consider the role of the public intellectual in relation to sport, culture and society;
- Question the values that are at the heart of global sport and the need to provide alternatives;
- Re-assert the question of sport's capacity, limited or otherwise, to promote social change and provide resources of hope.

In drawing this journey to a close let me start with two examples that serve to open a window on what has been covered in this book. In April 2002, George W. Bush told the Palestinian people that everyone must choose as to whether they were either with the civilised world or with the terrorists. Many people around the world might at the time have recalled Ghandi's famous reply when asked what he thought of Western civilisation – he replied that it would be a good idea. Almost three years later to the day since George W. Bush made this statement, another Indian leader, Dr Singh, invited the Pakistani President to join him at the New Delhi cricket ground to watch India play Pakistan. In April 2005, speaking after signing a joint peace agreement in the Indian capital Delhi, the two leaders Manmohan Singh and Pervez Musharraf agreed that peace between the two nuclear rivals was irreversible. On the same day, the two leaders watched the start of the final day of the one-day international cricket match between India and Pakistan. A match eventually won by Pakistan, a match in which the result had been secondary to the process of reconciliation and internationalism between two nuclear rivals. In comparing the two incidents many might be left wondering what are the values of Western liberal capitalist societies, in this case the neo-liberal consensus that underlay the war drives of the Washington and London administrations of the early twenty-first century. What form of civilised values reduces freedom to the right to buy and sell, equality to a legal form, replaces forms of solidarity with privatised individualism and threatens the very planet with warfare all in the name of democracy and freedom? If only a form of sporting diplomacy and internationalism could have been found to contribute to unlocking more recent global tensions as it did with South Africa during the apartheid era.

Should policy advisers, activists, researchers be excited about the possibilities that exist within the different worlds of sport? It is hoped that having read this book many may appreciate that the study of sport, culture and society is a point of entry into not simply reflecting upon the world in which we live, but also trying to do something about the injustices that unquestionably exist. The study of sport, culture and society, as indicated in the introduction, requires a sound grasp of sport but also a commitment to evidence, analysis and ultimately an attempt to contribute to social change and intervention. It is the interconnected nature of three initially straightforward questions that provide so much ground for the researcher, student, teacher and others interested in the limits and possibilities of sport. These are

i   the evidence – what is going on out there in the world of sport?
ii   analysis and explanation – how do I make sense of what is going out there in the world of sport?
iii social change and transformation – having completed points (i) and (ii) what am I going to do in order to make sport and the worlds in which sport is located a better place, a more just place, a more humane place, a more trusting, safe and secure place to be?

The structure, rationale and objectives behind the thinking in this book are not incidental in that it has attempted to do several key things that this author thought needed to be done. First, anyone working in the area of sport, culture and society over the past decade and more will have undoubtedly recognised the valuable contribution made by authors such as Jay Coakley in the numerous editions of the popular book *Sport in Society: Issues and Controversies*. Yet there has for some time needed to be an attempt to provide a comprehensive intervention which offers something other than an American perspective on sport, culture and society and one of the primary starting points for writing this book was just that. It provides an alternative reading and body of research that attempts to show that there is not only one American world of sport, culture and society but many worlds of sport. There can be a commitment to a single world but also an appreciation that there are many worlds of sport within it. Global sport, like globalisation, does not offer a single coherent challenge. It may even be a myth but certainly the debate about global sport within sport, culture and society, while recognising the local and the national, is almost silent on anti-globalisation, anti-capitalism, neo-liberalism and capitalism as if none of these were pertinent to the discussion about contemporary sport. A primary concern for those working in the field of sport, culture and society should be to question and move beyond any neo-liberal consensus that often characterises the debate about global sport.

Second, the almost obscene deafening silences in the academic world over certain aspects of sport today, such as the politics of cricket in Zimbabwe, occurs in a way that would almost have been unthinkable during the last quarter of the twentieth century. More than 20 years ago critical commentators on sport were enquiring regularly about the transforma-tive value of sport. Put simply can sport truly make a difference to people's lives? Or what limited capacity does sport and related areas of activity have for producing social change? Or how can sport be a progressive force throughout the first decade of the twenty-first century and beyond? It is almost as if there is a missing additional character from the sport, culture and society academy, namely the public intellectual, and yet there is a very real need to re-assert and prioritise as a question what is the capacity for sport to produce social change today? Not in a utopian way but, in a way that recognises the limited but progressive capacity of sport to produce change. The problems facing sport can often provide a basis for common ground with other calls for recognition, justice, redistribution and democracy in sport, particularly at the local level. A second concern within this book then has been to prioritise the question of social change and suggest that this needs to stay near the top of the agenda for researchers, teachers and students interested in sport, culture and society.

A third concern has been to question the plethora of research that has revolved around the notion of identity in sport as if identity is a worthy end in itself. It has been argued here that the concept is not sufficient or weighty enough to encompass all the differences or representations presented through sport. There is an urgent need to rethink recognition in sport. Contemporary struggles for recognition through sport often take on the guise of iden-tity politics. This is often aimed at championing the cause for a particular social difference or form of representation from disenfranchised or less powerful sections of sport and/or society. It has been suggested here that such approaches are misconceived on at least three accounts (i) the failure to foster authentic collective identities across differences has tended to enforce separatism, conformism and intolerance; (ii) the struggle for identity politics through sport has tended to replace struggles for economic justice and wealth redistribu-tion which condemns different sporting groups to suffer grave injustices and (iii) the failure to realise that while levels of social inequality between certain groups may be decreasing, levels of poverty may be increasing in many parts of the world. Identity politics in sport is not enough and alternative forms of thinking about recognition in sport that make a real difference need to be urgently addressed. Only by looking at alternative conceptions of redistribution and recognition can we meet the requirements of justice for all and question those accounts of identity in sport that view identity as an end in itself.

Much more could be done if researchers, students, teachers of sport regarded themselves less as academics and more as a public resource to help or intervene in some or all of the many worlds of sport. The notion of the public intellectual may not be perfect but it is a useful starter. The role of the public intellectual in sport is fundamentally different from the role of the academic. Public intellectuals, suggest Said (2001), are not only different from academics, but almost the opposite of them. Academics usually, but not always, plough a narrow disciplinary/conservative inter-disciplinary path whereas public intellectuals roam ambitiously from one area to another. Academics are interested in ideas, research and analysis whereas public intellectuals are more concerned with the intersection between research, analysis and public debate, ideas and helping ordinary people. The decisions about sport and the part of the social contract that involves matters of sport can only work if we have honest argument, real information and not the spurious confessions of spin-doctors or political puppets or researchers whose silence can be bought.

Writers such as Said (2001:8) are explicit about the role of the public intellectual which is to 'uncover the contest, to challenge and defeat both an imposed silence and the normalised quiet of unseen power' wherever and whenever possible. Said laid out a powerful case for regarding intellectuals as those who are never more themselves than when moved by metaphysical passions and disinterested principles of justice and truth, they denounce corruption, defend the weak and defy imperfect or oppressive authority. Sport has provided many such role models, Muhammad Ali, Nelson Mandela, Cathy Freeman, Arthur Ashe, Billy Jean King among others. There are too those who speak the truth to power – or at least expose silences – and refuse the constraints of disciplinarity and specialisation that Said believed tended to weaken and depoliticise the intellectual strengths of academic writing. Terms such as globalisation, global sport, free-market, privatisation, public/private funding for sport are readily bandied about and yet all of these need to be properly explained as they tend to be accepted tacitly as if they are pre-ordained or the only way to do things.

So much for analysis but what is to be done about this malaise in the worlds of sport, culture and society and beyond? It is up to teachers, students and researchers not only to help to reverse the unfortunate trends of anti-intellectualism but also to promote debate within and outside of the worlds of sport. It is not as if one is short of things to worry about. This book has drawn our attention to the plight of child labour in sport, the role of sport in promoting reconciliation and internationalism, social divisions in and through sport, the dangers of global sport, the changing nature of violence in sport and need to interrogate the nature of denial in sport, the way in which sport provides an escape from poverty or inhibits social mobility and the need to recognise the dangers and weakness of accounts of sport that separate identity from recognition and redistribution. As stated earlier, sport has always been an arena in which various social actors and groups can actively rework their relationships and respond to changing conditions as a whole. The resources to do this have invariably been uneven both between and within different groups and sports. There is no single agent, group or movement that can carry the hopes of humanity; but there are many points of entry or engagement into a debate about sport that offer good causes for optimism that things can get better. It is crucial that current and future students, teachers and researchers of sport, culture and society continue to recognise the socially situated nature of their work and engage with the future politics of sport.

Globalisation is a good example of a contested concept or idea. It is contested along two dimensions – explanatory and normative. Global sport is also a contested idea but all too often the alternatives to global sport remain silent as a result key silences about sport's role within alternative debates about internationalism, anti-globalisation, anti-capitalism, social movements and the power of the social within the world past and present. Some have suggested neo-liberalism is dead but the values often associated with neo-liberalism seem to be alive and well. Freedom is reduced to the right to buy and sell and reduces solidarity to privatised individualism. Yet historically the potential of sport lies not with the values promoted by global sport or particular forms of capitalism. The possibilities that exist within sport are those that can help with radically different views of the world perhaps based upon opportunities to foster trust, obligations, redistribution and respect for sport in a more socially-orientated humane world. Sport's transformative capacity must not be overstated, it is limited and it needs to get its own house in order, but possibilities do exist within sport to provide some resources of hope within a world that is left wanting on so many fronts. To ignore the capacity of sport to assist with social change is not an option, particularly for students, teachers and researchers of sport, culture and society. This has to be near the top of any research agenda for those working in this and related fields for the foreseeable future.

Bibliography

The bibliography presented here is the complete list of sources including books, articles, conference papers, newspaper sources, web-based sources, official reports, unpublished papers and dissertations used to research this study of sport, culture and society.

Afary, J. (1997). 'The War Against Feminism in the Name of the Almighty: Making Sense of Gender and Muslim Fundamentalism'. *New Left Review*, 24 (July/August): 1–21.

Ahmed, A. (2000). *Post-modernism and Islam*. London: Routledge.

Alabarces, P. (2000). *Peligro de Gol*: *Estudios Sobre Deporte Y Sociedad En America, Latina*. Buenos Aires: Clacso.

Alcock, P. (1997). *Understanding Poverty*. Basingstoke: Palgrave.

Alexander, T. (2003). 'Uniting Humanity – Strategies for Global Democracy and Progressive Globalisation'. *Fabian Global Forum*. London: Fabian Society at http://www.fabianglobalforum. net/forum/article026.html

Ali, T. (2003). 'Re-Colonizing Iraq'. *New Left Review*, 21 (May) 5–20.

Allison, L. (2005). *The Global Politics of Sport*: *The Role of Global Institutions in Sport*. London: Routledge.

Allison, L. (2002). 'Sport and Nationalism'. In Coakley, J. and Dunning, E. (eds). *Handbook of Sports Studies*. London: Sage, 344–356.

Allison, L. (2001). *Amateurism in Sport*. London: Frank Cass.

Anderson, P. (2002). 'Internationalism: A Breviary'. *New Left Review*, 14 (March/April): 5–25.

Appadurai, A. (1995). 'Playing with Modernity: The decolonisation of Indian cricket' in Breckenridge, C. (ed.) *Consuming Modernity: Pubic Culture in a South Asian World*. Minneapolis, MN: University of Minnesota Press, 23–48.

Arbena, J. (1999). *Latin American Sport*: *An Annotated Bibliography, 1988–1999*. Westport: Greenwood Press.

Archetti, E. (1999). *Masculinities*: *Football, Polo and the Tango in Argentina*. Oxford: Berg.

Armstrong, G. (2004). 'The Lords of Misrule: Football and the Rights of the Child in Liberia, West Africa'. *Sport in Society*, 7(3): 473–502.

Armstrong, G. and Giulianotti, R. (eds) (2004). *Football in Africa*: *Conflict, Conciliation and Community*. Basingstoke: Palgrave.

Armstrong, G. and Giulianotti, R. (1997). *Entering The Field*: *New Perspectives on World Football*. Oxford: Berg.

Arrighi, G. (2002). 'The African Crisis'. *New Left Review*, 15 (May/June): 5–39.

Australian Government (2004). Crime Prevention through Sport and Physical Activity, Australian Institute of Criminology. Paper 165. www.aic.gov.au/publications/tandi/tandi165.html

Back, L., Crabbe, T. and Solomos, J. (2001). *The Changing Face of Football*: *Racism, Identity and Multiculture in the English Game*. Oxford: Berg.

Bairner, A. (2001). *Sport, Nationalism and Globalization*. Albany: State University of New York Press.

Balakrishnan, G. (2002). 'The Age of Identity'. *New Left Review*, 16: 130–142.

Bale, J. (2003). *Sports Geography*. London: Routledge.

Bale, J. (2002a). 'Lassitude and Latitude: Observations on Sport and Environmental Determinism'. *International Review of the Sociology of Sport*, 37(2): 147–159.

Bale, J. (2002b). 'Human Geography and the Study of Sport'. In Coakley, J. and Dunning, E. (eds) *Handbook of Sports Studies*. London: Sage, 170–186.

Bale, J. (2000). 'The Rhetoric of Running: the Representation of Kenyan Body Culture in the Early Twentieth Century'. In Hansen, J. and Nielsen, N. (eds) *Sports, Body and Health*. Odense: Odense University Press, 123–133.

Bale, J. (1998). 'Capturing the African Body? Visual Images and Imaginative Sports'. *Journal of Sports History*. 25(2): 234–252.

Bale, J. (1994). *Landscapes of Modern Sport*. London: Leicester University Press.

Bale, J. and Cronin, M. (2003). *Sport and Post-colonialism*. Oxford: Berg.

Bale, J. and Philo, C. (eds) (1998). *Body Cultures*: *Essays on Sport, Space and Identity*: *Henning Eichberg*. London: Routledge.

Bale, J. and Sang, J. (1996). *Kenyan Running*: *Movement, Culture, Geography and Global Change*. London: Cass.

Barros, C., Ibrahimo, M. and Szymanski, S. (eds) (2002). *Transatlantic Sport*: *The Comparative Economics of North American and European Sports*. Northampton: Edward Edgar.

Bass, A. (2002). *Not the Triumph but the Struggle*: *The 1968 Olympics and the Making of the Black Athlete*. Minneapolis: University of Minnesota Press.

Bauman, Z. (2001). *Community*: *Seeking Safety in an Insecure World*. Cambridge: Polity Press.

Bauman, Z. (2000a). *Liquid Modernity*. Cambridge. Polity Press.

Bauman, Z. (2000b). 'Whatever Happened to Compassion in the Global Era?'. In Bentley, T. and Stedman Jones, D. (eds) *The Moral Universe*. London: Demos, 51–57.

Bauman, Z. (1990). *Thinking Sociologically*. Cambridge: Basil Blackwell.

Bauman, Z. and May, T. (2001). *Thinking Sociologically*. Oxford: Blackwell.

Baylis, J. and Smith, S. (2001). *The Globalization of World Politics*: *An Introduction to International Relations*. Oxford: Oxford University Press.

Beacom, A. (2000). 'Sport in International Relations: The Case for Cross-disciplinary Investigation'. *The Sports Historian*, 20(2): 1–25.

Beal, B. (1996). 'Alternative Masculinity and its Effects on Gender Relations in the Subculture of Skateboarding'. *Journal of Sport Behaviour*, 19: 204–220.

Beal, B. (1995). 'Disqualifying the Official: An Exploration of Social Resistance through the Subculture of Skateboarding'. *Sociology of Sport Journal*, 12(4): 252–267.

Beaumont, P. (2001). 'Kidnapped Children Sold into Slavery as Camel Racers'. *The Observer*, 3 June: 27.

Beer, S. (2002). 'Better Faith, Better Ethics?'. *Fabian Review*, Spring: 8–12.

Begg, Z. (2000). 'What the Olympics Really Celebrate' at www.greenleft.org.au/back/2000/441717p14.htm

Bell, M. (2003). 'Another Kind of Life'. In Rinehart, R. and Sydnor, S. (eds) *To the Extreme*: *Alternative Sports Inside and Out*. Albany: Suny Press, 219–257.

Bellos, A. (2003) 'The President wins the Midfield Battle'. *New Statesman*. 3 November: 32–34.

Benedict, J. (1997). 'Arrest and Conviction Rates of Athletes Accused of Sexual Assault'. *Sociology of Sport Journal*, 17(2): 171–197.

Bentley, T. and Stedman-Jones, D. (2001). *The Moral Universe*. London: Demos.

Bhabha, H. (1983). 'The Postcolonial Critic'. *Arena*, 96: 47–63.

Billings, A. and Tambosi, F. (2004). 'Portraying the United States vs. Portraying a Champion: US Network Bias in the 2002 World Cup'. *International Review for the Sociology of Sport*, 39(2): 157–167.

Blackshaw, I. (2002a). 'Law and Human Rights'. *SportsBusiness International*, November: 42–44.

Blackshaw, T. (2002b). 'The Sociology of Sport Reassessed in the Light of the Phenomenon of Zygmunt Bauman'. *International Review of the Sociology of Sport*, 37(2) 199–218.

Blackshaw, T. and Crabbe, T. (2004) *New Perspectives on Sport and Deviance*: *Consumption, Performativity and Social Control*. London: Routledge.

Blaikie, A., Sartan, S., Hepworth, M., Holmes, M., Howson, A. and Inglis, D. (2003). *The Body*: *Critical Concepts in Sociology*. London: Routledge.

Blanchard, K. (2002). 'The Anthropology of Sport'. In Coakley, J. and Dunning, E. (eds) *Handbook of Sports Studies*. London: Sage, 144–157.

Bliers, H. (2003). *Communities in Control*: *Public Services and Local Socialism*. London: Fabian Society.

Booth, D. (2004). 'Surf Lifesavers and Surfers: Cultural and Spatial Conflict on the Australian Beach'. In Vertinsky, P. and Bale, J. (eds) *Sites of Sport*: *Space, Place Experience*. London: Routledge, 115–131.

Booth, D. (2003). 'Expression Sessions: Surfing, Style and Prestige'. In Rinehart, R. and Sydnor, S. (eds) *To the Extreme*: *Alternative Sports Inside and Out*. Albany: Suny Press, 315–337.

Booth, D. (2001). *Australian Beach Cultures*: *The History of Sun, Sand and Surf*. London: Frank Cass.

Borish, L. (2002). 'Women, Sport and American Jewish Identity in the Late Nineteenth and Early Twentieth Century'. In Magdalinski, T. and Chandler, T. (eds) *With God on Their Side*: *Sport in the Service of Religion*. London: Routledge,71–98.

Bourdieu, P. (1990a). *In Other Words*: *Essays Towards a Reflexive Sociology*. Cambridge: Polity Press.

Bourdieu, P. (1990b). *The Logic of Practice*. Cambridge: Polity Press.

Bourdieu, P. (1978). 'Sport and Social Class'. *Social Science Information*, 17(6): 819–840.

Boyle, R. and Haynes, R. (2004). *Football in the New Media Age*. London: Routledge.

Boyle, R. and Haynes, R. (2000). *Power Play*: *Sport, the Media and Popular Culture*. Essex: Longman.

Brackenridge, C. (2004). 'Women and Children First? Child Abuse and Child Protection in Sport'. *Sport in Society*, 7(3): 322–337.

Brackenridge, C. (2002). 'Men Loving Men Hating Women: The Crisis of Masculinity and Violence to Women in Sport'. In Scraton, S. and Flintoff, A. (eds) *Gender and Sport*: *A Reader*. London: Routledge, 255–269.

Brackenridge, C. (2001). 'Gender, Abuse and Violence: Men Loving Men Hating Women – The Crisis of Masculinity in Sport'. In Ruskin, H. and Lammer, M. (eds) *Fair Play*: *Violence in Sport and Society*. Jerusalem: Magnes Press, 127–158.

Bradley, H. (2000). 'Social Inequalities: Coming to Terms with Complexity'. In Browning, G., Halcli, A. and Webster, F. (eds) *Understanding Contemporary Society*: *Theories of the Present*. London: Sage, 476–489.

Bradley, J. (ed.) (2004). *Celtic Minded*: *Essays on Religion, Politics, Society, Identity and Football*. Glendaruel: Argyll Publishing.

Bradley, J. (1999). 'British and Irish Sport: The Garrison Game and the G.A.A. in Scotland'. *The Sports Historian*, 19(1): 81–96.

Brennan, T. (2003). *Globalization and its Terrors*: *Daily Life in the West*. London: Routledge.

Brennan, T. (2001). 'Rooted Cosmopolitan v International'. *New Left Review*, 7: 75–85.

Bricknell, P. (2000). *People before Structures*. London: Demos.

Britcher, C. (2004a). 'Virtual Horses for Virtual Courses'. *Sport Business International*, 88 (February): 28–30.

Britcher, C. (2004b). 'MLB Upwardly Mobile'. *Sport Business International*, 86 (January): 25–28.

Brownell, S. (1999). 'The Body and the Beautiful in Chinese Nationalism: Sportswomen and Fashion Models in the Reform Era'. *China Information*, XIII (2/3): 36–58.

Brownell, S. (1995). *Training the Body for China. Sports in the Moral Order of The People's Republic*. Chicago: Chicago University Press.

Browning, G., Halcli, A. and Webster, F. (2000). *Understanding Contemporary Society: Theories of the Present*. London: Sage.

Burki, R., Elsasser, H. and Abegg, B. (2003). 'Climate Change and Winter Sports: Environmental and Economic Threats' at www.google.co.uk/search?q=cache:cyMNECTWTnm8J:www.unep.org/sport_en/Documents/toribuerki.doc+SPORTS%2ENVIRONMENTS&hl+en

Burnett, J. (2000). *Riot, Revelry and Rout: Sport in Lowland Scotland Before 1860*. East Linton: Tuckwell Press.

Callaghan, T. and Mullin, M. (2000). 'This Sporting Lie'. *Index on Censorship*. April: 37–47.

Cammack, P. (2002). 'Attacking the Global Poor'. *New Left Review*, 13 (January/February): 125–136.

Cameron, M. and Macdougall, C. (2004) 'Crime Prevention through Sport and Physical Activity'. Australian Government: Australian Institute of Criminology Paper 165 at www.aic.gov.au/publications/tandi/tandi1165.html

Campbell, D. (2004). 'Game Over For Former Olympic Events'. *Observer*, 3 October: 5–6.

Cantelon, H. and Letters, M. (2000). 'The Making of the IOC Environmental Policy as the Third Dimension of the Olympic Movement'. *International Review of the Sociology of Sport*, 35(3): 249–308.

Carlin, J. (2003). 'Rwanda's Magic Moment'. *Observer*, 13 July: 14.

Carrington, B. and McDonald, I. (2001). *Race, Sport and British Society*. London: Routledge.

Cashmore, E. (1997). *The Black Culture Industry*. London: Routledge.

Castells, M. (1998). *The Information Age: Economy, Society and Culture*, Vol. 111. Oxford: Blackwell Publishers.

Chaker, A. N. (2004). *Good Governance in Sport*. Strasbourg: Council of Europe.

Chatterjee. P. (1993). 'Clubbing South East Asia: The Impacts of Golf Sports Development' at http://multinationalmonitor.org/hyper/issues/1993/11/mm1193_13.html

Chiba, N., Ebihara, O. and Morino, S. (2001). 'Globalization, Naturalization and Identity: The Case of Borderless Elite Athletes in Japan'. *International Review for the Sociology of Sport*, 36(2): 203–221.

Chisari, F. (2004). 'Shouting Housewives!: The 1966 World Cup and British Television'. *Sport in History*, 24(1): 94–109.

Chung, H. (2003). 'Sport Star Vs Rock Star in Globalizing Popular Culture: Similarities, Difference and Paradox in Discussion of Celebrities'. *International Review for the Sociology of Sport*, 38(1): 99–108.

Clapson, M. (1986). *A Bit of a Flutter: Popular Gambling and English Society, c 1823–1961*. Manchester: Manchester University Press.

Clarke, J. and Critcher, C. (1985). *The Devil Makes Work: Leisure in Capitalist Britain*. London: Macmillan.

Coakley, J. (2003). *Sport in Society: Issues and Controversies*. Boston: McGraw Hill.

Coakley, J. and Dunning, E. (2002). *Handbook of Sports Studies*. London: Sage.

Coalter, F. (2000). *Role of Sport in Re-Generating Deprived Urban Communities*. Edinburgh: Scottish Executive Publications at http://www.scotland.gov.uk/crukd01/blue/rsrdua-00.htm

Cohen, S. (2001). *States of Denial: Knowing About Atrocities and Suffering*. Cambridge: Polity Press.

Cole, C. (2002). 'Body Studies in the Sociology of Sport'. In Coakley, J. and Dunning, E. (eds) *Handbook of Sports Studies*. London: Sage, 439–460.

Coleman, J. (1988). 'Social Capital in the Creation of Human Capital'. *American Journal of Sociology*, 94: 95–119.

Collins, T. (1996). 'Myth and Reality in the 1895 Rugby Split'. *The Sports Historian*, 16: 33–41.

Council of Europe (2000). 'Background Studies on the Problem of Sexual Harassment in Sport, Especially With Regard to Women and Children'. *9th Council of Europe Conference of Ministers Responsible for Sport*. Bratislava. Slovakia. 30–31 May.

Cronin, M. (1999). *Sport and Nationalism in Ireland*: *Gaelic Games, Soccer and Irish Identity since 1884*. Dublin: Four Courts Press.

Cronin, M. and Bale, J. (2003). *Sport and Post-colonialism*. Oxford: Berg.

Crosset, T. (1995). *Outsiders in the Clubhouse*: *The World of Women's Professional Golf*. Albany: New York University Press.

Cunningham, J. and Beneforti, M. (2005). 'Investigating Indicators for Measuring the Health and Social Impact of Sport and Recreation Programs in Australian Indigenous Communities'. *International Review for the Sociology of Sport*, 40(1), 89–98.

Da Costa, L., Lamartine, P. and Miragaya, A. (2002). *Worldwide Experience and Trends in Sport for All*. Munich: Meyer and Meyer Sports Books.

Danish Ministry of Culture (1996). *Politics of Culture in Denmark*. Arhus: Danish Ministry of Culture.

David, P. (2005). *Human Rights in Youth Sport*: *A Critical Review of Children's Rights in Youth Sport*. London: Routledge.

Davies, H. (2005) 'The Fan'. *New Statesman*, 14: 59–60.

Deacon, B. (2003). 'Global Social Governance Reform'. *Fabian Global Forum*. London: The Fabian Society at http://www.fabianglobalforum.net/forum/article033.html

Department of Sport and Recreation (1997). 'Pulling it Together: Developing A Sport and Recreation Policy That Meets The Needs of the Nation'. South African Department of Sport and Recreation. Cape Town: Unpublished Paper.

Dimeo, P. (2005). 'Cricket and the Misrepresentation of Indian Sports History'. *Historical Studies*, 20: 98–111.

Dimeo, P. (2004). '"A Parcel of Dummies?" Sport and the Body in Indian History'. In Mills, J. and Sen, S. (eds) *Confronting the Body*: *The Politics of Physicality in Colonial and Post-Colonial India*. London: Anthem, 39–57.

Dimeo, P. (2002). 'Colonial Bodies, Colonial Sport: "Martial" Punjabis, "Effeminate" Bengalis and the Development of Indian football'. *International Journal of the History of Sport*, 19(1): 72–90.

Donnelly, P. (2003). 'Sport and Social Theory'. In Houlihan, B. (ed.) *Sport and Society*: *A Student Introduction*. London: Sage, 1–28.

Donnelly, P. (2002). 'Interpretative Approaches to the Sociology of Sport'. In Coakley, J. and Dunning, E. (eds) *Handbook of Sports Studies*. London: Sage, 77–91.

Donnelly, P. (1993). 'Sub-cultures in Sport: Resilience and Transformation'. In Ingham, A. and Loy, J. (eds) *Sport in Social Development*: *Traditions, Transitions and Transformations*. Illinois: Human Kinetics, 119–147.

Donnelly, P. (1988). 'Sport as a Site of Popular Resistance'. In Gruneau, R. (ed.) *Popular Cultures and Political Practices*. Toronto: Garamond Press, 69–82.

Donnelly, P. and Petherick, L. (2004). 'Workers Playtime? Child Labour at the Extremes of the Sporting Spectrum'. *Sport in Society*, 7(3): 301–321.

Dunning, E. (1999). *Sport Matters*: *Sociological Studies of Sport, Violence and Civilization*. London: Routledge.

Dunning, E. and Rojek, C. (1992). *Sport and Leisure in the Civilizing Process*: *Critique and Counter-Critique*. London: Macmillan.

Dunning, E., Murphy, P. and Malcolm, D. (2004). *Sports Histories*: *Figurational Studies in the Development of Modern Sport*. London: Routledge.

Dunning, E. and Sheard, K. (1979). *Barbarians, Gentlemen and Players*: *A Sociological Study of the Development of Rugby Football*. Oxford: Martin Robertson.

Dyck, N. (2000). *Games, Sports and Cultures*. Oxford: Berg.

Dyck, N. and Archetti, E. (2003). *Sport, Dance and Embodied Identities*. Oxford: Berg.

Dyreson, M. (2001). 'Maybe It's Better to Bowl Alone: Sport, Community and Democracy in American Thought'. *Culture, Sport, Society*, 4(1): 19–30.

Dyson, S. (1994) 'Be Like Mike: Michael Jordan and the Pedagogy of Desire'. In Giroux, H. and McLaren, P. (eds) *Between Borders*: *Pedagogy and the Politics of Cultural Studies*. Routledge: New York, 119–127.

Eichberg, H. (2004). *The People of Democracy*: *Understanding Self-Determination on the Basis of Body and Movement*. Arhus: Klim.

Eilling, A., De Knop, P. and Knoppers, A. (2003). 'Gay/Lesbian Sport Clubs and Events: Places of Homo-Social Bonding and Cultural Resistance'. *International Review for the Sociology of Sport*, 38(4): 441–456.

Eitzen, D. (2003). *Fair and Foul*: *Beyond the Myths and Paradoxes of Sport*. New York: Rowan & Littlefield Publishers.

Elias, N. (1983). *The Court Society*. Oxford: Blackwell.

Elias, N. (1978). *What is Sociology?* London: Hutchinson.

Fabian Review (2003). 'Non-economic Boycotts'. Spring: 8–10.

Fabian Society (2003). 'Human Rights'. *Fabian Global Forum*, London: Fabian Society at http://www.fabianglobalforum.net/knowledge/article002.html

Fan Hong (1997). *Footbinding, Feminism and Freedom*: *The Liberation of Women's Bodies in China*. London: Frank Cass.

Fasting, K. (1989). 'Women's Leadership in Sport'. In *Women and Sport Taking the Lead*. London: Council of Europe, 6–17.

Field, J. (2003). *Social Capital*. London: Routledge.

Foster, K. (2000). 'How Can Sport be Regulated?' In Greenfield, S. and Osborn, G. (eds) *Law and Sport in Contemporary Society*. London: Frank Cass, 268–285.

Foucault, M. (1988). *The History of Sexuality, Volume 1*: *An Introduction*. New York: Vintage.

Foucault, M. (1977). *Discipline and Punish*. New York: Pantheon Books.

Fraser, N. (2003). 'Social Justice in the Age of Identity Politics'. In Fraser, N. and Honneth, A. (eds) *Redistribution or Recognition?* London: Verso, 45–61.

Fraser, N. (2000). 'Re-thinking Recognition?' *New Left Review*, 3 (May/June): 107–120.

Fraser, N. (1995). 'From Redistribution to Recognition? Dilemmas of Justice in a Post-Socialist Age'. *New Left Review*, 12 (July/August): 1–24.

Fraser, N. and Honneth, A. (2003). *Redistribution or Recognition?* London: Verso.

Frazer, E. (2000). 'Communitarianism'. In Browning, G., Halcli, A. and Webster, F. (eds) *Understanding Contemporary Society*. London: Sage, 46–58.

Fukuyama, F. (1992). *The End of History and the Last Man*. Harmondsworth: Penguin Books.

Fukuyama, F. (1989). 'The End of History'. *The National Interest*, 16: 3–18.

Gardiner, G. (2003). 'Black Bodies–White Codes: Indigenous Footballers, Racism and the Australian Football League's Racial and Religious Vilification Code'. In Bale, J. and Cronin, M. (eds) (2003). *Sport and Post-colonialism*. Oxford: Berg, 29–45.

Gardiner, S., James, M., O'Leary J., Welch, R., Blackshaw, I., Boyes, S. and Caiger, A. (eds) (2001). *Sports Law*. London: Cavendish Publishing.

Gems, G. (1995). 'Blocked Shot: The Development of Baseball in the African-American Community of Chicago'. *Journal of Sports History*, 22(2): 135–148.

Gen Doy, A. (1996). 'Out of Africa: Orientalism, Race and the Female Body'. *Body and Society*, 2(4): 17–45.

Giddens, A. (2001). *Sociology*. Cambridge: Polity Press.

Gillis, R. (2001). 'Ready to Board?' *SportsBusiness*. August: 14–17.

Gillon, D. (2004). 'Candle who Brings a Ray of Hope'. *Herald*, 24 November: 12.

Gillon, D. (2003). 'A Winner who Had to Admit Defeat'. *Herald*, 19 July: 15.

Giroux, H. and McLaren, P. (eds) (1994) *Between Borders*: *Pedagogy and the Politics of Cultural Studies*. Routledge: New York.

Gitlin, T. (1993). 'The Rise of Identity Politics an Examination and Critique'. *Dissent*, Spring: 172–179.

Giulianotti, R. (2005). *Sport. A Critical Sociology*. Cambridge: Polity Press.

Giulianotti, R. (ed) (2004). *Sport and Modern Social Theorists*. Basingstoke: Palgrave Macmillan.

Giulianotti, R. and McArdle, R. (eds) (2005). *Sport, Civil Liberties and Human Rights*. London: Routledge.

Goldman, R. and Papson, S. (1998). *Nike Culture*. London: Sage Publications.

Gorman, J. (2003). *Rights and Reasons*: *An Introduction to the Philosophy of Rights*. Chesam: Acumen Publishing.

Goudsblom, J. (1977). *Sociology in the Balance*. Blackwell: Oxford.

Gourley, B. (2002). 'In Defence of the Intellectual'. Stirling: Stirling University, Robbins Papers.

Gray, J. (2002a). 'When the Forests Go, Shall We Be Alone?' *New Statesman*, 22 July: 27–30.

Gray, J. (2002b). 'The Myth of Secularism?' *New Statesman*, 20 December: 69–70.

Gray, J. (2001). 'The Era of Globalisation is Over'. *New Statesman*, 24 September: 25–27.

Greenberg, E. (2004). 'Coach: Title IX Protects Me From Retaliation' at http://www.cnn.com/2004/LAW/12/01/jackson/

Grenfell, C. and Rinehart, R. (2003). 'Skating on Thin Ice: Human Rights in Youth Figure Skating'. *International Review for the Sociology of Sport*, 38(1): 79–98.

Grundmann, R. (1991). 'The Ecological Challenge to Marxism'. In *New Left Review*, 187 (May/June): 1–15.

Gruneau, R. (1999). *Class, Sports and Social Development*. Illinois: Human Kinetics.

Gruneau, R. (1988). 'Notes on Popular Culture and Political Resistance'. In Gruneau, R. (ed.) *Popular Cultures and Political Practices*. Toronto: Garamond Press, 1–33.

Gruneau, R. (1976). *Canadian Sport*: *Sociological Perspectives*. Toronto: Addison-Wesley.

Gruneau, R. and Whitson, D. (1993). *Hockey Night in Canada*: *Sport, Identities and Cultural Politics*. Toronto: Garamond Press.

Guha, R. (2002). *A Corner of a Foreign Field*: *The Indian History of a British Sport*. London: Picador.

Gunnell, R. (2004). 'Religion: Why Do We Still Give a Damn?' *New Statesman* 3 (May): 18–22.

Guttmann, A. (1996). 'Sumo'. In Levinson, D. and Christensen, K. (eds) *Encyclopaedia of World Sport*. Oxford: ABC-CLIO, 380–381.

Guttmann, A. (1978). *From Ritual to Record*: *The Nature of Modern Sport*. New York: Colombia University Press.

Guttmann, A. and Thompson, L. (2001). *Japanese Sports*: *A History*. Honolulu: University of Hawaii Press.

Habermas, J. (1989). *The Structural Transformation of the Public Sphere*: *An Enquiry into a Category of Bourgeois Society*. Cambridge: Polity Press.

Hague, E. and Mercer, J. (1998). 'Geographical Memory and Urban Identity in Scotland: Raith Rovers FC and Kirkaldy'. *Geography*, 83(2): 105–116.

Hall, A., Slack, T., Smith, G. and Whitson, D. (1991). *Sport in Canadian Society*. Toronto: McClelland and Stewart.

Hall, S. (1981). 'Notes on Deconstructing the Popular'. In Samuel, R. (ed.) *People's History and Socialist Theory*. London: Routledge, 227–240.

Hansen, J. and Nielsen, N. (2000). *Sports, Body and Health*. Odense: Odense University Press.

Harding, G. (2003). 'Bosman in Baghdad'. *Observer*, 23 March: 12.

Harding, L. (2003). 'The Big Match Unites a Country of Two Halves'. *Guardian*, 1 March: 1.

Hargreaves, I. (1999). *New Mutualism*: *In From the Cold*. London: Trafford Press Ltd.

Hargreaves, J. (2004). 'Querying Sport Feminism: Personal or Political?'. In Giulianotti, R. (ed.) *Sport and Modern Social Theorists*. Basingstoke: Palgrave, 187–207.

Hargreaves, J. (2000). *Heroines of Sport*: *The Politics of Difference and Identity*. London: Routledge.

Hargreaves, J. A. (1994). *Sporting Females*: *Critical Issues in the History and Sociology of Women's Sports*. London: Routledge.

Hargreaves, John (1986). *Sport, Power and Culture*. Cambridge: Polity Press.

Hari, J. (2002). 'Yahoo Boo to a Daily Mail Myth'. *New Statesman*, September, 23–25.

Harris, J. (1998). 'Civil Society, Physical Activity and the Involvement of Sport Sociologists in the Preparation of Physical Activity Professionals'. *Sociology of Sport*, 15(2): 138–153.

Harris, O. (1999). 'The Rise of Black Athletes in the USA'. In Riordan, J. and Kruger, A. (eds) *The International Politics of Sport in the 20th Century*. London: E&FN Spon, 150–177.

Harris, P. (2002). 'Jumping the Gun'. *Observer*: *Sports Monthly*, March: 27–34.

Harvey, J. (2003). 'Sports and Recreation: Entertainment or Social Right?', http://polyresearch. gc.ca/page.asp?pagenm=v5nl_art_07

Harvey, J. and Cantelon, H. (eds) (1988). *Not Just A Game*: *Essays in Canadian Sport Sociology*. Ottawa: University of Ottawa Press.

Hashemi, F. (2000). 'Flying the Chador'. *Index On Censorship*: *This Sporting Lie*, 4: 70–73.

Hawkins, B. (1998). 'Evening Basketball Leagues: The Use of Sport to Reduce African American Youth Criminal Activity'. *International Sports Journal*, 2(2): 68–77.

Hay, R. (2003). 'The Last Night of the Poms: Australia as a Postcolonial Sporting Society'. In Bale, J. and Cronin, M. (eds) *Sport and Post-colonialism*. Oxford: Berg, 15–28.

Henry, I. (2001). *The Politics of Leisure Policy*. Basingstoke: Palgrave.

Henry, I. and Thedoraki, A. (2002). 'Management, Organizations and Theory in the Governance of Sport'. In Coakley, J. and Dunning, E. (eds) *Handbook of Sport Studies*. London: Sage, 490–503.

Henry, I., Amara, M. and Al-Tauqui, M. (2003). 'Sport, Arab Nationalism and the Pan-Arab Games'. *International Review for the Sociology of Sport*, 38(3): 295–311.

Heywood, A. (2004). *Political Theory*: *An Introduction*. Basingstoke: Palgrave.

Hill, J. (2002). *Sport, Leisure and Culture in Twentieth Century Britain*. Basingstoke: Palgrave.

Hill, J. (1996). 'British Sports History: A Post-Modern Future?'. *Journal of Sports History*, 23(1): 1–19.

Hill, J. and Varsasi, F. (1997). 'Creating Wembley: The Construction of a National Monument'. *The Sports Historian*, 17(2): 28–44.

Hirst, P. and Thompson, G. (1999). *Globalization in Question*. Oxford: Polity Press.

Hoberman, J. (1997). *Darwin's Athletes*: *How Sport Has Damaged Black America and Preserved the Myth of Race*. Boston: Houghton.

Hobsbawm, E. (1997). *On History*. London: Weidenfeld & Nicholson.

Hogenstad, H. and Tollisen, A. (2004). 'Playing Against Deprivation: Football and Development in Nairobi, Kenya'. In Armstrong, G. and Giulianotti, R. (eds) *Football in Africa*: *Conflict, Conciliation and Community*. Basingstoke: Palgrave, 210–229.

Holt, R. (2000). 'The Uses of History in Comparative Physical Culture'. In Tollener, J. and Renson, R. (eds) *Old Borders, New Borders, No Borders*: *Sport and Physical Education in a Period of Change*. Oxford: Meyer and Meyer Sport, 49–57.

Holt, R. and Mason, T. (2000). *Sport in Britain 1945–2000*. Oxford: Blackwell.

hooks, b. (2000). *Talking Back*: *Thinking Feminist, Thinking Black*. Boston: Southend Press.

Houlihan, B. (2003). *Sport and Society*: *An Introduction*. London: Sage.

Houlihan, B. (2002). 'Politics and Sport'. In Coakley, J. and Dunning, E. (eds) *Handbook of Sports Studies*. London: Sage, 213–227.

Hunt, D. (2001). *Communities in Control*: *Public Services and Local Socialism*. London: Fabian Society.

Hwang, T. (2001). 'Sport, Nationalism and the Early Chinese Republic 1912–1927'. *The Sports Historian*, 21(2): 1–20.

Jackson, S. (1996). 'Lacrosse'. In Levinson, D. and Christensen, K. (eds) *Encyclopaedia of World Sport*. Oxford: ABC-CLIO, 219–222.

James, C. L. R. (1983). *Beyond a Boundary*. London: Stanley Paul.

James, M. and McArdle, D. (2004). 'Player Violence or Violent Players? Vicarious Liability for Sports Participants'. *Tort Law Review*, (12)3: 131–146.

Jameson, F. (2004). 'The Politics of Utopia'. *New Left Review*, 25 (January/February): 35–54.

Jarvie, G. (2005). 'The North American Émigré and Highland Games in International Communities'. In Ray, C. (ed.) *Transatlantic Scots*. Alabama: University of Alabama Press, 80–96.

Jarvie, G. (2004). 'Sport in Changing Times and Places'. *British Journal of Sociology*, 55(4): 579–587.

Jarvie, G. (2003a). 'Internationalism and Sport in the Making of Nations'. *Identities*: *Studies in Global Culture and Power*, 10(4): 537–551.

Jarvie, G. (2003b). 'Sport, Communitarianism and Social Capital: A Neighbourghly Insight into Scottish Sport'. *International Review for the Sociology of Sport*, 38(2): 139–153.

Jarvie, G. (2002). 'Sport, Racism and Ethnicity'. In Coakley, J. and Dunning, E. (eds) *Handbook of Sports Studies*. London: Sage, 334–343.

Jarvie, G. (ed) (1999). *Sport in the Making of Celtic Cultures*. London: Leicester University Press.

Jarvie, G. (1997). 'Sport and Social Problems in Unprincipled Societies'. In Nardis, P., Mussino, A. and Porro, N. (eds) *Sport, Social Problems, Social Movement*. Milan. Edizioni Seam, 16–28.

Jarvie, G. (1994). 'Play, Pleasure and Nostalgia: Some Critical Comments on Madness'. *Working Papers in Sport and Society*, Warwick: University of Warwick, 1–10.

Jarvie, G. (1993). 'Sport, Nationalism and Cultural Identity'. In Allison, L. (ed.) *The Changing Politics of Sport*. Manchester: Manchester University Press, 58–83.

Jarvie, G. (1991). *Highland Games*: *The Making of the Myth*. Edinburgh: Edinburgh University Press.

Jarvie, G. (1985). *Class, Race and Sport in South Africa's Political Economy*. London: Routledge.

Jarvie, G. and Burnett, J. (2000). *Sport, Scotland and the Scots*. East Lothian: Tuckwell Press.

Jarvie, G. and Macintosh, T. (forthcoming). 'The Promise and Possibilities of Running in and Out of East Africa'. In Pitsiladis, Y. and Bale, J. (eds) *East African Running*. London: Routledge, 1–15.

Jarvie, G. and Maguire, J. (1994). *Sport and Leisure in Social Thought*. London: Routledge.

Johnston, G. and Percy-Smith, J. (2003). 'In Search of Social Capital'. *Policy and Politics*, 31(3): 321–334.

Jones, S. (1988). *Sport, Politics and the Working Class*: *Organised Labour and Sport in Interwar Britain*. Manchester: Manchester University Press.

Jones, S. (1986). *Workers at Play*: *A Social and Economic History of Leisure, 1918–1939*. London: Routledge.

Kaldor, M. (2001). 'New Wars and Morality in the Global Era'. In Bentley, T. and Stedman Jones, D. (eds) *The Moral Universe*. London: Demos, 43–51.

Katwala, S. (2004). 'Political Footballs'. *Fabian Review*: *The Age of Terror?* 116(2): 14–16.

Katwala, S. (2001). 'Can Sport be Reformed?' at www.observer.guardian.c....ort/issues/story/0,11839,72182500.html

Katwala, S. (2000a). *Democratising Global Sport*. London: The Foreign Policy Centre.

Katwala, S. (2000b). 'The Crisis of Confidence in Global Sport' at www.observer.co.uk/Print0,3858,4421203,00.html

Kay, J. and Vamplew, W. (2002). *Weather Beaten; Sport in the British Climate*. Edinburgh: Mainstream Publishing.

Kay, T. (2003). 'Sport and Gender'. In Houlihan, B, (ed.) *Sport and Society*: *An Introduction*. London: Sage, 89–104.

Keene, J. (1988). *Civil Society and the State*. London: Verso.

Kenny, M. (2004). *The Politics of Identity*. Cambridge: Polity Press.

Kidd, B. (1996). *The Struggle for Canadian Sport*. Toronto: University of Toronto Press.

Kidd, B. (1982). *Athletes' Rights in Canada*. Toronto: Ministry of Tourism and Recreation.

Kidd, B. and Donnelly, P. (2000). 'Human Rights in Sport'. *International Review for the Sociology of Sport*, 35(2): 131–148.

King, A. (2002). *The End of the Terraces*. London: Leicester University Press.

Kinnock, G. (2003). 'It's All About Justice'. *Fabian Global Forum For Progressive Global Politics* at www.fabianglobalforum.net/forum/article027.html

Klein, N. (2001). 'Reclaiming the Commons'. *New Left Review*, 9: 81–90.

Kluckohn, T. (1951). 'Dominant and Substitute Profiles of Cultural Orientation'. *Social Forces*, 28:376–393.

Knoppers, A. and Elling, A. (2004). 'We Do Not Engage in Promotional Journalism: Discursive Strategies Used by Sports Journalists to Describe the Selection Process'. *International Review for the Sociology of Sport*, 39(1): 57–75.

Krieger, J. (2000). *British Politics in the Global Age*: *Can Social Democracy Survive*. Cambridge: Polity Press.

Kruger, A. and Riordan, J. (1996). *The Story of Worker Sport*. Champaign, IL: Human Kinetics.

Kusz, K. (2004). 'Extreme America: The Cultural Products of Extreme Sports in 1990s America'. In Wheaton, B. (ed.) *Understanding Lifestyle Sports*: *Consumption, Identity and Difference*. London: Routledge, 197–215.

Laberge, S. and Sankoff, D. (1988). 'Physical Activities, Body Habitus and Lifestyles'. In Harvey, J. and Cantelon, H. (eds) *Not Just A Game*: *Essays in Canadian Sport Sociology*. Ottawa: University of Ottawa Press, 268–286.

Lacombe, P. (2001). 'The Breton Body in Culture and Religion'. *Culture, Sport and Society*, 14(3): 27–40.

Lafeber, W. (1999). *Michael Jordan and the New Global Capitalism*. New York: W.W. Norton and Company.

Landman, T. (2003). 'Swapping Debt for Education' at www.fabianglobalforum.net/forum/article012.html

Leadbeater, C. (2002). 'Globalisation: Want the Good News'. *New Statesman*, 1 July: 29–31.

Leader, S. (2003). 'Why Boycott Zimbabwe but not China?'. *New Statesman*, 6 January: 4–5.

Lenskyj, H. (2000). *Inside the Olympic Industry*: *Power, Politics and Activism*. New York: New York University Press.

Lenskyj, H. (1990). *Sex Equality in the Olympics*: *A Report to the Toronto Olympic Task Force*. April.

Leseth, A. (2003). 'Dance, Sport and Politics in Dar-es-Salaam, Tanzania'. In Dyck, N. and Archetti, E. (eds) *Sport, Dance and Embodied Identities*. Oxford: Berg, 231–249.

Levinson, D. and Christensen, K. (1996). *Encyclopaedia of World Sport*. Oxford: ABC-CLIO.

Lister, R. (2004). *Poverty*: *Key concepts*. Cambridge: Polity Press.

Lloyd, M. (1996). 'Feminism, Aerobics and the Politics of the Body'. *Body and Society*, 2(2): 79–98.

Low, M. (2000). 'Nationalism'. In Browning, G., Halcli, A. and Webster, A. (eds) *Understanding Contemporary Society*. London: Sage, 356–371.

Loy, J. and Booth, D. (2002). 'Functionalism, Sport and Society'. In Coakley, J. and Dunning, E. (eds) *Handbook of Sports Studies*, London: Sage, 8–28.

McCarthy, H., Miller, P. and Skidmore, P. (2004) 'Network Logic', Special Edition. *Demos*.

McCrone, D. (2000). *A Sociology of Nationalism*. London: Routledge.

McGovern, P. (2000). 'Globalization or Internationalization? Foreign Footballers in the English League, 1946–95'. *Sociology*, 36(1): 23–42.

McKibben, R. (1994). *Ideologies of Class*: *Social Relations in Britain 1880–1950*. Oxford: Clarendon Press.

McLean, I. (1996). *Oxford Concise Dictionary of Politics*. Oxford: Oxford University Press.

McMillan, J. (1995). 'Somewhere Over the Rainbow in the Real World'. *Scotland on Sunday*. 19 March: 16.

Macpherson, C. B. (1965). *The Real World of Democracy*. Toronto: CBC Merchandising.

Magdalinski, T. (2004). 'Homebush: Site of the Clean/sed and Natural Australian Athlete'. In Vertinsky, P. and Bale, J. (eds) *Sites of Sport, Space, Place Experience*. London: Routledge, 101–114.

Magdalinski, T. and Chandler, T. (eds) (2002). *With God on Their Side*: *Sport in the Service of Religion*. London: Routledge.

Maguire, J. (2005). *Sport, Power and Globalisation*. London: Routledge.

Maguire, J. (2002). 'Sport and Globalisation'. In Coakley, J. and Dunning, E. (eds) *Handbook of Sports Studies*, London: Sage, 357–370.

Maguire, J. (1999). *Global Sport*: *Identities, Societies, Civilizations*. Cambridge: Polity Press.

Maguire, J., Jarvie, G., Mansfield, L. and Bradley, J. (2002). *Sport Worlds*: *A Sociological Perspective*. Illinois: Human Kinetics.

Markovits, B. (2003). 'The Colours of Sport'. *New Left Review*, 22: 151–160.

Marquand, D. (2004). *Decline of the Public*. Oxford: Polity Press.

Marquand, D. (2000). 'The fall of Civic Culture'. *New Statesman*, November: 27–30.

Marquand, D. (1988). *The Unprincipled Society*. London: Jonathan Cape.

Marqusee, M. (2000). 'Sydney and the Olympics: Corruption and Corporatism Versus a Positive Social Role for the Olympics'. In Workers Liberty Australia Newsletter, October at archive. workersliberty.org/Australia/Newsletter/Oct00/olympics.html

Marshall, G. (1998). *Dictionary of Sociology*. Oxford: Oxford University Press.

Marshall, T. (1963). *Sociology at the Crossroads*. London: Allen & Unwin.

Martin, L. (2004). 'Lewis Hands Surfers Never on Sunday Warning'. *Observer*, 8 August:13.

Mason, T. (1993). 'All the Winners and the Half Times'. *The Sports Historian*. 13 (May): 3–11.

Mason, T. (1988). *Sport in Britain*. London: Faber and Faber.

Maynard, M. (2002). 'Race, Gender and the Concept of Difference in Feminist Thought'. In Scraton, S. and Flintoff, A. (eds) *Gender and Sport*: *A Reader*. London: Routledge, 111–126.

Mertes, T. (2004). *A Movement of Movements*: *Is Another World Really Possible?* London. Verso.

Mertes, T. (2002). 'Grass-Roots Globalism'. *New Left Review*, 17 (September/October): 101–112.

Metcalfe, A. (1996). 'Sport and Community: A Case Study of the Mining Villages of East Northumberland 1800–1914'. In Hill, J. and Williams, J. (eds) *Sport and Identity in the North of England*. Keele: Keele University Press, 13–40.

Metcalfe, A. (1991). *Canada Learns to Play*: *The Emergence of Organised Sport, 1807–1904*. Toronto: McClelland and Stewart.

Mewett, P. G. (2003). 'Conspiring to Run: Women, their Bodies and Athletics Training'. *International Review for the Sociology of Sport*, 38(3): 331–349.

Meyer, T. (2002). 'Towards a New Political Regime'. *Fabian Review*, Winter: 16–19.

Middleton, K. (2000). 'European Community Law Sport'. In Stewart, W. (ed) *Sport and the Law*: *The Scots Perspective*. Edinburgh: T&T Clark, 79–100.

Midol, N. and Broyer, G. (1995) 'Toward an Anthropological Study of New Sports Cultures: The Case of Whiz Sports in France'. *Sociology of Sport Journal*, 12: 204–212.

Mills, C. W. (1970). *The Sociological Imagination*. Middlesex: Penguin Books.

Mills, J. and Dimeo, P. (2003). 'When Gold is Fired it Shines: Sport, the Imagination and the Body in Colonial and Postcolonial India'. In Bale, J. and Cronin, M. (eds) *Sport and Post-colonialism*. Oxford: Berg, 107–122.

396

Miyoshi, M. (1997). 'Sites of Resistance in the Global Economy'. In Pearson, K., Parry, B. and Squires, J. (eds) *Cultural Readings of Imperialism*. London: Lawrence and Wishart, 49–66.

Moffat, G. (2000). 'The Secret Golf Club'. *New Statesman*. 20 September: 33.

Moller, J. and Andersen, J. (1998). *Society's Watchdog – Or Showbiz' Pet? Inspiration For a Better Sports Journalism*. Vingsted: Danish Gymnastics and Sports Association.

Morris, P. and Spink, K. (2000). 'The Court of Arbitration for Sport'. In Stewart, W. (ed.) *Sport and the Law: The Scots Perspective*. Edinburgh: T&T Clark, 61–76.

Morrow, S. (2003). *The People's Game? Football, Finance and Society*. Basingstoke: Palgrave.

Morrow, S. (2000a). 'Mutual Sport and Trust: The Case Study of Celtic *PLC*'. *Irish Journal of Accounting*, 15:14–27.

Morrow, S. (2000b). 'If You Know The History: A Study of Celtic'. In *Singer and Friedlander Review 1999–2000*, London: Singer and Friedlander.

Morrow, S. (1999). *The New Business of Football*. London: Macmillan.

Nash, K. (2001). 'The Cultural Turn in Social Theory: Towards a Theory of Cultural Politics'. *Sociology*, 35(1): 77–92.

Nauright, J. (1997). *Sport, Cultures and Identities in South Africa*. London: Leicester University Press.

New Statesman (2004). 'After Switch Over: What Next for Public Service Television?' 15 November: i–xv.

Niethammer, L. (2003). 'The Infancy of Tarzan'. *New Left Review*, 19 (January/February): 79–91.

Nixon, H. and Frey J, (1996). *A Sociology of Sport*. Albany: Wadsworth.

Novick, J. (2004). 'World of Sport'. *Herald*, 15 October: 24.

Nuttall, J. (2002). *An Introduction to Philosophy*. Cambridge: Polity Press.

Ogi, L. (2004). 'Sport Serving Development and Peace', unpublished address to the ISCA World Congress on Sport For All 2004. 21 May, Copenhagen: Denmark.

Ouellet, J. G. and Donnelly, P. (2003). 'Sport Policy, Citizenship and Social Inclusion' at http://policyresearch.gc.ca/page.asp?pagenm=horsunset_06_01

Ozawa-De Silva, C. (2002). 'Beyond the Body/Mind? Japanese Contemporary Thinkers on Alternative Sociologies of the Body'. *Body and Society*, 8(2): 21–38.

Pacione, M. (2001). *Urban Geography: A Global Perspective*. London: Routledge.

Palm, J. (2003). *Global Perspectives on Sport, Community and Inclusion: Sport for All in Policy and Practice*. London: Routledge.

Paraschak, V. (1995). 'The Native Sport and Recreation Programme, 1972–1981: Patterns of Resistance, Patterns of Reproduction'. *Canadian Journal of the History of Sport*, 26(1): 1–18.

Paraschak, V. (1990). 'Organised Sport for Native Females on the Six Nations Reserve, Ontario, 1968–1980'. *Canadian Journal of the History of Sport*, 21(1): 70–80.

Parratt, C. (1998). 'About Turns: Reflecting on Sport History in the 1990s'. *Sport, History Review*, 29(1): 4–17.

Parratt, C. (1989). 'Athletic Womanhood: Explaining Sources for Female Sport in Victorian and Edwardian England'. *Journal of the History of Sport*, 16(2): 140–157.

Parrish, R. (2003). *Sports Law and Policy in the European Union*. Manchester: Manchester University Press.

Paton, A. (2003). 'Surf's Up'. *Sunday Herald*, 5 October: 20.

Payne, G. (2000). *Social Divisions*. Basingstoke: Palgrave.

Pearson, B. (2003). 'Say Aloha to Sisters of Surf'. *Herald*. 12 April: 14.

Pfister, G. (1999). 'Physical Education – From a Male Domain to a Female Profession. The Controversy over Women as Physical Educators in Germany'. In Trangbaek, E. and Kruger, A. (eds) *Gender and Sport from European Perspectives*. Viborg: Olesen Offset, 69–84.

Pfister, G. (1990). 'The Medical Discourse on Female Physical Culture in Germany in the 19th and Early 20th Centuries'. *Journal of Sport History*, (17)2: 183–9.

397

Pilz, G. (1996). 'Social Factors Influencing Sport and Violence: On the Problem of Football Violence in Germany'. *International Review for the Sociology of Sport*, 31: 49–65.

Pink, S. (2003). 'She Wasn't Tall Enough and Breasts Get in the Way: Why Would a Woman Bullfighter Retire?' *Identities*: *Studies in Global Culture and Power*, 10(4): 427–450.

Pink, S. (1996). 'Breasts in the Bullring: Female Psychology, Female Bullfighters and Competing Femininities'. *Body and Society*, 2(1): 34–51.

Polley, M. (2003). 'History and Sport'. In Houlihan, B. (ed) *Sport and Society*. London: Sage, 49–64.

Polley, M. (1998). *Moving the Goalposts*: *A History of Sport and Society since 1945*. London: Routledge.

Pope, S. (1998). 'Sport History: Into the 21st Century'. *Journal of Sports History*, 25(2): i–x.

Portes, A. (1998). 'Social Capital: Its Origins and Applications in Modern Sociology'. *Annual Review of Sociology*, 24: 1–24.

Putnam, R. (2000). *Bowling Alone*: *The Collapse and Revival of American Community*. New York: Simon & Schuster.

Putnam, R. (1995) 'Bowling Alone: America's Declining Social Capital'. *Journal of Democracy*, 6: 65–78.

Ramsamy, S. (2002). 'Olympic Values in Shaping Social Bonds and Nation Building at Schools' at www.gov.za/Conf_Wshops_Events/Values/Sam_Ramsamy.htm

Randels, G. and Beal, B. (2002) 'What Makes a Man? Religion, Sport and Negotiating Masculine Identity in the Promise Keepers'. In Magdalinski, T. and Chandler, T. (eds) *With God on Their Side*: *Sport in the Service of Religion*. London: Routledge, 160–177.

Ray, C. (2005). *Transatlantic Scots*. Alabama: University of Alabama Press.

Ray, C. (2001). *Highland Heritage*: *Scottish Americans in the American South*. London: The University of North Carolina Press.

Reid, I. and Jarvie, G. (2000). 'Sport, Nationalisms and their Futures'. In Jones, R. and Armour, K. (ed.) *Sociology of Sport*: *Theory and Practice*. London: Longman, 83–96.

Rinehart, R. (2002). 'Arriving Sport: Alternatives to Formal Sports'. In Coakley, J. and Dunning, E. (eds) *Handbook of Sports Studies*. London: Sage, 504–519.

Rinehart, R. and Sydnor, S. (eds) (2003). *To the Extreme*: *Alternative Sports Inside and Out*. Albany: Suny Press

Rinehart, R. and Grenfell, C. (2002). 'BMX Spaces: Children's Grass Roots, Courses and Corporate Sponsored Tracks'. *Sociology of Sport Journal*, 19(3): 302–314.

Riordan, J. and Kruger, A. (eds) (1999). *The International Politics of Sport in the 20th Century*. London: E & F N Spon.

Roberts, K. (2005). 'Taking the Local Approach to International Sporting Opportunities'. *SportsBusiness*, 101 (April): 25–27.

Roberts, K. (2002). 'Sport's Helping Hand'. *SportsBusiness International*, November: 24–26.

Robertson, R. (1995). 'Globalization: Time-space and Homogeneity-Hetero-geneity'. In Featherstone, M., Lash, S. and Robertson, R. (eds) *Global Modernities*. London: Sage, 25–44.

Robertson, R. (1992). *Globalization*: *Social Theory and Global Culture*. London: Sage.

Rojek, C. (1995). *Decentring Leisure*: *Rethinking Leisure Theory*. London: Sage.

Rowe, D. (2003). 'Sport and the Repudiation of the Global'. *International Review for the Sociology of Sport*, 38(3): 281–295.

Rowe, N. and Champion, R. (2000). *Sports Participation and Ethnicity in England*: *National Survey 1999/2000*. London: Sport England at www.english.sports.gov.uk

Russell, D. (1997). *Football and the English*: *A Social History of Association Football in England, 1863–1995*. Preston: Carnegie Publishing.

Russo, G. (2004). 'Brutal History of a Beautiful Game'. *Herald*, 11 December: 5.

Ruthven, M. (2000). *Islam*: *A Very Short Introduction*. Oxford: Oxford University Press.

Sader, E. (2002). 'Beyond Civil Society'. *New Left Review*, 17 (September/October): 87–101.

Said, E. (2001). 'The Case for the Intellectual'. *The Age*, May: 5–12.

Said, E. (1993). *Culture and Imperialism*. London: Chatto and Windus.

Sassoon, D. (2002). 'On Cultural Markets'. *New Left Review*, 17 (September/October): 113–126.

Scheerder, J., Vanreusel, B. and Renson, J. (2002). 'Social Sports Stratification in Flanders 1969–1999'. *International Review for the Sociology of Sport*, 37(2): 219–245.

Schontz, L. (2002). 'Fast Forward: The Rise of Kenya's Women Runners'. *Pittsburgh Post Gazette*, 22 October: 1214.

Scott, J. (2000). 'Class and Stratification'. In Payne, G. (ed.) *Social Divisions*. Basingstoke: Palgrave, 20–55.

Scott, S. and Morgan, D. (1993). *Body Matters*. London: Falmer Press.

Scottish Executive Publications www.scotland.gov.uk/crukd01/blue/rsrdua-00.htm

Scottish Executive (2005) *Record of the Summit on Sectarianism*. Edinburgh: Scottish Executive Publications.

Scraton, S. and Flintoff, A. (eds) (2003). *Gender and Sports*: A Reader. London: Routledge.

Seabrook, J. (2003) 'Don't Punish the Poor for Being Poor'. *New Statesman*, 23 September: 6–7.

Settle, D. (2004). *Fighting Poverty*: The Facts. Swindon: ESRC.

Shilling, C. (1993). *The Body and Social Theory*. London: Sage Publications.

Sloane, P. (2002). 'The Regulation of Professional Team Sports'. In Barros, C., Ibrahimo, M. and Szymanski, S. (eds) *Transatlantic Sport*: The Comparative Economics of North American and European Sports. Northampton: Edward Edgar, 50–69.

Slowikowski, S. (1993). 'Cultural Performance and Sport Mascots'. *Journal of Sport and Social Issues*, 17(1): 23–33.

Smith, A. and Westerbeek, H. (2004). *The SportsBusiness Future*. Basingstoke: Palgrave Macmillan.

Smith, M. (2002). 'Muhammad Speaks and Muhammad Ali: Intersections of the Nation of Islam and Sport in the 1960s'. In Magdalinski, T. and Chandler, T. (eds) *With God on Their Side*: Sport in the Service of Religion. London: Routledge, 177–196.

Southgate, B. (1996). *History*: What and Why? Ancient, Modern and Postmodern Perspectives. London: Routledge.

Spivey, P. (1985). *Sport in America*: New Historical Perspectives. Westport: Greenwood Press.

Sport England (2003). *Sports Volunteering in England 2002*. London: Sport England.

Sportsengland (1998). *The Social Value of Sport*. London: Sportengland.

Sportscotland (2001). 'Sports Participation in Scotland 2000'. *Research Digest 84*. Edinburgh. Sportscotland.

Sports Policy Research Initiative Canada at http://policyresearch.gc.ca/page.asp?pagenm= horsunset_06_01

Stephen, D. (2000). 'What's in a Game? Class and History'. *New Statesman and Society*, June: 20–22.

Stevenson, D. (1997). 'Olympic Arts: Sydney 2000 and the Cultural Olympiad'. *International Review of the Sociology of Sport*, 32(3): 227–238.

Stewart, W. (ed.) (2000). *Sport and the Law*: The Scots Perspective. Edinburgh: T&T Clark.

Stoddart, B. (1998). 'Other Cultures'. In Stoddart, B. and Sandiford, K. (eds) *The Imperial Game*. Manchester: Manchester University Press, 135–149.

Stoddart, B. and Sandiford, K. (1998). *The Imperial Game*. Manchester: Manchester University Press.

Stolle, D. (1998). 'Bowling Together, Bowling Alone: The Development of Generalized Trust in Voluntary Associations'. *Political Psychology*, 19(3): 497–525.

Stone, E. (2001). 'Disability, Sport and the Body in China'. *Sociology of Sport Journal*, 18(1): 51–68.

Stranger, M. (1999). 'The Aesthetics of Risk: A Study of Surfing'. *International Review for the Sociology of Sport*, 34(3): 265–276.

399

Struna, N. (2002). 'Social History and Sport'. In Coakley, J. and Dunning, E. (eds) *Handbook of Sports Studies*. London: Sage, 187–203.

Stubbs, S. and Chernushenko, D. (2004). 'Guidelines for Greening Sports Events' at www. committedtogreen.com/guidelines/greening.htm

Sugden, J. (1996). *Boxing and Society*: *An International Analysis*. Manchester: Manchester University Press.

Sugden, J. and Tomlinson, A. (eds) (2002). *Power Games*: *A Critical Sociology of Sport*. London: Routledge.

Sudgen, J. and Tomlinson, A. (1999). 'Digging the Dirt and Staying Clean: Retrieving the Investigative Tradition for a Critical Sociology of Sport'. *International Review of the Sociology of Sport*, 34(4), 385–397.

Sugden, J. and Bairner, A. (1993) *Sport, Sectarianism and Society in a Divided Ireland*. London: Leicester University Press.

Supiot, A. (2003). 'Dogmas and Rights'. *New Left Review*, 21 (May/June): 118–137.

Tait, R. (2005). 'The Little Schumacher who is Driving Iran Round the Feminist Bend'. *Herald*. 27 March: 21.

Tatchell, P. (2003). 'Ambassadors of Tyranny: Zimbabwe Cricket Tour'. *New Statesman*, 19 May: 16.

Taylor, I. (1987). 'Putting the Boot into a Working Class Sport: British Soccer after Bradford and Brussels'. *Sociology of Sport Journal*, 4(3): 171–191.

Theeboom, M. and De Knop, P. (1997). 'An Analysis of the Development of Wushu'. *International Review for the Sociology of Sport*, 32(3): 267–282.

Therborn, G. (2001). 'Into the 21st Century'. *New Left Review*, 10 (May): 87–111.

Tiger Club Project (2003) *Annual Report 2003*. Kampala: Uganda.

Tönnies, F. (1963). *Community and Association*. London: Routledge & Kegan Paul.

Tormey, S. (2004). *Anti-Capitalism*. Oxford: Oneworld Publications.

Turner, B. (2000). 'The Cartesian Myth of Mind and Body'. In Hansen, J. and Nielsen, N. (eds) *Sports, Body and Health*. Odense: Odense University Press, 1–19.

Turner, B. (1996). *Body and Society*. Oxford: Blackwell.

Vamplew, W. (1998). 'Facts and Artefacts: Sports Historians and Sports Museums'. *Journal of Sports History*, 25(2): 268–283.

Vamplew, W. (1988). *Professional Sport in Britain, 1875–1914*: *Pay Up and Play the Game*. Cambridge: Cambridge University Press.

Vamplew, W. and Stoddart, B. (1994). *Sport in Australia*: *A Social History*. Cambridge: Cambridge University Press.

Van Ingen, C. (2003). 'Geographies of Gender, Sexuality and Race: Reframing the Focus on Space in Sport Sociology'. *International Review for the Sociology of Sport*, 38(2): 201–216.

Vaugrand, H. (2001). 'Pierre Bourdieu and Jean-Marie Brohm: The Schemes of Intelligibility and Issues Towards a Theory of Knowledge in the Sociology of Sport'. *International Review of the Sociology of Sport*, 36(2): 183–200.

Vertinsky, P. (1994). 'The Social Construction of the Gendered Body'. *The International Journal of the History of Sport*, 11(2): 147–171.

Vertinsky, P. and Bale, J. (eds) (2004). *Sites of Sport, Space, Place Experience*. London: Routledge.

Vidacs, B. (2003). 'The Postcolonial and the Level Playing Field in the 1998 World Cup'. In Bale, J. and Cronin, M. (eds) *Sport and Post-colonialism*. Oxford: Berg, 147–158.

Walia, S. (2001). *Edward Said*: *Writings and Interpretations*. London: Icon Books.

Wallerstein, I. (2002). 'New Revolts Against the System'. *New Left Review*, 18 (November/December): 29–41.

Walseth, K. and Fasting, K. (2003). 'Islam's View on Physical Activity and Sport: Egyptian Women Interpreting Islam'. *International Review for the Sociology of Sport*, 38(1): 45–61.

Watters, R. (2003). 'The Wrong Side of the Thin Edge'. In Rinehart, R. and Sydnor, S. (eds) *To the Extreme*: *Alternative Sports Inside and Out*. Albany: Suny Press, 257–267.

Wearing, B. (1998). *Leisure and Feminist Theory*. London: Sage.

Weiss, O., Norden, G., Hilscher, P. and Vanreusel, B. (1998). 'Ski-Tourism and Environmental Problems: Ecological Awareness Among Different Groups'. *International Review for the Sociology of Sport*, 33(4): 367–369.

West, P. (2004). 'The Philosopher as Dangerous Liar'. *New Statesman*, 28 June: 24–25.

Whannel, G. (2002). 'Sport and the Media'. In Coakley, J. and Dunning, E. (eds) *Handbook of Sports Studies*. London: Sage, 291–308.

Whannel, G. (1992). *Fields of Vision*: *Television Sport and Cultural Transformation*. London: Routledge.

Wheaton, B. (ed) (2004). *Understanding Lifestyle Sports*: *Consumption, Identity and Difference*. London: Routledge.

Wheaton, B. and Beal, B. (2003). 'Keeping it Real: Sub-Cultural Media and the Discourses of Authenticity in Alternative Sports'. *International Review for the Sociology of Sport*, 38(2): 155–176.

White, J. (2004). Interview with Haile Gerselassie at http://sport.guardian.co.uk/athleticsstory/0,10082,680623,00.html

Wilner, D. (2004). 'The Media Value Problem'. *SportsBusiness*, March: 12–14.

Wilson, D. (2004). 'Cricket's Shame: The Inside Story'. *New Statesman*, 6 December: 27–31.

Woodward, K. (2002). *Identity and Difference*. London: Sage Publications.

World Health Organization (WHO) (2002). *World Report on Violence and Health*. Krug, E., Dahlberg, L., Mercy, J., Zuri, A. and Lozano, R. (eds) Geneva: WHO.

Wynsberghe, R. and Ritchie, I. (1998). '(Ir)relevant Ring: The Symbolic Consumption of the Olympic Logo in Postmodern Media Culture'. In Rail, G. (ed.) *Sport and Postmodern Times*. New York: State University of New York Press, 367–384.

Index

References to Tables, Figures and illustrations have been printed in **bold**.

405

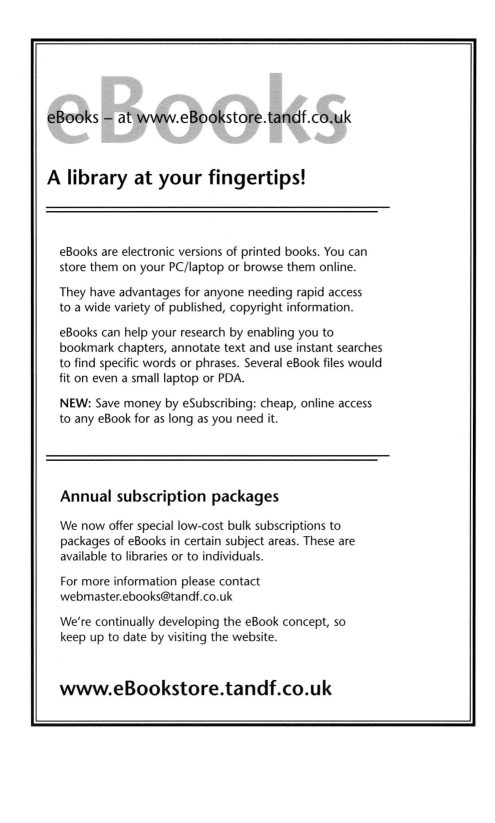